SYMBOLISM AND
MODERN LITERATURE

SYMBOLISM AND MODERN LITERATURE

studies in honor of
Wallace Fowlie

edited by Marcel Tetel
Duke University Press
Durham, N. C. 1978

Printed in the United States of America
by Heritage Printers, Inc.

Contents

[v]

41383

PART V. Symbolism and after

Foreword

Already a legend in his lifetime, Wallace Fowlie figures as a High Priest of French literature. He has initiated thousands of students to these rites both through the classroom and through his voluminous critical studies. An itinerant teacher-scholar, dedicated to the cult of French letters and of literature as a whole, from Yale to Chicago, to Bennington, to Colorado, to Duke, he is leaving behind him a teeming crowd of admiring students and colleagues. On campus, his public comprises not only the French major or the Dante lover but also those who thirst for an acculturation and a system of values. Among his peers he reaches those interested not only in the modern periods but also in the earlier ones, and the generalist as well. His name, usually associated with the Symbolist and Surrealist poets, and with Proust, Cocteau, Claudel, Mauriac, Gide, or Jacob, can also be related to Stendhal, Pascal, Molière, Scève, or Villon.

In lettristic circles, Wallace Fowlie associates with American and French poets and with such francophiles as Anaïs Nin and Henry Miller (with whom he entertains a lively correspondence, since published). For Wallace Fowlie then, literature is not just the human experience through the written word but through personal relationships with the creators of the word. Indeed, a distinguishing trait of Wallace Fowlie is his ability to view every matter, ultimately, in human terms; the personalized and human factor emerges invariably behind the event, behind a friendship, or a novel, a poem. No wonder therefore that his friends have responded enthusiastically to honor him.

In the name of those friends, and of many others, we pay homage to you, Wallace Fowlie—teacher, scholar, humane person.

M. T.

PART I

Essays in homage

Austin Warren

A Boston friendship

Wallace Fowlie and Howard Blake, the former ten years my junior, the latter fifteen years, were both met—I delight to trace back how particular friendships have been made—through superior students of mine at the College of Practical Arts.[1] Wallace's poet cousin, Pauline, a shy, proud, palely beautiful girl, mentioned her cousin in an essay or conversation or both, probably as a poet and lover of music (the name of Debussy was one signal I caught); and, in writing an essay on Poe, another young woman, the daughter of a state senator from Maine, described a young poet friend of hers whose dress and pallor and nocturnal habits resembled Poe's, were perhaps modelled on his. The requisite first meetings were arranged.

Both of these younger men were, like me, native Yankees, both from the middle class, both bookish, literary, musical, artistic: in a sense, younger Austins, but with the distinct advantage over me of being, so I soon felt, far more focused and clear of aim—not, as I was, on the boundary, "torn between" options and alternatives. Neither had more energy than I; neither perhaps had as much; but theirs they did not disperse or squander—these fortunate young artists, who were sure that they were literary men, writers even.

My habitual epigraph for myself is "Desiring this man's art and that man's scope." I envied these young men their assurance, their clear sense of vocation, their never doubting that they were writers. Was it their influence which made me, despite my waverings and self-doubts, settle upon "writer" as the name for my own vocation? In drawing away from B . . . and being drawn towards these two young writers, my juniors, I was certainly, at the least, choosing the direction in which I willed to move, choosing my influence.

The matter of influence was not of course one-sided, for there were things I had to impart as well as to receive, even though I was ever far more conscious of what I received. There was something very New England about both of these friendships: each teaching what he knew best to his

1. Boston University.

friend; each friend grasping every opportunity to learn from his own private tutor. What real education I have received has come mostly through my friends.

Wallace was and is for me a unique combination of artist and pedagogue, the two existing side by side without seeming conflict. A born ritualist as well as symbolist, he had, in his apartment, a black desk at which he corrected his students' exercises, and a white writing-table at which to compose his novels and poems.

For public teaching as well as private, he had a passion; and I occasionally heard him lecture—a treat, for his "lessons" (as, after the French fashion, he liked to call them) were elegant as well as lucid, elegantly lucid, carefully planned, proportioned, timed so as, exactly, to end on the hour; often memorized; delivered with eloquence and precision of enunciation. His model for these performances was his Harvard teacher André Morize, a master of the French *explication de texte*; and, even in his early twenties, Wallace—or Michel, as I must now begin to call him (for his private, his secret name, which I always used, was French, Michel Wallace)—was already a minor master at the same half-pedagogic, half-aesthetic mode of discourse.

Michel taught me how to make French onion soup. He also sought to teach me to drive an automobile though he gave up, without a word, after the first lesson. He likely tried to teach me handball, for it was through him, already a member, that I joined the Health Club. He was better rounded and balanced than I, and far more sensible and practical and systematic: here, New England and his adopted France collaborated.

Even his writing was systematic, regular, habitual: so many pages a day; so long at his desk—generally early in the morning. From time to time, I tried to emulate his habits of regularity at the writing table, generally unable to persist for long. My own writing, of which I did much, was done chiefly by spurts and at irregular hours. When I had an assignment, a commission, as I liked to have, the deadline served me as a point at which to start spurting, while Michel had regularly ready his manuscripts (neatly typed by himself) well in advance of any publisher's need.

Michel had just graduated from Harvard College when I first met him and was pursuing his graduate studies at Harvard and doing part-time teaching at a private school. He had an excellent memory, a fine and early trained ear for languages, and a docility, real or feigned. Under his academic coloring and standard, his unbohemian, almost businessman, certainly professional exterior, he has remained undistorted, almost un-affected, by the methods, routines and aims of academic scholarship.

His prime ambition was to write—and to publish; and, to do both, he, no more than I, needed the conventional academic incitations. And, busi-nessman as well as artist, already, when first I knew him, he knew how to separate the writer from the salesman. When he received manuscripts back, he immediately sent them out again and continued to circulate them till they were placed. If he could not find an American publisher, he found an English or a French. Bilingual, he could and would, if necessary, translate his book just written in one language into another. This last was a practice I could not follow; but I was fortified, if not influenced, by Michel's assiduity in marketing his wares into a similar and equally suc-cessful persistence in the disposition of my own.

In one matter which concerns writing we differed. I was accustomed to having my productions criticized, and, with whatever wincing at some of the judgments offered, desired criticism; but Michel soon made it clear to me, and in so many words, that he wished no analysis or advice, even "constructive." I desisted. But that was a part of a larger difference: he was, it seemed, almost entirely intuitive in his mental operations; I, some-thing of a dialectician or arguer as well.

Between friends, there is likely to be some special form of sharedness, some mode of communication. Ours was an affectionate afternoon of French, "poetry" and diction and criticism; such sessions went on for several years. Those were memorable more or less weekly afternoons. Michel shared with me his treasures and devotions. We read together Gide—*Les Nourritures terrestres*, Baudelaire, Rimbaud, Mallarmé; we talked of Proust, of whose *madeleine* and *tisane* Michel had memorially partaken, and of Proust's "asthma jacket," of which Michel had an equiv-alent to wear when he wrote. The pattern of these afternoons included reading the texts aloud. The reading was accompanied by commentary, Michel contributing, as I recall, what he had learned from his Harvard professors and French scholarship, and I improvising explications and interpretive comments on my critical own. Michel's French was, then, like that of the few other American-born French scholars I have known, man-darin: precise and elegant beyond that of the French-born.

Michel and I had many tastes and interests in common, even a native religiosity of temperament and the movement towards Catholicism. I could see how he, though the most tender, respectful and dutiful of sons, had been drawn out of the Baptist and Fundamentalistic religion in which he had been reared, and out of his suburban environment and class by the intensity of his devotion to two causes—France and "Poetry." It would be hard to say which of these came first, either chronologically or metaphysically, causally, psychologically. In a sense, "Poetry" stood for France, and France for poetry, each being a transcendent incarnate.

Chronologically, French seems to have come first, for Brookline, the Boston suburb where Michel grew up, had early introduced the study of French into the grammar school: and he began his French in the sixth grade under charming and ardently Francophile teachers. "French" was his initiation into the exotic and Romantic, the first evocation of all which was not suburban. And everything connected with France had its magic: the words, the morphology, history, geography, cuisine, music. He could imagine it all before ever he paid his first visit to Paris; and when I once asked him whether, on that first visit, he found what he had expected, he replied, "Exactly." He received no surprise, only glad confirmation. I could see clearly how this early attachment to France had "educated" my friend —as other attachments to other civilizations, Italy or Greece, have educated other Americans. And I in turn had the prized advantage of seeing France, and reading French literature, through Michel's expert and addicted eyes.

Olivier Revault d'Allonnes

Francis Picabia le loustic

à Michel, en souvenir de notre Henriette

Loustic? Mot aujourd'hui un peu désuet, mais toujours léger, savoureux, sautillant, et qui sent sa gaminerie. L'étymologie ne saurait faire de doute, et tous les dictionnaires le font venir de l'adjectif-adverbe allemand *lustig*, "gai, joyeux." Au XVIIIe siècle, les Français l'écrivent *loustig*, ce qui atteste la filiation: le mot, substantivé en français, désignait alors originellement le bouffon attaché aux régiments suisses, probablement donc aux mercenaires des guerres de Louis XV. Puis il s'est mis à désigner, par exemple chez Balzac, l'amuseur attitré d'une compagnie: "le boute-en-train du bourg, le loustic." Lautréamont, lui, parle "des écrivains ravalés, dangereux loustics, farceurs au quarteron." A l'époque où Picabia emploie ce mot, il est devenu plus familier et quelque peu péjoratif, et ne désigne plus nécessairement le bouffon ou l'amuseur d'un groupe. Le loustic est toujours le farceur, le plaisantin, voire le meneur d'un chahut de potaches, mais c'est aussi le petit bonhomme astucieux mais peu digne de confiance ou d'estime, celui qui ne respecte rien et se fait même un malin plaisir de transgresser sans cesse les usages, et de "contester," comme on dit maintenant, les valeurs reçues. Pas méchamment: par la dérision, par une malice sans vraie malignité, et au seul moyen de quelques contorsions et pirouettes, toujours accomplies avec un sourire adressé au public comme pour solliciter sa connivence.

Loustic, Francis Picabia l'est donc bien, et très exactement, dans toute sa vie, dans sa peinture, dans ses écrits, dans son film *Entracte*, dans ses relations avec les critiques et les marchands de tableaux comme dans ses amitiés souvent éphémères, et jusque dans son rapport avec les choses, automobiles ou bateaux, qu'il traite tour à tour avec respect et avec désinvolture. Il n'est pas jusqu'à la connotation péjorative du loustic que Picabia n'ait assumée volontairement, lui qui signait aussi Pharamousse, qui commence comme Pharaon et finit irrespectueusement comme frimousse; ou bien Francis le Raté; ou bien, plus vulgairement encore, Pipicabia, voire Picacabia....

Encore un mot sur *loustic*: je regrette, quant à moi, de devoir à la vérité
de reconnaître l'étymologie suisse allemande. J'aurais préféré, comme
pour bien des mots un peu argotiques qui commencent par un *l*, pouvoir
incriminer l'argot des bouchers de La Villette, cette langue à demi secrète
qui s'est formée au XIXe siècle, et dont la règle unique de création du
vocabulaire consiste en ceci:[1] on prend un mot qui commence par une
consonne; on rejette cette consonne à la fin du mot, et on la remplace par
un *l*; on ajoute ensuite un suffixe, *-ique*, *-oque*, *-uche*, *-alte*, *-ème*, etc., et
plus tard *-tingue*. C'est ainsi qu'un boucher devenait un *loucherbème*, mot
qui s'est mis à désigner cette langue spéciale elle-même. Le français
moderne doit à ce parler un mot fort employé et qui n'est pas sans noblesse,
c'est *loufoque*, très régulièrement construit à partir de *fou*. Huysmans, peu
familier de La Villette, l'écrit avec deux *f*. Il existe même la variante
louftingue; et puis, le suffixe peut tomber, comme chez Queneau: "t'es pas
louf?"; et tous les dérivés sont possibles, puisque Gide parle de "la loufo-
querie de la conversation." Le loucherbème a aussi donné des mots argotiques de construction non régulière ou aberrante, comme le vilain *lardeuss*
où l'on retrouve encore son pardessus.

Mais hélas, lorsque j'opère sur loustic à l'inverse de la composition du
loucherbème, pour retrouver le mot français, et si je considère *-ic* comme
un suffixe possible, j'obtiens: *tous*, et ma recherche s'arrête là. Car enfin, il
est hautement improbable que Picabia ait eu connaissance de loucherbème,
bien que d'un autre côté il ne soit pas impossible qu'il ait voulu faire
entendre que nous sommes "tous" des "loustics." Conclusion que pourrait
admettre une exégèse caricaturale. Passons.

J'étais encore gamin, et parfois un peu loustic, lorsque Michel Wallace
Fowlie, sans doute à la demande de ma mère Henriette Psichari, toujours
soucieuse de mes études, me donna quelques leçons de français. J'en ai
retenu notamment ceci, que la langue française est une langue pauvre, en
ce sens que son fonds sémantique est réduit, son vocabulaire restreint
relativement à d'autres langues comme l'allemand et l'anglais, mais aussi
à d'autres langues latines comme l'italien ou l'espagnol. Racine emploie
quelques centaines de mots là où Shakespeare utilise plusieurs milliers.
Une fois faite la part de la volonté de l'un de limiter, et de l'autre d'élargir
son vocabulaire, il reste encore largement à incriminer la relative rareté
des mots en français: ce que Raymond Queneau ira jusqu'à appeler
la "famine linguistique." Le français a donc été contraint de se "débrouil-
ler" avec ce qu'il avait, et de faire de son manque une ressource. La dispari-

---

1. Schwob et Guieysse, *Mémoires de la Société de Linguistique*, t. VII (1892).

tion des cas du latin a conduit le français, depuis la *Chanson de Roland* jusqu'à la Renaissance et après, à multiplier prépositions et formules prépositionnelles, à affiner sans cesse leur emploi jusqu'à constituer l'abondante panoplie du français classique et du français moderne. C'est ainsi que cette langue, enrichie de tournures allemandes, occitanes, bretonnes, puis anglaises, est devenue la plus révolutionnaire des langues latines. C'est ainsi que le sens, dans toute sa subtilité et toutes ses nuances, a dû se dire dans la structure de la phrase et dans le style, dans l'esprit de la parole et de l'écriture, autant et plus que dans la matérialité des termes. Un professeur français ne m'eût peut-être pas fait sentir aussi fortement cette situation, et surtout ne m'eût pas communiqué comme l'a fait Michel la passion pour un mode d'expression qui fait de sa pauvreté richesse, et de l'astuce linguistique un art.

Mais revenons à Picabia. Lui aussi, comme écrivain, s'est trouvé dans la situation où sont, qu'ils le sachent ou non, tous ceux qui parlent ou écrivent le français. Ajoutons à cela qu'il voulait en outre non pas casser, mais déborder l'outil linguistique comme il cherchait à déborder l'outil pictural. La peinture étalée à la brosse ne lui suffit pas: il lui faut coller sur la toile allumettes, boutons, épingles à cheveux pour tout à la fois élargir et ridiculiser le geste du peintre. Ecrivain, il se heurte sans cesse également aux barrières de l'usage et du sens; il lui faudra tour à tour les contourner, les franchir ou les détruire. Il en appellera par exemple à la prononciation contre l'orthographe, quand il écrira: "mes *dessins*, comme ceux de la Providence, sont impénétrables." Ou bien lorsqu'il écrira les mots à l'envers, de sorte que Suzanne devienne Ennazus. Ou bien lorsque, de retour de New York, il transformera *wrong wrong* en Ron-ron.[2] Les à peu près, les jeux de mots, les calembours souvent volontairement médiocres, sont innombrables sous sa plume. Il s'agit, comme en peinture, de faire rendre à l'outil plus qu'il ne peut donner, de débusquer le sens ou du sens au delà même du sens, dans le non-sens ou le contresens. Il s'agit de triturer la matière jusqu'à la défigurer, pour en faire jaillir l'esprit, mais cela de façon absolument libre, improvisée, imprévisible, sans aucun de ces procédés que tentera de codifier le surréalisme, nouvelle "chapelle" à laquelle Picabia n'adhéra jamais. Bref, il s'agit d'être un vrai loustic.

Lorsque j'entrepris voici dix ans de rassembler les innombrables écrits de Francis Picabia, publiés par lui pendant quarante ans dans cent journaux et revues, et dans des livres et brochures devenus rares (d'autant que

---

2. *Poésie Ron-ron*, publié à Lausanne en 1919, réédité dans: F. Picabia, *Ecrits* (Paris, 1975), pp. 131–57. Le tome deux et dernier paraîtra en 1978 chez le même éditeur.

l'une de ces brochures fut tirée à trois exemplaires!) le découragement a d'abord failli me paralyser. Et puis, de texte en texte, j'allais de stupeur en découverte, d'amusement en trouvaille, et à chaque fois je tombais sur un Picabia "semblable" à lui-même, c'est-à-dire entièrement différent: capricieux, déguisé de frais, recommencé de pied en cap. Il n'est pas jusqu'au genre le plus inattendu de sa part qu'il n'ait pratiqué: le genre sérieux! Etre loustic à ce point....

Dans cette quête que j'aurais pu craindre lassante, mais qui fut palpitante, j'ai souvent pensé à Michel et à ses enseignements. Je suis heureux de pouvoir le lui dire aujourd'hui publiquement. Mais voici que le courrier m'apporte d'outre-océan une photographie de Michel chez lui, et j'entrevois dans les lointains le coin d'un tableau de Picabia. Décidément, il n'y a pas de hasard, il n'y a que des complicités spirituelles, qui finissent toujours par se manifester. Picabia le Loustic a poussé très loin l'effort de renouvellement et de dépassement du geste, de la pensée, de l'écriture. Et cela dès l'année 1908, qui l'a vu rompre avec l'impressionnisme, où du reste il réussissait. Il est toujours resté inquiet, à l'affût du tout autre, à l'écoute de ce qui peut surgir, assoiffé de recommencer une nouvelle vie. Mais sous cet esprit primesautier, on se tromperait si l'on croyait qu'il n'y a pas une très large et très exacte connaissance de ce qui se passe, de ce qui se fait et se dit. Seulement, ce savoir scrupuleux n'est jamais académique (j'allais écrire: sorbonnard, mais peut-être la Sorbonne aussi ressuscitera-t-elle), ce savoir n'est jamais étouffant, jamais suffisant ni tranquillisant. Il est toujours vécu immédiatement comme dérangeant. Il n'est pas archive de greffier, mais aventure humaine qui me sollicite, m'interroge, me met en demeure de me situer moi-même face à elle. C'est ma propre aventure qui est en question, ma propre responsabilité qui est ouverte. Il ne doit pas y avoir d'oreiller du savoir. Il ne doit y avoir que des recherches et des inquiétudes, même et surtout si l'on ignore l'objet de leur quête. La voilà, la leçon, surtout pour celui que son métier conduit à enseigner: rester toute sa vie un étudiant, plus fasciné par les régions à défricher que par les routes parcourues. La leçon qui sauve des mauvais démons de l'érudition impersonnelle et du coup, inutile. La leçon de vie et de jeunesse.

Mais je m'arrête là, parce que je m'égare. Je croyais parler de Picabia, et voici que j'esquisse un portrait de Michel.

PART II

Critical essays

Francis Fergusson

Poetry and drama

One must realize quite soon that it would be very hard to talk sensibly about Poetry in general, or Poetry in itself. For we know that there are many kinds of poetry, which have flourished at different periods in our tradition, and that poetry in the widest sense usually includes everything from the shortest epigrams through sonnets, odes, narratives, to a great deal of the best fiction and drama, though that may often be written in prose. We cannot point to the concrete reality of poetry, and we lack a definition which would apply to all its forms.

Nevertheless if one is committed to a discussion of poetry one needs to have some actual poetry in mind, and I have therefore fairly arbitrarily decided to concentrate on four poems of medium length as examples of poetry. They are from four very different periods. They are quite different from each other, but I think nearly everyone would agree that they are all really poems. The first is a chorus from Sophocles' *Antigone*; the second a *canzone* of Dante's; the third a short lyric passage from Shakespeare's *Antony and Cleopatra*; and, to conclude, Eliot's "Gerontion." From these four a general conception of poetry should emerge, and my title, "Poetry and Drama," should be clarified.

I said that *almost* everyone would agree that these four are really poems. But we all know that at the moment all sorts of writings which are not poetry as I understand the term are classified as poetry. These forms, or non-forms, seem to be due to boredom with the tradition, or sometimes to mere laziness. Those who still try to write "real" poetry tend to be concealed or engulfed by the current movements. Perhaps we are about to lose poetry altogether. But I return to my remarks about poetry as it used to be understood.

The conception I shall use is the one that Aristotle explains in the *Poetics*, that the arts are imitations of action. Two thousand years later Coleridge was to agree with Aristotle. He writes in his essay on *Othello*: "The unity of action is not properly a rule, but in itself the great end, not only of drama, but of the lyric, epic, even to the candle-flame of the epigram—not only of poetry, but of poesy in general, as the proper generic term inclusive of all the fine arts as its species."[1] Aristotle assumes that drama is the fundamental art, and the *Poetics*, as everyone knows, is devoted largely to the analysis of Sophoclean tragedy. I wish to look quickly at Sophocles' *Antigone*, and then at the first chorus in the play, which may be considered as a separate lyric. I hope, thus, to indicate a relation between lyric poetry and drama.

The *Antigone*, you remember, is set in Thebes just after the war in which Oedipus' two sons, Eteocles and Polyneikes, fought for the city, Eteocles defending and Polyneikes attacking it. The two brothers killed each other, and when the play opens their uncle Creon has just become the ruler of the city. He announces that he will leave Polyneikes' corpse for the birds to devour, while he buries Eteocles with full honors. The Greeks believed that if a man was not properly buried he could never rejoin his family in the next world, but must exist in a kind of exile; and Antigone insists on burying her brother in spite of Creon. When she is caught in the act and brought before her uncle she maintains that the family past and present must be restored, as love and the gods themselves decree; but Creon insists that it is his duty to defend the city by punishing its attacker. The issue between them cuts very deep; it is between the divine authority of the ruler and the equally divine authority of the laws of the dead.

The chorus consists of fifteen elders. It first rejoices that the city has been saved, but then it must watch as Creon announces his punishment of Polyneikes, and the guard of Polyneikes' corpse comes to report that it has been buried already. Creon, in rage, threatens whomever is guilty, and the chorus is left to think over what it has just seen. As the chorus gropes for understanding, its sense of the secret burial induces in its mind images of the wonderful and terrible motives of mankind. I cite the choral ode as it appears in the translation by Fitts and Fitzgerald:

> Numberless are the world's wonders, but none
> More wonderful than man; the storm-grey sea
> Yields to his prows, the huge crests bear him high;
> Earth, holy and inexhaustible, is graven
> With shining furrows where his plows have gone
> Year after year, the timeless labour of stallions.
>
> The lightboned birds and beasts that cling to cover,
> The lithe fish lighting their reaches of dim water,
> All are taken, tamed in the net of his mind;

1. Coleridge, *Othello*, in *Lectures on Shakespeare* (London, 1931).

The lion on the hill, the wild horse windy-maned,
Resign to him; and his blunt yoke has broken
The sultry shoulders of the mountain bull.

Words also, and thoughts as rapid as air,
He fashions to his good use; statecraft is his,
And his the skill that deflects the arrows of snow,
The spears of winter rain: from every wind
He has made himself secure—from all but one:
In the late wind of death he cannot stand.

O clear intelligence, force beyond all measure!
O fate of man, working both good and evil!
When the laws are kept, how proudly his city stands!
When the laws are broken, what of his city then?
Never may the anarchic man find rest at my hearth,
Never be it said that my thoughts are his thoughts.[2]

It is evident, I think, that this ode may be read apart from the play as an independent lyric. Its verse-forms are more elaborate than those of the dialogue, and it was chanted to the accompaniment of musical instruments, perhaps flutes and percussion. It emerges from the situation in the play, but its action is contemplative, "to see the meaning for me of the images of man which come to me." It moves from the wonders of the intelligent creature to the only wind, that of death, that he cannot stand, and then it sees the terrible dangers of getting caught in the laws which man has himself devised. This thought brings its contemplation back to the immediate situation and ends the lyric.

We shall see presently that the other lyrics I discuss also move through visions which come of their own accord. Each lyric has its *persona* who speaks it, corresponding to Sophocles' chorus, and each one arises from a situation outside the poem. The action is always "to see" or "to understand" the emotionally charged images which come to it unwilled. This ode is thus a real poem, and so may be read apart from its play.

The ode is however also an essential part of *Antigone*. Aristotle remarks that the Sophoclean chorus is like a character in its play, sharing in the action. The *Antigone*'s action is "to restore the right order in Thebes": that is what both Creon and Antigone want, and their conflicts arise from their different interpretations of "the right order." The chorus also wants the

2. *Antigone*, trans. Dudley Fitts and Robert Fitzgerald.

right order, but it is not wedded like the others to a narrow view of what that would be. Moreover, it cannot act like Creon or Antigone to get order, but must realize its action only in watching, praying, and trying to see. It is mainly Creon who moves the play ahead with his strong purpose, and only when he suffers a frustration can the chorus's contemplative action begin. The action of the play moves in a repeated rhythm from Purpose, to Pathos, to the Perception of the chorus.

Antigone—the whole play—is of course itself a poem. The chorus represents a recurrent moment in its development. That distinguishes this ode from Dante's *canzoni* and Eliot's "Gerontion," both of which embody contemplative actions; but both are dependent on a *persona* and an implicit situation outside the poem, like the situation in Thebes.

I wish to glance next at Dante, who is often taken as the model for modern poets who wish to learn to write. I shall try to see what he thought poetry was. Dante discusses poetry in various ways in the course of his life. But he must have known, directly, what poetry was, since he wrote it all his life, from the *Vita Nuova* straight through to the *Commedia*. After Beatrice's death, when he was living in exile and reading the classical philosophers, he wrote two great prose works, *De Volgare Eloquentia* and the *Convivio*, where he elaborated a completely rational account of poetry which reminds me of the neoclassicism of Dryden or Racine. In this period he regarded the ultimate vision of philosophy as the height of life, at least for himself. His *persona* at this time was a mature, responsible, reasonable citizen, and he endeavors to make both his prose and his verse fit that.

De Volgare Eloquentia[3] seeks the best Italian—"illustrious Italian" as he calls it—and he thinks poetry is superior to prose because, as he says, it "seems to serve as a pattern to prose writers." He then analyzes the *canzone*, which is generally regarded as the noblest form of poetry, embodying whole poetic art. Only the three greatest human themes, "Safety," by which he means warlike heroism, "Love" and "Virtue" are to be handled in *canzoni*. They are "tragic" by which he means only their verbal style; an eloquence subdued by the manners and the decorum of an elite, disciplined by reason, and refined by familiarity with the ancient masters. When he comes to the form of the *canzone* he tells us that "poetry is nothing else but a rhetorical composition set to music." And the analysis of the *canzone* which follows is a severe technical treatise on metrics.

If one read only *De Volgare Eloquentia* one might think that Dante

3. Dante, *De Vulgare Eloquentia* (London, 1929).

didn't recognize poetry at all. But most of the *canzoni* which he was writing at this time are just what we mean by poetry, and a couple of years later he wrote the *Convivio*,[4] in which he is definitely concerned with his *canzoni* as *poems*. He did not have Aristotle's *Poetics*, which was not rediscovered for a hundred years after his time; probably the definition he offered of the *canzone* represents his effort to give an Aristotelian account of poetry on the basis of the *Rhetoric* only. But in the *Convivio* he comes close to a theory of poetry like that of the *Poetics*, probably because he made careful use of the rest of Aristotle's philosophy. I shall illustrate by considering the third treatise of the *Convivio*, which is an elaborate analysis of his Canzone III, in the Temple Classics edition.

This *canzone* starts as follows:

> Amor, che nella mente mi ragiona
> della mia donna disiosamente—

Love, which in the mind discourses to me of my lady, longingly, moves things about her often, so that my intellect loses its way about them.

He then tells us that Love speaks of her so sweetly that he wishes that he could tell it all to us; but can't understand much of it, and so he must confine his rhymes to a small part of what he hears. So ends the first part of the *canzone*; it serves to introduce the mystery of the lady whom Love is discussing.

Parts II, III, and IV tell us about the lady. In part II we learn that the sun illuminates her beauty, and her maker gives her the power to reach all who see her. In part III we hear of a spirit which comes down to her from heaven, giving her speech the power to call upon love, and strengthen our faith. In part IV we see that some of the joys of paradise are revealed to us in her eyes and in her smiling mouth, and her beauty rains like flamelets upon us, shattering the inborn vices of those who see her.

Part V is the *tornata*, and it explains that in a previous ode he had called this lady cruel and disdainful, but that was only what she seemed to *him*: it terrified him; but actually she is like the sky which is always clear behind the clouds, and he asks permission to speak of her everywhere.

Although the beauty of this poem depends on Dante's Italian and the subtle music he makes of it, I still wish to point out its analogies to the Sophoclean choral ode. It has its own *persona*, Dante as the rational citizen he was then trying to be. It comes from Dante's own worldly situation,

4. Dante, *The Convivio* (London, 1924).

when Beatrice was fading away and the new lady was taking full possession of his thoughts and feelings. Its action contemplates various abilities of the lady: to bring love to those who see her, to reveal some of the joys and some of the terrors of paradise; and finally, in the *tornata*, it turns to itself, apologizing for contradicting the previous poem; and so it ends, like the Sophoclean ode, by returning us from the visions inspired by Love to the *persona* in the actual world.

As Dante tells us in the first line, this ode is inspired by Love. And a large part of his analysis is an explanation of Love, according to his scholastic philosophy. "Everything," he tells us, "hath its specific love," by which he means the forces, like gravitation, which move the physical world, and the forces that move plants, animals and man. In man, "Love . . . is nought else than a spiritual union of the soul and the loved thing; to which union the soul, in virtue of its own nature, runs swift or slow according as it is free or impeded."[5] Love is the inspiration of the poem: he sees love in the eyes and in the mouth of his lady and is impelled to celebrate it in his verse.

But when he comes to the allegorical meaning he tells us that the lady signifies philosophy. This part of his explanation may distress us, because the lady certainly feels like a real woman, probably the one he fell in love with after Beatrice's death, when she looked at him out of her window. However, he pursues philosophy, moved by love, and gradually rises from physics or biology to the most abstract truths, just as he proceeds from his lady's physical beauties to a more direct sense of her soul. He saw the reasoned structure of philosophy as the summit of human experience, the ultimate object of love; and his lady, as he slowly contemplates her by way of her beauties, represents the highest object which the rational soul can reach.

When Dante turned away from his humanistic rationalism, he returned to Beatrice and put everything into the writing of the *Commedia*. I don't propose to discuss the poetry of the *Commedia* (you will be glad to hear); but I wish to point out a few bits which show how his conception of poetry changed when he accepted God, rather than philosophy, as the supreme object of human love. Even in his rationalistic phase he saw poetry as a matter of the *concrete* movements of love, or action; but when he wrote the *Commedia* he was free to discuss everything in his universe and to write not only in the limited high style of his *canzoni* but in the style or styles

5. Ibid.

which best conveyed what he was talking about. And he understood very clearly what he was doing.

Thus in *Inferno* II,[6] as he is about to follow Virgil into Hell, he suddenly realizes the contrast between his own little strength and the appalling journey ahead of him, where only Aeneas and St. Paul had been before: "But I, why do I come here? Or who permits it? I am not Aeneas, I am not Paul; neither myself nor others deem me worthy of it" (lines 31–33). Virgil reassures him: it is not his own strength but the grace of God that he must rely on. That is the role and the *persona* he accepts, both in his journey and in the writing of it to follow.

It is in his *Letter*[7] dedicating the *Paradiso* to Can Grande that Dante explains the style of the *Commedia* in two ways. He will abandon the tragic style of the *Canzoni*, for with "respect to the method of speech," he writes, "the method is lax and humble, for it is the vernacular speech in which very women communicate." At the same time it must be able to serve every purpose, and "The form or method of treatment is poetic, fictive, descriptive, digressive, transumptive; and likewise proceeding by definition, division, proof, refutation, and setting forth of examples." These terms, which cover both the emotive and the metaphorical, and the conceptual and logical uses of language, are apparently derived from the *Rhetoric*. They may remind one of the *Poetics*: "Under thought is included every effect which has to be produced by speech, the subdivisions being— proof and refutation; the excitation of the feelings, such as pity, fear, anger and the like; the suggestion of importance or its opposite" (XIX).[8] Neither Aristotle nor Dante in his maturity thinks of poetry as requiring a special poetic language. And in the *Commedia* Dante makes poetry of every kind of language, from the tough vulgarities of Hell to the quiet, elegant order of Virgil's philosophy or Beatrice's theology.

That is because Dante, like Aristotle in the *Poetics*, understands poetry as the imitation of action, and action for him means Love, the Love I discussed above. In the *Purgatorio* he meets the poet Bonagiunta who asks him whether he is the author of the lines beginning "Ladies who have intelligence of love." Dante replies (in Sinclair's translation): "I am one who, when Love breathes in me, take note, and in that manner which he dictates within go on to signify" (XXIV).[9] "I see well how your pens

6. Dante, *Inferno* (London, 1934).
7. Dante, *Epistola X, Latin Works* (London, 1929).
8. Aristotle, *Poetics* (New York, 1961).
9. Dante, *Purgatorio* (London, 1932).

follow close behind the dictator," says Bonagiunta, "which assuredly does not happen with us." Bonagiunta is talking, at least at first, about the poems in the *Vita Nuova*, but Dante speaks as the writer of the *Commedia*, where love breathes in him in every manner, from that of the lost in Hell to that of the saints in Paradise. He is free to note the infinitely various movements of love in his own inner being, and then imitate what he notes there, in his verse.

By the time Dante wrote the *Commedia* he had become a model for all poets, but that was partly because of his Christian vision, and shortly after his death the poets that followed him could not accept or understand him. In our time we often hear that his thirteenth-century Christianity makes him inaccessible to us. But the late Erich Auerbach has demonstrated what he calls his Christian "realism," and a number of subsequent poets have shared that.[10] Among them are Shakespeare three hundred years after Dante, and Eliot, in 1920. I wish next to look briefly at a passage from Shakespeare.

The passage I want to cite is a small bit of *Antony and Cleopatra* which I think may be taken as a poem, like the ode from *Antigone*. It is the beginning of Scene 14, Act IV, just after Antony has lost a crucial battle with Caesar, when Cleopatra's fleet sailed away. Antony, like the Theban elders in *Antigone*, has withdrawn, after the battle, with his attendant Eros, to contemplate his fate. He thinks Cleopatra is to blame for the flight of her fleet and that she has betrayed him. As he meditates quietly we remember his wavering course throughout the play in pursuit of Cleopatra:

ANTONY: Eros, thou yet behold'st me?
EROS: Ay noble lord.
ANTONY: Sometime we see a cloud that's dragonish,
           A vapour sometime, like a bear or lion,
           A towered citadel, a pendant rock,
           A forked mountain or blue promontory
           With trees upon't that nod unto the world
           And mock our eyes with air. Thou has seen these signs;
           They are black vesper's pageants.
EROS: Ay my lord.
ANTONY: That which is now a horse, even with a thought
           The wrack dislimns, and makes it indistinct
           As water is in water.
EROS: It does my lord.

10. Erich Auerbach, *Mimesis* (Princeton, 1953).

ANTONY: My good knave Eros, now thy captain is
Even such a body. Here I am Antony,
Yet cannot hold this visible shape, my knave.
I made these wars for Egypt, and the Queen,
Whose heart I thought I had, for she had mine;
Which whilst it was mine had annexed unto't
A million moe, now lost—she, Eros, has
Packed cards with Caesar, and false-played my glory
Unto an enemy's triumph.[11]

I think you will see at once that this passage is analogous to the Sopho-clean choral ode, though of course it is simpler. Antony is its *persona*, and his action is to see through the cloudy shapes before him to himself, as he really is. When he sees *that*, he too cannot hold his visible shape; the lyric ends, and he sees Cleopatra as the cause of his non-entity. As he speaks we remember his wavering course throughout the play, and the shifting actions of his antagonists, who tried to keep up with him. His vision, or daydream, illuminates both his action and that of the play.

The most recent school of poetry in this country is that of Pound, Eliot, and their distinguished followers, including Ransom, Tate, Robert Penn Warren, Wallace Stevens, Blackmur, and others. Of course I realize that a number of recent poets object to this group, and I know that it is very diverse for a "school." But it was they who first made us aware of poetry in our time, and moreover they sometimes succeeded in creating first-rate poetry themselves. The conception of poetry which I am endeavoring to explain is derived ultimately from them. To conclude, I remind you of Eliot's "Gerontion," which, "modern" though it is, illustrates much of what I have been saying.

"Gerontion" was first published in 1920, after the early poems and a couple of years before *The Waste Land*. The title is a Greek word meaning "little old man," and the poem is a larger and subtler version of "The Love Song of J. Alfred Prufrock." The epigraph,

Thou hast nor youth nor age,
But as it were an after dinner sleep
Dreaming of both,

is taken from the Duke's speech to Claudio in *Measure for Measure*. The first stanza, a prologue introducing the *persona*, is like the first act of a drama:

11. Shakespeare, *Antony and Cleopatra* (New York, 1961), p. 181.

Here I am, an old man in a dry month,
Being read to by a boy, waiting for rain.
I was neither at the hot gates
Nor fought in the warm rain
Nor knee deep in the salt marsh, heaving a cutlass,
Bitten by flies, fought.
My house is a decayed house,
And the jew squats on the window sill, the owner,
Spawned in some estaminet of Antwerp,
Blistered in Brussels, patched and peeled in London.
The goat coughs at night in the field overhead;
Rocks, moss, stonecrop, iron, merds.
The woman keeps the kitchen, makes tea,
Sneezes at evening, poking the peevish gutter.
                    I an old man,
A dull head among windy spaces.[12]

This *persona* and his dreary dwelling are implicit throughout the poem
and are explicitly returned to several times. They prepare us for the action,
which is expressed directly in the next line: "Signs are taken for wonders.
'We would see a sign!' " The old man is commencing to seek among his
dreams and memories some sign, something to see and follow, and that
action will persist, in various ways, until the end of the poem.

The first sign he investigates is *the* sign, Christ, who comes, an ironic
answer to his quest, in a modified quotation from Eliot's favorite, Bishop
Andrews:

The word within a word, unable to speak a word,
Swaddled with darkness. In the juvescence of the year
Came Christ the tiger

    In depraved May, dogwood and chestnut, flowering judas,
To be eaten, to be divided, to be drunk
Among whispers; by Mr. Silvero
With caressing hands, at Limoges
Who walked all night in the next room;

By Hakagawa, bowing among the Titians;
By Madame de Tornquist, in the dark room
Shifting the candles; Fräulein von Kulp
Who turned in the hall, one hand on the door.
        Vacant shuttles
Weave the wind. I have no ghosts,
An old man in a draughty house
Under a windy knob.

Notice the structure of this sequence, which finds and rapidly loses Christ. It begins with the traditional "Christ the tiger," next identified with the excitement of spring, Eliot's season, the time of fragrant flowers, the Dionysian rituals which he will use in *The Waste Land* and thereafter. The eating, dividing, and drinking of Christ, which is accomplished by the unidentified figures who may be dealers in religious pictures, leave us with nothing: no Christ, not even any ghosts, only the wind in the house, and the lost old man.

In the next stanza the old man investigates a series of images of history, which come to him out of his quest for a sign. He is seeking to understand the historic process which has brought us here:

After such knowledge, what forgiveness? Think now
History has many cunning passages, contrived corridors
And issues, deceives with whispering ambitions,
Guides us by vanities. Think now
She gives when our attention is distracted
And what she gives, gives with such supple confusions
That the giving famishes the craving. Gives too late
What's not believed in, or if still believed,
In memory only, reconsidered passion. Gives too soon
Into weak hands, what's thought can be dispensed with
Till the refusal propagates a fear. . . .

History's course is both mocking and deceptive, it shows us nothing. The stanza ends with a picture of our failure, which suggests much contemporary literature, especially the French:

                    Think
Neither fear nor courage saves us. Unnatural vices
Are fathered by our heroism. Virtues

Are forced upon us by our impudent crimes.
These tears are shaken from the wrath-bearing tree.

The whole stanza is, I think, an extraordinarily skillful dramatization of Gerontion's desperate reading. We see him scanning the books which we can almost recognize, becoming gradually frustrated, finally terrified. But he is not reading now. He is thinking over his past years of reading, in the revealing light of his actual situation.

The next two stanzas are much shorter. They represent two phases near the end of Gerontion's action, as he withdraws from his lost seeking for a sign. He realizes that he has not intentionally willed the elements of his show, and he sees himself as having been removed, quite without his will, from all human contact. The two stanzas remind one of the fourth acts of Shakespeare's tragedies, when the characters have done all they can, and now must pause, dreaming, awaiting the fatal but still unseen result. I cite the first of these stanzas:

The tiger springs in the new year. Us he devours. Think at last
We have not reached conclusion, when I
Stiffen in a rented house. Think at last
I have not made this show purposelessly
And it is not by any concitation
Of the backward devils.

He is now ready to address his reader directly:

I would meet you upon this honestly.
I that was near your heart was removed therefrom
To lose beauty in terror, terror in inquisition.
I have lost my passion: why should I need to keep it
Since what is kept must be adulterated?
I have lost my sight, smell, hearing, taste and touch:
How should I use them for your closer contact?

The passage remembers a Jacobean tragedy by Middleton, and modern subjective idealism, notably that of Bradley. It establishes once more the isolation of Gerontion, but places him in a nightmarish historic context like that of our time.

The last stanza returns us to the opening scene, Gerontion in his windy house, between terror and his dry quiet:

These with a thousand small deliberations
Protract the profit of their chilled delirium,

Excite the membrane, when the sense has cooled.
With pungent sauces, multiply variety
In a wilderness of mirrors. What will the spider do,
Suspend its operations, will the weevil
Delay? De Bailhache, Fresca, Mrs. Cammel, whirled
Beyond the circuit of the shuddering Bear
In fractured atoms. Gull against the wind, in the windy straits
Of Belle Isle, or running on the Horn,
White feathers in the snow, the Gulf claims,
And an old man driven by the Trades
To a sleepy corner.
                                        Tenants of the house,
Thoughts of a dry brain in a dry season.

This finale contrasts with all the preceding stanzas, which are rich with human imagery: here the small deliberations are like a sauce to the sense or mirrors to the eye; and all is quickly wiped out in the implicit cosmic explosion, to end in the silent inhumanity of the white feathers in the snow.

"Gerontion" is the last poem I shall discuss. It is of course very different from any of the others. After the opening picture of the old man in his dreary kitchen it depends entirely on dreamlike figures, or on abstractions. Christ the tiger fades rapidly through depraved May and Mr. Silvero and his colleagues. In the third stanza an unseen history, inconceivable in itself, exists for the *persona* only as a series of cruelly teasing "givings." That *persona* who in the next two stanzas addresses us directly is not as real for us even as Prufrock is. We feel him, rather, as a metaphor for the author. In the last stanza he reappears as the old man in his sleepy corner, and he serves, there, to belittle the author after the tragic diction of the preceding stanzas. Eliot did not have the classically "real" human beings of Sophocles or Shakespeare, nor the objective philosophy of Dante. He did not have a recognizable situation in the real world, and therefore he lacked a *persona* capable of all the thought and experience in the poem. But he had, as his authentic inspiration, the perpetually failing action, "to see a sign." He sensed that action so deeply that it brought him the extraordinarily varied imagery and the dramatic unity of the poem, which I have tried to indicate. The poem is thus analogous to the others I have discussed: it is the imitation of a contemplative action.

Acknowledgment
I wish to thank the Trustees of the Witter Bynner Foundation, for which this essay was originally written, for their permission to print it here.

Arthur R. Evans, Jr.

Ernst Jünger's *Auf den Marmorklippen:* a sketch toward an interpretation

Le principal ennemi de l'homme... c'est la forêt.
Malraux, *L'Espoir*

Ernst Jünger's allegorical novel depicts a model of world harmony, a cosmos destroyed by brutish, anarchical forces. It opens on a nostalgic note, evoking the poignant memories of a way of life founded on fraternity, civil order, the rhythm of nature, and a respect for the traditional pieties. The mood is autumnal and, appropriately, reference is made to the festivals celebrated once upon a time in conjunction with the yearly harvests. The new wine is tasted, nuts are eaten, there is time for bird shooting, and crowds congregate along the shores of the Grand Marina to carouse and joust with one another in displays of wit. At early morning the sun rises over Alta Plana, situated to the south, beyond the waters of the Marina, just as the sun will set, at the end of the novel—to rise again, we know— upon the prosperous homestead of Ansgar up on the mountains of Alta Plana. On a bright day the eye can see all the way to the borders of New Burgundy where the high-born family of Sunmyra, representative of the declining aristocracy, lives and farms its estates. On their way home at dawn from the fall feastings, the two brothers now and then catch a glimpse of some startling scene or image having the power to call up, but only for a moment, the archaic, preternatural spirit of the land, fecund yet terrible in its promise of unnamed menace.

There were celebrations, too, which usher in the spring equinox. Here the brothers and townspeople of the Marina, dressed up as clowns decked out in bird feathers, join in the merriment by attaching themselves to the guild of the woodpeckers. Meanwhile, the crowd sets up in the old market-place the traditional tree of fools. In mocking, discordant accompaniment to the general festivity are the shrill call and answer of the authentic birds of the area. Their ominous cry is to the rites of spring what the chilling

[26]

images of nature's secrets are to the winemaking holidays: a sign of fore-boding amidst the general air of abundance and well-being.

The narrator and Bruder Otho live in the Rue Cloister (*Rautenklause*).[1] To get to their home from the Marina one passes through the Cock Gate, from which on the left loom up the Marble Cliffs, the cloister itself being situated on the edge of the cliff in close proximity to long stretches of grapeland. During the spring the hyacinth blooms and in fall the wild cherry, but all year long the silver-green rue bushes give off their pungent odor. *Ruta*, herb of grace in the lore of flowers, possesses powers against evil spells: formerly, a branch of rue was used to sprinkle holy water in churches, and the ancients, according to Pliny, believed that the plant not only improved the physical strength of the eye but bestowed, as well, an inner vision, a second sight.[2] The Rue Cloister consists of a library, which opens onto the garden where the golden lily is in flower, and, on the second floor, an herbarium. Here the brothers are engaged, with the aid of Lin-naeus' *Systema Naturale*, upon a lifetime's labor of collecting and classify-ing the flora of the region.[3] Living with the two of them is Lampusa, who acts as a housekeeper and tends the kitchen placed in the lower recesses of the Marble Cliffs, and Erio, the illegitimate child of the narrator, whose mother is Silvia, daughter of Lampusa. The boy and his grandmother have been brought to the Cloister by Bruder Otho who has the knack of winning people's confidence, a gift for bringing out the best in them. Lampusa is the Terrible Mother, a telluric force, one who knows the dark, generative— and destructive—secrets of nature. She entertains Belovar, the just herds-man, in her cliff cellar but at the same time is on good terms with the

1. In his war journals, Ernst Jünger refers to the family house at Kirchhorst, just out-side of Hanover, where he lived from 1939 to 1950, as "die Klause." See *Gärten und Strassen* (Berlin, 1942), p. 79. The choice of name for the narrator's brother would seem to have been dictated by exclusively aesthetic considerations, for Jünger writes: "Es fiel mir noch kein rechter Name für die Gestalt des Bruders ein, den ich zunächst Profundus nannte, welcher Dreiklang indessen zu schwer im Satze wiegt. Deshalb setzte ich vorläufig Felix für ihm ein, was reichlich farblos wirkt. Vielleicht entschliesse ich mich zu Otto oder Otho, was rein vokalisch sich in jede Wendung einfügen lässt" (No better name struck me for the figure of the brother whom I called Profundus, but its triple syl-lables weighed too heavily in the sentence. Then I thought of Felix, but this was much too colorless. Perhaps I should settle for Otto or Otho, which in its pure vocalic sound can be used at any turn in the narrative). *Werke*, II (Stuttgart, n.d. [1962]), 43. The text we have used for the *Marmorklippen* is that of *Werke*, IX, Erzählende Schriften I (n.d. [1960]), 189–298. All translations are ours.
2. See Alice M. Coats, *Flowers and Their Histories* (London, 1968) pp. 301–3.
3. During the early thirties, Jünger collaborated in a desultory fashion with an entomologist teacher of his in the compiling of a *fauna* of Goslar in Lower Saxony. See the chapter, "Goslar im Harz," in *Subtile Jagden* (Stuttgart, 1967).

Oberförster's ruthless huntsmen. Lampusa communicates with the lance-head vipers who dwell in the crevices of the Marble Cliffs and, at sunset, descend to the court of the cloister to drink the milk which she sets out for them. Distinguished from the rest by her brass-burnished scales and jewel-like green head is the leader of the viper train, Griffin, who becomes the special pet of Erio, the divine child or *puer senex*, a model of strength and purity whose presence invigorates the brothers while at their work. Whenever these serpents join company with Erio, they gather about him in the form of a sun disk.

Hard by the Rue Cloister, on the southern, Marina side of the Marble Cliffs, stands the monastery of the Falcifera, dedicated to Maria Lunaris. She, in the words of Bruder Otho, combines on a higher plane the virtues of Fortuna and Vesta and must be seen as a beneficent counterforce to the baleful charms of Lampusa. The monastery houses the eminent botanist Father Lampros, who, as a specialist on the symmetry of fruits, can help the brothers currently at work on a study of how plants, in their growth, form a circle around an axis. Obedient to nature's ways, as is indicated by his other name Phyllobius, he who lives with leaves, and by the motto engraved on his cornelian ring, "meyn geduld hat ursach" (patience is my strength; i.e., I bide my time), Lampros has been initiated into the nutritional, curative, and integrating properties of plant life. First met by the brothers with a gladiola in hand (*Siegwurzrispe*) and light streaming from the transept window on his white mantle, this priest is the great force for good, for the sustaining recreative virtues of spirituality in the face of the destructive powers unleashed by the *Oberförster*. Lampros and Maria are, respectively, the solar and lunar principles at work, a *hieros gamos* or union of the blazing sun of science and the twilight of imagination and mystery. Both the Rue Cloister and the monastery, then, are fully achieved centers of being, for at the brothers' house it is they who represent the conscious, rational mind, whereas Lampusa incarnates infrarational, chthonic drives. The force joining and transcending the two realms, and the link between cloister and monastery—in his messages to the brothers, Lampros will entrust their dispatch only to him—is Erio, the mystic, heroic child. And the configuration of the sun disk formed by the serpents under Erio's spell—"coiled into a circle, [the serpent] symbolizes the self-sufficiency and oneness which are associated with God's preservative power"[4]—finds its parallel in that mysterium revealed in the monastery garden by Lampros to the two brothers, the green circlet of leaves and the vibrant, radiant

4. Philip Wheelwright, *The Burning Fountain* (Bloomington, Ind., 1959), p. 134.

center of the otherwise quite inconspicuous plantain, *Plantago major.*
Coiled snake and plantain, like Bruder Otho's golden lily and the gladiola
of Lampros, are thus mandalas, Indian circular images signifying, in modern psychoanalytic terms, that wholeness which the human personality
strives to attain.[5] The contemplative stillness of the monastery enclosure, the
bright blue sky and strong sunlight which are the atmospheric setting for
the disclosure of the hidden, restorative virtualities of the plantain flower,
form a pastoral landscape, a *locus amoenus*, lying at the extreme opposite
to the horrible forest clearing of Köppelsbleek with its instruments of
torture and perversion, lost in mist, and haunted by the mocking cry of
the cuckoo bird and the whispering of bats.

This place of infamy, the source from which terror will spread out over the
land—"die üble Küche, aus der die Nebel über die Marina zogen"—lies
to the north of the Marble Cliffs, on the far side of the Campagna, just
beyond the marshlands where the domain of the *Oberförster* begins. On
days when the brothers are pleased with the progress of their research,
they will climb to the summit of the Cliffs and enjoy the sublimity of its
panoramic view. At other times, tired and depressed, the two will set out
on botanical excursions in search of a new specimen. One such field trip,
undertaken to find a variety of Linnaeus' *rubra*—the woodland orchid
(*Rote Waldvögelein*)—brings them deep within the Campagna, past the
three poplars and the obscene image of the Red Steer, to the sickle-shaped
Flayers' Copse (the depraved antitype of Mary's cloister, the Falcifera,
"sickle-bearing," "sickle-shaped"). To their delight they discover the flower—but at the same time, too, the ghastly spectacle of Köppelsbleek with
its stakes and hooks, rattling skulls, and singing dwarf hard at work. Terrified, the impulse is to flee the place, but catching hold of themselves, they
are reminded of their obligation as scientists to enter a description of the
woodland plant and its natural setting in their journal. Here again the
flower functions as a mandala, an image of the potentialities of the self.
In the juxtaposition of orchid and skull, beauty in its vital growth and
radiance resists the destructive power of evil.[6]

5. See the excellent essay of Peter Uwe Hohendahl, "The Text as Cipher: Ernst Jünger's
Novel, *On the Marble Cliffs,*" in *Perspectives in Literary Symbolism*, ed. Joseph
Strelka (University Park, Pa., 1968), pp. 128 ff., to which we are also indebted for the
etymology of proper names referred to below.
6. " 'Köppelsbleek' oder besser 'Köppelesbleek' ist eine Stätte, auf der die Schadel
bleichen. . . . Ich verwendete hier einen Goslarer Flurnamen" ('Köppelsbleek' or better
yet, 'Köppelesbleek' is a place where skulls whiten. . . . I used here a dictionary of flowers
for the Goslar region), Jünger, *Werke*, II, 325; cf. the description of the home of Jünger's
entomology teacher: "Ein schönes Haus mit Garten am Stadtrand, gegenüber von Köppels-

Linked with the mandala as a conserving, integrative force are the lamp and mirror of Nigromontanus (necromancer), used at the discretion of Bruder Otho, the pure blue flame of which acts as a caustic burning objects down to their very essence. In the "time of troubles" which has overcome the land of the Marble Cliffs, the brothers must be ready at any moment to set fire, as eventually they will, to herbarium and library. Nigromontanus' mirror with its device, "Und sollte die Erde wie ein Geschoss zerspringen/ Ist unsere Wandlung Feuer und weisse Glut" (And were the earth to explode like a shot/ In our transformation we have become fire and a white glow), is assurance that their painfully acquired spiritual acquisitions will not fall prey to base powers, but instead be preserved in a higher order. If the mandala is an expression of the organic, curative virtues of nature, then the mirror translates the transforming power of art in its victory over the forces of destruction. These agents of conservation gather to themselves a whole series of such efficacious symbols. At moments of fatigue and discouragement, the narrator and Bruder Otho close the doors of the cloister, drink wine, breathe the fragrance of stored-up leaves and flower petals, light the pure-grained candles of the Provençal knight Deodat, which call to mind the sunset hour in Rhodes; they will page through the books of trusted authors and browse among old letters from cherished friends. These varied, intimate sensations and nostalgic musings nourish an idealizing memory which shores up the fragments of the past and protects them against the erosion of time. The brothers are fond, too, of composing gnomic couplets or doggerel lines which sum up, in their pithiness, nature's laws. Scribbled down on slips of paper, they serve in the evening as points of departure for serious conversation, after which they are discarded. These sibylline jottings join mandala and mirror and the various stimulants to memory as steps in a contemplative ritual dedicated to moral order, heightened awareness, and the effort to discern a pattern in the manifoldness of nature.

The present course of events occurs some seven years after the war against Alta Plana to which the brothers ascribe the ills that have ever since slowly infected the land. During the war they were enrolled in the Purple Riders, an elite squadron of the order of the Mauretanians, and it was here that they knew and frequented the company of the *Oberförster*,

---

bleek" (A lovely house with a garden on the edge of town, across from the Köppelsbleek). *Subtile Jagden*, p. 203. Some of Jünger's readers have been tempted to find in the name a key for "*Goebbels-Bleek.*" See *Werke*, III (n.d. [1963]), 451. For Goebbels and Braquemart, whom we shall discuss later, see ibid., p. 450.

who was for a time commander of all Mauretania. Prior to their enlistment, the brothers were living at loose ends; distracted and jaded by a way of life which had no meaning for them, they joined this far-flung order dedicated to the pursuit of power for its own sake. The Mauretanians are cool, disabused realists, the managerial strategists of Jünger's *Der Arbeiter.* Disciplined, endowed with keen practical intelligence, these men are committed to a ruthlessly detached view of political power. The philosophy of action which they espouse is a peculiarly abstract, efficient one intent only upon the manipulation of tangible forces: *a priori* values and inherited loyalties count for nothing in its calculations. These ascetics of the will, with their single-minded vision, exercise a strong attraction on the brothers wandering about feckless and apathetic.

Thus the Mauretanian order and the regimen of the Rue Cloister lie at opposite poles from each other, yet their extremes meet. The Rue Cloister:

> Vielleicht war es *die starke Luft der Rautenklause,* die unserem Denken eine neue Richtung gab, gleich wie im reinem Sauerstoff die Flamme steiler und heller brennt (p. 203: The new direction which our thought took was no doubt owing to the bracing air of the Rue Cloister, just as in pure oxygen the flame burns higher and brighter).

And the Mauretanians:

> Bei den Mauretanieren . . . herrschte unberührte Stille wie im Zentrum des Zyklons. Wenn man in den Abgrund stürzt, soll man die Dinge in dem letzten Grad der Klarheit wie durch überschärfte Gläser sehen. Diesen Blick, doch ohne Furcht, gewann man in *der Luft der Mauretania,* die von Grund auf böse war (p. 208: An undisturbed stillness as in the center of a cyclone prevailed among the Mauretanians. When we plunge into the abyss, we see things in their highest degree of clarity, just like looking through a sharply focused lens. This is the kind of vision, but without fear, that one attained to in the air of Mauretania which [nevertheless] was evil from the ground up).

The discipline of each of these separate ways of life, active and contemplative, calls for lucidity of outlook and the strict dedication to an ideal. The common denominator is an ethic which will both concentrate and liberate vital energies. Something of the element of play in its detachment and gratuitousness, its release of powers within very fixed limitations, enters into both spheres. Each of these styles is radically set apart from the normal, commonplace routines of life and demands from its initiates the virtues which we normally associate with solitude: a freedom from distraction, perseverance, and a steady reliance upon one's own moral resources. Given, then, the factors common to these two pursuits, the conquest of power, on the one hand, and the search for truth, on the other, both by nature radically alien to a bourgeois existence, though directed to entirely opposite ends, it is not surprising that they should appeal to the two brothers at different periods in their life, just as, indeed, they have to Ernst Jünger himself, warrior and contemplative, the author and actor of *In Stahlgewittern* and *Subtile Jagden*. On the level of biography, of *la vie romancée*, an essential though not, of course, the most important vantage point from which to read our novel, the campaign in Alta Plana with its sorry aftermath is a near-literal translation of Ernst and Friedrich Georg Jünger's engagement in the First World War and their subsequent conviction, never in doubt, that Germany's series of humiliating setbacks in the twenties must be seen as a result of the fatherland's disastrous defeat and the succeeding injustices of the Versailles Treaty. The boredom with life as it is felt by narrator and Bruder Otho transcribes fictionally the Jünger brothers' disdain for the Weimar Republic's experiment in parliamentary democracy, with its assumed concessions to mass opinion, as well as their fear of the growing rationalization and vulgarization of all areas of life in contemporary Germany. Even such a detail in the story as the magnanimity shown by the brothers towards Ansgar, the enemy soldier, finds its real-life counterpart in Jünger's gallant attitude and gestures towards his English enemies on the western front during the Great War and in his desperate efforts generally to imagine some kind of chivalry in even the bloodiest moments of trench fighting.[7]

7. The different personal accounts of Jünger's participation in the First World War make up the initial volume of the *Werke: Tagebücher I, Der erste Weltkrieg*, 1961. Jünger's own relationship to the events narrated in *Auf den Marmorklippen* is, necessarily, a complex one. The novel was finished on July 28, 1939, and published in the fall of that year. Reminiscing upon it six years later, at the end of the Second World War, he writes, "Bei Ausbruch des Krieges erschien 'Auf den Marmorklippen,' ein Buch ... das die Vorgänge in Deutschland zwar in seinem Rahmen passten, das es aber nicht speziell auf sie zugeschnitten war. Ich sehe es daher auch heute ungern als Tendenzschrift aufgefasst. Den Schuh konnten und können sich manche anziehen. Dass es auch bei uns geschehen wurde, war mehr als wahrscheinlich, und dass ich gerade hier als Augenzeuge Anregungen erfahren hatte, liess sich nicht abstreiten.... Später, inmitten der Katastrophe, wollte es mir zuweilen scheinen, als ob der Traum, die Ahnung das Künftige selbst in den Einzelheiten eindringlicher erfasst hätten, als es sich in Erlebnis verwirklichte" (At the outbreak of the war *The Marble Cliffs* appeared, a book ... which fit in very well with the preceding events in Germany, but was not expressly tailored to them. Even today I don't like to see it interpreted as in any way tendentious. The shoe could and can still fit many people. That it could also happen to us was more than likely, and that right here as an eyewitness I had experienced these disturbances cannot be denied.... Later on, in the midst of the catastrophe it seemed to me at times as if dream and presentiment had

Yet for all the points of similarity between the way of the Cloister and that of Mauretania, it is the differences which are crucial and must be stressed. The latter has as its purpose self-aggrandizement achieved through means which depend upon aggression, domination, and exploitation; the other, to which the brothers have become converted, calls for a renunciation of self, an openness to natural laws and processes which transcend the individual person and serve to integrate him in an indivisible order, at once physical and spiritual. The grandmaster of the Mauretanians is the Chief Ranger—the *Oberförster*.[8] His extraordinary presence, alluded to in the very first pages of the novel, shadows the entire narration without his ever once making an actual appearance. We hear his trumpeting laughter at the moment when he unleashes Chiffon Rouge and the bloodhound pack, and can envision the ilex-leaf pattern of his coat as he rides with arrogant assurance through his domains. He is the prince of darkness, "der Geist, der stets verneint." From his various strongholds deep within the forest interior, he sends forth his "glowworms," huntsmen, and mercenaries to spread suspicion, pick quarrels, aggravate troubled situations, abet corruption, and perpetrate acts of terrorism. Since the days of Charlemagne the Marina has often been invaded and occupied by foreign troops; but manners, customs, and even the physical setting of the area have changed very little. It is only now with the end of hostilities against Alta Plana that a perceptible deterioration has come about in the quality of life and the general look of things. The time-honored ways of the vintner, poet, and philosopher are despised in favor of the raw, boisterous behavior of the Campagna herdsmen. Once the privilege of heros, the sacred funeral rites of *elegeion* and *eburnum*, severely set forth and devoutly attended to, have become profaned, being now nothing better than raucous wakes to which any common bootlicker is entitled. One-time citizens of the Marina, who as refugees from

---

seized upon the future, even in its details, with more penetration than was actually realized in experience). *Werke*, III, 639. For Jünger's political and ideological activity between the wars, see the monumental work by Jean Pierre Faye, unsympathetic to Jünger, *Les Langages totalitaires* (Paris, 1972).

8. Jünger observes, in commenting upon the English translation of his novel (1940): "[Stuart] Hood schlägt 'Chief Ranger' für Oberförster vor. Das deutsche Wort sollte den Ordnungscharakter treffen, der untergründig wird, ähnlich wie bei Hoffmanns Geheimraten" ([Stuart] Hood recommends "Chief Ranger" as an equivalent for *Oberförster*. The German word was intended to capture the sense of an order which becomes subversive, just as with Hoffmann's *Special Advisers*). *Werke*, III, 577–78. In the French version, *Sur les falaises de marbre* (Paris, 1942), the translator, Henri Thomas, uses the name "le Grand Forestier." The *Oberförster* and Mauretania recall Stefan George's "Der Widerchrist": "Der Fürst des Geziefers verbreitet sein reich/Kein schatz der ihm mangelt. Kein glück das ihm weicht..." (The Prince of Vermin extends his kingdom. No treasure escapes his grasp. No happiness recedes before him...). *Werke*, I (Munich, 1958), 258.

justice have fled to the bogs and meadows of the Campagna, keep up connections with the homeland, thus making possible a continuous intrusion of alien, questionable practices. Progressively, the constabulary of the local police chief, Biedenhorn, himself open to corruption, has been infiltrated by bullies and criminal types dispatched from the "back of the beyond." For life in the Campagna, too, has degenerated. Because of the sinister influence of the *Oberförster*, the native, barbaric elements have become unruly, prone to yield to the darker, vicious sides of their nature. The kind of rude but fundamentally decent code of social behavior as represented by Belovar and his son Sombor, who stand for the older, authentic morality of the Campagna, is fast disappearing. A debilitating fever, a general failure of nerve paralyze the whole area, from the confines of the Campagna down beyond the Marina's shore to the holiday islands of the Hesperides where in happier times people used to row over, during the autumn, to enjoy the festivities of St. Peter's Fish and to delight in the sight and fragrance of the roses which bloom all year. Only the Rue Cloister and the Convent of Maria Lunaris, both close by the Marble Cliffs and oases of the spiritual life, remain immune against this corrupting malaise. Yet even here the menace is very real: Lampusa's ambiguous presence inhabits the lower depths of the white peaks.

During their tour of duty with the Mauretanians, the narrator and Bruder Otho would, on occasion, drink and ride with the *Oberförster*. His grand manner and the charismatic authority which he wielded fascinated them. His person, if somewhat ridiculous, possessed a genuine compelling force, all the more dominating for standing out in such contrast to the inertia of the times. Here was a creature possessed by some daemonic power, capable, one feared, of appalling acts; yet demanding from us, however grudgingly and qualified, our admiration. As the brothers remark upon listening to the ruthless exploits of the Capitano, who was later to introduce them to the *Oberförster* and to Mauretania: "Lieber noch mit diesem stürzen, als mit jenen leben, die die Furcht im Staub zu kriechen zwingt" (Better to fall with this fellow than to live with those whom fear brings to their knees in the dust).[9] Nor do the brothers question the rightness of the war they engage in against the Alta Plana. For them it is a matter, in the last resort, of doing their duty—and duty is itself a source of order, of inner strength. Nevertheless, they sympathize with these people who were defending their

9. Mauretania is the ancient, Latin name for Morocco. In Caesar's time the inhabitants belonged to the Berber strain of the Moors, lived as nomads, and had the reputation of being very belligerent.

freedom against foreign oppression. It is perhaps the encounter with Ansgar and the mercy they show him that first prompt a decisive change of heart. From their present point of view, absorbed in the life of the Rue Cloister, they see that the two of them could have risen high in the ranks of Mauretania were it not for their sense of outrage at its repressive measures against the suffering and the weak. The fundamental inhumanity of the order was intolerable to them and they had to leave. That change of heart brought on by the meeting with Ansgar in the treacherous mountain passes of the Bergland is steadily reinforced and brought to a firm resolution in the close association with Pater Lampros. They have renounced the use of force and put off forever the way of the Mauretanians. This is apparent in the brothers' refusal, after momentarily weighing their decision, to join Belovar in ridding the area through violent means of the *Oberförster*'s terrorist gangs. Aided by Lampros' example, they are determined to resist the present tyranny by remaining unswervingly devoted to a life of study and contemplation.

The choice they have made is summed up in the meeting with Braquemart (short, broad-bladed sword) and Sunmyra (he who does not speak).[10] Each of the two is only half a person: the first, the epitome of the Mauretanian outlook, is a technician of power but with no feeling for the affective, infrarational bases of our existence; the other a sensitive, noble spirit but without the force to act upon his fine impulses. The two, nihilist and aristocrat, have come together to challenge in his very seat of authority the despotic rule of the *Oberförster*. Their well-intentioned, futile, and ultimately tragic union points to the deep, seemingly irreconcilable divisions in contemporary Western culture between a conservative humanism which has lost confidence in itself and is powerless to shape the dynamic forces released by contemporary civilization, and an arrogant, runaway technocracy, heedless of spiritual values and revealing itself in certain of its grander conceptions to be grimly antihuman. "Tout ce que nous savons, tout ce que nous pouvons," Valéry writes, "a fini par s'opposer à tout ce que nous sommes." As the two men walk up the Marble Cliffs, the Prince of Sunmyra scarcely pays attention to the magical lance-head vipers, while Braquemart contemptuously steps aside from their path. Head and heart have been severed from each other, and the "two cultures" go blindly each its own way. The pathetic, frustrated efforts of Sunmyra anticipate with astonishing foresight the deliberations and abortive attempts of the German

10. The short broadsword can be seen as the symbolic opposite of the long sword of chivalry, lying in his father's house far to the north, which the narrator recalls using in the great, memorable battles of the past, but which he would scorn to handle against the minions of the *Oberförster*.

aristocracy, such men as Claus von Stauffenberg, Count Helmuth James von Moltke, Peter Yorck von Wartenburg, and Adam von Trott zu Solz, to resist and overcome Hitler.[11] It had been Jünger's forlorn hope, often commented upon in his journals of the World War II years, that the aristocracy, the Prussian landed gentry, would provide the moral leadership for a "conservative revolution" against the modern ideologies of capitalism and communism, thus preventing the rise to power and consolidation of National Socialism. Lampros' intercession on Sunmyra's behalf and the preservation of the latter's head in the petal-strewn amphora represent Jünger's sympathies with the traditional values of the German nobility, the bearers of that "Third Force," so called from the vantage point of the political right. Hearing on May 1, 1945, of Hitler's death, Jünger remarked—referring to Stauffenberg's abortive attempt at assassination the year previously—upon his own early awareness that any serious try on Hitler's life would have had to be made by one born of the old aristocracy and that, paradoxically, the dramatic and spiritual effect of such an act would lie only in its failure. "I pointed this out in detail with the figure of Sunmyra in 1939."[12]

Sunmyra is scarcely twenty years old, yet already stooped in body and world-weary in mind. He shows interesting resemblances to and differences from the thaumaturgic child Erio, wise far beyond his years and a never-failing source of joy. When the narrator sets out on his perilous search for the young prince, he takes with him the reassuring smile of Erio. It is the brother's hope, disappointed by events, that Sunmyra can come under the care of Father Lampros, for they are confident that this counselor of souls can restore to the tired scion of an old Burgundy family the faith, purpose,

11. In the extracts culled and translated in French from Jünger's World War II journals, *Strahlungen*, under the dateline 2 avril 1946, there is the curious notation: "C'était surtout la visite nocturne d'un certain M. von Trott zu Solz, destiné, par la suite, à devenir l'une des victimes du 20 juillet, qui m'avait laissé une impression funèbre. *J'avais pensé à lui en décrivant le prince de Sunmyra.*" *Journal de Guerre et d'Occupation 1939–48* (Paris, 1965), p. 483. Our italics. This passage has subsequently been suppressed in the Stuttgart *Werke*. See also Martin von Katte, "Adam von Trott zu Solz," in *Wandlung und Wiederkehr, Festschrift zum 70. Geburtstag Ernst Jüngers* (Aachen, n.d.), where Adam's admiration for Jünger is stressed; and Christopher Sykes, *Tormented Loyalty* (New York, 1969), p. 203. The model for our couple, Sunmyra-Braquemart, could very well have been suggested by the pairing of Prince Stavrogin and the terrorist Piotr Stepanovitch in Dostoevski's *The Possessed*, a favorite book of Jünger's. See, in this connection, "Das erste Pariser Tagebuch," 6. Januar 1942, in *Werke*, II, 297, and Jünger's novel, *Heliopolis* (Tübingen, 1955), p. 351.

12. "Ich habe das 1939 an der Gestalt Sunmyras im einzelnen ausgeführt." *Werke*, III, 436. Cf. the historian and essayist Reinhold Schneider: "Die Initiation der Revolutionen ist Privileg der Aristokraten, das letzte; sie lassen es sich nicht aus den Händen reissen; noch einmal sind sie voraus" (The initiation of revolutions is the privilege of aristocrats, the last one; they won't let it be snatched from their hands; once more they're out in front). *Winter in Wien* (Freiburg i.B., 1973), p. 26.

and resolve to check the disorders raging all about and to build anew. They do join each other in spirit, priest and dreamer, in the spectacular scene of apotheosis capping the catastrophic events which overtake the Grand Marina. While the Cloister of Maria Lunaris goes up in flames, the brothers hold aloft to Lampros amidst the wreckage the embalmed head of Sunmyra; the hierophant, as a sign of consecration, returns this invocatory gesture by raising his hand with the cornelian ring (bearing the motto, "I bide my time"). The nobleman's sacrifice has been made wholly acceptable, a pleasing gift. The large rose window in the transept, where the brothers first met the priest, falls in upon Lampros, its green tracery reproducing in outline the wondrous plantain flower of the monastery garden. The prince's head, purplish in cast from its preservative of wine and roses, and the glowing stained-glass window complete the series of mandalas and thus set a seal upon the exchange of sacred gestures. In the general holocaust which sweeps the country, the young Sunmyra's death is an offering in prayer for a new beginning.

Braquemart is Jünger's embodiment of a specifically modern form of evil, rootless, without allegiance, scientifically trained but one-dimensional; contemptuous of sentiment, resentful by instinct, he is bent upon destruction—even if it means, as by the logic of his character it must, self-destruction. He belongs, like Koestler's Gleitkin, to the race of the Neo-Neanderthals. In the play of forces, ideological and psychological, Braquemart sides with the *Oberförster*, though there are important differences between them. As the principle of evil, the Chief Ranger belongs, mythologically, to an ancient heritage which includes the various personifications of Satan as well as the archvillains of the Gothic novel and the Romantic imagination. A creature of the twilight, he has a wisdom of the ways of beast, wind, and rain. He is the dark, gnostic power of all the many versions of a Manichaean view of life (cf. his countertype, Lampros, the Greek word for "brilliant," "effulgent"). However real his menacing presence, there is, as a creation of myth, something fanciful and literary about him. Though both men are possessed by a frenzy to destroy, Braquemart is a different matter. He is a peculiarly modern phenomenon, conceived and analyzed imaginatively in Dostoevski's novels, heralded in Nietzsche, and realized in the revolutions and wars of our century.[13] His

13. In this connection, referring to the modern Russian experience, Berdyaev comments: "Un des caractères frappants de la révolution bolchévique fut l'apparition de nouveaux visages dont on ignorait l'expression auparavant. D'autres, connus, s'étaient métamorphosés. On n'avait jamais rencontré de types semblables parmi le peuple russe. Un nouveau type anthropologique, sans bonté, sans la molesse ni le vague des traits russes d'antan se

nihilism is the product of a dehumanized rationalism which thrives in our modern age of capitalist enterprise, vast urbanized conglomerates, relentless technocratic advances, bureaucratization, and sophisticated advertising. The complexity and nervous rhythms of today exasperate his sensibilities and turn him inward, creating a mood of sullenness and self-hate. Hence Braquemart's urge to make *tabula rasa* of everything: his natural climate is the desert, just as the forest is the habitat of the *Oberförster*.[14] Jünger insists upon the fact that *der Alte* of the forest is a man of action, whereas Braquemart is a theorist. In any confrontation the modern city-bred nihilist is no match for the anarchist from the deep, primeval interior; the former, as the inheritor of all the dark secrets of the *selva oscura*, is simply too old in experience to be outdone by such a latecomer. And so, quite predictably, the latter's joint expedition with Sunmyra ends in disaster. Upon the arrival of the pair in the evening at the Rue Cloister, the Japanese lilies have opened up, displaying in their flawless beauty six slender stamens set in a circle about the pistil; when they take leave of the brothers at dawn, the lily's purity has been flawed: night moths have done it violence, and as the narrator makes this discovery, he detects in the

---

dessinait: des visages glabres, bien rasés, durs.... Le nouveau type d'homme était issu de la guerre et c'est elle qui a fourni les cadres bolchévistes. C'est un type aussi militarisé que fasciste." *Essai d'autobiographie spirituelle* (Paris, 1958), p. 288.

In alluding to a certain naval officer, v. L., who had served in part, along with Goebbels, as the model for Braquemart, Jünger writes, "In L. begegnete ich zum ersten Male jener Mischung von Menschenverachtung, Atheismus und grosser technischer Intelligenz, von Eigenschaften, die aufeinander ausgerichtet sind" (In L. I met for the first time that mixture of contempt for humanity, atheism, and exceptional intelligence—of traits, that is, which go well together). *Werke*, III, 450. And he adds that Reinhard Heydrich, the sinister S.S. commandant and one of the architects of the "final solution," belongs to this type as well.

14. On the relationship between Braquemart and the *Oberförster*, it is worth quoting at some length Jünger's comments in *Strahlungen* about the metaphysical meaning of Mauretania: "Es ist zu schildern, wie im Niedergange, so sich viel dumpfe Materie häuft, der Rationalismus das entschiedenste Prinzip vertritt. Sodann: Wenn sich um eine Doktrin von amoralischer Technizität Zirkel bilden, werden sich ihnen dank ihrer Bösartigkeit autochthone Kräfte zugesellen, um mit deren Hilfe die alte Macht wieder zu verwirklichen, nach der die Sehnsucht ja immer auf dem Grunde ihres Herzens lebt. Auf diese Weise leuchtet in Russland das alte Zarenreich hindurch. So auch der Oberförster; in solchen Figuren findet der Nihilismus seinen Herrn. . . . Der Techniker versucht, sich mit dem Autochthonen zu verbunden, im Gefühl seines Mangels an legitimer Kraft" (What has to be depicted is how in times of decline, when so much waste material is heaped up, rationalism steps in as the most decisive principle. Furthermore, whenever certain circles are attracted to a doctrine of amoral technics, then, because of its inherent vileness, autochthonous forces will join in order to realize, with the doctrine's help, that old power for which they have always yearned at the bottom of their hearts. In just such a way the old czardom shines through in Russia. So it is with the *Oberförster*; in figures like him nihilism finds its master. The technocrat strives to bind himself to the autochthonous in his awareness of a lack of legitimate power). *Werke*, II, 28–29.

distance the cuckoo bird's call, its mocking sound not having been heard since that horrendous afternoon at Köppelsbleek.

This ghoulish site serves at the end of the novel as the meeting ground for the deadly struggle between Belovar and the *Oberförster*, the autochthonous forces of the Campagna pitted against the barbarous anarchy of the forest. Here, in the natural scheme of things, the contest is more evenly matched, and it is only because of greatly superior numbers that the Chief Ranger is finally able to rout his opposition. Their savage encounter engages the two dog packs, the Molosson mastiffs of Belovar led by Leontodon and the *Oberförster's* red-and-black Cuban bloodhounds with the dreaded Chiffon Rouge at their head. The dog of story and legend, Anubis, Cerberus, Xolotl, has been traditionally associated with death and the underworld, and these dogs of the *Marmorklippen* are hellhounds. Their tearing at each other, in this Night of the Long Knives, is the final, convulsive release of all the pent-up fury and agitation, intrigue and suspicion which have been plaguing the country. The discharge of brutish force, of hot blood, must be seen as setting off the general destruction by fire which sweeps the entire area. The war between the Campagna and Forest, in which the narrator takes part almost in spite of himself—dedicated as he has been to the pursuits of peace—is a psychomachy, a death struggle between the powers of good and evil which explodes into holocaust. From the top of the Marble Cliffs where the narrator had been given in privileged moments of the past a vision of world harmony, he sees, laid out in front of him as far as the eye can reach, a view of total conflagration. The old order of things has gone up in smoke, and together with it the Rue Cloister, consumed by the flame of Nigromontanus' lamp, and the Convent of Maria Lunaris.

In Chiffon Rouge's deadly pursuit of the narrator, it is Erio who comes to the latter's aid. Lampusa, in league with the *Oberförster*, scorns to give help to the oppressed, while Bruder Otho, preoccupied with mirror and lamp, is lost in thought and not to be distracted by any concern for his brother's physical safety: these are witch and scientist transfixed by their own obsessive concerns and closed to any call from outside. The narrator leaps over the garden wall, falling in the lily bed, whereupon at a signal from Erio the lance-head vipers, Griffin in the lead, descend the steps of the Marble Cliffs. The bejeweled serpent strikes at Chiffon Rouge, who drops dead among the lilies, while the remaining vipers, in describing a golden circle about the feeding bowl, move out in stately, martial rhythm and strangle in a flash both bloodhound and men. The boy leaves then, smiling at the narrator, and we never hear from him again. Erio, like Lampros, has acted as a psychopomp for the brothers, initiating them into the mysteries. Griffin (*Greifin*), the name of the magnificent queen of the vipers, is an allusion to the mythical beast of antique and medieval lore (m. *Greif*) whose twin nature, lion(ess) and eagle, binds together in a single whole earthly and celestial energies. The rich, complex symbolism adhering to this serpent makes her a figure of harmony, and thus a salvific force. With the extermination of the hellhound Chiffon Rouge, the sinister powers released by the *Oberförster* have been brought under control, and life can now begin anew on the Grand Marina.[15] As an emphatic sign of resurrection, Bruder Otho restores to its former dignity the sacred ritual of the *eburnum* while participating in funeral services for Sunmyra at the old family chapel. Yet if there are hesitant steps toward a return to normality and hope, the dangers to existence persist: Biedenhorn, the sycophantic police captain, always alert to which way the wind is blowing, has run up over the town fortress the flag of the red boar's head, an emblem, like night moth, dog, and cuckoo bird, of the *Oberförster*'s menacing presence.

Our parable's schematic alignment of good and evil forces finds its metaphoric counterpart in the studied use of narrative moments rendered antithetically in light and dark: the smile of Erio and Lampusa's surly glance; the gold lily and the shimmering bodies of the lance-head vipers as contrasted with the blood-stained, weathered imagery and dark fauna of Köppelsbleek; the periods of joy in scientific study accompanied by excursions to the summit of the cliffs, followed by intervals of depression and the outings into the grey Campagna marshlands. Appalled by the sight of the decapitated Sunmyra, the narrator falls into a trance, a traumatic seizure in which his right arm is paralyzed; it is in such a state that he participates in the great regenerative destruction by burning and sees the gardens of the Rue Cloister, while being chased by Chiffon Rouge, as in a magical, metallic light. It is only when the serpents have assumed the mandala shape just prior to their attack that the narrator is roused from his dream and his arm quickened to life. Indeed the two principal centers of action, symbolic poles in this fable, are conceived in terms of *chiaroscuro*: the gleaming Marble Cliffs and that heart of darkness, the forest lair of

15. Jünger intended, originally, to call his novel *Die Schlangenkönigin*. See *Werke*, II, 27; and the richly informative essay of Henri Plard, "Ex Ordine Shandytorum: Das Schlangensymbol in Ernst Jüngers Werk," in *Freundschaftliche Begegnungen, Festschrift für Ernst Jünger zum 60. Geburtstag* (Frankfort a. M., 1955), pp. 95 ff. With regard to the encounter between the serpents and the dog pack, Jünger writes, "Im Treffen der Hunde mit den Schlangen schwebt mir die Begegnung des Blutes mit einer seiner Quintessenzen, dem Gifte, vor" (In the confrontation of dogs with snakes, I was put in mind of the meeting of blood with one of its quintessences, poison). *Werke*, II, 53.

the Chief Ranger.[16] The motif of light as a symbol of harmony is complemented by a strong if discreet colorist sense which presents in rich array efficacious objects and phenomena. Their virtuality for good is mirrored forth in vivid, pleasing color. Consider only the dramatic moment of the ruin by fire of Rue Cloister and Maria Lunaris late in the novel; chromatic values and hues are set off against each other with rich yet restrained effect: lilies and roses, the white of Deodat's candles and the wine-purple trophy of Sunmyra's head, Lampros' vestments and cornelian ring placed in the green setting of the cloister window, and the pure, steady, resonant blue of Nigromontanus' lamp. These colors burst forth, then, and are burned out in the awesome incandescence of the final, apocalyptic fires which sweep the country.

The purging holocaust brings with it the hope of a new life. The Alta Plana for which the brothers set sail succeeds, as a spiritual landmark, to the Marble Cliffs of the Grand Marina, just as Ansgar *père et fils*, who welcome them to their farmstead, now replace Belovar and his son Sombor. The barns, stalls, and family dwelling are all, within the shadow of the live oak, set together in one complex—the image of a unitary, organic scheme of life, and similar in this singular grouping to the brothers' family house in the north where the sword of chivalry lies. As in a spiraling climb, like that about the margin of the White Cliffs, we have come back to a point from where we started but on a higher level of ascent. In moments of deep contentment, narrator and brother are in the habit of climbing the marble peaks to watch the sun play upon sea and countryside.

Wenn wir vom hohen Sitze auf die Stätten schauten, wie sie der Mensch zum Schutz, zur Lust, zur Nahrung und Verehrung sich errichtet, dann schmolzen die Zeiten vor unserm Auge innig ineinander ein. Und wie aus offenen Schreinen traten die Toten unsichtbar hervor. Sie sind uns immer nah, wo unser Blick voll Liebe auf altbebautem Lande ruht, und wie in Stein und Ackerfurchen ihr Erbe lebt, so waltet ihr treuer Ahnengeist in Feld und Flur (p. 213: When we look out from high places upon the abodes of man, and consider how they have been erected in his honor and for his enjoyment, protection, and sustenance, then before our view all time fuses into a single moment. And the dead step forward, invisible, as though from open shrines. They are always close to us wherever our eye rests, full of

16. It is well to recall here the name of Hitler's hideaway at Rastenburg in East Prussia where the famous July 20th attempt on his life took place: *Wolfsschanze* (Wolf's lair). "Der Wald," writes Jünger, "ist ein grosses Todessymbol" (The forest is a great symbol of death). *Werke*, III, 548.

affection, upon the land cultivated from old, and just as their inheritance lives in stone and furrow, so the true ancestral spirit presides in field and meadow).

From this priviliged prospect, the different periods of the past merge into a single span, and time is seen under the sign of infinity, *sub specie aeternitatis.* "I live in the leaf" (which buds and withers), says Lampros for whom all scientific theories have their validity because each one, in turn, brings its contribution to the great mystery of genesis. Disintegration and reintegration, the recurring cycle of cosmos and chaos, catastrophe and rebirth, in individual lives as well as among nations and civilizations, define the underlying pattern of historical enactment which Ernst Jünger studies from the top of the Marble Cliffs. Individual fate functions as type and symbol, while the single occurrence in time is charged with depth and gravity, being conceived as the manifestation of a supratemporal order of recurrence.[17] In this allegorical meditation on world harmony, the vision of which is gnostic, mythic, and archetypal, Jünger belongs squarely to the tradition of German romanticism: his *Naturphilosophie*, with its organicism, Platonic resonances, and delight in symbol and faraway incident, makes him a *frère spirituel* of Goethe and Novalis.

"Dreieinig sind das Wort, die Freiheit und der Geist" (The Word, Freedom, and Spirit are triune). This solemn, trinitarian affirmation occurring in the very middle of our narration gives witness to Jünger's credo in the power of civilizing energies to overcome evil—an act of faith nourished by a perennial philosophy which equates order with *logos.* Hence the studied, disciplined care with which the novel is composed, Jünger assuming, in the manner of his master, Nietzsche, a prophetic, monumental, apodictic tone. Archaisms and exotic touches reinforce the timelessness of this fable in which automobiles make their way through feudal settings. Sentences are deliberately weighed against each other to assure a full, steady, cadenced effect, while a telling image or an aphorism of gnomic import rounds off the individual paragraphs unanimated by any conversation and, in their unremitting gravity of mood, giving the semblance of marble stelae.[18] Ritual, choice artefacts, beautiful natural forms, contem-

17. See Hohendahl, pp. 134–35; cf. Malraux's meditation at the close of *Les Chênes qu'on abat*: "Staline, regardant tomber par la fenêtre du Kremlin la neige qui ensevelit les chevaliers teutoniques et la Grande Armée . . ." (Paris, 1971), p. 222.

18. In reflecting, at the time of composition, upon the extremely conscious effort which was going into the writing of the *Marmorklippen*, Jünger comments, "Die Arbeit schreitet langsam vor, weil ich mir Mühe gebe, den Text vollkommen und in jedem Satze durchzustechen. . . . *Leider fehlt mir dazu die Nonchalance*" (The work is moving along slowly

plative leisure, and scientific research—in a word, all of the ingredients and values of a classic, high culture—are celebrated in a book completed on the eve of Hitler's invasion of Poland and just a few weeks before Jünger himself, resignedly, will report for military service as a captain in the *Wehrmacht*. His aestheticism and detachment, which have been strongly criticized and do at times lapse into a cold preciosity, are intended to serve as charms which ward off malign forces threatening to overwhelm philosophic composure and the rule of reason.[19]

---

because I'm taking great pains to go over the text as a whole and each sentence, too.... *Unfortunately, what I don't have for this is nonchalance*). *Werke*, II, 58; italics ours. "Qui donc a dit qu'il lui manquait ce que précisément il aimait tant chez les autres: la désinvolture?" Banine, *Portrait d'Ernst Jünger* (Paris, 1971), p. 251. Cf. Rainer Gruenter, "Formen des Dandysmus. Eine problemgeschichtliche Studie über Ernst Jünger," *Euphorion*, 46 (1952), 170–201.

19. Against the reproach that he is guilty of intellectual dilettantism in the midst of the horrors of our age, Jünger defends himself as follows: "Ces contradictions sont notre monde même: la dimension onirique ou cauchemardesque de l'existence moderne. Voyez les actualités: au même instant, explose une bombe atomique, une mère se sacrifie pour un enfant, des alpinistes tombent dans un gouffre. . . . Les événements ne se succèdent pas d'une façon systématique, ils s'enchevêtrent, et parfois ils sont horribles. J'ai toujours été fasciné par les facettes multiples de notre monde. Lorsqu'un terrible danger vous menace, pourquoi ne lirait-on pas Hölderlin, ou n'observerait-on pas l'évolution d'un insecte dans la boue? Cela m'est arrivé, dans les tranchées de la Première Guerre mondiale, ou en 1940, sur les routes. On peut oublier alors la guerre, le lieu, le temps, la consigne, et je crois que cela existe sur tous les fronts. Cette possibilité de s'abstraire dans son destin personnel, c'est parfois tout ce qui nous reste." "Va plus loin avec Ernst Jünger," *L'Express*, 11–17 Jan. 1971, pp. 68–69.

Edouard Morot-Sir

L'idéalisme philosophique et les techniques littéraires au vingtième siècle

I. Philosophie et littérature

Il n'y a pas de littérature sans engagement philosophique, explicite ou non. Les célèbres "engagements" existentiels, pascalien ou sartrien, ne sont pas plus universels que peut l'être l'engagement philosophique d'une expression littéraire quelconque. Le refus de participer aux entreprises d'un groupe est action. Techniquement, il n'y a pas d'ensemble verbal à prétention littéraire, sans intervention de mots et d'expressions à vecteur philosophique; et il est aisé de voir que la plupart des mots généraux d'une langue, quand ils ne désignent pas telle ou telle espèce d'êtres ou d'objets (le primate, le caporal, la viande, le tennis, etc.), invitent à la réflexion philosophique, vague ou précise: y a-t-il un moyen de présenter un texte littéraire sans faire intervenir, à un moment ou un autre, des mots tels que *être*, *existence*, *amour*, *moi*, *nous*, *eux*, etc.? Admettons donc l'existence d'un langage philosophique, ou au minimum, l'existence de mots et de phrases appartenant à d'autres langages (reconnaissons ici que la linguistique actuelle n'est pas assez avancée pour nous aider à identifier ces diverses espèces de langages; seuls les logiciens pourraient être de quelque secours en cette circonstance). En bref, la présence de la philosophie dans toute expression littéraire, longue ou brève, est inévitable et universelle.

Observons ensuite les aspects d'un usage conscient de la philosophie par des écrivains non-philosophes—poètes, romanciers, dramaturges, critiques, etc. Le langage philosophique intervient alors dans le jeu littéraire et participe, parfois au premier plan, à l'action et à l'effet littéraires cherchés. Il s'agit d'exploitations de thèmes philosophiques. Les procédés varient à l'infini, depuis l'illustration mythique d'une théorie (tels les mythes platoniciens) jusqu'à l'espérance poétique d'aller au-delà de la philosophie elle-même, et de la surexprimer. Le XVIIIe siècle français a même défendu l'idée que toute langue tend à s'achever dans une forme analytique qui est celle du langage philosophique, de telle sorte que la littérature, en son histoire, évoluerait vers l'expression philosophique: les genres littéraires, une fois dégagés des origines gestuelles et émotionnelles du langage (voir, par exemple, la théorie de Condillac), trouveraient leur ultime raison d'être comme illustrations communicables de la pensée philosophique. Il est vrai que cette conception de la relation entre philosophie et littérature porte en elle-même les germes de la destruction de la littérature, car cette forme dernière et analytique du langage n'est autre que le langage scientifique, lui-même destructeur de toute forme littéraire. Quoiqu'il en soit de ce danger permanent d'auto-destruction, le fait est général: la plupart des écrivains utilisent, systématiquement ou non, des formes philosophiques pour donner à leurs productions leur maximum d'effet et de rayonnement.

Il arrive aussi que l'œuvre entière d'un écrivain, d'un groupe, d'une génération, soit la conséquence de principes esthétiques formulés par une école ou un écrivain, ou encore empruntés à un philosophe. L'action du cartésianisme sur l'esthétique classique, par exemple, est aussi indéniable qu'elle est difficile à déterminer. L'existentialisme de Sartre est simultanément une psychanalyse existentielle, une théorie du langage et une esthétique concentrée sur le problème de la théorie de la littérature: le passage de *L'Etre et le Néant* à *Qu'est-ce que la littérature?* fait partie du développement naturel du langage sartrien, de telle sorte qu'il serait ridicule de se demander si ce passage d'une œuvre à l'autre est de l'ordre de la déduction, comme si l'expression littéraire choisie—nouvelle, roman, pièce, essai— était la conséquence d'un système; elle peut en être l'illustration ou la justification, mais rarement la déduction!

Les précédentes remarques montrent que la relation entre langage philosophique et expressions littéraires est infiniment plus complexe qu'il ne le semble au premier abord,—en tous cas, d'une complexité qui n'a pas été reconnue jusqu'à présent par les écrivains, par les philosophes eux-mêmes, et surtout par les historiens de la littérature qui ont tendance à réduire ce problème à une vague et confuse étude d'influence. Pour échapper à cette manière de poser le problème—et ici je ne vise pas l'écrivain lui-même pour qui la relation entre philosophie et littérature est un problème de technique littéraire, mais l'historien qui prétend expliquer et résoudre ce problème en termes d'objectivité scientifique—il n'y a, je crois, qu'une seule issue: poser le problème en termes de langage, ce que j'appellerai adopter une attitude linguistique généralisée, et ainsi refuser de le formuler en termes d'histoire des idées, ou en termes psycho-sociologiques. Une telle attitude implique le postulat suivant: la philosophie est un langage possible à partir d'une langue donnée; ce langage est reconnaissable par un certain vocabulaire que l'on trouve dans les lexiques ou dictionnaires de philosophie; de plus ces mots sont assemblés en phrases qui elles-mêmes se groupent en ensembles verbaux appelés essais, traités, systèmes.

Qu'on me permette ici une remarque personnelle: je tiens à souligner le caractère hasardeux de mes hypothèses; ma seule excuse est la quasi absence de précédents dans ce domaine de recherche qui pourtant me paraît central en théorie de la littérature. La plupart des historiens ou critiques partent d'une philosophie préalable, avouée ou non; et ainsi, au lieu d'analyser le problème, ils nous proposent une interprétation de la relation littérature-philosophie adaptée à la propre philosophie de leur langage critique! Je ne prétends certes pas faire mieux. Je cherche simplement à repartir de zéro, plus exactement, à ressaisir le problème à son point de départ: comment des mots ou des expressions, les uns et les autres reconnus philosophiques, interviennent-ils dans des formes reconnues littéraires? A cette question deux solutions formelles sont possibles: l'intervention se fait par *collage* ou par *intégration*. Par "collage" je veux dire ceci: l'expression philosophique (un mot ou un groupe de mots) a une existence distincte à l'intérieur d'un langage—par exemple, poétique, romanesque, théâtral, etc.—, elle y subsiste dans son originalité philosophique (que celle-ci soit une allusion philosophique, le commentaire d'un personnage dans une conversation, une maxime: l'inventaire systématique de ces collages reste évidemment à faire).

Par "intégration" je désigne tout autre procédé qui n'est pas de l'ordre du collage. C'est dire que le mot *intégration* cache divers procédés qui sont à identifier. Je propose de distinguer deux types d'intégration de langage philosophique en milieu littéraire: l'*insertion théorique* et l'*intégration technique*. La première est l'insertion d'un exposé philosophique à l'intérieur d'un récit, d'une pièce, d'un poème. *Louis Lambert, Séraphita* consacrent de longues pages à des développements théoriques. En forme plus ramassée, l'Oreste des *Mouches* présente la théorie sartrienne de la liberté. Les sermons de l'abbé Paneloux de *La Peste* sont des morceaux de théologie morale chrétienne. Les célèbres pages de Proust dans *La Prisonnière* et dans *Le Temps retrouvé* sur sa conception de l'art, de la littérature et des cultures humaines, sont aussi des exemples d'enclaves théoriques d'une certaine pensée philosophique dans le mouvement même d'un genre littéraire.—On objectera peut-être que cette insertion théorique pourrait ne différer que par degré du collage philosophique, puisque dans un cas comme dans l'autre, quelle que soit l'habileté technique de l'écrivain, la référence philosophique subsiste par elle-même comme un corps étranger au récit, au drame, au poème, même s'il en est l'aboutissement. Toutefois l'insertion d'un langage philosophique (dans un roman par exemple) crée une situation paradoxale, dont Proust, mieux que tout autre, a été conscient: il a reconnu la disparité de cette insertion quand il a attribué au récit les temps verbaux du passé, et à l'indicatif présent le temps d'expression de la pensée théorique: n'était-ce pas avouer que son œuvre, et même toute œuvre littéraire, ne peut être que la juxtaposition d'une trame philosophique et d'une navette faite d'un langage concret et particulier?

J'appelle *intégration technique* l'intervention de principes philosophiques dans la structure même d'un genre: par exemple, pour le roman, dans la composition des descriptions, des dialogues, du récit; au théâtre, dans le traitement des personnages ou le développement dramatique; ou encore dans la formation des images lyriques ou épiques. Alors la pensée philosophique cesse d'être théorique, elle n'est plus le résultat de cette conduite linguistique que l'on appelle "philosophie"; elle agit comme procédé de composition littéraire; elle renvoie au langage lui-même, et non, comme le fait normalement une philosophie, à la réalité, humaine ou autre.

En conclusion, *l'effet* proprement littéraire du langage philosophique est obtenu par le collage ou par l'intégration technique. Quand le langage philosophique intervient en quelque sorte démasqué, avoué et même revendiqué, il se présente alors dans sa propre vocation d'être un langage dernier, qui rassemble tous les autres,—la forme définitive et achevée de toute littérature, à moins que, suivant Proust, on concède l'indépendance de deux langages, l'un concret, l'autre abstrait, et qu'on se résigne à leur coexistence.... Dans la suite de cette étude nécessairement limitée, et comme exploration préliminaire, j'examinerai exclusivement le problème du collage. Je m'excuse de le redire une dernière fois: cette étude a pour objet de souligner l'importance critique de la relation entre littérature et philosophie; elle commence la prospection en insistant sur les questions de techniques d'écriture et de recherches des effets; heuristique, elle ne prétend être ni systématique ni exhaustive.

II. L'idéalisme philosophique

Pour sortir de ces généralités et les éprouver par l'examen d'un problème plus délimité, je vais étudier le cas d'une théorie philosophique assez bien définie, du moins par les dictionnaires et les histoires de la philosophie, *l'idéalisme*. J'ai précisé "philosophique" afin d'indiquer qu'il ne s'agit pas du sens courant du mot *idéalisme*, avec son adjectif et son verbe, dans sa portée morale et sentimentale.

Reportons-nous d'abord au *Vocabulaire technique et critique de la philosophie* d'André Lalande (édition de 1956). Nous y apprenons que le mot a été employé pour la première fois vers la fin du XVIIe siècle, et Leibniz est cité. L'article comprend trois sections de très inégale importance—une longue analyse du sens métaphysique, et deux brefs paragraphes sur les sens moral et esthétique. Il est reconnu que le mot, dans sa généralité, désigne *une tendance intellectuelle qui consiste à ramener toute existence à la pensée,* au sens le plus large de ce mot (tel qu'il est notamment employé par Descartes pour qui il dénote aussi bien les sensations que les sentiments ou les idées, et ainsi, aussi bien la pensée confuse de l'expérience sensible que la pensée mathématique la plus rigoureuse). Ensuite Lalande énumère les sens spécifiques, en tant qu'ils qualifient telles ou telles théories philosophiques: idéalisme platonicien, idéalisme immatérialiste de Berkeley, idéalisme empirique (l'expression, qui vient de Kant, vise les philosophies de Locke, Hume, Condillac), idéalisme transcendantal de Kant, puis les idéalismes subjectif de Fichte, objectif de Schelling et absolu de Hegel, l'idéalisme de Renouvier, et enfin l'idéalisme critique de Brunschvicg. Cette énumération suffit à montrer la variété des sens possibles pour l'historien de la philosophie! Lalande ajoute une section critique où il souligne la principale difficulté de cette philosophie: sa référence à la pensée vise-t-elle la pensée d'un individu ou une pensée universelle? Dans la première hypothèse, comment peut-on éviter le solipsisme d'une pensée incapable de sortir d'elle-même? Et dans l'autre cas, comment ne pas se reporter à un esprit universel, et ainsi revenir vers un réalisme spiritualiste? Lalande alors conseille "de faire le moindre usage possible d'un terme dont le sens est aussi indéterminé." Fort heureusement ce conseil donné par Lalande n'a pas été suivi: le mot "idéalisme" a été l'un des plus utilisés dans la pensée française du XXe siècle; il l'est encore de nos jours, même quand il est employé par les marxistes pour désigner une philosophie périmée.

Un coup d'œil à un ouvrage récent, *Dictionnaire des grandes philosophies,* sous la direction de Louis Jerphagnon (1973) prouve l'importance et l'activité actuelles du mot, bien que l'auteur de l'article "idéalisme" rejoigne Lalande pour reconnaître la confusion du mot et la grande variété de ses applications. Toutefois il note que la philosophie moderne se caractérise par une "exigence idéaliste" qui a sa source dans Descartes, et qui s'oppose au réalisme thomiste et aristotélicien.

Si l'on regarde maintenant la situation philosophique pour notre siècle, on constate que le mot idéalisme a organisé son champ sémantique en un ensemble d'oppositions qui se sont répercutées dans l'usage littéraire du mot: d'abord l'opposition globale entre idéalisme et réalisme—ce dernier mot désignant tantôt le réalisme d'origine thomiste et aristotélicienne, tantôt le réalisme scientifique, tantôt le réalisme marxiste (on reconnaîtra aisément ici, dans cette triple opposition, les trois problèmes les plus aigus de notre époque, au moins pour la culture française: l'idéalisme a été et est encore l'objet d'attaque de la part des grandes *orthodoxies* contemporaines—catholique, scientifique et marxiste). —Ensuite les oppositions structurent le champ idéaliste lui-même: opposition entre idéalisme absolu (d'inspiration hégélienne) et idéalisme critique (d'origine kantienne),—opposition entre idéalisme empirique (qui se rattache surtout à Berkeley, Hume, et englobe Condillac, Taine) et idéalisme transcendantal avec Kant, puis Husserl et sa méthode phénoménologique. Si nous ajoutons qu'à la fin des années 30, Hegel a exercé une influence considérable sur la pensée française au moment même où l'existentialisme de Sartre commence à attaquer violemment les idéalismes, alors triomphants, de Brunschvicg et du mouvement de la "Philosophie de l'Esprit," on comprendra que l'accusation de confusion faite par les lexicologues n'est pas vaine, et on se demandera aussi comment des écrivains non-spécialistes pouvaient trouver leur chemin dans un domaine où les philosophes eux-mêmes donnaient des exemples d'une superbe variété!

Pourtant l'action littéraire des philosophies idéalistes est indiscutable! On pourrait certes déclarer que certains philosophes ont été abusivement dénommés "idéalistes," par exemple Hegel, Schopenhauer, Husserl, Kierkegaard, etc. La présence, qui n'est guère contestable, de ces philosophes dans la vie littéraire du XXe siècle, s'expliquerait alors par l'existence, dans leurs pensées, d'éléments qui ne se rattachent pas à "l'exigence idéaliste." De telles discussions sont oiseuses, et invitent à penser que le problème d'influence est toujours mal posé. Reconnaissons aussi que la plupart des écrivains, quand ils ne sont pas philosophes de profession et n'ont pas besoin de marquer certaines oppositions personnelles ou théoriques, ne se soucient guère de se savoir ou de s'affirmer idéalistes, hégéliens, phénoménistes, phénoménologues, critiques, etc. Ils ont à résoudre des problèmes d'écriture qui impliquent des références à des langages philosophiques, mais non des prises de position philosophique.

Le vrai problème ne réside donc pas dans un engagement pour ou contre l'idéalisme, selon le contenu reconnu au mot. Il concerne la relation entre certains principes ou méthodes plus ou moins reliées à l'un ou l'autre des idéalismes reconnus par les vocabulaires ou dictionnaires, et leurs effets sur tel ou tel genre littéraire. Par exemple, le problème n'est pas vraiment de savoir si Baudelaire était un vague disciple de Platon, mais de saisir l'effet poétique qu'il tirait d'une référence, implicite ou non, au platonisme dans un vers ou un poème. Tout idéalisme, même restreint, même s'il admet l'existence d'un monde extérieur réel et matériel, commence par dire que toute expérience de réalité se fait par l'intermédiaire de la conscience ou de l'inconscient. Ce disant, il enlève aux mots leur charge réaliste commune, et les ramène vers une expérience intérieure: le mot *chaise* ne désigne plus un objet réel en dehors de moi, mais un groupe de sensations, ou même un modèle idéal de la chaise. L'écrivain—poète ou romancier—peut alors chercher à traduire ses expériences plutôt que de laisser son langage dominé par le postulat de l'existence d'un monde extérieur matériel. On comprend facilement que les techniques de narration et de caractérisation vont changer considérablement. Pour le moment contentons-nous d'admettre que l'idéalisme invite à chercher un effet de *déréalisation* (par rapport à la croyance commune à l'existence d'un monde extérieur) qui conduira à un effet inverse de *surréalisation*: ce qui est peut-être la condamnation de l'idéalisme comme philosophie, mais ce qui n'a été possible que grâce à l'attitude initiale de toute critique idéaliste. Est-ce par hasard—et je ne le crois pas—qu'André Breton écrit, quand il commence à chercher un langage théorique pour le Surréalisme, une *Introduction au discours sur le peu de réalité?*[1] Pensant sans doute à la célèbre déclaration de Mallarmé sur "l'absente de tous bouquets,"[2] il lance une proclamation antiréaliste:

> L'existence dûment constatée à l'avance de ce bouquet que je vais respirer ou de ce catalogue que je feuillette devrait me suffire: eh bien non. Il faut que je m'assure de sa réalité, comme on dit, que je prenne contact avec elle. L'erreur serait de retenir cette mimique pour seule expressive. En dépit de ces multiples accidents, *ma pensée* a son allure propre....[3]

Mais le problème technique de l'écrivain n'est pas résolu par une simple déclaration de foi philosophique. Il ne suffit pas de faire un exposé de philosophie idéaliste ou de dire: attention, quand j'emploie le mot *forêt* je ne vise pas simplement la forêt que votre sens commun réaliste vous fait

1. *Point du jour* (1934).
2. "Crise de vers," *Œuvres complètes*, Bibliothèque de la Pléiade, p. 368.
3. P. 11; je souligne.

croire réelle, mais j'évoque un au-delà de votre vie quotidienne. Il faut encore trouver les effets stylistiques qui fassent sentir la déréalisation idéaliste. L'écrivain comprend alors—et pour cela il n'a pas besoin d'être philosophe de profession—que tout idéalisme (la philosophie réaliste correspondante l'est aussi) est composée de trois théories qui se constituent en trois modes de langages possibles: le langage de la *perception* (les signes appliqués à des objets supposés extérieurs), le langage de la *réflexion* (les signes exprimant un monde intérieur en dehors des catégories sensorielles et spatiales), et le langage de *relation* (les signes se distinguant les uns des autres ou communiant entre eux selon des lois d'appartenance et de différenciation qui ne sont peut-être pas celles auxquelles nous sommes habitués dans notre réalisme vulgaire). Ainsi l'opération de déréalisation du langage peut se faire à trois niveaux—perception, réflexion, relation—avec la possibilité d'une fusion de niveaux: par exemple l'opération proustienne de déréalisation perceptive qui substitue le souvenir à la perception directe, et donne aux images une valeur métaphorique, est solidaire d'une déréalisation de la pensée qui s'installe dans le mouvement narratif d'un monologue intérieur: perception et réflexion sont alors fondues dans une même opération d'écriture. Le poète romantique, en déployant son univers métaphorique, est à la recherche d'un monde différent du monde extérieur,—un monde qui fourmille en relations analogiques, en communications subjectives qui prennent leur sens dans une réflexion greffée sur la perception naïve des objets extérieurs.

En résumé, les données de notre problème se précisent à l'aide des concepts suivants: (i) toute présence d'un langage philosophique quelconque dans un ensemble littéraire se fait par *collage, insertion,* ou *intégration*; (ii) l'intervention de l'idéalisme philosophique se caractérise par une opération de *déréalisation* qui détruit le langage associé au réalisme du sens commun; (iii) cette opération s'exerce à trois niveaux de langage—*perceptif, réflexif, relationnel.*

III. Le collage philosophique

Des exemples peuvent en être trouvés partout dans la littérature du XXe siècle,—le roman, la poésie ou le théâtre (j'écarte l'essai qui lui-même devrait être considéré comme une forme dérivée de littérature philosophique, et qui soulève un problème voisin, mais distinct de celui que je pose dans cette étude): je ne connais pas d'écrivain important de cette période qui n'ait fait intervenir dans son œuvre des noms de philosophes, ou des pensées, ou même, par allusion, des théories philosophiques. Leur fréquence est assurément plus grande dans le roman que dans la poésie ou le théâtre.

Le collage est le plus souvent le nom d'un philosophe, le titre d'une œuvre,—l'un ou l'autre souvent accompagné d'une brève référence à la vie ou à la pensée du philosophe. En voici quelques exemples. Dans *A la recherche du temps perdu*, on relève 25 allusions à des philosophes: presque tous sont d'orientation spiritualiste; quelques-uns sont idéalistes, selon l'un des sens que nous avons reconnus; mais le plus souvent ils sont cités pour des raisons qui n'ont rien à voir avec leur idéalisme. Ainsi Schopenhauer est mentionné deux fois, pour ses idées sur la musique. Kant est cité quatre fois, en référence à sa morale de la liberté. Platon apparaît neuf fois, mais par allusion aux jeunes gens, à Aspasie et à Socrate. Hegel est purement et simplement nommé. Descartes est reconnu une seule fois, pour son affirmation sur l'universalité du bon sens. Sur trois mentions de Leibniz une seule vise la théorie de la monade comme reflet individuel de l'univers. Il en va de même pour Taine, quoique l'une des quatre références à ce nom est bien curieuse et mérite d'être citée:

> Au reste, dans la limpide folie qui précède ces sommeils plus lourds si des fragments de sagesse flottent lumineusement, si les noms de Taine, de George Eliot n'y sont pas ignorés, il n'en reste pas moins au monde de la veille cette supériorité d'être, chaque matin, possible à continuer, et non chaque soir le rêve.[4]

Enfin il est peut-être significatif de noter que les deux seuls noms cités en relation avec la théorie idéaliste du monde extérieur sont ceux de John Stuart Mill et de Lachelier dans le même passage:

> Un philosophe qui n'était pas assez moderne pour elle [Marquise Renée de Cambremer], Leibniz, a dit que le trajet est long de l'intelligence au cœur. Ne quittant la lecture de Stuart Mill que pour celle de Lachelier, au fur et à mesure qu'elle croyait moins à la réalité du monde extérieur, elle mettait plus d'acharnement à chercher à s'y faire, avant de mourir, une bonne position.[5]

Ces échantillons suggèrent que les allusions proustiennes aux philosophes n'ont pas d'intention directement philosophique; elles évoquent un nom, une œuvre par rapport aux personnages de l'univers proustien, et elles donnent aux philosophes cités une présence réelle sur laquelle s'appuient les

4. Proust, éd. Pléiade, III, 123.
5. Ibid., II, 924.

êtres imaginaires de *La Recherche*. Dans le texte ci-dessus les noms de philosophes et leurs pensées produisent un effet contradictoire. Leibniz explique comment Madame de Cambremer peut à la fois croire au caractère apparent du monde extérieur, et chercher à fortifier sa position dans cet univers illusoire. Mill et Lachelier sont condamnés pour l'inefficacité de leurs idéalismes. Certes Proust, qui s'en prend ici à Madame de Cambremer, aurait pu se contenter de souligner la contradiction entre les idées de cette dame et ses décisions pratiques. Quel est alors l'effet obtenu par les trois noms? L'ironie est étendue; elle passe du monde du roman au monde réel de la philosophie,—Madame de Cambremer est située par rapport à des êtres réels; les uns en font une disciple, quelque peu naïve et snob, de la philosophie idéaliste; l'autre pose le problème du décalage entre la pensée et l'action. Nous trouvons aussi une autre indication: Proust oppose indirectement les grands philosophes de l'antiquité et de la période classique aux philosophes modernes.

Finalement ces collages proustiens concernent moins une certaine philosophie que la philosophie en général et les philosophes avec leurs mœurs et leurs formules, comme si Proust admettait implicitement l'existence d'un éclectisme philosophique dont Platon serait l'inspirateur. Ce ne serait donc pas par hasard si Platon est plus souvent cité que les autres philosophes: neuf fois, et sept fois Socrate. L'allusion qui renvoie à des individualités d'une culture passée, lointaine ou proche, force le lecteur attentif à sortir du texte, qui se trouve annulé dans sa prétention à devenir réel. Comme le collage cubiste, le collage philosophique est un avertissement magique, du genre de: attention, la réalité est ailleurs! Et pour Proust, on le sait, cette réalité est l'univers des cultures en devenir, dont les constellations sont des noms propres, révélateurs de signes, de langages et de pensées.

Les collages de référence idéaliste les plus intéressants se trouvent chez trois auteurs qui vont nous éclairer sur la fonction littéraire secrète de ce procédé: Breton, Gracq, Beckett.—Dans *Nadja* André Breton cite Berkeley et ses *Dialogues entre Hylas et Philonous*. La manière dont le collage intervient mérite attention. Les premières rencontres entre Breton et Nadja ont lieu entre le 4 et le 12 octobre 1926. La plus importante est sans doute celle du 6 octobre où le poète et Nadja, après s'être croisés par hasard, vont à la Place Dauphine. Ils marchent dans le quartier, se dirigent ensuite vers le Louvre. Sur le quai, ils regardent la Seine et Nadja demande: "Cette main, cette main sur la Seine, pourquoi cette main qui flambe sur l'eau?" Plus tard ils s'arrêtent devant un jet d'eau au Jardin des Tuileries, et Nadja commente: "Ce sont tes pensées et les miennes...." Alors Breton s'écrie: "Mais, Nadja, comme c'est étrange! Où prends-tu justement cette image qui se trouve exprimée presque sous la même forme dans un ouvrage que tu ne peux connaître et que je viens de lire?" Intervient alors ce collage qui est caractéristiquement mis entre parenthèses:

> (Et je suis amené à lui expliquer qu'elle fait l'objet d'une vignette, en tête du troisième des *Dialogues entre Hylas et Philonous*, de Berkeley, dans l'édition de 1750, où elle est accompagnée de la légende: "*Urget aquas vis sursum eadem flectitque deorsum*," qui prend à la fin du livre, au point de vue de la défense de l'attitude idéaliste, une signification capitale.)

Breton ne nous dira pas quelle est cette signification capitale. Il enchaîne immédiatement, comme pour montrer que selon lui, l'effet cherché a été produit: "Mais elle ne m'écoute pas, toute attentive qu'elle est au manège d'un homme...." Le lecteur peut adopter une attitude réaliste et penser: Breton rend compte d'une de ces coïncidences comme les surréalistes les aiment, et il nous donne en même temps un bel exemple de hasard objectif. Je crois qu'il faut partir d'une telle lecture réaliste,—ne pas se laisser prendre à la tentation de l'allégorie, celle-là même que pratique Nadja en comparant les mouvements de la pensée à ceux du jet d'eau. Mais nous sommes informés que Breton lit Berkeley et s'intéresse à son idéalisme,— que dans ce compte-rendu objectif qu'est *Nadja* la philosophie idéaliste a une importance particulière. Les précisions données (troisième dialogue, vignette, édition de 1750, maxime en latin) accentuent à la fois l'objectivité du récit et son étrangeté. Il serait trop simple de dire que Breton veut nous avertir de l'importance de l'attitude idéaliste pour le Surréalisme. La parenthèse est plus qu'une directe invitation au lecteur: "lisez Berkeley, avec moi!" Elle est comme un trou dans la continuité du récit,—un trou ou, si l'on préfère, une fenêtre qui s'ouvre et se referme aussitôt sur le monde philosophique. Il y a donc collage, et non pure fidélité à une situation de faits.

Il y a plus qu'un éclairage donné obliquement sur les arrière-plans du Surréalisme. Cet avertissement, cette indication surprennent, comme une rupture de réalité à double effet: un homme, un livre, des détails du livre sont désignés; ils sont réels, mais ils visent la pensée de l'irréalité du monde extérieur, et paradoxalement ils sont ouverture sur le monde extérieur par rapport au monde intérieur du récit. En bref un tel collage a un double effet positif et négatif. Aurait-il été possible avec n'importe quel autre auteur ou livre? Peut-être. Mais à mon avis, seule une telle allusion à l'idéalisme, au centre même de l'aventure Breton-Nadja, donne au collage berkeleyen un pouvoir d'explosif mental (pour employer une expression surréaliste): le récit, écrit apparemment comme un rapport médical, s'abolit devant une allusion philosophique, tout en se maintenant comme seul langage légitime. Dans ce contexte le vrai collage littéraire ne peut être qu'idéaliste. L'humour vient aussi de ce que cet immatérialisme, comparé à l'éclatement de l'eau en gerbes de gouttes qui montent et descendent, est en fait appuyé sur la réalité d'un homme et d'un livre. Le collage pourrait être, en recours ultime, le désespoir de toute littérature.

Voici maintenant d'autres collages idéalistes, cette fois avec Hegel, dans le premier récit de Julien Gracq, *Au château d'Argol*. On pourra contester la qualification de collage pour ces allusions philosophiques dans l'œuvre de Gracq. A première vue celles-ci semblent être des insertions qui jouent le rôle d'indications utiles, comme on en trouve en tout roman qui donne des informations sur l'apprentissage intellectuel d'un héros. Cependant le problème du langage philosophique dans ses relations avec le récit y est impliqué, de sorte que l'intégration théorique ou insertion, telle que je l'ai définie plus haut, ne serait ici qu'apparente. L'intention de collage est, à mon avis, plus forte; elle est littéraire par ses effets sur le lecteur. Voici les trois collages:

1) Il [Albert] s'était fixé pour tâche de résoudre *les énigmes du monde des sens et de la pensée*. Il lut Kant, Leibniz, Platon, Descartes, mais la pente naturelle de ses goûts le poussait vers *les philosophies plus concrètes* et certains osèrent dire plus courageuses qui, prenant le monde comme à bras-le-corps et généreusement, et non contentes d'y faire pénétrer le rapon de telle lumière particulière, lui demandaient sa vérité et son explication *totales* en le dénombrant en ses parties composantes, comme Aristote, comme Plotin, comme Spinoza. Mais surtout il s'était pris d'une curiosité passionnée pour le prince des génies de la philosophie, Hegel; à ce roi de l'architecture et de la science des ensembles, à celui pour qui les plus brillants systèmes philosophiques ne sont que les nébuleuses dont il compose sa gigantesque voie lactée, il venait de vouer une prédilection énergique: il tenait la dialectique pour ce levier demandé par dérision par Archimède et qui soulèverait le monde, et *il emportait Hegel dans son manoir solitaire de Bretagne* pour y remplir surabondamment les journées, qu'il prévoyait mornes et arides, d'une contrée mélancolique.[6]

6. *Au château d'Argol*, éd. José Corti, pp. 18–19.

J'ai tenu à citer ce texte dans sa totalité, car il est une sorte de prise de position à l'égard de la philosophie occidentale—les plus illustres philosophes étant séparés entre ceux qui ont cherché à construire de brillantes et partielles abstractions, et ceux qui ont tenté de saisir par le langage la totalité concrète des expériences possibles et vécues, le plus grand d'entre ceux-ci étant Hegel. On reconnaîtra que ce long commentaire sur une formation et des préférences philosophiques n'a de portée explicative que secondaire; sa véritable intention, et en un collage relativement important, est de rendre à la fois immensément présent et absent le langage philosophique pour les "événements" dont le récit commence. —Hegel est cité une deuxième fois (pp. 30–40), dans une allusion à une image du philosophe:

> Albert portait une riche curiosité aux mythes qui ont bercé l'humanité dans sa longue histoire, il en recherchait avec passion la signification intime; aussi un matin fut-il tout à fait surpris de voir que Hegel, malgré son aversion déclarée pour les *exemples*, s'était attaché à donner une explication du mythe de la Chute de l'homme.

Gracq, qui a souligné lui-même le mot *exemple*, donne alors une longue citation de Hegel—19 lignes, sans référence, et qui se termine par une phrase mise en italiques: *"La main qui inflige la blessure est aussi celle qui la guérit."* Cette image, avec sa puissance expressive, est au cœur du récit. Il y a comme un progrès entre la première allusion et celle-ci. L'une fait de Hegel le prince du concret, et ici il devient, comme tel, le maître des images, et l'image de la main apparaît à la fin d'un raisonnement purement abstrait dont Gracq a tenu à donner la phase finale.

De nouveau l'ambiguïté du collage reparaît. L'image est-elle exemple simple ou au-delà de l'intelligence? Le récit, à la fois, se justifie face à la philosophie, mais semble s'effacer devant elle: Gracq honnêtement fournit un échantillon de langage hégélien. Deux autres citations suivent (pp. 40 et 41): elles concluent en faveur d'un apparent triomphe de la philosophie comme langage dialectique. —Le troisième collage, à la page 46, poursuit l'hommage rendu à la dialectique, qui cette fois s'applique au trio du récit, Albert, Heide et Herminien:

> Peut-être Hegel eût-il souri de voir marcher auprès de chacun d'eux, comme un ange ténébreux et glorieux, le fantôme à la fois de son double et de son contraire, et se fût-il alors interrogé sur la forme d'une *union* nécessaire que ce livre entre autres buts ne saurait avoir que de finalement élucider.

(L'italique est de Gracq.) De nouveau le collage signifie l'existence d'un langage à la fois plus fort et plus faible que le livre lui-même qui constitue ce récit; l'allusion directe au livre dans cette référence suffit à prouver qu'il n'y a pas intégration, mais contraste,—une sorte de fantastique et double mise en abyme—,absorption du livre dans la citation de Hegel, et inversement récupération de la plus haute philosophie dans un exemple haussé à la dignité du mythe.

Vers la fin du livre on relève encore une allusion d'autant plus curieuse que Hegel n'est pas cité sauf par sous-entendu. Gracq parle des goûts métaphysiques d'Herminien, l'ami d'Albert, et il note que les inclinations d'Herminien l'orientent spécialement vers "la fin de la philosophie alexandrine et les premières lueurs de ce qu'on a convenu d'appeler l'idéalisme allemand, et qui brille d'un éclat sibyllin à travers l'œuvre glorieuse de Schelling et Fichte" (p. 160). Contrairement à Albert, Herminien ne va pas jusqu'à Hegel. Bien des interprétations sont possibles pour ceux qui connaissent les philosophies de Fichte et de Schelling. Mon objet n'est pas de poursuivre cette élucidation. Mais cette citation, je crois, confirme l'hypothèse initiale: les allusions à Hegel sont plus que des prises de position philosophiques; elles ont la valeur de collage et font intervenir dans le texte des éléments qui sont en même temps plus réels et moins réels que lui-même, c'est-à-dire des éléments qui détruisent la portée du livre en le renvoyant à un autre langage, concret et total, mais qui, par leur opacité même, ne sont plus pour le lecteur que des bornes peu précises au début de ce vrai chemin qui est le livre. Hegel, le prince de l'idéalisme absolu et dialectique, est à la fois le signe de la futilité et de la nécessité de la littérature.

Ces collages prennent alors une valeur exemplaire. Ils autorisent l'intervention des mots philosophiques dans l'organisation du récit. On pourrait objecter que la présence spécifique de Hegel est contingente, et qu'ainsi tout autre nom de philosophe et de philosophie ferait l'affaire. Je ne le crois pas: les écrivains français du XXe siècle (et ils ne sont pas les seuls) sont fascinés, voire obsédés par Hegel, par le fait même que son idéalisme justifie et condamne simultanément les entreprises littéraires. De là aussi le caractère paradoxal de ces collages qui consistent à faire du philosophe de la totalité le reflet d'une intention ou la nuance d'une atmosphère!

Avec Samuel Beckett le collage philosophique, au moins aussi important, a pour matière de référence, non plus l'idéalisme allemand, mais les cartésiens, grands et petits, et la tradition empiriste anglaise. Les collages apparaissent dans les poèmes, les romans et le théâtre. Cependant, parmi les grands écrivains du XXe siècle, Beckett est peut-être celui qui a donné au problème de la relation entre les langages philosophique et littéraire sa plus profonde signification, comme conflit entre les deux fonctions logique et esthétique de tout langage, de sorte que les collages dont nous allons donner quelques exemples ne sont pas isolés: ils se situent à l'intérieur d'une solution plus générale du problème littéraire. Et il est notable que Beckett voit dans l'idéalisme moderne sous toutes ses formes l'attitude philosophique à laquelle l'écrivain du XXe siècle doit se confronter. Il n'est donc pas étonnant qu'au début de sa carrière, l'auteur de *Whoroscope* multiplie les allusions à des noms de philosophes se rattachant à la tendance idéaliste. Notre problème est alors de comprendre la raison de ce collage où le nom propre prend lui-même une opacité mystérieuse.

Voici quelques exemples dans chacun des genres où Beckett a cherché la solution et justification de l'écriture. D'abord dans ses *Poems* (je ne cite pas bien entendu *Whoroscope*, tout entier consacré à Descartes, et qui appartient ainsi à ce que j'ai appelé plus haut l'insertion théorique et l'intégration technique): le poème intitulé *Dortmunder* se termine par les deux vers suivants: "Schopenhauer is dead, the bawd/ puts her lute away." Parmi les poèmes 1938–39 publiés d'abord dans *Les Temps Modernes* (Novembre 1946) le poème sans titre qui commence "ainsi a-t-on beau," évoque, après les périodes glaciaires et la grande chaleur du XIIIe siècle, "sur Lisbonne fumante Kant froidement penché." Tels sont les seuls collages philosophiques relevés dans les poésies. Au contraire les romans de la période pré-française en fourmillent. Ainsi *Murphy* cite les noms de 14 philosophes et donnent une phrase de Spinoza: entre autres, Démocrite, Berkeley, Descartes, Geulincx, Hegel, Manès, Pythagore, Socrate.[7] De loin le plus important collage dans ce roman concerne le philosophe préféré de Beckett, Geulincx, dont le nom s'accompagne d'une citation qui, selon Beckett, est une des clés de toute son œuvre: "How should he tolerate, let alone cultivate, the occasions of fiasco, having once beheld the beatific idols of his cave? In the beautiful Belgo-Latin of Arnold Geulincx: *Ubi nihil vales, ibi nihil velis.*"[8]

Les références de ce type deviennent rares à partir de la trilogie, mais leur rayonnement a d'autant plus de valeur. Ainsi dans *Molloy* Geulincx apparaît de nouveau en collage: "Moi j'avais aimé l'image de ce vieux

7. *Samuel Beckett: The Art of Rhetoric*, ed. E. Morot-Sir, H. Harper, and D. McMillan, III, 201 et suiv.
    8. *Murphy*, Grove Press, p. 178.

Geulincx, mort jeune, qui m'accordait la liberté, sur le navire noir d'Ulysse, de me couler vers le levant, sur le pont."[9] Un autre occasionnaliste cartésien, Malebranche, a les honneurs d'une mention dans *Comment c'est*: "... nous voilà partis nez au vent bras se balançant le chien suit tête basse queue sur les couilles rien à voir avec nous il a eu la même idée au même instant du Malebranche en moins rose les lettres que j'avais...."[10] Dans ces exemples beckettiens la déréalisation s'exerce sur la structure déterministe du monde, le principe de causalité ou l'indifférence aux valeurs. Mais on reconnaîtra aisément que les allusions philosophiques proprement dites n'ont pas de nécessité intellectuelle. Et il est difficile de croire que Beckett, tel un honnête érudit, ait tenu à citer ses sources! Peut-être ce sentiment est-il présent, mais il n'est pas essentiel, et il ne saurait justifier la présence de ces noms propres, de ces citations ou références; d'ailleurs dans *Comment c'est*, Beckett, en se moquant de lui-même, nous met en garde devant une interprétation aussi simpliste. Nous sommes reportés par l'intermédiaire du nom propre à un autre langage possible, inévitable même. Dès ses premières réflexions critiques Beckett aperçoit, au cœur de l'écriture littéraire un conflit entre philosophie et philologie: dans le premier paragraphe de son article "Dante...Bruno. Vico..Joyce," il compare la philosophie et la philologie à "a pair of nigger minstrels out of the Teatro del Piccoli," et il note immédiatement que Vico "insisted on complete identification between the philosophical abstraction and the empirical illustration." Dira-t-on que le collage est alors une illustration? Non, il faut dire au contraire que le collage est la technique beckettienne pour remplacer l'illustration; ce qui lui permet d'éviter la glissade irrésistible vers les allégories. Le collage serait ainsi une illustration qui objecte d'être assimilée à une allégorie. Le texte est refusé dans sa tentation de prosélytisme doctrinal; et le nom du philosophe brille d'une lumière équivoque pour nous avertir du danger du langage philosophique, tout en reconnaissant son existence inévitable.

Un tel collage a une structure analogue à celle des collages relevés chez Proust, et surtout chez Breton ou Gracq, mais l'effet cherché est opposé, pour la raison suivante: tandis que les autres écrivains qui le précèdent sont tous portés par un optimisme littéraire sans angoisse ni doute hyperbolique, Beckett se sert du collage pour mettre son propre texte dans une situation intenable: l'allusion philosophique se renie tout en niant le texte où elle apparaît: pour Proust la dualité des langages est heureusement consentie;

9. *Molloy*, Editions de Minuit, p. 76.
10. *Comment c'est*, Editions de Minuit, p. 37.

pour Breton et Gracq elle est mise en circularité dialectique, de sorte que la négation de l'un est l'affirmation de l'autre: le récit survit à la présence insidieuse du collage philosophique, qui lui-même triomphe à sa manière. Avec Beckett il y a toujours circularité dialectique, mais elle s'opère entre deux négations, également destructrices, également nécessaires: la littérature rejette le langage des philosophes, qui eux-mêmes, par leur seule existence, ridiculisent les prétentions des littérateurs. Le collage ainsi compris rappelle, pour le cas où l'écrivain et le lecteur seraient tentés de l'oublier, que le langage littéraire est un être androgyne dont un côté se porte vers la droite quand l'autre tire à gauche. C'est comme si Beckett nous disait: cette enclave ne peut être qu'enclave, ne la prenez pas pour la reconnaissance d'un gentleman's agreement entre le philosophe et l'écrivain; elle dit tout le contraire. Mais, objectera-t-on, Beckett n'est-il pas occasionaliste, comme Geulincx et Malebranche? Ne tient-il pas à leur rendre hommage de façon indirecte? Cette question est évidemment capitale, et la plupart des interprètes la résolvent de façon positive. Je ne veux pas dire que Beckett adopte une attitude contraire à celle de l'occasionnalisme. Loin de là! Tout simplement Beckett n'est pas philosophe, et ainsi il n'est ni occasionaliste, ni le contraire, ni quoi que ce soit d'autre. Mais il utilisera l'occasionnalisme comme technique littéraire de juxtapositions verbales sans connexions logiques. Cette technique rentre sous la catégorie que j'ai appelé "intégration technique" de la philosophie à la littérature.

Le collage, comme référence ouverte à des noms et à des pensées philosophiques, a un tout autre rôle littéraire. Il semble qu'au XXe siècle le collage soit typiquement idéaliste (il n'y a guère de collage marxiste, mais il y a des œuvres qui essaient d'être des transpositions littéraires de cette idéologie—tels sont les romans d'Aragon de confession marxiste), et sa fonction est de créer un moment "anomalique" dans le texte. Je me suis servi des métaphores du trou et de la fenêtre pour désigner cette rupture ambiguë dans une continuité verbale. Ses effets, avons-nous vu, sont circulaires, alternativement négatif et positif (et il y a sûrement des nuances entre l'usage proustien et l'usage surréaliste) ou doublement négatifs avec Beckett. Je ne prétends que ce soient là les seuls effets possibles du collage idéaliste, et plus généralement philosophique. D'autres sont certainement possibles. Seule sa forme subsistera: un arrêt bref du continu textuel, qui met en cause la réalité et la valeur du texte,—qui du même coup introduit des doutes sur la qualité et les droits philosophiques de l'écrivain, sur la vocation de vérité que revendique communément toute littérature, et finalement sur la légitimité du passage allégorique de l'abstrait au concret.

Certains surréalistes, analysant les effets des premiers collages cubistes, ont souligné leur caractère *magique*. Il y a certes, au niveau le plus superficiel du langage, une magie de l'allusion philosophique par noms propres ou pensées ramassées en ellipse. Comme si l'écrivain cherchait à éblouir le lecteur par le prestige de cet être mystérieux qu'est un philosophe, ou par l'éclat d'une formule à la profondeur fascinante! Mais ce n'est là que le premier effet,—celui de la surprise. L'effet essentiel réside dans cette circularité que nous avons décelée: l'intervention magique du philosophe et de la philosophie renforce et annule le texte qui, cependant, transforme en accessoire linguistique une exceptionnelle expression de la réalité et de la vérité!

Dépassant les effets de collage philosophique, certains écrivains n'hésitent pas à revêtir la livrée philosophique au moins pour certains moments de leurs œuvres; ils se servent des formes de l'aphorisme, du commentaire, de la méditation, du dialogue. Une telle option est fréquente, et elle ne va pas sans confusion: l'écrivain-philosophe est-il, ou essaie-t-il de passer pour le philosophe-écrivant et choisissant telle ou telle technique d'expression, pour son bonheur ou la satisfaction du lecteur souhaité? Ici sentiments de supériorité et d'infériorité alternent ou se mêlent, et sans doute sont-ils présents déjà dans le collage! Mais mon objet n'est pas de psychanalyser le collage idéaliste! Je n'ai cherché à montrer que sa forme, son importance et sa contribution à la recherche de l'effet littéraire.

Qu'on me permette, en guise de conclusion, quelques remarques générales. Tout d'abord, la référence à l'idéalisme, à ses philosophes et à ses langages divers, dans la littérature du XXe siècle, est d'une fréquence supérieure à la moyenne des allusions philosophiques possibles et prévisibles dans un texte littéraire. De plus cette intervention n'est pas simplement référentielle et thématique. Elle aboutit à des "effets" techniques dans les rhétoriques de la description, de la caractérisation et de la narration. Ainsi, en prenant conscience de cette opération idéaliste aux multiples aspects, on doit mieux comprendre l'évolution littéraire des deux derniers siècles; et ce qu'on pourrait appeler l'anti-réalisme de la littérature contemporaine prend des significations et des valeurs précises.... Il est vrai que les partisans du réalisme marxiste ou du réalisme néo-thomiste contesteront l'interprétation historique de mes analyses. Puis-je préciser ma position critique: elle n'est pas philosophique; je ne prétends pas que l'idéalisme ait été seul à dominer la pensée du XXe siècle; il est même possible que son action ait servi à féconder le réalisme et à permettre le passage du réalisme traditionnel à un réalisme matérialiste et dialectique, ou encore qu'il annonce et prépare un renouvellement souhaitable de la pensée et eschatologie chrétiennes. N'appartenant, pour ce texte, à aucune orthodoxie déclarée, je ne soutiens pas que l'idéalisme est la philosophie dominante et "indépassable" de notre temps! A d'autres le soin de décider si ces possibilités linguistiques de l'idéalisme dévoilent les aspects d'une idéologie bourgeoise en train d'agoniser, ou si elles annoncent des formes nouvelles de culture par delà les trois orthodoxies dont les signes de déclin sont décelables dans les productions littéraires qui ont renouvelé les puissances esthétiques de la poésie, du roman et du théâtre. Je me borne à constater le fait suivant: les philosophes idéalistes sont cités, leurs idées ont été utilisées et exposées, et leurs théories ont changé les êtres et les conduites des grandes espèces du langage littéraire.

PART III

Nineteenth-century
French literature

Richard M. Chadbourne

Chateaubriand's aviary: birds in the *Mémoires d'Outre-Tombe*

In the *Génie du Christianisme* birds are one of the "marvels of nature" which "prove the existence of God," and the bird is "the true symbol of the Christian here below" (le véritable emblème du chrétien ici-bas) because "il préfère, comme le fidèle, la solitude au monde, le ciel à la terre, et sa voix bénit sans cesse les merveilles du Créateur" (Part I, Book v, Ch. 5). In *Atala* birds are an essential feature of the exotic American setting and contribute to an imagery designed to create "une atmosphère vaguement poétique et un peu sentimentale."[1] References to birds are few in *René*, but at the core of that story lies the comparison which the hero makes of himself to "un oiseau voyageur" and of man in general to a migratory bird waiting to unfold his wings and to be borne on the "wind of death" to the higher world for which he yearns.[2]

In the light of these and many other references to birds in earlier works, it would have been surprising if Chateaubriand had not featured them prominently in his masterpiece, *Mémoires d'outre-tombe*. The most famous bird in the work is probably the thrush (*la grive*), whose warbling, heard by the forty-four-year-old Chateaubriand one summer's day at Montboissier, near Chartres, stimulated memories of a thrush heard in his childhood in the woods of Combourg and led, as though by magic, to the series of chapters recreating Combourg (I, iii). No less an authority than Proust himself cited this passage as one of his sources for what has come to be known as *la mémoire involontaire ou affective*, and it has been the subject of considerable comment and debate.[3]

But the thrush is merely one of the many "petits oiseaux mémoriels," as Jean-Pierre Richard calls them, which serve as stimulants to Chateau-

1. Maija Lehtonen, *L'Expression imagée dans l'œuvre de Chateaubriand* (Helsinki: Société Néophilologique, 1964), p. 75.
2. Chateaubriand, *Œuvres romanesques et voyages* (Paris, 1969), I, 130.
3. For further discussion of this question, see Lehtonen, pp. 416–23, Merete Grevlund, *Paysage intérieur et paysage extérieur dans les Mémoires d'outre-tombe* (Paris, 1968), pp. 200–207, and Jean-Pierre Richard, *Paysage de Chateaubriand* (Paris: Editions du Seuil, 1967), pp. 105–11.

briand's memory and as leading threads through the complex time-strata of the *Mémoires*. "Peu d'animaux dans le bestiaire de Chateaubriand," writes Richard, "mais une infinité d'oiseaux, reconnus par leur apparence et par leur chant, nommés, replacés dans leurs habitudes propres, caressés du regard, toujours chéris."[4] In the *Mémoires* alone, I have counted more than 200 references to birds. Approximately 170 are to birds by name and an additional 30 or so to birds in general (*les oiseaux*). Total kinds mentioned number over 60. Most of the named birds, including the thrush, receive only two or three mentions, but a small number recur frequently, by which I mean from 10 to 20 times. These, in descending order (once again the figures are approximate), are the nightingale, *le rossignol*, 20; the raven, *le corbeau*, and the crow, *la corneille*, 20 (raven, 13, and crow, 7); the eagle, *l'aigle*, 15; the swallow, *l'hirondelle*, and the swift, *le martinet*, 13 (swallow, 10, swift, 3); and finally, the lark, *l'alouette*, 10.

The purpose of this essay is to determine the function of birds in the *Mémoires* more extensively than previous critics have found occasion to do.[5] The essay is divided into four parts: birds in literary and other references, birds in comparisons, "literal" birds, and bird symbolism.

Throughout the *Mémoires* one finds scattered references to birds in various literary and popular sources. Naturalists are represented by Aristotle on partridges, Pliny the Elder on Agrippina's talking thrush, Buffon on tropical birds. A Greek popular song about the return of the swallow is quoted, as well as the *Chanson de l'Epervier et de la Fauvette* beloved of an aunt of Chateaubriand disappointed in love. "Miraculous" or legendary birds are cited from medieval chronicles (the dove which descended on Clovis with the holy oil, the ravens carrying live coals which set fire to the French countryside) and from the saints' lives (the raven which brought food to Saint Paul the Hermit in the desert, the birds which were "brothers and sisters" to Saint Francis of Assisi). Literary references include Anacreon on the "prattling" swallow (a disparaging epithet rejected by Chateaubriand), a Greek epigram on the bird and the grasshopper, Virgil's Philomela or nightingale (based on the ancient Greek myth of Philomela and Procne), Ovid on quails, Lucretius on crows, Shakespeare's lark in

4. Richard, pp. 64, 66.
5. Lehtonen (bird imagery in the major works of Chateaubriand), Richard (the bird as "l'aventurier du vide," pp. 64–67, and the episode of the thrush, pp. 105–11), and Grevlund (birds as part of "les échos," pp. 181–89) have all touched on my subject, but in larger contexts and in less detail. I am indebted to their studies, however, as I also am, for ornithological background, to Edward A. Armstrong, *The Folklore of Birds*, rev. ed. (New York, 1970). My thanks, finally, to my colleague Dr. Gérard de Jubécourt for his kind assistance in interpreting certain passages of the *Mémoires* related to birds.

Romeo and Juliet (a bird, Chateaubriand suggests, which will be remembered long after the Congress of Verona is forgotten), and Rousseau's nightingales of "la nuit au bord de la Saône" (*Les Confessions*).

These references are on the whole fairly impersonal and do not appear to form any particular pattern, except perhaps to remind the reader, as the author goes about incorporating certain birds into his personal mythology, of the distinguished role which birds have played over the centuries in various mythical and literary traditions. One of the sources referred to, however, the legend of Saint Francis of Assisi, bears an intimate relationship to Chateaubriand's "myth" or poetic image of himself. Francis of Assisi was the patron saint of François-René de Chateaubriand, and strange though it may seem, the two men do share some traits, including their penchant for conversations with birds. "J'ai reçu de mon patron," wrote Chateaubriand with reasonable accuracy, "la pauvreté, l'amour des petits et des humbles, la compassion pour les animaux; mais mon bâton stérile ne se changera point en chêne vert pour les protéger" (II,861).[6] (This last, an allusion to the legend of Saint Francis's walking-stick transformed into a nesting tree for the turtledoves, is his way of saying that holiness was not one of the gifts he had received from the saint.)

Turning now to bird images (that is, similes and metaphors) of Chateaubriand's own invention, it is surprising to discover that only about one-fifth of the total references to birds use them in this way. Surprising not only because, according to Lehtonen, nature—including birds—provided Chateaubriand with most of his images[7] but also because his well-known admiration for Shakespeare might have led one to expect him to emulate the great master of bird imagery much as he emulated in him the vision of life which embraces both the tragic and the comic.[8] As an explanation for the relatively small number of these images, I hazard the guess that the author chose not to lessen the impact of the "literal" or "real" birds, which play a central role in the *Mémoires* (as we shall see), by using birds in too many comparisons.

Of the bird images one does find, a significant number occur in a political or military context. Some examples: the French habitually forsake

6. References are given to the two-volume Pléiade edition of the *Mémoires* (Paris, 1951). I have also consulted the four-volume Edition du Centenaire, 2e éd. revue et corrigée (Paris, 1964).

7. Lehtonen: "La *nature* reste la source principale d'images, dont les plus fréquentes sont celles de l'eau (y compris la navigation) et les images empruntées aux animaux et aux oiseaux" (p. 517).

8. For references to this last point, see *Mémoires* I, 952, II, 575, and the discussion of Shakespeare in the *Essai sur la littérature anglaise*.

yesterday's political favorites for new ones, "comme les pigeons d'une ferme s'empressent sous la main qui leur jette le grain" (II, 545); the fall of the "great eagle" Napoleon, the death of "l'aiglon," his son (the Duke of Reichstadt) left no eagles or eaglets on the French political horizon, and those promised by the July Revolution "sont descendus de leur aire pour nicher avec les pigeons pattus" (II, 584); France, upon the return of Napoleon from Elba, is compared to "a great nest of soldiers" belonging to armies hatched beneath "the wings of the fame of Marengo and Austerlitz" (I, 960).

The majority of avian images compares persons to birds, for example, Lucile and Pauline de Beaumont, in their last years, to dying swans (I, 512), Tasso (on his return to Ferrara and prison) to "l'oiseau fasciné [qui] se jette dans la gueule du serpent" (II, 803), and Napoleon (of course) to the eagle and also, in a phrase borrowed from Buffon and reminiscent of the Icarus myth, to "l'oiseau des tropiques, *attelé*, dit Buffon, *au char du soleil*, [qui] se précipite de l'astre de la lumière" (I, 1025). If pigeons are the vulgar comic foil for the noble eagle, it should be pointed out in passing that eagles are far from uniformly noble in the *Mémoires*. In one episode of humorous intent, for example, the author shows us the Duchesse de Berry and General Bugeaud engaged in a quarrel: "Ils criaient comme deux aigles" (II, 816).

No person is compared more frequently to a bird in the *Mémoires* than the author himself.[9] In the first such image, very early in the book, using the word *hibou* in the sense of a morose, solitary fellow, he writes: "Il fallut quelque temps à un hibou de mon espèce pour s'accoutumer à la cage d'un collège et régler sa volée au son d'une cloche" (I, 48). He thought of his whole family at Combourg, in fact, as a nest of birds: after the death of his father and the property settlement, "nous nous dispersâmes, comme des oiseaux s'envolent du nid paternel" (I, 122); later, when François and Lucile joined Julie in Paris, he called this reunion "une douce association des trois plus jeunes oiseaux de la couvée" (I, 136). At various times he compares himself to the hazel-grouse (*la gelinotte*), to the lark (I, 496), to "ce triste et petit oiseau de l'hiver qui chante, ainsi que moi, parmi les buissons dépouillés" (I, 819), and to "le vieil oiseau [qui] tombe de la branche où il se réfugie [et qui] quitte la vie pour la mort" (II, 383). He is also the bird who got away from Napoleon, that is, during the Cent Jours: "l'oiseau a déniché" (I, 942). Only once, however, does he refer

9. Lehtonen: "Dans les *Mémoires d'outre-tombe* Chateaubriand se compare le plus volontiers à un navigateur, à un voyageur, à un soldat et à un oiseau" (p. 508).

to himself as an eagle, when he attributes to himself as a diplomat "un regard d'aigle" (II, 356).

In the light of these comparisons, it may seem at first somewhat strange to hear him declare: "Mon exactitude tient à mon bon sens vulgaire; je suis de la race des Celtes et des tortues, race pédestre; non du sang des Tartares et des oiseaux, races pourvues de chevaux et d'ailes" (I, 621). But the contradiction is more apparent than real. The essential point is that he consistently *aspired* to a birdlike freedom, just as he dreamed of the freedom of an artist's life in Rome unburdened of his ambassadorial responsibilities:

> Je voudrais être né artiste: la solitude, l'indépendance, le soleil parmi des ruines et des chefs-d'œuvre, me conviendraient. Je n'ai aucun besoin; un morceau de pain, une cruche de l'*Aqua Felice*, me suffiraient. Ma vie a été misérablement accrochée aux buissons de ma route; heureux si j'avais été l'oiseau libre qui chante et fait son nid dans ces buissons! [II, 242].

Birds in comparisons are far outnumbered, as I indicated earlier, by "literal" birds, that is, birds that exist in narrative or descriptive passages as objects of representation in themselves. Of course the distinction between "literal" and "figurative" birds frequently breaks down. Often the sight of a real bird will suggest to Chateaubriand a simile or metaphor which he will then proceed to formulate. Or on the other hand, he will imply, for a real bird he is depicting, an extension into the metaphorical or symbolic realm, without developing an explicit comparison.

Several birds figure in episodes or anecdotes of a humorous nature. These tend to be the more prosaic, "ridiculous" birds such as magpies and assorted barnyard fowl. Young Chateaubriand's theft of the magpie's nest while at the Collège de Dol (I, 59–60) belongs to this category, as do Madame Suard's noisy rooster which annoyed Madame de Coislin (I, 580), General de Trogoff's obstreperous nightingales (II, 710, 724),[10] and Chateaubriand's mock-elegy for the young chicken (*la géline*) served to him for lunch in an Austrian inn ("Pauvre poussin! il était si heureux cinq minutes avant mon arrivée!"—II, 841).

In his descriptions of customs and manners the author frequently uses ornithological details to make his point. "Le vieux matelot ressemble au

10. Armstrong (pp. 186–87) points out that the sad nightingale of harmonious song is better known to poetry than to folklore, where the noisiness of the bird is more commonly stressed. Chateaubriand appears to reflect both sorts of tradition.

vieux laboureur.... A l'un, l'alouette, le rouge-gorge, le rossignol; à l'autre, la procellaria, le courlis, l'alcyon,—leurs prophètes" (I, 200).[11] In Germany he was struck by the widespread habit of caging songbirds as pets, and compared the "crows, sparrows, and larks" of the fields with the "nightingales, warblers, thrushes, and quails" which greeted him from their tiny prisons in the towns (II, 743). He felt that the traveler had much to learn about various peoples by observing carefully "la physionomie des animaux" (presumably this also included the birds) which shared their environment (II, 845).

His own "eagle eye" took in the smallest things in nature. Visiting Voltaire's house in Ferney, he seemed more interested in the flora and fauna of a little valley nearby than in the memory of Voltaire (II, 504–5). His lack of enthusiasm for mountains is well known: even the Alps visible from Ferney could not distract him from attention to the tiniest natural phenomena. In this particular passage the tiny things happen to be "une palmette de fougère... le susurrement d'une vague parmi des cailloux... un insecte imperceptible qui ne sera vu que de moi et qui s'enfonce sous une mousse," but there is no doubt that his keenness of observation extended to birds as well as to plants and insects.

In another passage involving mountains considered as landscape subjects, he argued that the most beautiful landscape paintings are those which are reshaped by the painter's memory and feeling, and that from this point of view the smallest subjects have as much aesthetic value as the largest. His list of possibilities—a tree, a flower, a stream, a piece of moss on a rock, a bit of sky—this time also includes "une mésange dans le jardin d'un presbytère" and "une hirondelle volant bas, par un jour de pluie, sous le chaume d'une grange ou le long d'un cloître." He concludes: "Toutes ces petites choses, rattachées à quelques souvenirs, s'enchanteront des mystères de mon bonheur ou de la tristesse de mes regrets" (II, 593). It is the painter, not nature, who creates the landscape. "Le paysage est sur la palette de Claude le Lorrain, non sur le Campo-Vaccino" (II, 593).

Of the many landscapes created by the poet-painter of the *Mémoires*, almost none is without its birds, whether these be the skylark (*l'alouette de champ*) and the sea-lark (*l'alouette marine*) which share the indistinct terrain between land and sea in Brittany (I, 41), the "sarcelles bleues" of the Azores (I, 207), the egret or tufted heron of the Ile Saint-Pierre (I, 213),

11. Cf. *Génie du Christianisme* (I, v, 8) : "Entre le rouge-gorge et le laboureur, entre la procellaria et le matelot, il y a une ressemblance de mœurs et de destinées tout à fait attendrissante." In the *Mémoires* Chateaubriand has worked out the affinity between birds and *his own* "mœurs" and "destinées," in more personal terms than in the *Génie*.

the cardinals, doves, and mockingbirds along the Hudson River (I, 230), the cranes, turkeys, and pelicans of Florida "[qui] marbraient de blanc, de noir et de rose le fond vert de la savane" (I, 261), the doves nesting in cypresses in a Constantinople cemetery, "sharing the peace of the dead" (I, 605), or the "millions of starlings" flying above the ruins of Carthage (I, 616), among many others.

It should come as no surprise that the birds which play the most important role in the *Mémoires* are those associated with its author's childhood in Combourg. As he moved from place to place in his extremely long life, it was these birds which reappeared in different contexts, recalling the distant past to him, providing an essential element of unity and continuity in his life and in his work, and serving as structural links between the various parts of the *Mémoires*.

The thrush, we saw, was one of these: "Le chant de l'oiseau dans les bois de Combourg m'entretenait d'une félicité que je croyais atteindre; le même chant dans le parc de Montboissier me rappelait des jours perdus à la poursuite de cette félicité insaisissable" (I, 76). Another was the *passereau-blanc*, a kind of sparrow, glimpsed in the woods of northern New York: "Un couple solitaire voltigeait seulement devant moi, comme ces oiseaux que je suivais dans mes bois paternels; à la couleur du mâle, je reconnus le passereau-blanc, *passer nivalis* des ornithologistes" (I, 235). Still another was the water hen (*la poule d'eau*), which formed part of "la caravane emplumée" of the nearby pond at Combourg (I, 97), whose cry he heard outside Ghent, during a stroll, at the same time as the distant cannon of the Battle of Waterloo (I, 962), and which turned up once more in Lucerne ("J'ai vu les poules d'eau privées; j'aime mieux les poules d'eau sauvages de l'étang de Combourg"—II, 579).[12]

The nightingale also belongs to this privileged company of thematic "memory" birds. Together with the swallow, the oriole, the cuckoo, and the quail, it is one of the five birds announcing the arrival of spring in Brittany (I, 40). Later Chateaubriand encountered it at a crossroad of a wood in northern France as he and his brother fled to join the royalist army (I, 310), in a café on the Champs Elysées which he frequented (perhaps nostalgically) "à cause de quelques rossignols suspendus en cage" (I, 446), in the countryside near Rome as a true "Philomèle de Virgile" whose song he found less shrill than that of the French nightingale (II,

12. The "poule d'eau" is one of the birds described in most detail in the *Génie*. In a chapter of his *Impressions de voyage* ("Les poules d'eau de M. de Chateaubriand"), Dumas Père describes his visit to Lucerne in the summer of 1832, where Chateaubriand showed him "les poules d'eau, ses amies." See note in Edition du Centenaire, IV, 112.

366), and in the garden of the Infirmerie de Marie-Thérèse in Paris, where its song "rivaled the hymns" heard in the outdoor religious processions and reminded him of his chapter on Rogation Day ceremonies in the *Génie du Christianisme* (II, 622).[13] The nightingale also appears in the lyrical digression—one of the many variations on the Sylphide theme—known as "l'Invocation à Cynthie" (II, 725). Only once, however, does Chateaubriand suggest a more specific link between nightingales and the memory of Combourg, and even in this case he does so very indirectly. I refer to his gently mocking description of the way in which spring arrives in a Berlin park as compared with his native Brittany: "La nature vivante se ranimait avant la nature végétale, et des grenouilles toutes noires étaient dévorées par des canards, dans les eaux çà et là dégelées: ces rossignols-là *ouvraient le printemps dans les bois* de Berlin" (II, 49).[14]

Sharing top honors in Chateaubriand's hierarchy of birds are the swift and swallow, and the crow and raven.

"A few swifts," along with some screech-owls at night, were the "only companions" of the boy in his tower room of Combourg castle, and therefore were intimate components of the situation of a child forced to adjust to solitude, to be brave, and to develop his imagination (I, 84). Swallows became part of the "caractère moral de l'automne" for him, when from his boat on the pond he used to watch their playful but purposeful maneuvers over the waters and on the shore as they prepared for their annual migration. "Je ne perdais pas un seul de leurs gazouillis," he notes. "Tavernier enfant était moins attentif au récit d'un voyageur" (I, 96–97).[15] And when he too left Combourg, like Adam exiled from Eden, the reeds on which these birds liked to alight ("les roseaux de mes hirondelles") were among the last things his gaze took in (I, 105). As a Peer of France, busily engaged in political activities but never turning his back on the world of dreams, he associated in one memory "l'hirondelle qui me réveillait dans ma jeunesse et les Muses qui remplissaient mes songes" (II, 17).

Swallows and swifts then disappear for many pages, but it is inevitable, according to the artistic logic of the *Mémoires,* that they should eventually reappear, to have their special moments in the recall of Combourg.

For the swift the scene is Hohlfeld, in Germany, where Chateaubriand stopped on his return from Prague to France in 1833. There the configuration of swifts and tower perceived during an evening stroll set off the

13. IV, i, 8.
14. The italicized phrase is quoted (slightly misquoted) from a letter of Madame de Sévigné to her daughter, Madame de Grignan.
15. Jean-Baptiste Tavernier (1605–1689), a celebrated French traveler.

memory. "Sur [un] rocher s'allonge un beffroi carré; des martinets criaient en rasant le toit et les faces du donjon. Depuis mon enfance à Combourg, cette scène composée de quelques oiseaux et d'une vieille tour ne s'était pas reproduite; j'en eus le cœur tout serré" (II, 731).

The climactic swallow scene occurs shortly thereafter, in Bischofsheim (again Germany), and goes far beyond the recall merely of Combourg: it takes the form of one of those recapitulatory passages, frequent in the *Mémoires*, in which the author casts a backward glance over the major places and events of his life. A swallow, "vraie Procné, à la poitrine rougeâtre," perches outside his open window "en me regardant d'un air de connaissance et sans montrer la moindre frayeur." By means of references to Greek myth, poetry, and song the author effects a skilful transition from the familiar, prosaic, "real" bird to the figurative, personified bird who engages in a dialogue with him, recalling all her ancestors whom he has known in his life and travels, from her "trisaïeule qui logeait à Combourg" and bade him farewell when he embarked for America, through the swallows of England and the Holy Land, to those of Italy. Reminding him that she herself had met him "sur l'ancienne voie de Tivoli dans la campagne de Rome," she invites him to fly away with her. In reply, Chateaubriand, "poor moulted bird" who has lost all hope of regaining his feathers, must decline her invitation, but not without reassuring her of their continuing affinity: "Comme toi, j'ai aimé la liberté, et j'ai vécu de peu" (II, 735–736).[16]

Among the corvine birds the magpie, as we saw earlier, lends comic relief, and the jay (*le geai*) appears in a brief poetic flash linking Brittany, the Holy Land, and Germany (II, 742). But these are far surpassed in thematic importance by crows and ravens.

For certain of their attributes, Chateaubriand drew on motifs of folklore and legend: their association with death, their role as carriers of messages and of objects, either for catastrophic or for beneficent purposes (setting fire to the countryside, but also bringing food to nourish the anchorites), and finally their ability to talk and to remember and preserve bits of extinct languages (he imagines a raven surviving the disappearance of French civilization and alone preserving phrases from Bossuet taught to

16. Lehtonen (pp. 418–19) points out a prior use of the swallow in *L'Itinéraire de Paris à Jérusalem* to link the scene at the time (aboard ship in the Syrian Sea) to America and Combourg. Compare Richard: "L'hirondelle... ponctuera de sa réapparition régulière les principaux moments—Combourg, Amérique, Grèce, Allemagne, Rome—de l'existence de Chateaubriand. A partir de ces retours prendra forme, et même conscience l'architecture d'une vie" (p. 67).

him by "le dernier curé franco-gaulois," and suggests that this may one day be the fate of his own work—I, 250).[17]

In more intimate fashion both crows and ravens appear from the outset of the *Mémoires*, in the Combourg sections, as part of the "caractère moral de l'automne," that is, the melancholy aspects of nature in this declining season which reflect man's own mortality and therefore possess "des rapports secrets avec nos destinées" (I, 96). According to the familiar Romantic paradox, such sad scenes are also pleasurable ("Mes joies de l'automne," the chapter is entitled). Included among the pleasures are "le passage des cygnes et des ramiers, le rassemblement des corneilles dans la prairie de l'étang, et leur perchée à l'entrée de la nuit sur les plus hauts chênes du grand Mail" (I, 96). Two chapters later, in "Tentation," the first ravens make their appearance, in a gloomy context, the adolescent Chateaubriand's death wish and temptation to suicide:

> Après avoir marché à l'aventure, agitant mes mains, embrassant les vents qui m'échappaient ainsi que l'ombre, objet de mes poursuites, je m'appuyais contre le tronc d'un hêtre; je regardais les corbeaux que je faisais envoler d'un arbre pour se poser sur un autre, ou la lune se traînant sur la cime dépouillée de la futaie: j'aurais voulu habiter ce monde mort, qui réfléchissait la pâleur du sépulcre [I, 99].

The successors to the crows of Combourg are numerous. In his flight through the Ardennes forest after being wounded at the siege of Thionville, he comes across "quelques corneilles" together with some larks and yellow buntings, who seemed to be in as much danger as he while they sat immobile eyeing a falcon circulating above them (I, 339). At Westminster Abbey, too poor to pay the entrance fee very often, he "turned round and round outside with the crows" (I, 355). At Chantilly it is "quelques corneilles" which fly ahead of him, guiding him through the woods to the ruined castle of the Prince de Condé, where he broods on the arrest and execution by Napoleon of Condé's descendant, the Duc d'Enghien (I, 538). After this passage crows are absent for many pages (to be replaced by ravens) until they return in the fourth and last part of the *Mémoires*, to establish still another link with Combourg. The scene is the Danube Valley as Chateaubriand travels toward Prague on his second mission to the exiled court of Charles X:

17. Most of these folkloric motifs are found in Armstrong, Ch. 5, "The Bird of Doom and Deluge." For what it may be worth in the present context I also call attention to Armstrong's remark that in Celtic lands, "the raven and crow have far greater significance than the eagle" (p. 130).

Le 25 [septembre 1833], à la nuit tombante, j'entrai dans des bois. Des corneilles criaient en l'air; leurs épaisses volées tournoyaient au-dessus des arbres dont elles se préparaient à couronner la cime. Voilà que je retournai à ma première jeunesse: je revis les corneilles du mail de Combourg; je crus reprendre ma vie de famille dans le vieux château: ô souvenirs, vous traversez le cœur comme un glaive! ô ma Lucile, bien des années nous ont séparés! maintenant la foule de mes jours a passé, et, en se dissipant, me laisse mieux voir ton image [II, 847].

Ravens present nothing quite to match the poignancy of this scene, but they too have their moments of poetic beauty, and their spiritual affinity with Chateaubriand was surpassed by that of no other bird, except perhaps the swallow. As with the swallow, he "conversed" with ravens. In 1804 in the Parc de Monceaux, near the *petit hôtel* he then lived in on the Rue de Miromesnil, "je ne m'occupais de rien," he observed, "tout au plus m'en-tretenais-je dans le parc avec quelques lapins, ou causais-je du duc d'En-ghien avec trois corbeaux" (I, 576). Escaping from Paris at dawn during the Cent Jours, he saw on the outskirts a flock of ravens descending from the elm trees to "take their first meal in the fields"; he envied them their indifference to Louis XVIII and Napoleon, the fact that they were not "forced to leave their fatherland," and their freedom of flight, which re-minded him of his own lost freedom as a child. "Vieux amis de Combourg!" he complained, "nous nous ressemblions davantage quand jadis, au lever du jour, nous déjeunions des mûres de la ronce dans nos halliers de la Bretagne!" (I, 927).[18]

In Berlin he fed "de vieux corbeaux, mes éternels amis," who perched in linden trees outside his window; he describes in detail their skill in manipu-lating large chunks of bread in order to feed on them, and dignifies their after-dinner song with a verse from Lucretius: "Le repas fait, l'oiseau chantait à sa manière: *cantus cornicum ut saecla vetusta*" (II, 48).[19] "Aller revoir mes corbeaux" was synonymous with the wish to return to his diplomatic post in Berlin (II, 64). One of the few things he enjoyed in Zurich was "un vieux corbeau et un vieil orme," for which he declared

18. Compare Grevlund: "Les corbeaux, inséparables de l'image de Combourg, sont toujours pour Chateaubriand un prétexte de célébrer la liberté de ses jeunes années" (p. 186).
19. "La voix des corneilles est comme la voix des siècles anciens." The original Latin reads "Et partim mutant cum tempestatibus una / Raucisonos cantus cornicum ut saecla vetusta" (*De rerum natura*, V, 1084–85), and Chateaubriand translates: "D'autres oiseaux font varier avec les aspects du temps les accents de leur voix rauque; telles les générations des corneilles vivaces" (Edition du Centenaire, III, 67 n.).

himself willing to exchange the whole history of that city (II, 596). The last glimpse we have of ravens in the *Mémoires* is in a delicately painted detail of a sunrise landscape in the Salzburg plain: "Des bandes de corbeaux, quittant les lierres et les trous des ruines, descendaient sur les guérets; leurs ailes moirées se glaçaient de rose au reflet du matin" (II, 844).

There remains one final function of birds in the *Mémoires* to be pointed out: their role as symbols. The symbolic motifs which I shall outline briefly are rarely presented explicitly by Chateaubriand; his usual pattern is to convey them by repeated association of certain birds, or of birds as a whole, with certain qualities or states.

Birds symbolize, in the first place, solitude, a very positive value for Chateaubriand, as we know. The earliest reference to birds in the *Mémoires* has this connotation. He describes how, as a boy in Saint Malo, too poor to buy playthings at the fair and afraid to be ridiculed for his poverty, he went off alone by the seashore, "loin de la foule," and there, "je m'amusais à voir voler les pingouins et les mouettes, à béer aux lointains bleuâtres, à ramasser des coquillages, à écouter le refrain des vagues parmi les écueils" (I, 31). The motif of the swifts and the tower is also part of this symbolism. Typical of the *Mémoires* are scenes of the author alone with a few birds, often among ruins, in a deserted churchyard, or in some other secluded site. "Mes compagnons étaient les morts, quelques oiseaux et le soleil qui se couchait" (I, 161). At L'Abbaye-aux-Bois "quelques oiseaux se venaient coucher dans les jalousies relevées de la fenêtre; je rejoignais au loin le silence et le solitude, par-dessus le tumulte et le bruit d'une grande cité" (II, 221). Among the ruins in Rome "il y reste quelques oiseaux et moi, encore pour un temps très court; nous nous envolerons bientôt" (II, 297). Passing by L'Abbaye de Saint Urbain in Switzerland, he muses: "Si j'eusse été libre et seul, j'aurais demandé aux moines quelque trou dans leurs murailles pour y achever mes *Mémoires* auprès d'une chouette" (II, 604).

In most of these passages the solitude which birds come to represent also carries with it thoughts of the vanity of human existence and a yearning for the peace of death.

A second symbolic meaning attributed to birds is that of freedom, the freedom to take flight, to be elsewhere. This significance is more than once assumed by migratory birds in association with clouds. "Comme aux oiseaux voyageurs, il me prend au mois d'octobre une inquiétude qui m'obligerait à changer de climat, si j'avais encore la puissance des ailes et la légèreté des heures: les nuages qui volent à travers le ciel me donnent envie de fuir" (I, 538). During Chateaubriand's first sojourn in Prague he was dining on the grounds of the estate of the Comte de Choteck when he realized that he felt out of place:

> Tandis que je m'efforçais d'être présent au repas, je ne pouvais m'empêcher de regarder les oiseaux et les nuages qui volaient au-dessus du festin; passagers embarqués sur les brises et qui ont des relations secrètes avec mes destinées; voyageurs, objets de mon envie et dont mes yeux ne peuvent suivre la course aérienne sans une sorte d'attendrissement. J'étais plus en société avec ces parasites errants dans le ciel qu'avec les convives assis auprès de moi sur la terre: heureux anachorètes qui pour *dapifer* aviez un corbeau! [II, 687].[20]

The reader will note here not only a reprise of the *oiseaux-voyageurs-nuages* motif but also a distant echo of the "rapports secrets avec nos destinées" of autumn in Combourg.

Thirdly, birds symbolize the world of dream and imagination,[21] which Chateaubriand opposes, as he does the world of nature as a whole, to the world of "realities," by which he usually means politics.

Occasionally the sight of a bird serves to bring him back to earth from some flight of fancy: "Le vent du soir qui brisait les réseaux tendus par l'insecte sur la pointe des herbes, l'alouette de bruyère qui se posait sur un caillou, me rappelaient à la réalité" (I, 95). (This particular bird, significantly, is touching down to earth himself rather than taking flight.) But more characteristically birds represent an invitation to, and help usher in, the world of reverie. Their mere flight or even coming to rest, without the need of song or other sound, suffices. It was the cessation of sounds of the fresh-water birds as night descended over *l'étang de Combourg*, together with the sound of the reeds in the wind and of the water lapping the shore, that led to the first "Incantation" or magic conjuring-up by the imagination of the poeticized ideal woman, the Sylphide (I, 97). "Une fleur que je cueille, un courant d'eau qui se dérobe parmi des joncs, un oiseau qui va s'envolant et se reposant devant moi, m'entraînent à toutes sortes de rêves"

20. Maurice Levaillant explains, "Le *Dapifer*, ou Sénéchal, était sous les premiers Capétiens le chef des quatre grands officiers royaux de la Cour et le chef du service de la table." According to Levaillant, Chateaubriand is alluding here to the legend of the raven who brought Saint Paul the Hermit a daily half-loaf of bread, and when Saint Anthony visited him, a whole loaf. He also reminds us of the echoes of *René* and the *Génie* in this passage: "Les thèmes ici réunis sont parmi les plus chers à l'imagination de Chateaubriand" (Edition du Centenaire, IV, 242–43).

21. "Generally speaking, birds, like angels, are symbols of thought, of imagination and of the swiftness of spiritual processes and relationships." J. E. Cirlot, *A Dictionary of Symbols*, trans. from the Spanish by Jack Sage (New York, 1962), p. 27.

(I, 485). Each meeting he attended as a politician left him "un peu plus homme d'Etat et un peu plus persuadé de la pauvreté de toute cette science," and he would lie awake nights picturing all those bald-headed, unkempt, and physically unattractive statesmen and remembering that other, poetic world in which he felt more at home, the world of "the swallow who wakened me in my youth and the Muses who filled my dreams" (II, 17).

Finally, birds represent, as does the whole natural system of which they form part, changelessness and permanence in contrast to the transitory nature of man and all his works. Grevlund points out how this theme is tied in with the theme of memory: "Sans parler encore de mémoire affective, il est tout naturel que les retours en arrière se produisent surtout aux rencontres de ce qui, dans le monde présent, semble avoir traversé les années sans subir d'altérations: fleurs, oiseaux, parfums, la mer, le ciel..." (p. 200). Man forgets and passes away; nature remembers and endures. Chateaubriand's own powerful determination to remember the dead, to "donner une existence impérissable à tout ce qu'il a aimé" (I, 526), to "faire vivre dans mes ouvrages les personnes qui me sont chères" (I, 629), is a central preoccupation of all his work and reaches its supreme expression in the *Mémoires. He* would not forget, and if others forgot, at least he and nature would remember.

This piety extended to the small as well as the great ("Puisque c'est ma propre vie que j'écris en m'occupant de celles des autres, grandes ou petites" —I, 1026). One of the most moving examples is the awesome evocation of the Napoleonic retreat from Moscow and of the countless dead soldiers left behind whose remains would disappear on the battlefield:

> Qui pense à ses paysans laissés en Russie? Ces rustiques sont-ils contents d'avoir été *à la grande bataille sous les murs de Moscou?* Il n'y a peut-être que moi qui, dans les soirées d'automne, en regardant voler au haut du ciel les oiseaux du Nord, me souvienne qu'ils ont vu la tombe de nos compatriotes [I, 818].

This passage seems to me to provide the serious counterpart to the semi-humorous stories about human languages surviving in "la mémoire d'un oiseau."

When Chateaubriand refers to ravens as "mes éternels amis," the adjective is not to be taken lightly. Birds, and the natural system to which they belong, represent a permanence, almost a kind of eternity, which man lacks—a view easier to hold in the nineteenth century than today, when man has revealed his power to alter nature radically and even to destroy it.

"Les oiseaux," observes Lehtonen, "qui, pour Chateaubriand, jouent un rôle important dans l'évocation du passé, sont également des symboles de la nature qui survivra aux civilisations humaines" (p. 457). She cites several variations on this theme from other works, in addition to the passages I have included in this essay, but correctly points out that its main symbolic expression is the stork (*la cigogne*), whose role she traces from an early book-review by Chateaubriand through the *Mémoires*. The storks in Athens had inspired this reflection on his part:

> [La] mobilité des choses humaines est d'autant plus frappante pour le voyageur, qu'elle est en contraste avec l'immobilité du reste de la nature: comme pour insulter à l'instabilité des peuples, les animaux mêmes n'éprouvent ni révolution dans leurs empires, ni changements dans leurs mœurs.[22]

In the *Mémoires* a striking little painting, almost in the manner of a Dutch master, serves both to link the storks of a Danube valley town with those seen many years earlier, on a minaret in Athens, and to illustrate the contrast between the fragility of man and his creations and the durability of the animal kingdom. A stork's nest on the chimney of a house; beneath it a woman watching passers-by from her window; and in a niche below the window the wooden statue of a saint; the moral: "Le saint sera précipité de sa niche sur le pavé, la femme de sa fenêtre dans la tombe: et la cigogne? elle s'envolera: ainsi finiront les trois étages" (II, 639).

With apologies to ornithologists for any inaccuracies in terminology and to the computer for any errors (at least serious ones) in bird count, I conclude with a summary of my findings.

Birds are present from one end of Chateaubriand's *Mémoires* to the other, with only a few breaks of any appreciable length. Their presence is in fact so habitual that the reader feels the weight of their absence when it does occur. Their identities and habits are noted with precision: what is unusual is the author's occasional inability to name them, not his ability to do so. His birds reflect ancient beliefs of folklore as well as the observations of naturalists and the imagery of poets. They form part of landscapes of several continents, enter into anecdotes, episodes, and scenes, and provide the basis of many comparisons. The most significant of his birds, however, are those associated with his childhood in Combourg, and above all, the nightingale, the lark, the swallow and the swift, the crow and the

22. Quoted in Lehtonen, p. 458, from Chateaubriand's review of Alexandre de Laborde's *Voyage pittoresque et historique de l'Espagne*, in *Le Mercure* of 1807.

raven. These rank among his favorite agents of recall to memory, his most persistent "echo" effects ("Mes souvenirs se font écho"—I, 61), and the strongest structural links uniting the various parts of this "temple de la mort élevé à la clarté de [ses] souvenirs," as he described the *Mémoires* (I, 7). Joined by other birds, they are also raised to the poetic dignity of symbols, representing especially solitude, freedom, the world of reverie, and the permanence and changelessness of nature as opposed to the ephemeral character of mankind.

The thematic treatment of birds, which can be traced back to Chateaubriand's earliest works, reaches its artistic culmination as well as its richest amplification in his *Mémoires*. Such an exalted place in his imagination could hardly have been possible for them had he not felt with them, as he felt with the flowers, trees, clouds, rivers, and seas which he so often associates with them, mysterious bonds of affinity, "des relations secrètes avec [ses] destinées."

Robert T. Denommé

French theater reform and Vigny's translation of *Othello* in 1829

The significant rise in the prestige of Shakespearian drama in France from 1827 to 1830 stemmed from a wider acceptance of the notion of literary cosmopolitanism and from the pressing need of Romantic writers to reform the French theater. Differences in political ideology and aesthetic orientation prevented conservative or ultraroyalist Romanticists from joining with their liberal counterparts in a concerted campaign to modernize and revitalize the Neoclassical theater during the Empire and the first ten years of the Bourbon Restoration. Despite periodic appeals for change by drama critics in such journals as *Le Mercure du XIXe Siècle*, *Les Lettres Normandes*, *L'Album*, and *Le Globe*,[1] an unmistakably Neoclassical bias continued to dominate the official national theater, the French Academy, the universities, and most of the periodical press. The fact that no Romantic playwright had written a successful drama by 1825 hardly enhanced the position of the opponents of Neoclassicism. To gain control of the theater, they would have to rally conservative and liberal Romanticists under the same banner. The respective essays or manifestoes of Guizot, Stendhal, and Hugo managed to effect the desired coalescence by making Shakespeare the champion and symbol of their cause. To convince the more articulate exponents of Neoclassicism that the modernization of the French theater would not mean its ruination, it would have to be shown that the plays of Shakespeare had a constructive role to play in such a renovation. Alfred de Vigny's translation of *Othello* as *Le More de Venise* in 1829 virtually accomplished this aim singlehandedly to the satisfaction of most critics and spectators.

The series of articles by the Neoclassical playwright Mély-Janin in the Ultraroyalist journal *La Quotidienne*, from 1819 to 1823, made it clear

---

1. In this respect, cf. Adolphe Thiers in *L'Album*, 6 (25 Sept. 1822), 104–5; Léon Thiessé in *Le Mercure du XIXe Siècle*, 1 (1823), 171; the unsigned article in *Les Lettres Normandes*, 10 (Feb. 1820), 55; and Paul-F. Dubois's "La réforme du théâtre" in *Le Globe*, 1 (12 Oct. 1824), 54.

that the fundamental Neoclassical objection to the kinds of alterations and innovations suggested in the dramatic system of Shakespeare derived as much from political as from strictly literary considerations. One of these essays categorically declared that any acceptance of Shakespearianism in the theater constituted a virtual endorsement of liberal constitutionalism, and warned: "de la confusion des genres naîtra nécessairement la barbarie, comme de la confusion des pouvoirs en politique résulte l'anarchie."[2] The political climate of 1820 and 1821 served only to exacerbate the uneasiness which both the staunchest Neoclassicists and conservative Romanticists experienced. The assassination of the Duke of Berry in 1820 unnerved the Ultraroyalists, and the death of Napoleon in 1821 rekindled memories of the French defeat at Waterloo. Many tended to view the English as the architects of an elaborate plot to undermine French supremacy in all major areas of endeavor.[3] The arrival of the Penley Company for performances of Shakespeare in English proved disastrous on all counts. A billboard on *Othello* offended the sensibilities of Neoclassicists and ardent nationalists, and provoked strident outcries of blind chauvinism,[4] while the 31 July performance at the Porte St.-Martin induced a near riot in the midst of clamorous chanting: "Parlez français! parlez français!" It was clear that the audience associated Shakespeare with the hated Duke of Wellington, and that whatever Romantic enthusiasm may have existed for Shakespeare had quickly disintegrated in the confusion of events. Convincing entreaties from forceful writers would be required to unite the apostles of reform and to give meaningful direction or focus to the *bataille romantique*.

When François Guizot and his wife, Pauline de Meulan, undertook to revise the Le Tourneur translations of Shakespeare for the Ladvocat publishing firm in 1820, few Frenchmen could claim any genuine familiarity with the actual plays of the English playwright.[5] As translator, Guizot spelled out his ambition in forthright terms: "de montrer Shakespeare dans

2. The following issues contained denigrations of Shakespearian drama: 6 May 1819; 26 Jan. 1821; 19 Feb. 1821; 14 Nov. 1822; 22 March 1823; 8 Dec. 1823. The quotation is taken from the 14 Nov. 1822 issue.

3. Paul Reboul, *Le Mythe anglais dans la littérature française sous la Restauration* (Lille, 1962), pp. 35–36.

4. Notices in the French press were overwhelmingly negative. Only the 2 Aug. 1822 issues of *Le Drapeau Blanc* and *Le Journal de Paris* chided the public for its chauvinism. For a fuller account, see J. L. Borgerhoff, *Le Théâtre anglais à Paris sous la Restauration* (Paris, 1912), pp. 12–14.

5. The Ladvocat series of translations were intended to illustrate the values of English and German literature to French readers. The series included translations of the works of Shakespeare, Byron, Schiller, Goethe, by such French writers as Guizot, Prosper de Barante, Benjamin Constant, Charles Nodier, and Charles de Rémusat.

sa nudité."[6] Even though these translations have been subsequently criticized for their slavish literalness and frequent inelegance,[7] it should be underlined that they did constitute the first reliable rendering of Shakespeare's dramas in French. The long essay which appeared as a preface to the first volume in 1821, "Sur la vie et les œuvres de Shakespeare"—and republished as separate pamphlets under various titles in 1822, 1823, and 1852—provided Romanticists with the types of arguments that would allow them to challenge, finally, the dominant Neoclassical viewpoint. In a real sense, Guizot's treatise marked a turning point in the *bataille romantique*, since it changed the direction of Shakespeare criticism in France.

Guizot argued from the perspective of history in order to tarnish the image of Neoclassicism. Wishing to illustrate that a new type of national theater was sorely needed in France which could foster the integration of all the people into a single, modern culture, he proceeded to describe the system of Voltaire as moribund in nineteenth-century France. By juxtaposing Voltaire and Shakespeare as spokesmen for two opposite artistic cultures, he went on to trace the respective evolutions of the literatures in question, and he begged the provocative question: "à savoir si le systéme dramatique de Shakespeare ne vaut pas mieux que celui de Voltaire."[8] He defined the mission of dramatic poetry: "C'est pour le peuple qu'elle crée, c'est au peuple qu'elle s'adresse, mais pour ennoblir, pour étendre et vivifier son existence morale, pour lui révéler des facultés qu'il possède, mais qu'il ignore."[9] Whereas ancient Greece and Elizabethan England had allowed dramatic poetry to serve as a bridge between the arts and society, eighteenth-century France failed to keep the national culture in tune with the needs of the masses.

In order to demonstrate as dramatically as possible the naturalness of the Elizabethan theater in opposition to the artificiality which characterized the French Neoclassical stage Guizot emphasized the indigenous preoccupations of the former and the obsessive concern with Antiquity of the latter.[10] In straying from their mission to the people, Voltaire and the ex-

6. François Guizot, "Notice sur Antoine et Cléopatre," in *Œuvres complètes de Shakespeare* (Paris, 1821–1822), III, 4–5. Guizot spelled Shakespeare's name: Shakspeare.
7. See Margaret Gilman, *Othello in French* (Paris, 1925), p. 82. For an excellent historical overview of the problem of Shakespeare in France, see Joseph R. LeBlanc, *Shakespeare and the Romantic Movement in France* (Diss., Univ. of Virginia, 1977).
8. All of my references to Guizot's tract are from a later edition, entitled *Shakespeare et son temps* (Paris, 1852), p. 1.
9. Ibid., p. 4.
10. Schlegel also gave an account of the origins of Elizabethan drama in his *Cours de littérature dramatique* of 1813.

clusively aristocratic Neoclassical drama merely succeeded in institution-
alizing a mediocre and lifeless form of art which perpetuates a culture that
remains removed from the majority of the people and from human nature
itself.[11] Because he wished his readers to learn from Shakespeare himself
rather than from any specific dissection of any part of a work, Guizot made
every effort to describe the organic dramatic structure of the playwright.
He never attempted to hold up any particular set of standards except those
of dramatic genius itself. His discussion of Shakespeare's use of genres, for
example, is founded on the dramatist's philosophical and poetic conception
of tragedy.

Guizot's analysis of Shakespearian drama showed a distinct influence
of Schlegel's interpretation. Yet, the originality of his essay rests on the
manner in which he daringly pitted Shakespeare against Voltaire, explained Shakespearian drama in terms of a flexible system, and attacked
Neoclassical criticism of Shakespearian drama by using Shakespeare's
plays to single out the glaring deficiencies of the French Neoclassical
theater. Guizot supplied the method by which a determined group of critics
and playwrights could use and eventually came to use Shakespeare to over-
throw the Neoclassical theater and bring about the modernization of French
drama. Guizot's translations made Shakespeare more readily accessible
to French readers, and his long prefatory essay raised the question of
Shakespearian drama as a timely and critical issue.

Indignant over the hostile reception accorded the Penley Company in
1821, Stendhal entered the literary controversy with the publication of two
manifestoes bearing the same title, *Racine et Shakespeare*, in 1823 and
1825. Both essays repeated essentially the same plea for theater reform and
modernization that Guizot had made two years earlier. Although not as
tightly argued as Guizot's long essay, *Racine et Shakespeare* attracted
wider attention largely because its more belligerent dialectical approach
gave the two tracts a quasi-galvanizing effect. In order to bring into sharp
focus the nature of the differences which polarized the Neoclassical viewpoint from the Romantic attitude, Stendhal cast his tracts in the form of
dialogues between an imaginary Classicist and Romanticist. But his assertion that Romanticism was better able to convey a more satisfying expression of experience[12] proved too vague to be of use to readers who
wished to understand the differences between the two ideologies in question. His strong identification of Romanticism with Modernism and the

11. *Shakespeare et son temps*, pp. 50–56.
12. Henri Beyle, *Racine et Shakespeare*, ed. Pierre Martino (Paris, 1928), p. 154.

situation of post-revolutionary France, however, held great appeal to those younger advocates of change who formulated their values in the aftermath of the French Revolution. Calling on the young liberals to align themselves with Romantic advocates of reform in order to win the battle to modernize France, Stendhal suggested that the *bataille romantique* was primarily a conflict between the generations. The frontispiece of the 1825 version of *Racine et Shakespeare* made this appeal unmistakably clear: "Dialogue. —Le Vieillard: 'Continuons.' —Le Jeune Homme: 'Examinons.' —Voilà tout le dix-neuvième siècle."

Stendhal's thesis that neither Shakespeare nor Racine should be emulated but that the study of Shakespeare, on the other hand, would liberate French playwrights from their slavish obedience to rigid Neoclassical rules had been more convincingly argued by Guizot. But the publicity surrounding *Racine et Shakespeare* doubtless contributed to a detectable coalescence around Shakespeare in 1824 and 1825 among conservative and liberal Romantic writers. Ironically, Stendhal's emphasis on ideology in 1825 proved already somewhat outdated, since liberal and doctrinaire Romanticists had begun to regard the conservative poets who frequented the various *cénacles* as allies rather than as useless proponents of maudlin melodramas.[13] An ardent admirer of Shakespeare, Charles Nodier made it a practice to invite young poets to his workshop at the Arsenal, where he encouraged them to air their views on theater reform, Shakespeare, and foreign literature.[14] He began his campaign to rally Ultraroyalist poets, liberal Romanticists and Doctrinaire intellectuals around the issues of freedom in art by way of Shakespeare as early as 1820 with his pointed articles in *Les Lettres Champenoises*, *Le Mercure*, and *Les Annales*. In 1821 he chided what he termed "liberal Neoclassicists" for their hypocrisy, since they readily identified themselves as liberals in political matters concerned with reforms and greater freedoms, but took refuge behind the cloak of a narrow Neoclassicism when it became a question of encouraging writers whose plays failed to conform to the exact restrictions of classical taste.[15] What emerged with bold evidence was that the literary and social climates had changed substantially, and that the slogan of *Le Lycée Fran-*

13. See Léon Séché, *Histoire des Cénacles de la Muse française*, I (Paris, 1909), 227.

14. Virginie Ancelot, *Les Salons de Paris* (Paris, 1858), pp. 126–127, and Victor Pavie, *Œuvres choisies*, II (Paris, 1887), 105–6. His *Pensées de Shakespeare* (1801) and the manuscript notebook of C. A. Dusillet on *Cours de littérature ancienne et moderne de M. Charles Nodier* (Bibliothèque de Dôle, Ms. 272 R7) attest to his great interest in Shakespeare in the opening decades of the nineteenth century.

15. Cf. *Le Mercure*, 3 (1821), 182, and *Les Annales*, 5 (1821), 219.

çais of 1819—"Le système dramatique se lie à notre système politique"[16] —no longer rang true in 1825.

The cause of Shakespeare and theater reform gained a powerful spokesman when *Le Globe*, despite all claims of eclecticism, began to publish three issues of newsprint weekly in 1824. Counting among its contributors such names as Charles de Rémusat, Charles Magnin, Ernest Desclozeaux, Ludovic Vitet, and Sainte-Beuve, all of them admirers either of Guizot and Stendhal or of Elizabethan drama, *Le Globe* embarked on a sustained campaign to destroy the lingering Neoclassical resistance to reform and renovation. The newspaper expounded a theory of progress through the dissemination of new ideas in philosophy, science, and literature. Desclozeaux set the tone of the campaign which would be waged to demolish the stagnant Neoclassical theater: "Il faut rendre Shakespeare accessible à tout le monde, en un mot le populariser."[17] The same writer devoted a series of six major articles to Shakespeare which purported to shed light on the playwright's dramatic system and explain his individual plays.[18] The reader would decide for himself which system proved superior and more effective in binding the people to a national culture. More articles, all of them taking up the ideas expounded earlier by Guizot and Stendhal, supplemented Desclozeaux's provocative essays, which left no doubt that for *Le Globe*, Shakespeare and theater reform were but a single issue.

By 1826 most of the Parisian press still expressed hostility to Shakespeare and to most proposals for theater reform, but *Le Globe*, with amazing regularity, reminded its readership that Shakespeare remained the key to the modernization of French drama. Political differences no longer blocked the coalescence of the two groups of anti-Neoclassicists who tended, for the most part, to frequent either Charles Nodier's Arsenal or Etienne Délécluze's drawing room. Both, conservatives and liberals, finally agreed about Shakespeare. The French Academy still condemned Shakespearianism through the Société des Bonnes Lettres, the Sorbonne, the influential *Constitutionnel*, and the *Journal des Débats*. The official national theater prospered until 1825 and Neoclassicism prevailed as the prestigious literary philosophy. From the Neoclassical optic, at least, there loomed no urgent reason for conservative playwrights to look beyond their own dramatic forms as long as the public continued to attend their theatrical productions. But so much talk of historical plays and patriotic dramas eventually made

16. *Le Lycée Français*, 1 (1819), 23.
17. *Le Globe*, 1 (26 Nov. 1824), 154.
18. The articles were published in the following issues of *Le Globe*: 27 Nov. 1824; 25 Dec. 1824; 5 Feb. 1825; 19 Aug. 1826; 9 Sept. 1826; and 19 Oct. 1826.

playgoers restless with the Neoclassical fare. As attendance dropped significantly in 1825 and 1826, government subsidies were increased to absorb losses in revenue.[19] The Neoclassical theater was in trouble, and more liberal publications such as *Le Globe*, *Le Mercure du XIXe Siècle*, and *Le Figaro* brought this to the attention of their subscribers. Among other press publications, *Le Journal des Débats* and *Les Annales* placed the blame squarely on the political censorship imposed in 1821 as the chief cause for staleness on the French stage.[20] Vitet asserted in his columns of *Le Globe* that Neoclassicists who dominated the reading committees at the national theaters were known for their arbitrary rejections of all scripts which deviated even slightly from the prescribed rules and forms.[21] Talma's death in 1826 compounded the blow, and the *Mercure du XIXe Siècle* speculated that the death of the celebrated actor might conceivably lead to the death of the Neoclassical theater.[22] The eclectic *Pandore* warned most aptly:

> Le besoin de réforme qui travaille la littérature et les arts se fait sentir au théâtre plus qu'ailleurs, et la tragédie surtout veut sortir de la routine.... Voilà la différence des deux systèmes. Nous ne dirons pas lequel est le meilleur; mais nous reconnaissons que celui de Racine n'est plus conforme au goût du public, aux besoins de la littérature et à l'état des arts.[23]

It would be a serious exaggeration to convey the idea that the Romanticists made no attempts whatever to back up their theories on the drama by writing actual plays for the theater. In 1825 and 1826 thirty-five new dramas were written and produced, but only four were kept in the repertory.[24] Most of these plays were little more than "scènes historiques" such as Vitet's own *Barricades* in 1826. The preface to his drama describes this hybrid genre: "ce n'est point une pièce de théâtre que l'on va lire, ce sont des faits historiques présentés sous la forme dramatique, mais sans la prétention d'en composer un drame." The best-known Neoclassical playwrights of the time—Ancelot, Arnault, Casimir Delavigne, and Lemercier

---

19. In 1821 government subsidies to the Comédie Française totaled 121,387 francs. These subsidies were increased to 175,000 francs in 1825, and to 200,000 francs in 1826. Cf. *Archives Nationales*. O³ 1599, Box I, No. 218.
20. See Victor Hallays-Dabot, *Histoire de la censure théâtrale en France* (Paris, 1862), pp. 254–77.
21. *Le Globe*, 1 (23 April 1825), 491–93.
22. *Le Mercure du XIXe Siècle*, 15 (1826), 273–74.
23. *La Pandore*, 6 Dec. 1826, p. 2.
24. For a fuller account see Jules Marsan, *La Bataille romantique* (Paris, 1912), pp. 158–62. See also Michèle H. Jones, *Le Théâtre national en France de 1800 à 1830* (Paris, 1975) on plays involved with the depiction of the history of France.

—began to sprinkle their plots with allusions to French history, but, by and large, none of these dramas won the favor of theater audiences. The Baron Taylor, director of the Comédie Française since 1825 and a personal friend of Nodier and Vigny, encouraged the members of the *cénacle* at the Arsenal to write Romantic dramas. He attempted to revive the 1825–1826 drama season with no fewer than twenty performances of Ducis's adaptations of *Hamlet, Macbeth*, and *Othello*.[25] Bruguière de Sorsum's translations of Shakespeare, a mixture of verse and prose, in 1826, came the closest, thus far, in capturing the flavor of *The Tempest, Macbeth, A Midsummer Night's Dream*, and *Coriolanus*. But these were translations only meant to be read as texts. Ironically, it would take the visit of the English troupe of Charles Kemble and Charles Abbott in 1827 to inject badly needed adrenalin into the French theater.

The performances by the English troupe of the actual plays of Shakespeare in English made a lasting impression on the French theatrical establishment. When the company left Paris in the summer of 1828, French Romantic playwrights had at last begun to write their own dramas. There could be little doubt that Alexandre Dumas père, Vigny, Emile and Antony Deschamps, Musset, and Berlioz left greatly influenced by these performances as their subsequent dramas and musical compositions have revealed to us. There could be no doubting, either, that the English performances had profoundly altered Shakespeare's image in France. The English actors, who included Charles Kemble and Harriet Smithson in several key roles, emphasized freedom and creativity in their interpretations of *Hamlet, Othello, Macbeth, King Lear, Richard III*, and *Romeo and Juliet*. Reactions to the first performance at the Odéon on 6 September ranged from cautious approvals in *La Quotidienne* and *La Pandore* to expressions of outrage in *Le Constitutionnel* and *Le Courrier des Théâtres*.[26] More importantly, the plays caused many influential French critics to discard some of their prejudices and misconceptions concerning Shakespeare. The critic of the staunchly Neoclassical *Moniteur* admitted somewhat reluctantly that the English bard was not as barbarous a genius as Voltaire had led the French to expect. There was general agreement that *Hamlet* emerged as a genuine tragedy with no loss of dramatic unity resulting from the mixing of comic and serious scenes. On 18 September, after a triumphant performance of

25. Christian A.-E. Jensen, *L'Evolution du romantisme: l'année 1826* (Geneva, 1959), p. 146.
26. Cf. *Le Constitutionnel*, 8 Sept. 1827, p. 4: "... ces sauvages!" and Charles Maurice's scathing review in *Le Courrier des Théâtres*, 7 Sept. 1827, p. 2.

Romeo and Juliet, La Pandore declared itself outright as a full-fledged partisan of Shakespeare.[27]

The première of *Othello* on 18 September proved to be the only serious setback suffered by the English actors during their stay in France. The depiction of Desdemona's strangulation in the final scene shocked audience and critics alike, who viewed it as an outrageous violation of good taste. The British company presented *Othello* again on 25 September, this time with considerably less emphasis on the actual murder which was more in line with the eighteenth-century French adaptation by Ducis. By the time the English performers left France in the summer of 1828, the majority of the critics had been won over to Shakespeare, and most agreed that the performances had suggested to discerning French spectators how the brilliance of the Elizabethan playwright might be fused with the grace of Corneille and Racine. Upon the arrival of the troupe of actors in the summer of 1827, six of the ten most prestigious press publications voiced an open hostility to Shakespeare; by the summer of 1828, only two of these journals still professed any hostility.[28] Overwhelming critical opinion echoed the view expressed earlier in *La Pandore* concerning the theatrical experiment: "C'est en comparant notre système dramatique à celui des Anglais que les auteurs parviendront à opérer les réformes dont notre théâtre a tant besoin."[29] Even the academic Neoclassical bastion at the Sorbonne recognized the value of the 1827–1828 theatrical season. Paul Duport, a student of Villemain, published a two-volume study of Shakespeare in which he declared: "Bien connaître Shakespeare est donc devenu un besoin presque indispensable pour nous."[30] The success of the English troupe did much to create an ambience in which Romantic playwrights could now hope to overcome nearly all serious Neoclassical resistance to their reforms in the theater.

It will be recalled that the poets of *La Muse Française* entered into the Shakespeare controversy when they began to meet regularly at Nodier's Arsenal in the mid 1820's. At that time, Victor Hugo manifested a decided predilection for melodrama, and the Baron Taylor encouraged him to write an historical drama on *Cromwell*. The *Préface de Cromwell* of 1827, which

27. Cf. *La Pandore*, 18 Sept. 1827, p. 2.

28. Only *Les Annales* and *Le Courrier des Théâtres* were hostile to Shakespeare in 1828; the *Journal des Débats* only voiced its opposition to the dramatic form. Meanwhile *Le Constitutionnel*, *Le Mercure*, and *La Quotidienne* shifted from essentially hostile views to approvals of Shakespeare by 1828.

29. *La Pandore*, 19 Sept. 1827, p. 2.

30. Paul Duport, *Essais littéraires sur Shakespeare*, 2 vols. (Paris, 1828). The quotation is from the preface in Vol. I, p. iii.

accompanied the play, constituted yet another manifesto which argued that Shakespeare had shown how drama could be the most effective vehicle for Romantic expression. The essay elaborated further upon the theories which Nodier, Stendhal, and the critics of *Le Globe* had previously enunciated.[31] It joined Stendhal in condemning the *tirade*, the Racinian device for reporting events which had been adopted on a major level in Neoclassical drama, and equated the new Romantic theater with realism and modernity. Hugo's own conceptualization of a unity of opposites—"le beau et le difforme"—enabled him to arrive at a positive definition of the Romantic drama. The *Préface de Cromwell* represented a dramatic about-face of Hugo's earlier views on Shakespeare expressed tersely in an 1820 article he contributed to *Le Conservateur Littéraire*: "Les pièces de Shakespeare et de Schiller ne diffèrent des pièces de Corneille et de Racine qu'en ce qu'elles sont plus défectueuses."[32] The treatise of 1827 betrayed a central preoccupation with Shakespeare. Indeed the example of the English bard hovers behind Hugo's notion of the history of literary progress and his interpretation of the three ages of man. Despite the wide publicity accorded the manifesto in the press,[33] the *Préface de Cromwell* won few converts among the Neoclassicists even though the English performances of Shakespeare forced them to moderate their positions on the theater. If nothing else, the preface and the closet historical drama on *Cromwell*[34] did embolden the advocates of reform, since they could now refer to Hugo as a playwright who introduced innovations in the French theater.

In their forceful references to the authority of Shakespeare, the French Romantic theorists succeeded in obliging Neoclassical critics to reconsider Voltaire's celebrated attacks on the Elizabethan playwright. In 1828 the balance of opinion shifted in favor of Shakespeare with the founding of two liberal publications, *La Revue Française* and *La Revue de Paris*.[35] When the leading Neoclassical journal, *Les Annales*, folded for lack of sufficient subscribers and financial backing in the same year, the editors

31. Cf. the thesis of Eunice M. Schenck, *L'Influence de Charles Nodier sur Victor Hugo* (Paris, 1914), which maintains that Hugo merely embellished the theories of Nodier in the *Préface de Cromwell*.

32. *Le Conservateur Littéraire*, 1 (March 1820), 355.

33. *Le Globe* devoted an entire issue to a discussion of the *Préface de Cromwell* on 6 Dec. 1827.

34. Cf. Jean Boorsch, "Hugo's Fraternal Genius," *Yale French Studies*, No. 34 (1964), 67: "[*Cromwell*] is the fountainhead of the plays which follow rather than a monument to Shakespearian influence. It shows a solidity of construction, a structural symmetry, a concentration of time and plot alien to Shakespeare."

35. The emergence of such doctrinaire publications as *La Revue Française* and *La Revue de Paris* resulted, at least in part, from the passage of a liberal press law in 1828.

launched their last bitter attack on "ces messieurs de la nouvelle école."[36]
Both *La Revue Française* and *La Revue de Paris*, in promulgating the same
theories on theater reform as those of *Le Globe*, built upon the momentum
established by the English troupe and the *Préface de Cromwell* to wage a
relentless campaign aimed at the destruction of the last vestiges of a wan-
ing Neoclassicism.

The 1828 theatrical season in Paris made it plain that the Shakespearian
dramatic system had left a considerable imprint on the French theater.
Frédéric Soulié's adaptation of *Roméo et Juliette, drame en cinq actes*,
represented a vast improvement over the only available Ducis version.
Despite several minor cuts and certain alterations in the roles of Friar
Lawrence and Juliet's nurse, Soulié's *Roméo et Juliette*, written in disciplined verse, preserved intact most of the flavor of Shakespeare's tragedy.
The generally mixed reaction of basically sympathetic critics, who re-
proached Soulié for his deviations from the original text, did not prevent
the dramatic adaptation from enjoying a fairly popular run during the
summer of 1828. In commenting on his own theatrical venture in *La
Quotidienne*, Soulié admitted that a more faithful translation would have
better served the cause of Shakespeare and the modern theater. More
importantly, he brought out some of the crucial problems involving such
translations-adaptations:

> En voyant ce que l'auteur a fait, on peut juger de ce qu'il a laissé à
> faire, si ce n'est à de plus habiles, du moins à de plus hardis, c'est-à-
> dire à ceux qui oseront embrasser le drame de Shakespeare dans tout
> ce qu'il y a d'énergique et de profond, sans dédaigner ce qu'il y a de
> tendre et de naïf, à le suivre même dans les scènes d'enjouement et de
> grâce sans affaiblir ce qu'il y a d'austère et de religieux. En un mot, la
> naturalisation du poète anglais que le public attend n'est pas complète
> encore, mais nous avons lieu d'espérer qu'elle le sera bientôt.[37]

The timid attempts by such Neoclassical playwrights as Népomucène
Lemercier, Jouy, and Ancelot to insert inconsequential innovations in their
historical dramas and tragedies succeeded only in irritating liberal and
Neoclassical critics alike.[38] None of the playwrights involved possessed a
satisfactory mastery of Shakespearian drama, and plays such as Ancelot's
L'Espion, written in a mixture of prose and poetry and in violation of the

36. *Les Annales*, 24 (March 1829), 67.
37. *La Quotidienne*, 14 June 1828, p. 4.
38. Cf. Magnin, *Le Globe*, 5 (5 Jan. 1828), 103–4 and *Les Annales*, 22 (16 Dec. 1828),
281.

unities, exasperated the audiences of the Comédie Française. Heeding the recommendation of Charles Magnin in *Le Globe* that translations rather than adaptations of Shakespeare be written for the French stage, Emile Deschamps and Vigny ironed out problems associated with their joint translation of *Roméo et Juliette*. Although their translation was never produced, Vigny set out to translate *Othello* for the Baron Taylor and the reading committee of the Comédie Française. It is this translation and adaptation of Shakespeare that would give the Romantic theater its first decisive triumph on 24 October 1829, preceding the Romantic victory of *Hernani* on 25 February 1830.

Most frequently accepted as the successful Romantic poet of the *Poèmes antiques et modernes* and the author of the popular historical novel *Cinq-Mars*, in 1826, Vigny scarcely impressed critics as a potentially revolutionary innovator in literature. By 1827 he revealed an eagerness to contribute to the modernization of the French theater without destroying the valuable traditions of its glorious past. By reason of his serious personal manner and his past literary practice, he appealed to observers as the writer who could reason with the Neoclassicists while rallying the Romanticists in their campaign for meaningful theater reforms. Vigny had begun to disavow the Ultraroyalist stand of his early career and grew increasingly indifferent to the regime of Charles X and the political issue of Legitimacy. By the time he had joined the Romanticists' campaign for a new theater, he had embraced the Doctrinaire idea of literary progress. The preface to the 1827 edition of *Cinq-Mars* brought his altered attitudes into public view. "Réflexions sur la vérité dans l'art" took issue, principally, with Stendhal's earlier point in *Racine et Shakespeare* that the French theater could successfully be reformed with dramas which translated the events of history with scrupulous accuracy. Vigny agreed with Stendhal that Shakespeare's historical dramas provided reformers with excellent examples to guide them in their renovation of dramatic forms, but added that historical accuracy did not necessarily characterize Shakespeare's dramatic reconstructions.

The preface to the 1827 edition of *Cinq-Mars* explained what Shakespeare understood as "vérité dans l'art" and "le vrai du fait," arguing that the playwright knew that artistic truth differed from factual truth. "Vérité dans l'art" did not attempt to portray any exact reproduction of reality, but rather suggested a characteristic representation of reality in all of its potential greatness and beauty. If "vérité" was an extraction of real life, it was certainly not a slavish imitation of its details. Good historical dramas did not merely recite or enumerate the details of past events, but instead projected onto the stage the mind of the playwright actively intervening in the creative process. Only the poet's imagination ascribed color and "vérité" to historical personalities. In Vigny's estimation the historical dramas of Shakespeare justified this point of the function of the imagination:

> Tant mieux pour la mémoire de ceux que l'on choisit pour représenter des idées philosophiques ou morales; mais, encore une fois, la question n'est pas là: l'imagination fait d'aussi belles choses sans eux; elle est une puissance toute créatrice; les êtres fabuleux qu'elle anime sont doués de vie autant que les êtres réels qu'elle ranime. Nous croyons à Othello comme à Richard III, dont le monument est à Westminster, à Lovelace et à Clarisse autant qu'à Paul et Virginie, dont les tombes sont à l'Ile de France.[39]

While he worked on his translations of *Othello*, *The Merchant of Venice*, and the last two acts of *Romeo and Juliet*, Vigny evolved his theory of translation and associated it with the larger issue of the modernization of French drama. For him, Shakespeare's plays did not assault all of the Neoclassical dictums head on. His own translation of *Othello*, for example, reduced the violations of the unities of time and place to a minimum. Likewise, a few minor changes in the order of certain scenes could simplify the action considerably. The reduction of the use of clowns, puns, and coarse language, at strategic intervals, would prove less distracting to audiences unaccustomed to such mixtures of comic and serious scenes. With Emile Deschamps, Vigny held that the new poetical styles developed by some Romantic poets could be applied with great benefit to the French stage. His often delicate alexandrine verse in *Othello* would prove this point. Since Shakespeare's dialogues were all structured around poetic lines, he felt that prose should be avoided, and that all the speeches should be converted into verse in order to preserve the flow of rhythm. The dexterity with which he manipulated the alexandrine to convey such a wide range of passion and fury in the final act of *Othello* stood as the most convincing corroboration of his theory. Vigny's reproduction of the hissing sounds and the violently abrupt rhythms of Othello's opening speech in the second scene captured all the flavor of Shakespeare's original:[40]

39. Alfred de Vigny, *Cinq-Mars ou Une Conjuration sous Louis XIII*, in *Œuvres complètes*, notes by Fernand Baldensperger (Paris, 1935), p. xii. All references to Vigny's work are from this edition.
40. V, ii: "It is the cause, it is the cause, my soul. / Let me not name it to you, you chaste stars."

C'est la cause, ô mon âme! et vous la connaissez,
La cause qui m'amène au meurtre! c'est assez!
Etoiles qu'on adore en votre chaste empire,
La cause, sous vos yeux je n'oserais la dire!
Je ne verserai pas son sang, et mon dessein
Ne me conduira pas à déchirer ce sein
Si beau, que l'on croit voir, à la lampe bleuâtre,
Sur un tombeau de marbre une image d'albâtre.

Vigny made every effort to translate Shakespeare's plays in the manner which was least likely to offend unduly the Neoclassicist's sensibility. He concurred with the latter on the prospect of seeing the official theater inundated with prose melodramas.

But Vigny also believed that the French Neoclassical theater had failed to depict satisfactorily the modern condition of man and to probe the psychological aspect of the soul. By insisting on the separation of genres, the Neoclassicists had imposed severe restrictions on the nineteenth-century playwright. The latter should be given free rein to portray human passions and to trace the evolution of the passions. As far as Vigny was concerned, the ideals of Boileau could be achieved without resorting to the strict observance of his dictums. The "Lettre à Lord ***" constituted Vigny's preface to *Othello*, and it appeared in print a few days after the première of *Le More de Venise*. The essay has the force of a veritable manifesto on the theater and nineteenth-century literature.

The correspondence and the *Journal d'un poète* of October 1829 underlined the fact that Vigny considered himself a spokesman for the younger generation in this theatrical venture. This was precisely the point in his career when he espoused, however loosely and temporarily, some of the progressive notions of the Doctrinaires and the Saint-Simonians.[41] Aware that his *More de Venise* risked offending advocates of the Neoclassical establishment, he defined his attitudes to Auguste Brieux in a letter which commented on the prospective opening of his translation of *Othello* at the Comédie Française:

J'attends une nouvelle liste de conjurés. Qu'elle soit bien nombreuse, je vous en prie; c'est la cause de la jeunesse et c'est une liberté de plus qu'elle m'aidera à conquérir. Cette vieille citadelle de la rue Richelieu va nous appartenir si nous ouvrons la brèche. Cette guerre, au bout du compte, est une plaisanterie assez amusante, et cette soirée

41. *Journal d'un poète*, I (1823–1841), 76–77.

nous divertira, quelque chose qui arrive, très assurément. C'est du mouvement, c'est de la vie; depuis que j'ai quitté le service, il ne m'arrive rien, cela m'ennuie. Je me suis fait là un petit événement.[42]

Vigny's commitment to progress and reform was so categorical in 1829 that, with Hugo and Emile Deschamps, he gave serious thought to founding a journal which he proposed to name *La Réforme de la Littérature et des Arts.*[43]

The "Lettre à Lord ***" began with the somewhat jarring declaration that "*Le More de Venise* ne doit pas se nommer autrement pour moi que le 24 octobre 1829." The subtitle to this prefatory letter set the tone for themes that would be developed: "Sur la soirée du 24 octobre 1829 et sur un système dramatique." The essay was, in fact, an aggressive attack on the unities and the notion of the separation of genres which constituted the cornerstones of the Neoclassical theater. Since the dutiful observance of such guidelines could not guarantee that specific overall impressions be produced in all the members of the audience viewing a tragedy or a comedy, it was useless to insist on any uniform observance of the rules. Dramas set out to convey an overall impression on some aspect of existence, and the plays either succeed or fail according to the quality of the overall impression that is communicated to the audience: "On ne peut donc le nier: faire jouer une tragédie n'est autre chose que préparer une soirée, et le véritable titre doit être la date de la représentation. Ainsi, d'après ce principe, au lieu de *As you like it*, comme écrivit Shakespeare un jour, j'aurais mis, dans l'embarras du choix, en tête de sa comédie: *6th January 1600.* Et le *More de Venise* ne doit pas se nommer autrement pour moi que le 24 octobre 1829."[44]

Boldly blaming the Neoclassical rules concerning the unities and the separation of genres for having created a *cul-de-sac* in the development of the theater, Vigny pointed out that he wished his translation-adaptation of *Othello* to leave something more than a favorable impression with the spectator. *Le More de Venise* would raise and attempt to answer a crucial question concerning the future direction of the French stage. If the theater

42. Letter of 9 Oct. 1829 in *Correspondance*, I (1816–1835), 197–98. See also Vigny's letter to the Baron Taylor: "Qu'elle [la Comédie Française] ne craigne pas de se compromettre en suivant les voies nouvelles, il n'y a de vie que parmi les vivants; la brèche est faite, si l'un tombe, l'autre montera, et le sort d'*Hernani*, qu'on semble attendre pour se décider, ne peut rien prouver ni pour lui ni contre d'autres œuvres; ils prouveraient seulement que les calculs envieux auront été plus ou moins heureux contre ce beau drame" (ibid., p. 197).
43. *Journal d'un poète*, p. 72.
44. Alfred de Vigny, *Théâtre*, I: *Pièces en vers*, p. 13.

public could accept a modern tragedy which aimed to portray the larger issues of reality without the encumbrances of restrictions regarding unities and the mixture of genres, then the modernization and expansion of the French drama could be undertaken with confidence and enthusiasm. This question could be answered more tellingly through the presentation of a translation of a well-known masterpiece than with a new play which might incite more controversy than objective examination.

Vigny defined the new or modern theater in terms of the overall impression achieved in the drama rather than by any specific set of rules or prescriptions observed: "Ecoutez ce soir le langage que je pense devoir être celui de la tragédie moderne; dans lequel chaque personnage parlera selon son caractère, et dans l'art comme dans la vie, passera de la simplicité habituelle à l'exaltation passionnée; du *récitatif* au *chant*."[45] Such a style, informed by a world view, constituted the real basis for the modern system of drama, which soars beyond the limitations imposed by Neoclassicism. By removing the barriers of time and space, the playwright would be free to develop his characters and his plots in such a manner as to enable him to depict or reproduce reality artfully. If Ducis's adaptation of *Othello* failed to depict reality and move the spectator, it was because of an overriding desire to modify Shakespeare's tragedy to make it conform to what he considered to be the good taste of his Neoclassical audiences and readers. Vigny resolved to adhere more closely to Shakespeare's original script because he wished his translation to communicate a powerful and truthful drama. His more loyal adaptation of *Othello* would allow all of the power inherent in the text to impress itself on the audience. The superiority of the modern system of drama would emerge clearly over the Neoclassical one through the example of Shakespeare's tragedy. Why Shakespeare and not a modern play to illustrate his thesis? Vigny provided the answer himself in 1829: "Je cherchais depuis 1817 un sujet moderne qui fût aussi beau, aussi calme dans ses formes que les sujets antiques: je ne l'ai pas trouvé. Les tableaux modernes sont tourmentés de détails plus passionnés et plus dramatiques que les antiques, mais moins grands et moins simples de forme, par conséquent moins durables."[46]

The truth of the matter was that Vigny's *More de Venise* attempted to combine the best features of Classicism with Modernism. "J'ai donc cherché à rendre l'esprit, non la lettre."[47] His translation sought to capture Shake-

45. Ibid., p. 15.
46. *Journal d'un poète*, pp. 56–57.
47. *Théâtre*, I, p. 35.

speare's epic dimension in Othello in a passionate, graceful, and poetic presentation. The combined talents of the Elizabethan playwright and the Romantic poet would try to fuse poetry with drama, discipline with freedom, Classicism with Modernity. Above all, Vigny did not set out to translate Shakespeare merely to point out the superiority of one system of drama over the other. What he wished to achieve in *Le More de Venise* was to graft Shakespeare's tragedy to the possibilities of modern drama. Unless Shakespeare's plays could be so modernized, they would remain useless to the cause of progress and reform in the nineteenth-century French theater. Because of the universality of its message, its dramatic sweep and its penetrating execution, *Othello* could be readily adapted, with only minor alterations, so that it would meet the exigencies inherent in the modern theater. "Lettre à Lord ***" linked the cause of Shakespeare and that of the theater reform to the theory of social progress: "un symbole parfait de cette inflexible *loi du progrès* dont la marche emporte sans cesse avec elle les trois degrés de l'esprit humain qui lui sont indifférents, et ne servent, après tout, qu'à marquer successivement ses pas vers un but, hélas! inconnu?"[48] If it could be argued that Guizot, Stendhal, and the critics of *Le Globe* had previously achieved such a goal with varying degrees of success, Vigny wanted to substantiate his theory on the modern theater with a play that would win to the cause of reform converts among the spectators at the Comédie Française.

It will be remembered that Vigny had not intended his *More de Venise* to be a literal translation of *Othello*. The translation-adaptation, which ran thirteen performances in 1829 and three more in 1830, was conceived more as a proving ground for the future of the Romantic drama. Rather than alienate the Neoclassicists who would doubtless constitute a segment of his audiences, Vigny sought to edit certain puns, coarse language, and scabrous allusions which might only serve to irritate unduly such conservative spectators. For the most part his omissions and alterations do not detract seriously from the tone and temper of Shakespeare's script.[49] It was clear that Vigny intended to win over as many converts to the cause of theater reform as possible. Beyond dispute was the fact that his translation of the major confrontations between the various protagonists captures with

48. Ibid., p. 40.

49. Vigny, for example cut part of the scene between Iago and Desdemona in II, i, 137–92; the clown scenes in III, i; and IV, i, 1–24. Act II ends with a dialogue between Iago and Roderigo. See also Stirling Haig, "Vigny and Othello," in *Yale French Studies*, No. 33 (1963), p. 55: "The French translator had to perform a very delicate balancing act and could expect to be condemned both for his timidities and his temerities."

often stunning effects the richly tragic dimensions in *Othello*. Utilizing, in most instances, the text of the First Folio edition of *Othello*,[50] Vigny succeeded admirably in finding the exact correspondences between French and English terms. Iago's brief soliloquy in Act III, just after he has planted the seed of jealousy in Othello's heart, underscored Vigny's talent in conveying extended imagery with felicitous results; for example:

> Look where he comes! Not poppy nor mandragora,
> Nor all the drowsy syrups of the world
> Shall ever medicine thee to that sweet sleep
> Which thou owedst yesterday

becomes in French:

> Va déchire ton cœur! Va, ni le feu, ni l'eau,
> Les boissons de pavots, d'opium, de mandragore,
> Ne pourront te guérir et te donner encore
> Ce paisible sommeil que tu goûtas hier.[51]

Whatever the minor inconsistencies and deviations from the original text which critics have pointed out in Vigny's translation, admiration for the poet's majestic rendering of Othello's celebrated farewell scene to his past military exploits has been quasi-universal. The translator's particularly adept handling of the alexandrine allowed him to capture the exact tone of the original version of the fatal dialogue. Vigny's alteration of the last three words of the speech were explained as a desire not to reduce the exalted station of the African warrior to a prosaic level. One becomes aware of the fact that *Le More de Venise* is the work of a first-rate poet and translator in such a passage:

> Adieu, joie et bonheur détruits par une femme!
> Adieu, beaux bataillons aux panaches flottants!
> Adieu, guerre! adieu, toi dont les jeux éclatants
> Font de l'ambition une vertu sublime!
> Adieu donc, le coursier que la trompette anime,
> Et ses hennissements, et le bruit du tambour,
> L'étendard qu'on déploie avec des cris d'amour!
> Appareil, pompe, éclat, cortège de la gloire!
> Et vous, nobles canons qui tonnez la victoire

50. See Margaret Gilman, *Othello in French*, pp. 99–100, for variations used by Vigny.
51. *Othello*, III, iii; *Le More de Venise*, III, viii.

Et qui semblez la voix formidable d'un Dieu,
Ma tâche est terminée! A tout jamais, adieu![52]

From the strictly objective or scholarly point of view of the modern
Shakespearian reader, however, there occurs in *Le More de Venise* a series
of alterations which appear to be the result of the translator's defective
comprehension of the English language. Yet such aberrations are relatively
few and of minor consequence, since they never detract seriously from the
overall sense of *Othello*. When Roderigo admits that he is not directly involved in the unfolding of the plot against Othello because of his ignorance
of certain facts: "I do follow here in the chase, not like the hound that
hunts, but as one that fills up the cry," Vigny's rendition insinuates, instead,
that Roderigo pursues a subtle strategy to win over Desdemona: "J'ai,
qu'enfin je me lasse/ De courir le pays comme un chien à la chasse."[53]
More frequently than not, however, Vigny's alterations emerge as deliberate attempts to tone down some expressions in *Othello* which might otherwise offend French sensibilities unaccustomed to such frankness on the
stage. The metaphor which Othello employs with respect to Desdemona
in Act IV, Scene ii, is a case in point. The fountain, which is Desdemona,
"to be discarded thence,/ Or keep it as a cistern for foul toads/ To knot
and gender in" becomes in *Le More de Venise* merely "un marais impur."[54]
What the audience of 24 October 1829 at the Comédie Française saw in
Le More de Venise was a minutely planned performance. Vigny received
advice for the staging from the English actor Young, who had been celebrated in England for his role of Iago.[55] Mlle Mars, despite her forty-nine
years, played Desdemona with vivacity and passion. Despite a minor out-
burst of laughter at the mention of "mouchoir," in Act IV, the audience
waited in eager anticipation for the climax. Where the touring English
actors in 1827 had offended French theatergoers with a detailed portrayal
of Desdemona's brutal suffocation by Othello, Vigny's Othello spared Desdemona—and also the audience—considerable agony by acceding to her
request for a swifter death. Neoclassical critic Duvicquet described the
reaction following the first performance of *Le More de Venise* as an actor
stepped forward to announce: "L'auteur de la traduction de la tragédie de
Shakespeare (applaudissements),... de la tragédie du GRAND Shakespeare

52. *Le More de Venise*, III, ix. Cf. *Othello*, III, iii, 345–54.
53. *Othello*, II, iii, 363–64; *Le More de Venise*, II, xvii.
54. *Le More de Venise*, IV, xii.
55. Jules Marsan, "Lettre inédite à M. Robert," *Revue de Littérature Comparée*, 5
(1925), 379.

(redoublement d'acclamations et de bravos), est M. Alfred de Vigny!"[56]

All other considerations aside, immediate critical reaction to the performances of Vigny's translation-adaptation made it plain that the Romantic battle to popularize Shakespeare had been won, and that the example of Shakespeare would actually provide useful directions for the much-needed reform of the French theater. Charles Magnin of *Le Globe* paced the other advocates for innovation: "Enfin, voilà ce que nous avons tant désiré! Voilà une première pièce de Shakespeare, non plus imitée, défigurée, travestie, mais fidèlement traduite! Voilà l'auteur d'*Othello* introduit sur notre scène par une main habile. Grâces soient rendues à M. Alfred de Vigny!"[57] The audiences attending the performances of *Le More de Venise* at the Comédie Française had ratified the triumphs of Shakespeare and the Romanticists. The easily detectable note of jubilation which punctuated most critical reactions to Vigny's translations conveyed with pride that the play's success had decided the whole question of Shakespeare once and for all, and that a literary revolution had been accomplished on 24 October 1829. "Cette révolution signalée s'est accomplie dans le goût même du public plutôt, ou du moins plus décidément, que dans ses doctrines."[58] *Le More de Venise* vindicated Vigny's prefatory "Lettre à Lord * * *" and established him in the vanguard of theater reform in France in the eyes of most Romantic innovators.

Of the various Neoclassical critics who voiced their opposition to Shakespeare during the theatrical season of 1827–1828, Duvicquet and Charles Maurice admitted they feared that the destruction of Neoclassicism would mean the triumph of the insipid melodrama in the French theater. Both critics attended performances of *Le More de Venise* and read Vigny's prefatory manifesto. What impressed Duvicquet, especially, was a genuine tragedy which had been translated skillfully into graceful and often melodic French. The experience compelled him to wonder aloud on the extreme positions embraced by both Classicists and Romanticists:

> Les classiques déclarent qu'il n'y a d'autre moyen de plaire, que de soumettre le génie à des règles sanctionnées par l'expérience, approuvées par la réflexion, défendues par l'exemple des grands maîtres aux époques les plus florissantes de l'art, et chez les peuples les plus universellement éclairés. Les romantiques répondent qu'ils ne connais-

56. *Journal des Débats*, 26 Oct. 1829, p. 3.

57. *Le Globe*, 7 (28 Oct. 1829), 683. For similar reactions, see *La Quotidienne*, 26 Oct. 1829, and the review dated 26 Oct. 1829 in *Le Mercure* 27, 172–76.

58. Broglie, *La Revue Française*, 13 (Jan. 1830), 64.

sent qu'une règle, celle de réussir et de plaire en dépit des règles. Aux chefs-d'œuvre de la Grèce, de l'Italie, de la France, ils opposent ceux de l'Angleterre et de l'Allemagne; aux noms de Corneille, de Racine et de Voltaire, ceux de Shakespeare, de Schiller et de Goëthe....[59]

Duvicquet's review posed the question: did this mean that perhaps Neoclassicists and Romanticists could adopt similar guidelines to produce good plays? "S'il m'était permis de présager l'avenir, j'oserais parier pour Shakespeare et pour M. Alfred de Vigny."[60] In his last articles for the *Journal des Débats*, Duvicquet came to accept Shakespeare as classical, and to appreciate the Romantic argument that great plays could be written under a different set of guidelines than those of Boileau.

A self-professed chauvinist and an inflexible defender of Neoclassicism, Charles Maurice redefined his position with respect to the Romanticists after viewing *Le More de Venise*: "Disons d'abord ce que c'est que *Le More de Venise*, ouvrage si remarquable et si singulier. Dans cet examen, n'oublions pas que son premier auteur est un homme de génie, et le second, un écrivain de beaucoup d'esprit."[61] The heretofore outspoken opponent of Shakespearian drama expressed the hope that other theaters would perform Shakespeare translations and adaptations rather than resort to the wholesale production of third-rate melodramas. From 10 November to 26 November, Maurice wrote articles daily on Shakespeare, echoing essentially the viewpoints enunciated by Villemain at the Sorbonne during the 1827 theatrical season: despite minor deficiencies in form, the English playwright wrote powerful and unforgettable dramas.[62] If Shakespeare did rank lower than Racine and Corneille as a dramatist, he certainly emerged superior to all of their imitators. Maurice's pondered about-face signaled the end of all serious opposition to Shakespeare and the dramatic system which differed radically from that of the French Neoclassicists.

By early winter of 1829 the Romanticists considered Shakespeare as the creator of modern drama and as their most articulate spokesman against Neoclassicism. For their part, the staunchest Neoclassicists learned to appreciate Shakespeare as a powerful and respected playwright whose plays never descended into melodrama. Those taken with the theater of the boulevard saw in his plots bizarre and gothic ingredients which could be quickly incorporated into their commercially successful melodramas. The

59. *Journal des Débats*, 26 Oct. 1829, p. 1.
60. Ibid., p. 2.
61. *Le Courrier des Théâtres*, 24 Aug. 1829, p. 2. See also Maurice's article in the 6 Sept. issue of that same year.
62. Ibid., 10 Nov. 1829, p. 2.

result of this widespread convergence was that the theatrical season of 1829–1830 featured several respectable translations and adaptations of Shakespeare, melodramas and operas which highlighted Shakespearian plots or motifs, and an impressive number of books and essays concerning the playwright's tragedies, histories, and comedies.[63] It is no exaggeration to claim that the plays of Shakespeare contributed significantly to the crumbling of Neoclassicism by 1829. The success of *Le More de Venise* softened the resistance of such critics as Villemain, Duvicquet, and Charles Maurice to Romanticism. Vigny's translation-adaptation of *Othello* in 1829 prepared the climate that would welcome such daringly new dramas as *Hernani* in 1830 and afterwards.

63. See Emma Sakellarides, *Alfred de Vigny, auteur dramatique* (Paris, 1902).

Germaine Brée

Le mythe des origines et l'autoportrait chez George Sand et Colette

*Pour Wallace Fowlie, un des premiers
critiques qui usa de la psychobiographie*

I

La critique psychobiographique affronte de nombreux problèmes aujourd'hui, dont le moindre n'est pas la "vaste confusion" qui, selon Serge Leclaire, règne à la fois dans les concepts et la terminologie. Nul secteur plus que le domaine de la critique féminine, souvent féministe à priori, le domaine le plus innovateur peut-être en France, n'est marqué par cette confusion. A propos d'Anaïs Nin,[1] Paul Kuntz posait récemment la question de l'impact qu'une connaissance approfondie de Freud ne peut manquer d'avoir sur le discours du "moi": l'autobiographie, l'autoportrait, les confessions, les mémoires sont-ils encore possibles? Bien hardi serait le critique qui tenterait de "démythifier" les textes d'Hélène Cixous et de Catherine Clément qui sont fondés sur une connaissance exceptionnelle des principes de la psychanalyse freudienne.

Pour George Sand et pour Colette cette question ne se pose pas. Nulle théorie ne s'interpose entre le discours qu'elles adressent au lecteur, la charge affective et le sens qu'il se propose de lui communiquer. C'est sans doute pourquoi ce qu'on appelle "l'arrière-monde du désir" des deux écrivains y apparaît en clair et informe, comme eût dit Gide, l'autoportrait qui, directement ou indirectement, est au cœur de leur œuvre tant fictive qu'autobiographique.

Ce sont quelques-unes des modalités de cet "arrière-monde" du désir que je tenterai de dégager, me limitant à certains écrits en principe autobiographiques—*Histoire de ma vie* de Sand et les nombreux écrits où, à partir de *La Maison de Claudine*, Colette rêve sur le monde de Saint-Sauveur et sur

1. "Art as Public Dream: The Theory and Practice of Anaïs Nin," *Journal of Aesthetics and Art Criticism*, 32 (Summer 1974), 525–37.

le couple Sido-Minet Chéri. Pendant un siècle, successivement, la personnalité de ces deux femmes a dominé l'imagination d'un public dont les bornes sont mal définies, mais qui n'est sûrement pas limité au monde "littéraire," ni au monde essentiellement féminin des lectrices de roman. Et, par un parallélisme curieux, toutes deux ont été récuperées par la légende populaire. L'image de la "bonne dame de Nohant" et celle de "Madame Colette du Palais-Royal" relèvent de celle, rassurante, de la "bonne sorcière" accordée à l'antique sagesse maternelle de la terre. C'est la présence du visage maternel que je tenterai de dégager dans les textes, et la manière dont s'esquisse chez Sand et Colette ce "roman des origines" dont Freud a souligné le rôle dans l'élaboration de mondes imaginaires.

George Sand avait cinquante ans quand parurent les premiers fascicules de son *Histoire de ma vie*, commencée sept ans plus tôt. On pourrait soutenir que déjà avec les quatre volumes de Claudine, Colette s'engage dans l'autobiographie. Cependant, je ne tiendrai compte que des textes de sa soixantaine, *La Naissance du jour, Sido, Ces plaisirs...* (intitulé plus tard *Le Pur et l'impur*) qui se prolongent dans les méditations fragmentaires toujours reprises qui accompagneront Colette jusqu'à sa mort. Colette elle-même les distingue des "fragments déformés de sa vie sentimentale" que, sous forme de fictions, elle livre à son public.

Célèbres toutes deux et déjà légendaires, elles s'adressent alors à un public présent et à venir en écrivains professionnels qui vivent de leur plume. Elles sont en pleine et sereine possession de leur métier et ne se trompent ni l'une ni l'autre sur l'ambiguïté de leur entreprise. L'épigraphe succinte de *La Naissance du jour* est bien connue: "Imaginez-vous à me lire, que je fais mon portrait? Patience: c'est seulement mon modèle." C'est ce que Sand, plus longuement, affirme dans le remarquable premier chapitre de l'*Histoire de ma vie* intitulé "Pourquoi ce livre?": "Je ne pense pas qu'il y ait de l'orgueil et de l'impertinence à écrire l'histoire de sa propre vie, encore moins *à choisir dans les souvenirs que cette vie a laissés en nous ceux qui nous paraissent valoir la peine d'être conservés.*"[2] Pas question chez Colette d'une "histoire," mais d'un "modèle," un portrait idéal. Chez Sand l'histoire sert le portrait. Comme la déclaration liminaire l'indique, et selon les rites propres au genre, s'il faut en croire Philippe Lejeune, Sand donne à son entreprise une valeur didactique: "Pour ma part je crois accomplir un devoir... en vue d'un enseignement fraternel";

2. *Histoire de ma vie*, dans *Œuvres biographiques* I, éd. de la Pléiade (1970), p. 3. C'est moi qui souligne. Toutes les citations se référent à ce texte. Et les épisodes retenus se retrouvent dans les parties III, IV et V de cette biographie.

elle propose de présenter "un stimulant, un encouragement et un guide pour les autres esprits engagés dans le labyrinthe de la vie." Il ne s'agit pas d'une auto-accusation à la Rousseau, mais, selon le climat humanitaire de l'époque, d'un témoignage dont la nature, par ricochet, dessine en filigrane le portrait de l'écrivain: "Charité envers les autres. Dignité envers soi-même. Sincérité devant Dieu. Telle est l'épigraphe du livre que j'entre-prends." C'est l'émergence de cette image du *moi* que trace en fait l'autobiographie avec une grande cohérence et une étonnante fermeté. Là, dans les premiers livres, l'image est liée au drame des rapports de l'enfant avec ses "deux mères" et se rattache à une interprétation de cette origine.

Colette qui n'évoquera sa vie que par fragments, est d'une autre époque et n'attache à son entreprise aucune valeur exemplaire; écrire, prétend-elle, était la seule voie qui lui permettait de gagner sa vie. "Née d'une famille sans fortune, je n'avais appris aucun métier. Je savais grimper, siffler, courir mais personne n'est venu me proposer une carrière d'écureuil, d'oiseau ou de biche. Le jour ou la nécessité me mit une plume en main et qu'en échange des pages que j'avais écrites, on me donna un peu d'argent, je compris qu'il me faudrait, lentement, docilement, écrire, patiemment concilier le son et le nombre, me lever tôt par préférence, me coucher tard par devoir" (*Journal à rebours*).[3]

Le mythe s'esquisse qui oppose le petit animal—enfant heureux et doux, écureuil, oiseau ou biche—à l'écrivain, exclu du paradis naturel, voué comme Adam et Eve après la chute, à un travail ingrat. Le but de la narration est de toute évidence de recréer dans l'espace textuel l'harmonie perdue: "concilier le son et le nombre" devient, arbitrairement, semble-t-il, d'abord un "devoir" non dicté par la seule nécessité. Mais Colette elle aussi écrit sous la contrainte d'une "mission," qu'elle perçoit comme un héritage maternel: "Elle [Sido] m'a donné le jour, et la *mission* de poursuivre ce qu'en poète elle saisit et abandonna, comme on s'empare d'un fragment de mélodie flottante en voyage dans l'espace" (*La Naissance du jour*). C'est Sido, mère réelle et mythique, qui définit donc, selon Colette, le domaine qui sera celui de l'écriture: "ma bondissante ou tranquille perception de l'univers vivant" et "l'impérieuse et secrète tendresse qui me liaient à la terre." L'image maternelle, terre et mère se confondant, est impérieuse. Et l'écriture est le chemin vers le domaine secret, partagé et, nous le verrons, locus d'une complicité originelle et profondément char-

3. Les éditions de Colette sont nombreuses. Les textes sont relativement courts, d'où le choix de ne mentionner que le titre du texte qui permet de retrouver la citation sans difficulté.

nelle. "Je sais," écrit Colette, "où situer la source de ma vocation." Et c'est par rapport à cette source maternelle qu'elle élabore le mythe du "pur" et de "l'impur" dont l'opposition sémantique régit son univers et son image d'elle-même: "Dans le cœur, dans les lettres de ma mère étaient lisibles l'amour, le respect des créatures vivantes. Je sais donc où situer la source de ma vocation, une source que je trouble aussitôt née, dans la passion de toucher, de remuer le fond que recouvre son flot pur." Ecrire, c'est donc échapper à l'impur, retrouver la source maternelle. Le projet de l'écrivain malgré certaines confessions mutées, n'est point de suivre stade par stade le développement du moi ou son refoulement. Mais, comme le dit assez étrangement Colette, de "renouer sa mère" à elle, c'est-à-dire de faire surgir les scènes qui réconcilient un "moi" présent, fragmentaire, avec un "moi" pur, le moi des commencements, sous l'égide de "Sido."

L'on pourrait dire que la stratégie de l'écrivain dans les deux cas est inverse. Pour Sand, sa fonction d'autobiographe est de procéder à partir de la conscience nette qu'elle a de son rôle présent. Le passé éclaire ce moi que l'organisation des épisodes dégage du chaos des faits. De chaque crise émerge une même résolution, une réaffirmation d'identité. L'autoportrait prend la forme de scènes dramatiques, fortement colorées, qui ponctuent la narration. Les évocations de Colette sont fragmentaires, rattachées à cette rêverie[4] qui semble naître au rythme du langage et appartenir à un niveau profond et immuable de l'existence du moi. Elles font appel aux "sortilèges" du langage, et se chargent de la nostalgie des paradis perdus.

Sand réanime par l'écriture les moments de rupture d'où émerge une personnalité qui surmonte les contraintes familiales; Colette recrée les moments heureux où le moi et le monde se confondent et dont le manque présent préside, selon Colette, à ce que Lejeune appelle "l'acte de naissance du discours." Il s'agit d'examiner de plus près la stratégie de l'écriture et ce qu'elle communique.

II

Sand, nous dit-elle, avait deux mères: sa mère, parisienne et fille du peuple; la mère de son père une aristocrate qui était fort consciente du sang royal dont elle héritait, et qui restait attachée au passé pré-révolution-naire par son mode de vie soit à Nohant, soit à Paris, et par sa culture. A la mort de son père, quand l'enfant avait quatre ans, le conflit se dessine qui domine les parties II, III, et IV de l'autobiographie sandienne, sou-

4. Voir Freud: "The Relation of the Poet to Daydreaming."

lignant son importance dans la "vie imaginative" (comme l'appelle Freud) de l'écrivain.

J'examinerai trois épisodes qui illustrent le mythe sandien des origines et le role qu'il joue dans l'autoportrait. Les trois épisodes sont déterminants et marquent chaque fois le passage d'Aurore à un nouveau stade de maturité. Tous trois mettent en jeu le triangle familial, modifié (grand'mère paternelle, mère, enfant) et les tensions qu'il comporte avec leur charge dramatique. La situation peut se résumer ainsi: après la mort du père, la petite Aurore vit heureusement à Nohant avec sa mère et sa grand'mère; ensemble elles constituent ce que je nommerai le "triangle heureux." L'amour des deux femmes converge sur l'enfant, médiatrice qui remplit le vide laissé par le fils et l'époux. Les trois scènes violentes et longuement décrites sont les conséquences de la destruction de cette situation mythique, la réalité des tensions familiales faisant irruption dans le monde du désir enfantin.

Dans une première permutation, la mère d'Aurore laisse la petite fille aux soins de la grand'mère en échange d'une pension, et la grand'mère tente de la séparer de ses attaches maternelles en refusant de recevoir une demi-sœur d'humble origine. L'enfant s'identifie alors passionnément avec l'image maternelle et subit une profonde occultation de sa vie affective. C'est dans ce cadre que Sand situe la première scène. Au moment où après une brève visite estivale à Nohant sa mère va la quitter, l'enfant lui écrit une lettre la suppliant de la garder et tire d'elle une promesse, une solution imaginaire au conflit insoluble pour l'enfant. Sa mère ouvrira un magasin qui lui permettra de se passer de la pension et où le rêve d'Aurore de vivre en communion heureuse avec une mère aimée et aimante sera réalisé. La mère absente et aimée joue le rôle de la "bonne mère" et la grand'mère celui de la "mauvaise." Le conflit est défini et intériorisé, et crée une division affective et l'hostilité vis-à-vis du "clan" de la grand'mère.

Mais la promesse n'est pas tenue. Le trouble affectif éclate et crée une nouvelle confrontation avec la réalité et une seconde permutation.

L'histoire est présentée ainsi: à treize ans Aurore vit dans une sorte de désespoir. La bonne de sa grand'mère, à la suite d'un léger acte d'insubordination, menace de la renvoyer à sa mère, déclenchant une explosion de colère qui s'exprime en une grande tirade qui s'étale sur dix-sept lignes. Elle se termine par une déclaration fervente d'amour pour la mère, accompagnée du vœu de vivre avec elle, de l'aimer seule et de lui obéir uniquement. Les conséquences sont dramatiques. Pendant trois jours personne ne parle à l'enfant. Puis, dans une "scène d'époque," la grand'mère convie

Aurore et lui révèle indirectement le genre de vie peu orthodoxe que mène sa mère. Le choc est profond. Aurore, muette, se retire dans sa chambre. Peu à peu la "mauvaise mère," la grand'mère, devient la bonne mère. La mère est occultée. Aurore s'identifie avec sa grand'mère qu'elle soigne avec dévouement.

Le troisième épisode a lieu lorsqu'à dix-sept ans Aurore hérite les biens de sa grand'mère. La grand'mère l'a placée sous la protection de sa famille paternelle. Le conflit éclate entre les deux familles. Aurore est sommée de choisir. Le conflit passe désormais sur le plan social. Il s'agit soit d'opter pour l'aristocratie et un mariage flatteur, soit de retomber dans l'inacceptable néant de la plèbe. Noblement, Aurore choisit sa mère et se voit abandonnée par la famille paternelle. Cependant la relation heureuse avec sa mère si ardemment désirée ne s'établit pas. Sa mère est tyrannique, violente, capricieuse, et finalement l'abandonne à une "bonne mère" adoptive. Donc à dix-sept ans Aurore n'a plus de liens familiaux; mais, Sand note, par la force d'une volonté inflexible elle avait maintenu son intégrité en restant fidèle à sa double appartenance; en refusant de renier son origine plébéienne elle était restée digne du code aristocratique de l'honneur. Mais chaque gain pour le "moi" amène une punition maternelle d'où découlent d'infinies conséquences.

Il y aurait beaucoup à dire sur le côté très évidemment romancé de cette narration qui par le scénario et les rôles relève du roman et de ses structures d'opposition. Les lettres à Aurélien de Sèze, antérieures d'une vingtaine d'années donnent une toute autre version des mêmes événements. Mais le portrait d'Aurore ne varie guère. Sa personnalité est née de la constance avec laquelle elle refuse de choisir entre les deux mères et rejette la séparation infligée.

Si nous voulions aborder le conflit de Sand selon un système d'oppositions binaires, symbolisé par les deux mères, la moisson serait riche: aristocrate, femme du peuple; ancien régime, républicaine bonapartiste; déiste voltairienne, chrétienne superstitieuse et passionnelle; rationalisme, irrationalisme; campagne, ville; passé, avenir. Et il est certain que la matrice du monde romanesque de Sand se rattache à la fois à la nostalgie du "triangle heureux" et à ce système d'oppositions. Le "moi" de l'autobiographe Sand par ailleurs, tel qu'elle le reconnaît, est lié à sa victoire sur le conflit personnel et social dont elle héritait. Les "mères" ont été réconciliées et dépassées, non rejetées, dans ces scènes d'auto-dramatisation intenses, où l'auto-justification est flagrante. Mais un autre schème se dessine sous ce "dessin optimiste," qui régit aussi bien les rapports internes de l'intrigue de nombreux romans que les incidents de la vie de Sand, et qu'elle semble reconnaître quant elle parle du "mal incurable" d'un cœur qu'elle ne peut maîtriser. Rien, nous dit Dominique Fernandez[5] ne peut compenser la perte de l'affection maternelle. Les "pères substituts" remplacent les mères ennemies dans la vie de Sand qui semble inlassablement tenter de rétablir le "triangle heureux" de l'enfant. Il ré-apparaît dans les fantasmes qui structurent les situations de nombreux romans donnant au trio classique et conventionnelle une nouvelle forme et une signification privée: le destin d'Indiana n'entraîne pas le choix entre mari et amant; mais entre l'amant fantasque et égoïste et Sir Ralph, homme mûr et ami raisonnable; celui de Lélia met en jeu le passionné jeune Sténio et l'ami sensé Trenmor. De *Rose et Blanche* à la *Confession d'une jeune fille*, les rapports avec la mère se chargent d'ambiguïté: la "mauvaise mère" de Rose "vend" sa fille qui la fuit, puis elle la trahit. Lucienne, la narratrice de la *Confession d'une jeune fille*, perd tout contact avec la sienne à quatre ans et, mystérieusement ramenée à sa grand'mère, grandira dans le doute sur son identité. C'est ainsi que les thèmes chers aux romans populaires—enfant perdu, aban-donné, dépouillé, trahi, substitué, se chargent chez Sand d'une signification nouvelle. Il est impossible de retracer leur cheminement souterrain dans les limites de cette étude.[6] Le fantasme personnel des origines persiste long-temps chez Sand: "Je suis la fille d'un patricien et d'une bohémienne" écrit-elle encore à Flaubert. Le jeune officier semi-aristocratique et la "pauvre enfant du vieux pavé de Paris" se sont transformés.

Le thème de la chute hors du milieu social qu'illustre la scène très évidemment fictive de la situation d'Aurore au seuil du mariage est, vague-ment, l'homologue de celle de la société en général. Ainsi Sand n'est pas seule "déclassée." La société où Sand se retrouve située ne sera celle ni de l'une ni de l'autre de ses deux mères: elle sera positiviste et bourgeoise. C'est donc sur un autre plan que se situera leur réconciliation: celui de cet être supérieur et hors-caste, l'artiste humanitaire annonciateur d'un nouvel accord social: Sand imagine l'avenir *contre* le mal qui vient de la société-mère, de sa tyrannie qui impose à la femme un rôle social. Sand a intellec-tualisé ainsi un conflit affectif qui remonte à sa petite enfance, et a résolu ainsi une crise profonde d'identité.

5. Préface de *L'Arbre jusqu'aux racines* (Paris, 1972), p. 11.
6. Cette analyse est développée dans la communication: "George Sand et les fictions de l'autobiographe," présentée par moi au colloque d'Amherst le 26 février 1976.

III

Le processus chez Colette est fort différent quoique ses textes soient aussi hantés par le thème d'une chute et d'un exil, mais c'est une chute irrémédiable qui scelle à jamais l'exil de la jeune femme. C'est un banissement voulu, un auto-banissement du monde originaire heureux dont Colette subit les conséquences: l'interminable écriture. Colette ne présente pas, comme Sand, une histoire continue que Sand fait remonter même à une préhistoire, celle de son père. Elle plonge plutôt à travers des couches de souvenirs vers une "région fabuleuse," un espace fermé qui l'habite. "J'appartiens à un pays que j'ai quitté..." "Il y avait dans ces temps-là de grands hivers, de brûlants étés..." "Qu'a-t-on fait de ces grands hivers d'autrefois, blancs, solides, durables, embellis de neige, de contes fantastiques, de sapins et de loups?" "Rien ne menaçait... mon heureux été de ciel et de cristal..." "donnez-moi ... un pinceau de fée... car il n'y a point de mots pour vous peindre, au-dessus d'un toit d'ardoise violette brodé de mousses rousses, le ciel de mon pays tel qu'il resplendissait sur mon enfance." On pourrait multiplier les citations. Le mythe du paradis situé à l'origine des temps prend chez Colette la forme du jardin où règne la mère mythique, Sido et son "glorieux visage de jardin" et où il n'est pas de serpent sauf, insidieuse, l'inévitable maturation qui dénoue le couple mère-fille heureux.

Combien ce jardin est mythique, immobilisé dans le "cristal" ou le diamant, le lecteur s'en rend compte qui note avec quel soin Colette, si précise, dit-on, en écarte tout ce qui mord, tue, détruit, inquiète. Elle-même nous en informe lorsqu'elle bannit délibérément, de l'espace de sa rêverie, les inquiétantes plantes tropicales. Le "jardin de mon enfance" est un jardin à la vie charmée, auquel Colette rattache, comme au visage maternel, son besoin "extra-humain" de la pureté: "Le mot 'pur' ne m'a pas découvert son sens intelligible. Je n'en suis qu'à étancher une *soif optique* de pureté, dans les transparences qui l'évoquent, dans les bulles, l'eau massive, et les *sites imaginaires retranchées*, au sein d'un *épais cristal.*"

L'écriture pour Colette, au niveau subjectif, servira toujours d'amorce à sa réapparition. Ce monde fabuleux des origines fait de la fille de Sido l'enfant "mythique" d'origine divine, l'enfant aimée dont Colette cherche à retrouver "l'éblouissement optique et olfactif," la connivence avec le jardin. L'écriture est donc pour elle une forme de sortilège, un rite sacré où, par l'intermédiaire du "visage de jardin" de Sido, elle remonte vers cette origine première, vers cette existence primordiale "paradisiaque" dont tout autre que le couple mère-enfant est exclu.

La chute, cependant, a eu lieu: avec le trouble sexuel et "la brûlante intrépidité sensuelle" de l'adolescente et l'initiation à ce que Colette, réticente, n'a livré qu'indirectement au lecteur—la vie "impure" du couple Colette-Willy: le paradis enfantin se referme, le monde de l'enfance s'occulte, monde "dont," dit Colette, "j'ai cessé d'être digne." Pour retrouver ce monde primordial et refoulé, il lui faudra recréer l'image tutélaire maternelle, qui la libère du trouble "impur" que les autres êtres humains remuent en elle. L'optique "d'éblouissement" dont elle a soif, naît de ce rêve éveillé. C'est elle la créatrice d'un univers sans faille, où la relation heureuse avec le monde ne comporte pas de culpabilité. Elle ouvre à Colette le monde d'avant "l'effraction," qui échappe à la sexualité, mais reste ouvert tout entier à la sensualité. La figure maternelle n'est pas pour Colette comme pour Sand une source d'angoisse et de drame. C'est la source unique de bonheur et de sécurité et d'une vision crystalline du monde dont l'origine est dans le regard fervent mais innocent de Sido.

Dans l'espace du texte où Colette rêve le dialogue avec Sido, c'est son propre portrait "d'écrivain caché" qu'elle trace, écartant d'elle-même la jeune femme dont Willy fut le créateur. Et c'est de la suzeraineté de la mère que relève aussi l'écriture née à l'origine d'une "longue rêverie" dirigée vers l'énigme de ce moi enfermé au jardin lointain de l'enfance et qu'il faut récupérer. C'est dans ses romans, dans les portraits d'amis, qu'elle fera passer les connaissances dues à Willy. Le monde de Colette mémorialiste se scinde en deux, l'anecdote, le portrait (de soi, des autres), d'une part, d'autre part le flot égal du langage harmonieux qui les distancie et les unit dans "un fragment de mélodie flottante" en voyage dans l'espace de la page, et les intègre au monde de l'écriture. Abstraits de la réalité, ils participent à "l'impérieuse et secrète tendresse," dépersonnalisée, qui par l'entremise de Sido lie Colette à la terre. Voilà, du moins semble-t-il, le mythe du "moi" qui alimente la vie affective profonde de Colette. L'écriture rend Colette à la solitude heureuse du paradis enfantin et à sa plénitude: "Solitude... c'est un mot à belle figure, son S en tête dressée comme un serpent protecteur. Je ne puis l'isoler tout à fait de l'éclat farouche de diamant." Le mythe du paradis renaît ici que *protège cependant* le serpent; renaît avec l'image de l'eclat, de la transparence qui l'accompagne toujours. La solitude est le domaine réservé dont tout autre être est exclu, monde dépolarisé et secret, ouvert à l'écriture exclusivement; là l'arrière-monde inconscient sous-jacent combinera, grâce au labeur patient, en de savantes phrases, les deux faces séparées de la vie de Colette et établira le droit légitime de Colette au titre de "fille de Sido."

"Women who write," notait Virginia Woolf, "think through their mothers" et les recréent, pourrions nous ajouter. Si différentes que soient les liens avec la mère que décrivent Sand et Colette, il semble bien que le désir inconscient profond qui oriente leur vie réelle et imaginaire est le fantasme de la fusion heureuse et sans faille du monde enfantin et du monde maternel. C'est à ce fantasme générateur que se rattachent les situations de prédilection sandienne, les prédilections secrètes qui assurent l'unité des écrits de Colette. C'est en termes de la perte puis du retour à la mère qu'elles ont l'une et l'autre fondé leur autoportrait et leur singularité. Pour différentes que soient leurs stratégies littéraires, dans ce qu'on appelle aujourd'hui l'archéologie de leur sensibilité existe une même vision secrète de bonheur liée au monde maternel des origines qui libère en elles la vie imaginaire. L'écriture chez elle est déclenchée moins par la hantise de la perte que par cette connaissance secrète; écrire est un rite d'affranchissement, grâce auquel par des voies fort différentes Sand et Colette retrouvent le langage et les désirs de l'enfance féminine heureuse: goût de la vie, joies de l'instant, liberté, solitude, univers d'avant l'arrivée et l'intervention de l'Autre: coercion sociale dans le cas de Sand; exigence sexuelle chez Colette. L'univers maternel désiré est celui qui accorde à l'enfance féminine la place qui par ailleurs lui est refusée. L'écriture est alors l'inverse d'une effraction, c'est un rite de préservation. Colette et Sand "renouent" leurs mères à elle et se créent libres et entières à partir d'une origine retrouvée.

Marcel Tetel

Gobineau et Rabelais: symbolisme et Renaissance

De prime abord une juxtaposition de Gobineau et Rabelais peut sembler bien étrange. Que peuvent avoir en commun cet aristocrate, auteur des *Pléiades*, et le père spirituel de ces vons géants, Gargantua et Pantagruel? Mais le rapprochement se resserre sensiblement depuis la redécouverte et la publication assez récente d'une nouvelle de Gobineau, intitulée *Les conseils de Rabelais*, qui n'a pas encore vraiment attiré l'attention des critiques.[1] Ce conte met en scène Odet de Châtillon, cardinal apostat, à qui Rabelais avait adressé son *Quart Livre* dans une longue dédicace; ce prince de l'Eglise dans le texte de Gobineau prêt à abandonner sa première religion et à se marier vient demander conseil au sage Maître François. Etant donné le rapport étroit entre la nouvelle gobinienne et l'œuvre rabelaisienne, il est donc permis de penser à une affinité d'esprit entre les deux auteurs. Par conséquent, une étude comparée devra se centrer sur: (i) le rapport entre la nouvelle et la dédicace "A très illustre prince et Révérendissime Monseigneur Odet, Cardinal de Chastillon," une sorte de premier prologue au *Quart Livre* qui est en somme la matrice de ce conte; (ii) la signification des *Conseils de Rabelais*, sa structure, son art, ses liens avec l'œuvre rabelaisienne; (iii) le rapport entre cette nouvelle et *La Renaissance*, une vaste fresque dramatique, que Gobineau continua à composer tout au cours de sa vie.

Jusqu'à présent cette nouvelle n'a guère reçu de jugement favorable; son éditeur même montre le chemin: "*Les conseils de Rabelais* sont une œuvre hâtive, écrite assez à la diable, d'une valeur littéraire inégale, néan-

---

1. Arthur de Gobineau, *Les conseils de Rabelais*, éd. A. B. Duff (Paris, 1962). Cette nouvelle, la deuxième qu'il ait jusqu'alors composée, parut les 22 et 23 octobre 1847 dans le *Courrier Français* lorsque l'auteur, âgé de trente et un ans, s'était exercé surtout à la fabrication de romans historiques situés au XVIe siècle et à l'époque des guerres de religion. Elle resta ensuite inédite jusqu'à nos jours. Il faut noter que dès l'âge de vingt-deux ans Gobineau commença à s'imprégner de la Renaissance. Dans une lettre du 23 juin 1838 adressée à sa sœur, il se dit "toujours fourré dans le XVIe siècle... [je] ne jure que par ces artistes-là, [je] ne vois qu'eux, [je] passe ma vie au milieu d'eux dans mon cinquième étage" (cité dans René Guise, "Aux sources de l'italianisme de Gobineau," *Revue de Littérature Comparée*, 40 [1966], 363).

moins bien composée: un diptyque et une sorte de moralité." Et plus loin il
continue à se demander si ce n'est pas une "œuvre mal venue," mais il
conclut "intéressante en tout cas, complexe, révélatrice."[2] Il ne s'agit pas
d'élever Gobineau au niveau d'un Stendhal ou d'un Flaubert, et malgré son
œuvre assez prolifique il n'atteint pas la vision d'un Balzac. En tant que
nouvelliste a-t-il le don d'un Maupassant ou d'un Voltaire, la verve d'un
Diderot, la finesse d'esprit d'une Marguerite de Navarre? Est-il l'émule
d'un Mérimée qu'il admirait? Or, sa gloire littéraire repose toujours sur
Les Pléiades, roman imposant qui par sa structure prismatique et son
abondance du monologue intérieur préfigure Proust et le nouveau roman;
dans ce sens l'ombre gobinienne plane sur une bonne partie du roman du
vingtième siècle.[3] Dans nombre de ses nouvelles, y compris *Les conseils
de Rabelais*, et dans *La Renaissance* aussi Gobineau n'est pas, et ne peut se
prétendre, créateur de personnages vifs et complexes mais plutôt formu-
lateur de symboles, simples portes-paroles d'idées favorites; dans ces cas
il s'allie au symbolisme de Vigny dont il partage également le pessimisme
foncier. En outre, Gobineau s'encadre dans l'esprit de la première moitié
du dix-neuvième siècle qui fait revivre la Renaissance où il recherche et
fait valoir ce que lui-même incarne: une énergie vitale vouée à l'échec et
une déification de l'art. Une étude des *Conseils de Rabelais* révèle déjà ce
genre de symbolisme et nous fait un tableau impressionniste, sinon elliptique, des passions d'une époque et d'un drame particulier et personnel.

Gobineau tire son Rabelais sage conseiller, c'est-à-dire bon médecin,
ainsi que l'espace temporel de la nouvelle, de la dédicace du *Quart Livre*
à Monseigneur Odet. Dans cette pièce liminaire Rabelais continue à se
disculper contre les fausses accusations de ses ennemis, tel qu'il l'a fait
depuis le *Pantagruel*, et vante au contraire les bienfaits et l'esprit chrétien
de son œuvre. Il définit sous le voile du médecin le rôle de l'écrivain qui
pour guérir, divertir et instruire, mêle le vrai au faux:

2. Ibid., pp. 3, 5. Un autre éditeur de nouvelles gobiniennes remarque que *Les conseils
de Rabelais* "ajoutent peu de choses à sa [Gobineau] gloire" et il cite la première opinion:
" 'Œuvre mal venue,' dit... M. Duff, dont on connaît la bienveillance extrême pour
l'auteur" (Arthur de Gobineau, *Le mouchoir rouge et autres nouvelles*, éd. Jean Gaulmier
[Paris, 1968], p. xi). Et encore, dans un ouvrage sur les nouvelles de Gobineau, l'auteur
ne consacrant que deux pages à la nôtre, conclut: "*Les conseils de Rabelais* with its faulty
organization and lack of unity can hardly, except for its brevity, be considered a short
story. However, the work is of documentary interest for it reveals Gobineau's lasting concern with two basic themes; the dichotomy between the elite and the masses, and the
power of love" (Rebecca M. Valette, *Arthur de Gobineau and the Short Story* [Chapel
Hill, N.C., 1969], p. 104).

3. L'art de ce roman, mais surtout du point de vue stylistique, a été habilement étudié
par Michael Riffaterre, *Le style des Pléiades de Gobineau* (New York, 1957).

Sus toutes choses, les autheurs susdictz ont au médicin baillé advertissement particulier des parolles, propous, abouchemens, et confabulations qu'il doibt tenir avecques les malades de la part desquelz seroit appellé. Lesquelles toutes doibvent à un but tirer et tendre à une fin: c'est le resjouir sans offense de Dieu et ne le contrister en façon quelconques.[4]

Cette fonction thérapeutique de l'écrivain se retrouvera dans la sagesse rabelaisienne qu'exalte le conte gobinien. Pour souligner cette sagacité bienfaitrice, Rabelais n'hésite pas non plus à se faire l'émule de Salomon. Au moyen de cette comparaison Rabelais se démontre sûr de lui-même, de son art, et de la portée de son œuvre, et de sa part, Gobineau transfère ces facultés, presque divines, à son personnage qui conseillera Monseigneur Odet. Tout comme le Rabelais de la nouvelle, l'écrivain-médecin, philosophe, Salomon, conseiller proverbial et extraordinaire, apparaît dans la dédicace à travers une retrospection historique; Salomon est en somme l'écrivain-mage:

... homme craignant et aymant, agréable à tous humains, de Dieu et des hommes bien aymé, duquel heureuse est la mémoire. Dieu en louange l'a comparé aux preux, l'a faict grand en terreur des ennemis; en sa faveur a faict choses prodigieuses et espoventables; en praesence des Roys l'a honoré; au peuple par luy a son vouloir déclaré et par luy sa lumière a monstré. Il l'a en foy et débonnaireté consacré et esleu entre tous humains. Par luy a voulu estre sa voix ouye et à ceulx qui estoient en ténèbres estre la loy de vivificque science annoncée [522].

Le Rabelais bon chrétien, sinon bon catholique, qui se dégage de la pièce liminaire se retrouve également dans la nouvelle. L'auteur du *Quart Livre* proteste qu'il est sans cesse mal interprété et par conséquent accusé d'hérésie.[5] De même le Rabelais gobinien n'approuve pas l'apostasie du cardinal: "Mais je ne crois pas un mot de ce que vous m'avez dit, et si tant est que vous vouliez vous faire huguenot et abandonner le paradis

4. François Rabelais, "A très illustre prince et révérendissime Monseigneur Odet," *Œuvres complètes*, éds. Jacques Boulenger et Lucien Scheler (Paris: Bibliothèque de la Pléiade, 1962), p. 519. Dorénavant nous citerons de cette édition.
5. "Car l'une des moindres contumélies dont ilz usoient estoit que tels livres tous estoient farciz d'hérésies diverses (n'en povoient toutesfois une seulle exhiber en endroict aulcun); de folastries joyeuses, hors l'offense de Dieu et du Roy, prou: c'est le subject et thème unicque d'iceulx livres; d'hérésies poinct, sinon perversement et contre tout usaige de raison et de languaige commun interprétans ce que, à poine de mille fois mourir, si autant possible estoit, ne vouldrois avoir pensé: comme qui pain interprétroit pierre; poisson, serpent; œuf, scorpion" (520).

pour l'enfer (je parle ici en théologien terrestre et qui sait pertinemment son thème)..."(14).

L'espace temporel de la première partie de la nouvelle se situe à l'époque où Rabelais se met à composer son *Quart Livre*, c'est-à-dire vers 1547. On le voit installé à l'abbaye de Saint-Maur-des-Fossés à Paris dans un milieu paradisiaque où l'intérieur, la chambre paisible et remplie de livres, s'accorde à un extérieur agréable, le jardin abondant en fleurs et retentissant du chant des oiseaux, afin de créer une atmosphère propice au travail artistique et aux "habitudes de voluptueuse méditation du nouveau chanoine" (9) qui se présente "surtout ami du cardinal Du Bellay" (8). La description idyllique de l'abbaye et l'allusion à Jean Du Bellay font penser de nouveau à un rapport étroit entre la nouvelle et la dédicace car ils se retrouvent dans la pièce liminaire:

> Cestuy évangile [bonne nouvelle] depuys m'avez de vostre bénignité réitéré à Paris, et d'abondant lorsque naguères visitastez monseigneur le cardinal Du Bellay qui pour recouvrement de santé après longue et fascheuse maladie, s'estoit retiré à Sainct Maur, lieu ou (pour mieulx et plus proprement dire) paradis de salubrité, aménité, sérénité, commodité, délices et tous honestes plaisirs de agriculture et vie rusticque [521].

Il faut noter que la même effervescence verbale présente dans la description de Rabelais se revoit chez Gobineau; bien que ce genre de tableau se prête à un enthousiasme descriptif, il est aussi permis de voir dans cette similarité stylistique un rappel précis de forme.[6] En outre, du point de vue temporel Gobineau se livre à un anachronisme, voulu semble-t-il, dans *Les conseils de Rabelais*. Lorsque le cardinal Odet de Châtillon fait profession ouverte de la religion réformée, en 1561, l'auteur du *Quart Livre* ne vit plus depuis 1553. Ce lapsus n'est pas une faiblesse narratrice de la part de Gobineau mais simplement une liberté à laquelle un conteur a le droit quand il manie un fond historique; on ne peut pas toujours s'attendre à des faits véridiques dans une fiction. En effet, une fonction de la littérature est de démythifier l'Histoire pour la réduire à l'échelle humaine.

La médecine et le rôle du médecin constituent l'étoffe métaphorique qui enveloppe la dédicace au *Quart Livre*, et de ce tissu figuré provient le schéma triangulaire de la nouvelle gobinienne: "De faict, la practicque de

---

6. "Dans la chambre, il y avait des livres doctes et joyeux, parlant médecine, théologie, astrologie, poésie et raillerie; mais dans le jardin, il y avait des colonies d'oiseaux de cent espèces, chardonnerets, pinsons, merles, rouges-gorges qui ne se taisaient qu'à la nuit tombée et encore pour laisser chanter à leur tour les rossignols" (9).

médicine bien proprement est par Hippocrates comparée à un combat et farce jouée à trois personnages, le malade, le Medicin, la maladie" (518). Précisément, dans la nouvelle le malade c'est le cardinal Odet de Châtillon, l'amoureux; le médecin, Rabelais qui tente mais échoue de guérir son illustre client; et la maladie, Elisabeth de Hauteville, maîtresse et ensuite épouse du cardinal. Mais par rapport à la dédicace au *Quart Livre* de Rabelais, Gobineau définit assez nettement et renverse même le rôle de ses personnages; Rabelais est le sage philosophe-médecin et monseigneur Odet est en proie à une incontrôlable crise spirituelle. Tandis que dans la dédicace, Rabelais, accablé d'années et de calomniateurs se tourne vers Odet comparé au sage Salomon, mais il se présente à la fois comme médecin-guérisseur au moyen de ses livres. Gobineau donc continue le mythe du sage Rabelais prévalant à travers les siècles et démythifie Odet.

Les conseils de Rabelais se divisent en trois parties. La première se compose de la scène entre Rabelais et Odet où ce dernier vient chercher quelque soulagement chez Maître François qui finit par le haranguer sur la condition de l'homme dans la société. La deuxième, séparée de la première par un nombre imprécis d'années, se centre sur un dialogue entre Odet et sa femme éxilés à la cour d'Elizabeth d'Angleterre; l'isolement, la passion et le culte du moi dominent cette scène. Cette partie d'ailleurs est la plus longue de la nouvelle. Par cet élargissement structural Gobineau insiste sur l'élément de la crise spirituelle des deux époux qui se trouvent bannis de France et exclus de la vie sociale à la cour anglaise. Le moi isolé mais supérieur, le fameux thème gobinien du fils de roi, est un des sujets de la nouvelle qui la relie au reste de l'œuvre gobinienne. Cette deuxième section se termine par l'empoisonnement de Odet trahi par ses gentilshommes; de nouveau échec, cette fois-ci d'une tentative de liberté individuelle. La troisième partie est sous forme d'épilogue où Rabelais, ici porte-parole de Gobineau, conseille au seul gentilhomme resté fidèle à Odet de se faire loup car les moutons sont toujours mangés, message cruel et pessimiste d'un Gobineau déjà marqué par l'amertume de la vie.

Le portrait de Rabelais qui se dégage de la nouvelle est celui d'un sceptique et d'un cynique, qu'il s'agisse de l'homme mûr de la première partie ou du vieillard de l'épilogue. Ces caractéristiques sont d'ailleurs les indices mêmes de sa sagesse et font de lui un "homme savant et l'oracle des vrais philosophes" (20). Il n'est donc pas outré de supposer que Rabelais incarne ici le pessimisme de Gobineau qui observe un monde où tout est bouleversé, où "les plus fous sont les plus sages" (10). Par conséquent les sots dominent la société et la trompent tandis que les gens d'esprit et les vertueux refusent de s'engager. Puisque l'homme qui cherche à échapper à cette condition humaine reste isolé, Rabelais prédit à Odet les événements de l'épilogue:

> ... les sots, c'est tout le monde en un chacun; à eux fut donné le royaume du ciel, comme il est écrit, et mieux encore le royaume de la terre; les sots font la foule, remplissent les rues, les maisons, les couvents, les parlements, les hôtels royaux, parfois même ils occupent le trône; c'est pour leur bon plaisir que l'on juge, ruine, et pend; vous avez tort de les dédaigner; quant à ce qui est de moi, je ne les affronte jamais... les gens d'esprit sont donc, par essence, de complexion timide, craintive, poltronne et nullement amie des hasards: tous ils vous abandonneront... Il vous restera pourtant des amis intéressés, qui deviendront un jour des ennemis altérés de votre perte [22–23].[7]

Gobineau réfute ironiquement l'engagement car en fin de compte il le préconise vraiment tout en réalisant que les tentatives échoueront; peut-on ou doit-on même sortir de son ornière individuelle. En effet, la sagesse consiste en cette acceptation d'une réalité hypocrite, et l'amertume se dévoile derrière les conclusions du Rabelais gobinien: "d'autant plus que je ne me ferai jamais brûler pour aucune cause" (23). Evidemment il y a là un rappel du fameux "Jusques au feu exclusif." Mais le sourire railleur du Rabelais de la Renaissance, sous-entendu dans cette dernière remarque, devient une grimace douloureuse chez le Rabelais gobinien. La résolution se trouve à l'intérieur de soi-même; chacun doit simplement dépendre de son moi et agir selon sa propre vérité intérieure, solution socratique qui résume aussi le *Tiers Livre*, et ce rapprochement n'est sans doute pas fortuit.

Gobineau pose la question traditionnelle, si répandue pendant l'antiquité romaine et ensuite au moyen âge, du *pro* et *contra* de la vie active ou de la vie contemplative. Il se trouve coincé dans un étau entre une volonté d'engagement et de liberté qui vont échouer et, d'autre part, la sérénité de la retraite ou solitude. Le portrait du vieux Rabelais, lecteur du *Banquet* en grec, vient appuyer les bienfaits d'une vie paisible résultant de sa sagesse, bien que Gobineau reste toujours tiraillé devant l'alternative: "un beau vieillard, figure réjouie et fine, ventre rebondi, qui dans un costume à

---

7. Cette même attitude envers les sots se retrouve dans la correspondance de Gobineau dont les sentiments politiques d'extrême droite, il était ultra-royaliste, expliquent le contexte suivant: il s'adresse contre "la faiblesse, la niaiserie, et pour tout dire, la sottise sublime de *son* cher parti... Nous n'étions représentés jusqu'ici que par des sots, nous allons l'être par l'intrigant de bas étage le plus diffamé qui existe"; de lettres à sa sœur (1843) et à son père (1845) soit deux et quatre ans avant la nouvelle. Cité dans Jean Gaulmier, *Spectre de Gobineau* (Paris, 1965), p. 132.

moitié laïque, et à moitié clérical, écossait des pois et plaisantait avec un petit garçon assis dans la poussière du chemin à ses pieds" (44). Cette scène idyllique rappelle le portrait rustique et bienveillant du vieux Grandgousier lorsqu'on vient lui annoncer le début de la Guerre Picrocholine.[8]

Odet de Châtillon incarne le fils de roi déchu, héros gobinien par excellence; il s'agit du personnage qui s'engage activement dans la vie quotidienne, le plus souvent dans la vie politique, se trouve d'abord couronné de succès mais inévitablement tombe de ses premières hauteurs et se perd dans le malstrom des fortunes humaines: "autrefois l'honneur et la splendeur de la cour de France, l'idole des savants et des poètes, l'arbitre du goût et de l'élégance, le plus grand seigneur du royaume après son oncle de Montmorency et le duc de Guise" (29). Ce qui rachète Châtillon pour le moment c'est son amour de Mlle de Hauteville pour laquelle il abandonne non seulement sa première religion mais aussi sa position privilégiée. Gobineau veut faire entendre qu'une passion authentique est une expérience purificatrice qui élève l'esprit au dessus de celui de la foule et libère l'individu des entraves de la société;[9] Platon non plus n'est pas très loin ici. Il suffit de citer les héros des *Pléiades* dont l'ascèse spirituelle s'opère de cette même façon pour noter la centralité de ce concept du bonheur chez Gobineau, élan vital dans la recherche d'un bonheur stendhalien voué à l'échec d'un Sorel. Mais il faut à tout prix sauvegarder cette bribe précieuse si chère à la Renaissance: la dignité humaine. Voilà pourquoi Odet de Châtillon se lamente auprès de sa femme:

depuis notre arrivée, j'ai remarqué que tous les honneurs qui sont dus à votre rang et à ma naissance ne vous étaient pas rendus. Sans doute, je suis un fugitif, un malheureux dépouillé injustement de sa puissance; mais tel qu'on me voit encore, je veux qu'on me respecte et vous avec moi... je suis un Châtillon, et cela non plus je ne puis l'oublier [33, 34].

Il appartient donc à cette élite dispersée et il est prêt à souffrir pour ne pas s'abaisser; la douleur, d'ailleurs, surtout celle provenant des passions, édifie l'âme et l'éloigne de la médiocrité des autres.

8. "...le vieux bonhomme Grandgousier, son père, qui après souper se chauffe les couilles à un beau, clair et grand feu, et, attendent graisler des chastaines, escript au foyer avec un baston bruslé d'un bout dont on escharbotte le feu, faisant à sa femme et famille de beaulx contes du temps jadis" (88).
9. "Oui, hier, enfin, las de combattre, convaincu de ma lâcheté, brûlant de me régénérer dans une vie nouvelle et d'être heureux, oh! oui, heureux sans crime, sans souillure, en suivant le droit chemin, en proclamant ce que je crois, j'ai résolu fermement d'abjurer la foi de Rome, d'épouser devant les hommes et devant le Seigneur la femme que j'ai choisie, et de parcourir ce qu'il me reste de jours avec la confiance d'avoir fait le mieux" (20).

L'intégrité et la probité du moi se voient chez Elisabeth de Hauteville. Le véritable moi, selon elle, est celui que l'individu perçoit à l'intérieur de lui-même sachant que ses actions sont sans reproche. Peu importe ce que pensent les autres car ils jugent seulement d'après leurs propres préconceptions. Gobineau voudrait réfuter une altérité sartrienne, nous sommes prisonniers des opinions des autres, mais ses héros finissent par en être les victimes puisqu'il sait bien que certaines lois de la société sont inexorables. Ce culte du moi permet à l'individu de devenir un être supérieur, condition temporaire en attendant la fin inévitable:

A-t-on surpris dans ma conduite ou dans mes paroles rien qui fît douter de ma droiture? Ai-je négligé quelque devoir? Suis-je sortie jamais de la réserve qui sied à l'épouse chrétienne? Non pas, que je croie. Laissez donc Elisabeth railler à son aise, et souhaitez-lui de descendre un jour au tombeau aussi vénérée qu'elle est crainte. Pour nous, Monseigneur, aimons-nous en Dieu comme nous avons fait et, sans chercher à rehausser notre gloire en ce monde, jouissons en paix de l'affection mutuelle qui ne s'est jamais obscurcie entre nous [37–38].

Le contraste entre les deux Elisabeth appuie la thèse que le moi intérieur l'emporte sur l'extérieur. La reine d'Angleterre, malgré sa condition importante, ne manque pas quand l'occasion se présente de se montrer mesquine et hypocrite envers les Châtillon.[10] Tandis que Elisabeth de Hauteville reste inaccessible à ces injures; l'honnêteté de son amour envers son mari l'élève bien au-dessus de ce que les autres pourraient penser d'elle.

Une passion honnête ennoblit l'âme et en même temps isole le moi des autres. Dans une situation fictive, et donc souvent idéalisée, telle que plus tard dans *Les Pléiades*, l'homme amoureux et spiritualisé arrive enfin au bonheur, mais dans le monde quotidien et vécu cet individu est en fin de compte anéanti par les lois de la société. En effet, Gobineau recherche l'absolu et retrouve sans cesse une réalité noire et implacable et Odet de Châtillon incarne précisément cette tentative et l'échec qui s'ensuit. De plus, l'orientalisme de Gobineau, ses *Nouvelles asiatiques*, reflète encore une fois ce recours au rêve et à l'évasion. C'est ainsi que s'explique également son affinité pour les idées chevaleresques car il refuse le réel, le monde qui l'entoure et opte en faveur de paradis artificiels.[11] Il n'est donc pas outré

10. "Je suis plus souvent frappé par cette femme qui est là au-dessus de moi, m'adressant de belles paroles quand on la regarde et des insultes quand les yeux sont ailleurs" (33).
11. Jean Boissel, *Gobineau, l'Orient et l'Iran (1816–1860)*, I (Paris, 1973), 47, 49.

de supposer que, à cet égard, la trame chevaleresque des deux premiers livres de l'œuvre rabelaisienne et le voyage spirituel et ensuite concret des deux derniers livres ont certainement dû saisir l'imagination de Gobineau. Dans *Les conseils de Rabelais* la recherche de l'absolu se traduit non seulement par la préconisation d'un amour libérateur et purificateur mais aussi par un plaidoyer pour une religion non-dogmatique. Le Rabelais gobinien, qui s'acharne contre un Calvin borné et contre tout théologien aveugle, se rapporte directement, même par l'emploi de paroles identiques, au Rabelais du *Gargantua*: "et encore, s'ils avaient connu notre bon ami Jean Calvin, auraient-ils rejeté bien plus loin l'idée de se mettre dans la peine pour plaire à une pareille *bête enragée*, non moins méchante en son espèce que tous les sorbonistes, frères mendiants et autres *papelards* que vous et moi apprécions ce qu'ils valent" (16). L'ironie de "notre bon ami Calvin" fait contraste à une ferveur sincère envers les Marot, les Des Périers et les Dolet, esprits libres et véritables amis de Châtillon, auxquels se réfère le *ils*. Le Rabelais gobinien conseille donc au cardinal de tâcher de réformer l'Eglise sans l'abandonner, autrement dit de suivre une position évangéliste. Mais Châtillon choisit une voix extrême, en grande partie parce qu'il aime: "je me fais confesseur de la vraie religion, il me semble que je me grandis et sors d'esclavage" (17); il suivra son inclination rebelle et refusera l'ordre qu'on lui impose. La question religieuse n'est qu'une autre métaphore pour démontrer l'échec de l'absolu. Gobineau se dédouble en ses personnages: Rabelais est tel qu'il devrait être s'il pouvait, et Châtillon représente la véritable personnalité, tragique, de l'auteur.

Pour qu'une œuvre littéraire soit réussie il faut que fond et forme s'intègrent; sinon il s'agit plutôt de rhétorique que d'art. Or, la forme des *Conseils de Rabelais* ne frappe guère par sa prépondérance car dans cette œuvre de jeunesse, Gobineau recherche surtout des débouchés pour ses idées favorites qui commencent à germer. Par conséquent, cet ouvrage devient un essai de nouvelle où les personnages sont des êtres très stylisés, c'est-à-dire des symboles, et cette entreprise se fait naturellement au détriment de l'art du conte ou plutôt sans en tenir compte. Gobineau ne sculpte pas ni ne cisèle; il dit tout simplement. L'élan vital de Châtillon s'oppose au cynisme clairvoyant de Rabelais, et l'idéalisme passionné de Elisabeth de Hauteville succombera aux pronostics de ce dernier.

En outre, une ironie plane sur la deuxième moitié de la nouvelle puisque nous savons déjà où aboutiront les tentatives de Châtillon. De nouveau, un parallèle s'impose ici avec le *Tiers Livre* car au début de cet ouvrage,

Panurge se met à la poursuite de son bonheur, doit-il se marier ou non, malgré les conseils indécis de Pantagruel: "Vostre conseil (dist Panurge) soubs correction semble à la chanson de Ricochet. Ce ne sont que sarcasmes, mocqueries et redictes contradictoires. Les unes destruisent les aultres. Je ne sçay ès quelles me tenir" (III, 361). Le Rabelais gobinien joue ainsi le rôle du sage Pantagruel dans le *Tiers Livre* tandis que le Châtillon impulsif fait écho au Panurge à la quête d'une réponse simpliste et catégorique à sa question tout en refusant les conseils d'autrui. D'ailleurs, il n'est pas fortuit qu'au début de la nouvelle le portrait d'un Rabelais bien avisé de son art et de sa pensée rappelle sa manipulation des personnages, et l'emploi du mot *sarcasmes* est l'indice même de ce rapprochement: "mettant sur le papier, non sans choix, ce qui lui venait dans l'esprit. Un matin, qu'il était ainsi occupé et qu'il broyait innocemment dans sa cervelle les sarcasmes de Panurge..." (10).

Quant à la structure du conte, elle est simple, même classique, et fait donc contraste aux meilleurs ouvrages de Gobineau. Dans *Les Pléiades*, par exemple, il préfère une structure prismatique plutôt que linéaire. Mais il faut noter qu'une quarantaine d'années séparent la nouvelle du roman; l'auteur a bien eu le temps de s'exercer à son métier. Les deux premières parties sont d'une longueur égale, plus ou moins, et chacune se centre sur un dialogue: dans la première entre Rabelais et Châtillon et dans la deuxième entre les deux époux; dans les deux cas il se dégage un manque de communication puisque les conseils de Rabelais sont négligés et le couple reste isolé du monde extérieur. Ensuite l'épilogue ne fait que renchérir sur le pessimisme établi dans le conte même. Par conséquent, la structure ne fait pas preuve de conflit thématique, de présentation dialectique ou antithétique, mais elle illustre plutôt un acheminement vers une inéluctable fin ironique car le résultat était annoncé dès le début. Ce manque de progression, ce mouvement circulaire, renforce le caractère acerbe du récit.

La langue de la nouvelle ne se distingue pas; en effet, le langage figuré, par exemple, fait à peine surface. L'allure de la phrase est simple car le style en général est direct, la syntaxe guère complexe. On a noté, cependant, dans la prose gobinienne globale l'emploi fréquent de l'asyndète, souvent sous forme de constructions tripartites. Ce procédé rhétorique, qui a été étudié dans *Les Pléiades* et dans les nouvelles, traduit l'élan vital de l'auteur, son énergie, ses convictions, l'intensité de son expressivité.[12] La même technique marque aussi le style rabelaisien, mais il ne s'agit pas évidem-

12. Cf. Riffaterre, pp. 116–63; Alexandre Lorian, "Remarques sur la phrase polycéphale de Gobineau," *Etudes Gobiniennes*, 5 (1971), 155–71.

ment d'en déduire l'influence de l'un sur l'autre.[13] Ce procédé se voit
d'ailleurs chez nombre d'auteurs, certains bien plus proches de Gobineau
tels que Hugo et Chateaubriand; il reflète par conséquent une affinité d'expressivité qu'exige un même tempérament. L'asyndète typifie dans une
grande mesure le style de la Renaissance car elle reproduit le côté exubé-
rant de cette époque que Gobineau admirait et cherchait à émuler. A cet
égard il s'allie aux romantiques qui redécouvrent le XVIe siècle où ils trouvent un terrain fertile pour leur nouveau credo.

Tout comme la Renaissance voulait atteindre, suivant Platon, une Beauté
idéale pour harmoniser un monde déchiré, Gobineau aussi recherche
l'Absolu pour combattre un monde dépravé, et l'asyndète par ses particu-
larités synonymiques exprime les tentatives vers ce but, tandis que par ses
qualité mimétiques elle traduit l'énergie qui presse l'auteur dans cette
direction. Bien qu'elle ne soit pas dominante, l'asyndète se remarque déjà
dans *Les conseils de Rabelais*:

> Je ne vous ferai pas l'histoire de ma passion, de ses désirs, de ses
> assauts, de ses combats. Toutes ces contradictions qu'elle rétorquait,
> tous ces obstacles qu'elle surmontait, tous ces refus qu'elle savait
> abattre lui donnaient plus de force, et victorieuse, impérieuse, elle
> finit per s'emparer de mon être... je l'étais jadis [philosophe] et, à
> mesure que l'âge avance, je le deviens plus encore, en voyant de plus
> près la mesure, le mérite et l'étoffe de toutes choses [19, 44–45].

Les polynômes permettent à Gobineau de saisir, ou tout du moins de tenter
de saisir, la totalité d'une expérience, d'un sentiment et expriment justement cette force intérieure qui va. Une vitalité intérieure se concrétise au
moyen d'une énergie verbale. Pendant la Renaissance, à commencer par
Jean Lemaire de Belges et les Grands Rhétoriqueurs, la polynomie, synonymique on non, indique aussi la recherche d'un nouveau langage et l'exploitation de la parole pour sa valeur significative, sonore et rythmique;
chez Gobineau on distingue plutôt le besoin intense de l'expressivité que
l'expérimentation du XVIe siècle.

Un auteur, romancier ou nouvelliste, extériorise sa pensée à travers ses
personnages. S'il ne fait que les ébaucher, sa pensée domine sur leur hu-

---

13. Pour Rabelais, voy. mon article "La tautologie chez Rabelais," *Le Français Moderne,*
31 (1963), 292–95, et mon *Etude sur le comique de Rabelais* (Florence, 1964), pp. 91–95,
129–36. Pour l'emploi de la polynomie synonymique et l'asyndète au XVIe siècle en général,
voy. Alexandre Lorian, *Tendances stylistiques dans la prose narrative du XVIe siècle*
(Paris, 1973), pp. 65–137, 295–301.

manisation car ils figurent surtout en tant qu'instruments philosophiques de leur créateur. C'est précisément cette fonction que Rabelais et Odet de Châtillon exercent dans *Les conseils de Rabelais*; le premier incarne le philosophe-artiste et le second, l'homme d'action. Et Gobineau donne raison à l'artiste, qui finit toujours par subsister, tandis que le succès de l'homme d'action reste éphémère. Cette formule de la supériorité de l'artiste à l'homme engagé constitue aussi la thèse fondamentale de *La Renaissance* à laquelle Gobineau avait commencé à travailler en 1841, quatre ans après la composition de la nouvelle, mais qui ne sera achevé qu'en 1874. Il n'est donc pas outré de supposer que *Les conseils de Rabelais* servent d'embryon thématique à *La Renaissance* qui est une succession de tableaux historiques où les personnages italiens, pour la plupart *condottieri* politiques ou religieux, illustrent l'échec de l'engagement par rapport à la permanence de la création artistique.

Les héros de *La Renaissance* sont des "fleurs d'or, les grandes merveilles de la vitalité humaine";[14] il va sans dire que le Rabelais gobinien et Châtillon appartiennent également à cette catégorie d'êtres supérieurs. Mais si cette vitalité s'exprime par un engagement politique et réformateur, elle ne se réalisera pas tandis que la solitude de l'artiste mènera à des résultats durables. En effet, les héros engagés dans la politique et les conflits religieux échouent, mais les peintres s'éternisent. En outre, les tableaux de *La Renaissance* suivent non seulement une courbe chronologiquement historique, de Savonarole au vieux Michel-Ange, mais aussi ascendante, d'une succession d'échecs (Savonarole, César Borgia, Jules II, Léon X) à une réussite (Michel-Ange). Evidemment ce sont les échecs qui dominent; cependant, l'œuvre se trouve encadrée de deux portraits d'êtres spirituels: l'idéaliste Savonarole qui voudrait réformer la morale et la théologie du

14. Arthur de Gobineau, *La Renaissance*, éd. Jean Mistler (Monaco: Editions du Rocher, 1947), p. 6. Cette notion se retrouve par exemple dans un autre ouvrage, une sorte de long poème chevaleresque, *Le roman de Manfredine*: "L'un s'appelait Robert, l'autre était Manfredine,/ Deux fleurs dignes en tout leur tige divine" (Paola Berselli Ambri, éd., *Poemi inediti di Arthur de Gobineau* [Florence, 1965], p. 171). Ce concept de la "fleur d'or" ou de l'être supérieur remonte au *génie* du XVIIIe siècle que les romantiques se plaisent à perpétuer et qui aboutit aux *phares* de Baudelaire. Il faut aussi noter que Gobineau avait d'abord voulu intituler *La Renaissance*, "Les Fleurs d'or." Dès sa jeunesse il se considérait membre d'une élite: "Les Sceltis [choisis] sont des esprits aventureux et hardis, de vrais condottieri; tu sais que cela a toujours été mon idéal"; d'une lettre du 22 octobre 1840, citée dans René Guise, "Aux sources de l'italianisme de Gobineau," p. 364. Pour concrétiser la réalité de l'être supérieur il avait même, vers la même époque, organisé une société: "Trois choses sont communes aux membres de la Sérénissime Société: l'ambition, l'indépendance d'esprit, les idées aristocratiques" (ibid). Plus tard cet état d'esprit le mènera à la composition d'un ouvrage auquel il doit une réputation ambiguë, son *Essai sur l'inégalité des races humaines*.

peuple florentin mais finit sur le bûcher, et Michel-Ange qui dévoue sa vie à l'art. Un rapport s'impose immédiatement entre le moine florentin et le cardinal Odet de Châtillon car ces deux individus ont tenté de réformer l'Eglise et leur défaite leur a coûté la vie.

La Renaissance incarne le culte de l'énergie, de l'action, et de l'individualisme; elle reflète donc la définition qu'en donne les romantiques, et un Michelet et un Burckhardt. Aussi les personnages agissent-ils soit par un engagement fébrile dans la vie quotidienne soit par la création artistique. La raison d'être d'un César Borgia est son besoin intense de dominer: "Tant que j'existe, le monde est à moi! j'ai le pied dessus!" (201). Le pape Jules II, malgré la certitude de l'insuccès, persiste et rappelle Picrochole par sa conduite de fantoche:

> Je manie un grand pouvoir, il est vrai. Mais je veux beaucoup plus que je n'atteins. Je suis dévoré de désirs par delà le possible... Voilà ce que je suis... je le comprends bien à cette heure: tout s'écroule, s'efface... Je bute à chaque pas... C'est un grand malheur... Mais quand on a quelque énergie, on peut se relever de tout... Ecris encore. Le siège de Ferrare, il faut le presser! Ecris à Marc-Antoine Colonna, aux Vénitiens, aux Suisses, que ma volonté est inébranlable. J'ai besoin de l'argent; dis-le leur!... Il faut aussi en finir avec le gouvernement de Florence et son chef imbécile, Soderini! Prends ceci en note... Bon... Le cardinal Jean de Médicis commandera l'armée de l'Eglise dans cette occurrence... Nous aurons pour nous les partisans de sa maison... [284, 285].

Quant au tableau du pape Léon X c'est une apologie de la Réforme, mais la fin du chapitre est marquée de nouveau par la désillusion et l'effort toujours maté: "L'amour des lettres, si puissant autrefois pour amuser mes loisirs, a perdu de son prestige; la Religion seule me soutient; elle a bien des menaces à côté de ses promesses" (367). En effet, Gobineau avait fait resplendir le début de ce chapitre; c'était la fête des lettres et des inventions. Mais comme dans les autres chapitres, sauf le dernier, la chute reste inévitable.[15] Toute apogée ou réussite devient par conséquent ironique

15. Cf. aussi le chapitre sur Jules II où Rafaël exprime son enthousiasme des arts: "La joie, la vie, la fécondité nous enlèvent; nous nageons, nous autres, dans un éther olympique! Et les savants, et les poètes, et les littérateurs, et les antiquaires, et les imprimeurs, et les peintres, les sculpteurs, les architectes, les graveurs, les tailleurs d'images, les enlumineurs, tout, tout, tout ce qui dans une forme, d'une manière quelconque, est devenu capable d'exprimer une pensée, une nuance de la pensée, un atome tout mince et tout réduit d'une idée, tout est à l'œuvre, travaille, ne se laisse pas déranger, accumule les effets sur les effets, et traverse les désastres, la lumière du génie sur le front, le sourire aux lèvres et son œuvre à la main" (pp. 280–81).

puisque nous savons dès l'abord que les événements se précipiteront vers un abîme. Malgré la trajectoire croulante des actions humaines, il ne faut pas abandonner l'engagement; en fin de compte, les tentatives importent autant sinon plus que le résultat ou les réussites. Après la mort de Léon X, un autre pape, Adrien VI, apparaît aidé de Charles V; Gobineau fait un autre, même un dernier, sursaut: "ne faiblissez pas, ne reculez pas, ne tombez pas!... Car, moi, j'irai toujours en avant, et si l'Eglise fléchit ou hésite, je la traînerai malgré elle!" (372).

Le rapport entre Machiavel et Michel-Ange dans *La Renaissance* illustre de nouveau le contraste semblable entre Odet de Châtillon et Rabelais dans *Les conseils de Rabelais*; dans les deux cas la vie créatrice l'emporte sur la vie active politique ou religieuse. L'amertume et la désillusion règnent chez le chancelier florentin qui incarne ici les sentiments de Gobineau même envers sa patrie et la société; l'auteur du *Prince* s'adresse ici au peintre des fresques de la chapelle Sixtine:

> Pour moi, je ne suis pas un artiste dont la vraie patrie est le monde; je ne suis pas un savant qui peut trouver en tous lieux l'honneur et l'entretien; je suis un misérable fonctionnaire du plus misérable des Etats, et je hais cet Etat, et je hais Florence... Quand le Frère Jérome Savonarole vint prêcher sa doctrine, j'étais un jeune homme; j'aimais les humains; j'aimais ma patrie; j'aimais l'Italie; je croyais à la possibilité de la raison et à celle de la vertu. J'ai épuisé tous mes efforts afin de leur bâtir un nid. Quel fut le succès de ces espérances? N'en parlons pas [408, 409].

Gobineau traduit l'idéal de l'homme de la Renaissance qui cherche à s'éterniser au moyen de la création artistique; il aurait voulu que la participation à la vie publique, un autre idéal humaniste, fût aussi un moyen de laisser sa trace sur la terre, mais cette tentative mène toujours à une impasse; il tire cette conclusion d'ailleurs de sa propre vie. Machiavel, son dédoublement fictif, finit par être un personnage pitoyable et tragique, un potentiel qui ne s'est pas réalisé, une force qui n'a pas été comprise:

> Je ne suis qu'un grabeleur d'idées, et le fait prouve que je n'ai été qu'un rêveur. Il y a loin de voir juste à créer vrai. De la laideur même, vous faites l'immortelle beauté, comme avec la glaise la plus vile il vous est donné de modeler des formes enchanteresses; votre monde peut périr, vous restez dieu et vous vivez. Mais, moi? J'ai compris ce qu'il fallait essayer de produire; j'ai montré ce qui était désirable.

L'a-t-on exécuté? Non! que reste-t-il de moi? Un pauvre homme courbé en deux qui va disparaître, et tout sera dit! [410].

Bien que l'art reste supérieur à la vie publique, le choix est tout autant forcé que voulu; la supériorité de l'un ne devrait pas être aux dépens de l'autre. Suivant l'idéal de la Renaissance les deux devraient coexister pour réaliser la plénitude de notre séjour sur la terre. Cet avortement de l'énergie et la contrainte du choix imposé par les limites et la bêtise humaines produisent l'amertume et le pessimisme de Gobineau.

Le culte du moi est la force intérieure qui fait agir le héros gobinien, et la création artistique se fait valoir non seulement en tant que but intrinsèquement noble mais aussi en fonction de cet égocentrisme. Le moi se définit par l'art qu'il façonne, et la gloire, déité humaniste, s'ensuit. En juxtaposant l'Arétin à Titien, Gobineau oppose la réalité dans la littérature, qui est surtout intériorisée et impressionniste, à la réalité dans les arts plastiques, qui est, selon lui, essentiellement extérieure et objective puisque l'artiste dépeint tout simplement ce qu'il voit autour de lui. Il ne cherche pas à démontrer la supériorité de l'une sur l'autre mais plutôt à déployer la gamme de différents moi qui s'en dégage. Dans le domaine littéraire le moi influe sur la réalité tandis que dans les arts plastiques c'est le contraire. Bien que cette distinction puisse sembler un peu superficielle, elle reflète l'esprit dialectique de Gobineau; mais en est-il convaincu lui-même? Gobineau souligne plutôt la notion de disponibilité et l'importance d'une recherche incessante qui développent le moi à travers la création artistique: "Je serai grand, moi qui suis ton Raphaël, parce que j'apprends partout et de tous, je ne m'arrête jamais dans ma recherche. Il m'importe médiocrement de fouiller sous les racines de l'arbre à fruit que chacun possède, mais je veux l'arbre et je veux les fruits, et voilà pourquoi... je suis moi..." (242-43). A la Renaissance il y a une confluence d'épistémologie et d'ontologie qui attire Gobineau et s'accorde avec son propre esprit. Dans *Les conseils de Rabelais*, l'auteur-philosophe du *Quart Livre* incarne cette intégrité, or sa réussite et sa sagesse, tandis que Odet de Châtillon, limitant sa disponibilité et l'envergure de sa recherche religieuse, échoue.

Les conseils de Rabelais constituent en fin de compte un fragment, une ébauche même, de *La Renaissance*. Les personnages de cette fresque illustrent le *pro* et *contra* de la vie publique engagée ou de la vie artistique, tout comme Odet de Châtillon et Rabelais dans la nouvelle. Du point de vue idéologique, donc, la Renaissance n'est plus cette époque qui se prête éperdument au changement car les tentatives de réforme religieuse ou politique (Savonarole, Machiavel, Odet de Châtillon) ne réussissent pas. Evidemment cette optique ne résulte pas d'une historicité scientifique mais reflète plutôt les observations et les expériences personnelles de Gobineau qui préconisait toujours, et sans succès, une politique de droite, la cause royaliste, et qui a éprouvé maintes désillusions amoureuses. Il n'est pas étonnant que l'art finit par l'emporter sur la vie; ce n'est pas un art pour l'art, malgré les énoncés dans *La Renaissance*, mais une activité créatrice qui rend la vie vivable, supportable. Il se dégage, par conséquent, une définition moderne de l'ère de Machiavel et de Michel-Ange puisque cette époque n'est plus marquée par la joie et l'enthousiasme qu'on attribue généralement à la Renaissance; en dépit du culte du moi et de l'énergie, la résignation, le stoïcisme, et la désillusion finissent par dominer la Renaissance gobinienne. Cette sobriété transforme les personnages en symboles, car ils n'existent qu'en fonction de cette pensée mélancolique et obsédée de leur auteur. Le Rabelais gobinien, Odet de Châtillon et le *dramatis personae* de *La Renaissance* ne sont pas des caractérisations animées d'individus dont nous suivons minutieusement le drame de leur vie, mais des incarnations fixes du conflit que Gobineau éprouve lui-même entre la vie engagée publique et la vie de la création artistique ou littéraire, dilemme qui confrontait tout humaniste et que Rabelais aussi fait ressortir dans son prologue du *Tiers Livre*.

Or, il s'agit chez Gobineau d'un symbolisme assez simple où les personnages figurent en tant que phénomènes et suivent une courbe prédéterminée. Dans ce domaine on est bien plus proche de Vigny que de Mallarmé; comme Gobineau, le poète de "Moïse" rend évident le parallélisme entre sa vie, sa pensée, et les actions de son personnage. Tandis que dans "L'après-midi d'un faune," par exemple, on procède par association et le symbole se crée, par l'enchevêtrement de métaphores et d'intuition, au fur et à mesure que la pensée pérégrine. Un Vigny, tout comme l'auteur des *Conseils de Rabelais*, ne se pose pas de doute sur la validité de son engagement littéraire car la plume rachète le pessimisme d'une existence misérable. D'autre part, suivant une tradition platonicienne, Mallarmé fonde en grande partie la substance de sa poésie sur les doutes à l'égard de son art— les difficultés et l'insuffisance du langage et de la création poétique; Rabelais avait eu les mêmes préoccupations. Mais douter ne veut pas dire réfuter la littérature et sa fonction médicinale pour l'esprit. Le symbolisme rationalisé de Gobineau implique tout simplement une vision dialectique, un peu trop nette, de l'univers et un dévouement moins assidu envers la création littéraire à laquelle manque une fureur bachique.

Gobineau était historien, sociologue, orientaliste, poète, critique littéraire, romancier, journaliste, sculpteur, diplomate. Voilà aussi pourquoi la multiplicité de l'homme de la Renaissance l'attirait; cet idéal le poursuivait tandis qu'il voulait donner tous les débouchés possibles à sa propre énergie. Mais les Leonardo da Vinci et les Michel-Ange restent exceptionnels et divins. Et Gobineau, lui, reste humain par sa prise de conscience résultant de son besoin de rêver et d'émuler les dieux.

Robert J. Niess

Zola's *Au Bonheur des Dames:* the making of a symbol

Although it is risky to speak of authorial intention, we can be fairly sure that we know what Zola meant to do in composing *Au Bonheur des Dames* (1883), eleventh novel of the Rougon-Macquart series and the first major work in French to treat commerce in modern terms. The book itself, and more especially the apparatus that accompanied it—notes, sketches, plans and the like—make it clear that he meant to show the rise of the "new" large-scale commerce, product of the young capitalistic system, and the fall, the "death" of the old commerce of traditional kind that had so long been characteristic of French urban life, represented by the little *boutiques* of all kinds that lined the streets of Paris, the shops so picturesquely described in Balzac's novels. The movement described in *Au Bonheur des Dames*, symbolized in the entity of the department store which bears the name of Au Bonheur des Dames, had actually been in process for a half-century or a little more in 1883; but some lengthy interruptions in its progress make its origins in the twenties of the past century appear to us now as a little premature, which is to say that Zola was undoubtedly right in locating the real beginning of the new commercial methods somewhere in the era of the Second Empire.[1]

The process of change was an enormous one and to describe it adequately was in itself a major task. But, as happened to him on more than one occasion, Zola appears to have been swept along by the momentum of his idea, and *Au Bonheur des Dames* gradually became not only the fictionalized record of an historical economic process but a Darwinian depiction of the social and economic struggle implicit in the laissez-faire system then in vogue, and more, a prophecy of the continuation and expansion of this Darwinism in which the new commerce is seen as existing only by virtue of the death of the old methods and the old techniques.

1. For a discussion of the history of Parisian commercial techniques in the nineteenth century, see Henri Mitterand, "Etude" of *Au Bonheur des Dames*, in *Les Rougon-Macquart*, Edition de la Pléiade (Paris, 1964), III, 1672 ff. All quotations in the present study are taken from this edition and page numbers are indicated after each quotation.

As sometimes happens in the Rougon-Macquart series, the plot of this novel is not really very interesting or significant for us today—save that it contains a good deal that is important for students of the modern woman's liberation movement—and it might fairly be said of it that it serves mainly as a pretext for introducing the milieu, the trade, the movement that Zola wished to depict. Briefly, it recounts the adventures of a young girl, Denise Baudu, who comes up to Paris to seek employment to enable her to care for her two younger brothers. She obtains a place as salesperson in the department store named Au Bonheur des Dames, which occupies a position just across the street from Le Vieil Elbeuf, the musty fabric shop maintained by her uncle, old Baudu, apostle of traditional commercial methods and hence doomed to destruction by the new competitor. Denise gradually establishes herself by dint of unflagging efforts and uncomplaining virtue and gradually wins the heart and eventually the hand of the owner of Au Bonheur des Dames, Octave Mouret, a collateral descendant of the Rougon-Macquart family and as much an apostle of the new commerce as Baudu is a representative of the old. Denise's rise in the organization of Au Bonheur des Dames exactly parallels the store's vast expansion, which is typified in three great scenes, the sale of "nouveautés d'hiver," the second sale, of "nouveautés d'été," and the third sale, an enormous "white" sale in which Zola accomplishes a real tour de force in descriptive art. It should be added that Denise's victory over Mouret, who like some of the more active heroes of the Zola canon is a confirmed womanizer, represents a symbolic revenge of the female sex on the man who had built his commercial empire on the merciless exploitation of woman's weakness in the domain of fashion and elegant materialism.

But while it is clear that Zola is much interested in Denise, who is one of a series of female paragons each more perfect than her predecessor in his work and each, correspondingly a little less credible, what really lay closer to his heart was the "grand magasin" itself, the Darwinian devourer, the representative of the new economic system and hence of changing human society in the Occidental world. So it was that the realistic description of a large department store gradually became the creation of a huge and powerful symbol of tomorrow's world, of today's mortal competition, and of yesterday's defeat at the hands of what Zola considered to be progress.

Zola was no novice at the creation of such large symbols. As early as *La Curée* (1872), the second novel of the series and a wonderfully animated depiction of the real estate speculation which accompanied Haussmann's rebuilding of Paris, he had created a symbolic building, a lavish mansion in which the lust and greed which he thought characteristic of the Second Empire might find expression; in *Le Ventre de Paris* (1873) he had done much the same thing, but on a larger scale, for the Halles Centrales, embodying in that new creation the "fatness" and hatefulness of the Empire; in *La Faute de l'Abbé Mouret* (1875) he had conceived an enormous animistic creation, a forest-garden to be the cradle and symbol of the power of Eros; in *L'Assommoir* (1877) he had created a symbolic apartment house in which misery and alcohol would reign; and in *Nana* (1880) he had made an apartment—and more specifically a bed—in which once again the Second Empire's appetite for the flesh would find itself epitomized, as indeed it does in the colossal figure of Nana herself, the largest and most perfect of his symbolic humans. After *Au Bonheur des Dames* the symbolic, the mythic tendency continues and even grows, in *Germinal* (1885), where the mine personifies the devouring nature of modern industrial capitalism, in *L'Œuvre* (1886) where the Ile de la Cité becomes "le cœur de Paris," and in *La Terre* (1887) the earth and the Beauce come to stand for nature's eternal creativity and goodness, sign of fecundity and sexuality. These are his best novels, by and large, and the symbolic height they attain is in great measure responsible for their artistic and critical success and their popularity with the public.

In other novels he seems to have tried, unsuccessfully, to accomplish these same symbolic and mythic ends—in *La Conquête de Plassans*, for instance, where the central building, a house, never acquires transcendent value, or in *Son Excellence Eugène Rougon*, where the Chambre des Députés never attains the kind of stature it might have had. In some later books he may have failed too, as in *L'Argent*, where he never succeeded in giving the Bourse the kind of higher existence the subject seemed to demand.

But in some novels of the series, not many, there is no apparent attempt at any such elevation of the subject to the level of myth. In *Pot-bouille* (1882), for example, the novel immediately preceding *Au Bonheur des Dames*, the apartment which is almost the sole scene of the action is never rendered in any terms except immediately realistic; there is no transcendence of any kind and the whole work remains on the level of its theme, the dirty adultery of the pious bourgeoisie. And nothing is more instructive of the double talent of Zola, the talent for Balzacian analysis and rendition of everyday "truth," and the talent, more modern, more primitive, for raising his observation into the range of myth by the creation of powerful and mobile symbols.

The techniques which Zola employed in creating these epic entities, these symbols, were always the same, though in each novel they appear on different levels of importance. All of them depend, in various ways, on three rhetorical devices which have always been associated with the epic, from Homer to Faulkner: personification, a reflection of the animism that is the most characteristic tendency of Zola's mind; hyperbole, product of his constant desire to break away from reality and to enter other, higher realms; and impressionism, reflection of his early deep involvement in the artistic movement of the sixties and seventies and of his endeavor to create an effective device for the depiction of the complex world he found around him. These major elements are backed by a wide range of metaphors, developed and recurring comparisons of all types, most of them created out of Zola's need to support his rhetorical devices by references to the level of experiential reality, but called up also by his animism, his tendency to "grossissement" and his partial, light-dominated view of the real.

Animism is everywhere here, and for an excellent reason that transcends Zola's deep native devotion to its principle, the clearest part of his romantic heritage: it is everywhere because *Au Bonheur des Dames* depends for its very existence, intellectually, on an antithesis, the contrast between the old commercial institutions of the quarter, the *boutiques*, which represent the dead hand of tradition and the end of the old world, and the new commerce, the commerce of the huge institutions of modern days, where low profits and high volume are the rule, where desire is created by advertising, where woman is the source of success—the commerce of the future, in a word. This antithesis is constantly expressed in terms of Darwinian struggle, that is, in terms of life and death, with life depending on death and the dead feeding the living.

True to his Hugolian tendencies, Zola establishes in the first pages of the novel the elements of the "struggle for life" that his book will contain, posing on one side of the street the dark, gloomy, damp, and discouraged fabric shop, Le Vieil Elbeuf, owned by Denise's uncle, and on the other, the second incarnation of the department store which will eventually "kill" him as it will kill every other merchant around the *îlot*, as Zola calls it, the parallelogram bounded by the rue du Quatre-Septembre (which appears in the novel under its original name, rue du Dix-Décembre) and the rue Saint-Augustin (which at the time of the novel was called rue Neuve-Saint-Augustin) on its longer axis and by the rue de la Michodière and the rue de Monsigny on its shorter sides. We see in these first pages the second incarnation of Au Bonheur des Dames because the first incarnation was itself a *boutique* in the old style, owned first by the father of Octave Mouret's first wife, Mme Hédouin, now dead, and then by her first husband, and rebuilt by Octave into this first approximation of a department store in the new manner, that is, the manner of the Magasins du Louvre and Au Bon Marché, which provided Zola with a large number of the details of his novel.

Our first glimpse of Au Bonheur des Dames emphasizes its living quality, its "notes vives," the piece of blue fabric in the window, the activity of the window-dressers, the buzzing of its personnel preparing for the day (389). Already three appeals are made to our sense of life—the colors to the eye, the activity to the mind, the noise to the ear—and all through the novel Zola will take the greatest care to step up this assault on our perception, striking us from every direction at once. As the work goes on, activity will become animation, sometimes confusion; and nothing in the store will be depicted as static—stasis is death, it lodges on the other side of the street—and perhaps in no novel of Zola's do the characters cover so many linear feet of space in their professional capacities as in this one. We have constant glimpses of people working or buying, a "pullulement" (414), "une agitation de chantier" (423), life attracting life, as Mouret says (613). And colors—the novel glows with them, colors "bariolées, chinées, rayées" (391), an "incendie d'étoffes" (434), "une débauche de couleurs" (469), "un rayonnement d'astre" (470), and as the store grows the colors become more frequent, more brilliant, more central, just as they brighten and grow more dominant, symbolically, as the new sections of the store are built, passing from the solid sobriety of the past, the neutral shades of traditional manufacture, to brilliant reds and greens "au milieu d'une prodigalité d'or, des flots d'or, des moissons d'or" (626–27). And in all the splendor of the colors, colors of the Orient, of all the flowers of the Western world, of fire and flame and ember, red and gold will constantly predominate, these colors so long associated with passion, blood, and sexuality. True enough, red and gold were, historically, the favorite "public" colors of the Second Empire, as a thousand paintings will testify, but Zola sees them too frequently to allow us to believe that he is simply copying reality here. Across the street the shutters are down, the blinds are drawn.

Where there is color, there must be light, and indeed there is light in *Au Bonheur des Dames*, in a surprising volume and variety; not so much as in *Le Ventre de Paris*, perhaps, where Zola came close to abusing his impressionistic techniques, but a great deal nonetheless. It is obvious that so much light represents a deliberate effort on his part to reinforce the contrast he makes between the old commerce and the new and that it plays a strong symbolic role in supporting the life-death antinomy that is central to his philosophy. Much of the light in the novel is sunlight, a little unexpectedly, for nearly all the action is interior to the building, but so much sunlight—and it appears in all forms, pale winter light, blazing summer, soft spring—calls to our attention one of the capital facts about the building which houses the store: its large amount of glass, itself an innovation in urban construction at the time, and of course indicative of the presence of life, for it admits the sun, source of all existence, and permits the store to "live" on the street, so to speak. At all events, light fills the store, it is a "flamboiement" (403) changing the great central "nave"—the term is Zola's—into a "foyer d'ardente lumière" (414), into a vision, almost a hallucination: "[le] Bonheur des Dames flambait au fond des ténèbres comme un foyer colossal" (597)—a "foyer," incidentally, where the ruin of the small merchants is being forged. And when the great white sale takes place, it creates within the store "la flambée blanche d'un incendie en plein feu" (768). Not all the light effects in the novel are so brilliant—or so hyperbolical—for many are more Flaubertian, more modest, single spots of gaslight in dark corridors, exit signs, and the like. But given the limited kinds of light which the technology of the time provided him, Zola renders a stunning impression of invading light, seeking out every murky corner and transmuting it into still another center of the life that will build the future.

More primitive appeals to our sense of life are there too, and in good number. Department stores are notably warm places in reality, but Zola makes of heat an effective recurrent reminder that life does not exist without heat, which again he contrasts to the cold damp of the old *boutiques* around Au Bonheur des Dames. This is one of the most certain signs of his belief that a "living" entity like the great store exists in the same conditions as humans do. Odors and noise contribute too. During his lifetime Zola was often mocked by his critics for introducing so many odors, most of them disagreeable, into his novels; they seemed to believe that this habit of his was only another example of his ineradicable vulgarity. But Zola apparently realized, as Baudelaire had before him, that the sense of smell, the earliest of our senses to appear and the least intellectualized (it does not even have its own vocabulary) was our swiftest and surest guide to the presence of life and that even a stinking gutter or a reeking hallway in a miserable apartment house betrayed more surely than any other signal could the presence of the living, from bacteria to humanity. Noise in this novel, like most of the other effects, is on the colossal scale: we hear the vast hum of the crowds, thousands of footsteps on the iron stairways, the racket of the stock reception chutes, the whole roar and rumble of the huge machine that Au Bonheur des Dames becomes as the clients storm its departments. Soft sounds, like soft light, hardly exist, for this is a book about masses, the society of the future, of our time now, and there is no place for the quiet and the muted. Moments of calm, of silence are rare; they serve mainly as antithetical elements to set off the vast movement of life that the great sales generate.

Most of the principal metaphors, or metaphorical systems, of the novel support the animistic principle illustrated in all this emphasis on life, Zola's first step in the creation of his symbolic entity. These chief metaphors are provided by references, in about equal numbers, to machines, military life, and water; a fourth principal metaphorical complex, derived from the imagery of religion, does not apply to this aspect of the novel, but has great relevance in another aspect, hyperbole. Military imagery, one of the "imperialistic" Zola's favorite resources in all his novels, is probably the most numerous of these chief clusters of metaphor, and its frequency here is of course fitting in the Darwinian scheme of things as Zola saw it. I believe it to be connected to the animistic theme because, as Zola employs it, it emphasizes attack and conquest, movement of "troops," i.e., sales-people, and battle strategy and tactics, and lays little stress on less mobile aspects of military life, encampment, repose after battle, and so on, though it should be added that some of the military metaphors do represent Au Bonheur des Dames as a ravaged city, prostrate after an attack, the "attack" of the clientele during the sales. At all events, verbs like "envahir," "attaquer," "dominer," "ravager," "conquérir," and "vaincre" are common all through the novel, and these verbs of course imply conflict, which in turn implies motion and hence life, just as some of the most significant nouns, like "triomphe," "défaite," "saccage," "victoire," imply past action of equally violent kind.

Mouret's most characteristic position during the three sales is at the top of the monumental stairway in the center of the building, a position where he can survey his "troops," direct the "tactics" of his battle with the clientele, and thus carry out the "strategy" prepared in anticipation of the struggle, a plan which will bring him victory, not only over the women, who are crushed into slavelike submission by the store's assault on their senses, but eventually also over his competitors of the small shops of the quarter. It might be remarked that this position of Mouret's looks a good deal like a position adopted more than once by Napoleon, who often watched the progress of his battles from the vantage point of a small hill; and surely Zola wants us to understand that men like Mouret, the "generals" of the new commercial movement, are the Napoleons of the modern age. But whether or not Zola meant us to see Mouret as a new Napoleon, the fact remains that battle plays a strong role in *Au Bonheur des Dames* and battle, conflict, means life (and death too, its other face) and life means movement, action, change.

About as frequent as military metaphors and perhaps more important are machine images. Here again, Zola called upon one of his favorite sources to support his animistic themes, for machine imagery becomes constantly more frequent and more central in the Rougon-Macquart series after the appearance of *Le Ventre de Paris*, becomes in fact the source of some of his most powerful symbols, as in *Germinal* and *La Bête humaine.*

Modern readers have been schooled to regard machines as man's opposite—they are tireless, emotionless, heedless, soulless, and predictable —and even as his enemy—machines put men out of work (this of course is not strictly true, but makes good folklore), they tempt man to overproduce, they dehumanize our work and our world, and so on. So we sometimes have difficulty in accepting Zola's factory and machine imagery as examples of his tendency toward animism. But while he seems to recognize some of the threatening aspects of machine technology, he always tends to see machines in human (or monstrous, but the difference is slight here) terms. One has only to think of the personality he attributes to La Lison, the powerful and beautiful locomotive of *La Bête humaine,* or of the toiling, blowing, almost human stationary engine of *Germinal,* to realize what little difference he occasionally made in his depiction of laborer and machine and how much he was inclined to describe machines in human terms, much more than to describe men in terms of machine.

At all events, the total entity of Au Bonheur des Dames, building and people, is very frequently compared to some kind of technological creation, usually a steam engine, which, it might be remarked, is a more "human" kind of machine than our modern electrically driven and computer-controlled equipment, for the steam engine acts a little like a man in the clutches of his toil: it blows, it sweats, it strains, it seems to breathe and almost to suffer. Denise, on seeing the interior of the store for the first time, feels its enormous power and almost immediately begins to think of it as a steam engine "fonctionnant à haute pression, et dont le branle aurait gagné jusqu'aux étalages" (402). A little later she sees the store again and has the same impression: "La machine ronflait toujours, encore en activité, lâchant sa vapeur dans un dernier grondement" (414). When she visits Au Bonheur des Dames to apply for a position she arrives a little early and finds the "machine" still "au repos"; but by afternoon "la machine menait la danse des clients et leur tirait l'argent de la chair" (492). This example is the first instance in the novel of a tendency which will become almost obsessive with Zola as the work progresses, the tendency to see the machine, which in its first appearances was relatively neutral, even friendly, as a weapon, a tool, a menacing element in a book already heavy with threat and struggle.

On one or two other occasions the "machine" is presented as being, if not precisely hostile to man, utterly indifferent to his fate, as a tyrannical master might be. It was the practice at Au Bonheur des Dames, as it undoubtedly was in reality at all the "grands magasins" of Paris, simply to dismiss employees when business declined seasonally; any pretext would suffice, and sometimes no pretext at all was invented to justify these cruel dismissals. The employees themselves accepted the system: "L'usine chômait, on supprimait le pain aux ouvriers; et cela passait dans le branle indifférent de la machine, le rouage inutile était tranquillement jeté de côté, ainsi qu'une roue de fer" (535). This Darwinism rendered in mechanistic terms appears at least once again, toward the close of the novel. Competition is the lifeblood of the new commerce, competition between commercial entities of all kinds, old and new, large and small, conservative and innovative, as we see in the duel between Mouret and the old shopkeepers of the quarter. But competition exists within the store too, among the clerks, even among the administrators. Bourdoncle, the second in command, hopes to "manger" Mouret as Mouret has devoured so many others: "Cela était dans l'air de la maison, dans cette bataille pour l'existence, dont les massacres continus chauffaient la vente autour de lui. Il était emporté par le jeu de la machine" (747).

It might be added that Zola occasionally concretizes the machine symbol by introducing real machines into his narrative. He seems to have been much interested by the chutes in the receiving department, since he mentions them on several occasions, and it may be that they attracted him because their smoothness, their speed, and their efficiency represented the qualities which he wanted to convey as typical of his fictional department store. The brilliant passage in which he describes the prodigious effort of demolition and rebuilding that the expansion of the store requires is a good example of this double symbolism. Here the real machines of the contractors tear down the old buildings of the *boutiquiers*, excavate a huge emplacement for the foundations and basement, build the new structure day and night and in their efforts bring home heartlessly to Mouret's competitors the exact sense of what such a Darwinian invasion as he is planning will mean to them: their ruin is in the very plaster dust which arises from the fallen edifice and sifts through their decayed walls to damage the merchandise on their shelves.

Water metaphors, though very frequent, are not so striking as machine or military images. It goes without saying that the idea of water is very nearly ideal for rendering the sense of life, for not only is it constantly in motion, as life is, but also we have kept our primordial feeling that water was the medium in which our ancestors first rose to the sense of life. Water is seen in *Au Bonheur des Dames* in forms that emphasize its movement: the sea, the tide, the river, the flood, rain; it is true that one or two examples can be found of expressions like "un lac de verre" to describe a roof, images, that is, which emphasize stasis, but these are rare. The receiving chutes well illustrate the concept of movement: they are like a river, a flood; they hurry along a "débâcle de marchandises" that is compared to the stones rolling in the bed of a torrent (422, 426); the merchandise at the counters is a rising sea (485), in the wools a "nappe bouillonnée" falls from above, the fabrics roll like water, "à flots grossis," they are a "cataracte lâchée" (487), the crowd is a river (491). After one of the sales the departments are an ocean of rolls of material, piles of rolls are like houses half-destroyed "dont un fleuve débordé charrie les ruines," there are "banquises de serviettes" (500). The crowd, seen from above as hats and hair, is again a sea (627), the receiving chutes once more appear as a "lit de fleuve, où le continuel flot de marchandises roulait avec la voix haute des grandes eaux" (708), and the crowd produces the enormous voice of a river "qui charrie." Strangely, water images are never used in this novel to reinforce the sexual theme that is so prominent a part of its economy; their function seems to be only to support the sense of animation, of motion, of life.

Certainly the best example of Zola's persistent efforts at personifying the great store is given by the series of important metaphors describing Au Bonheur des Dames as monster, ogre, devourer—devourer not only of its clients and of its workers but also of the whole quarter and finally of the whole city of Paris. Nearly all the chief symbolic elements of Zola's works, especially in the latter part of his career, give the central symbol some threatening aspect, an element of danger and menace—the mine, in *Ger-*

minal, is a devourer, the land in *La Terre* eats men until she is sated, La Lison brings about the destruction of her "lover" in *La Bête humaine*. In *Au Bonheur des Dames* the metaphor is not quite so dramatized, but verbs like "manger," "dévorer," "avaler" are very common, and it is apparent that Zola wishes us to see the store not only as machine but as devouring machine for which the only food is humanity—everywhere in the store can be heard "un gros bruit de mâchoires" (542). The single most active use of this metaphor of threat, for that is what it clearly is, appears in the recurrent references to the blood of Mme Hédouin, Octave's first wife and daughter and widow of its successive owners. She had died in a fall into the excavation for a new foundation, leaving some of her blood there, and Zola evidently wishes us to see in this blood, mentioned a half-dozen times and a symbol in itself, a reminder that commerce in the new manner is a battle to the death, that a great organization like Au Bonheur des Dames destroys all that stands in its way, as it consumes the very people who animate it, and that, in strictly Darwinian terms, there is no life without prior death, that the future lives on the blood of the past.

But in this symbolic novel it is not only the impression of life, of movement and conquest, that counts, it is the size of that life, its proportions above the proportions of reality. In nearly all his novels Zola aggrandizes the principal elements—people, buildings, objects, events—and everywhere one can see an attempt to create a fictional structure larger than the life that was its origin. But in no novel more than in *Au Bonheur des Dames* does this hyperbolical tendency more clearly appear and in none does it play a greater role in establishing the essential symbol. It is very nearly true that everything here is larger than life, save perhaps the small (but also symbolic) figures of the *boutiquiers* whom Mouret "kills." Denise is more pure, more long-suffering, more courageous than any woman has a right to be. Mouret is a Napoleon of his *métier*, a Balzacian *arriviste* who manages to arrive. True enough, the secondary figures are prosy and drawn to human scale, perhaps a little smaller, but the people who make the novel move are far above our normal moral dimensions. And so also the store. Everything about it grows steadily and rapidly: the building itself is enlarged so much that it swallows the whole *îlot*, the personnel rises from a few hundred to three thousand, the clientele grows in really astronomical terms until quite literally all Paris comes through the oriental vestibule to the main hall. The colors are all the brightest; the light is fire, flame, blazing embers; the dominant adjectives are "colossal," "énorme," "vaste"; individuals are constantly lost in the overpowering crowds; the total effect is one of almost incredible size, surpassing reality by no one knows what proportion.

Zola arrives at this impression of vastness by some ordinary techniques into which he pumps a good deal of exaggerated rhetoric and hyperbolical language. If a stronger, more colorful, more violent or more dramatic word is available in a choice of near-synonyms, he always rejects the weaker, the more prosaic—and often the more "real." But he does other things too. He returns constantly to the dimensions of the building, for instance: in our first glimpse of it the store appears large chiefly by contrast with the squat, crumbling shops around it; then the wide display windows are described at length, then he turns to interior views, where it appears "vaste comme une église" (596); its main door is as high as "un porche d'église" (611), the central gallery is like "une nef de gare" (626), the kitchen for the employees' meals is big enough to hold "des grils à faire griller des martyrs, des casseroles à fricasser un mouton... des éviers de pierre larges comme des piscines" (663). Mouret finally sees his building creating a greater shadow over Paris than the Louvre itself—"ceci tuera cela," as Victor Hugo had said a half-century earlier. At the time of the white sale the "vaisseau énorme" offers a prodigious spectacle: "une échappée boréale, toute une contrée de neige, déroulant à l'infini des steppes tendues d'hermine" (768).

Sometimes Zola is a little more artful than this, though certainly equally hyperbolical: occasionally, though not often enough, he does not tell us of the building's size, he demonstrates it—the spectacle of the clerks wildly working at inventory time "semblait se perdre au fond des rayons, dans un lointain confus d'émeute" (690), and on another occasion he shows us some clients returning from the cutting rooms upstairs as though they had been on such a long journey that they had completely lost their bearings. In a somewhat similar way a fine impression of great height is produced by the fairly frequent descriptions of the ironwork stairways and galleries, an innovation in the technique of construction which interested Zola deeply and which he had previously employed as the basis for a whole range of metaphors in *Le Ventre de Paris*, where the cast-iron and steel structure is made to represent the "new" in architecture as the stone cathedral represents the "old." It should be added that Zola's effective use of mirrors, and generally of glass, in *Au Bonheur des Dames* adds to the impression of size and multiplicity, though by far the most effective technique he introduces to obtain the effect of limitless variety—one of the chief advantages of the department store over the old, specialized *boutiques*—is contained in the almost endless lists the novel contains of all kinds of merchandise, fabrics, gloves, umbrellas, white goods, coats, feathers, furs, rugs, even furniture. These lists, of really epic size (and of course recalling the epic enumerations), give as no other device can an idea of the inexhaustible range of objects in a modern department store and by extension some idea of the physical size necessary to encompass so many things. The same technique had served with great success in *Le Ventre de Paris*—one has only to remember the magnificent "symphonie des fromages" to realize how effective such lists can be—and had also served as the structural basis of the long central description of the forest-garden of Le Paradou in *La Faute de l'Abbé Mouret*.

So size is everywhere: the new flower and feather department, one of Mouret's innovations, offers "sous la lumière vive du vitrage, une floraison énorme, une gerbe blanche, haute et large comme un chêne" (787). The display windows become wide enough to "exposer le poème entier des vêtements de la femme" (764) and soon Au Bonheur des Dames becomes, in Zola's gargantuan terms, a worldwide force. Mouret inaugurates the technique of sending catalogues to provincial and foreign customers for mail-order sales and mounts a vast new advertising campaign: "C'était un débordement d'étalages, le Bonheur des Dames sautait aux yeux du monde entier, envahissant les murailles, les journaux, jusqu'aux rideaux des théâtres" (613). The ogre, the monster gives the impression that there can be no limit to its growth, and never does it lose its threatening character for the little shopkeepers who surround it: "ce cube énorme, ce colossal bazar leur bouchait le ciel, leur paraissait être pour quelque chose dans le froid dont ils grelottaient, au fond de leurs comptoirs glacés" (611).

And of course all manner of metaphors support this impression of size, imperialism, and grandeur. The store is "la réalisation moderne d'un palais de rêve, d'une Babel entassant des étages, élargissant des échappées sur d'autres étages et d'autres salles, à l'infini" (626); it is like a city, "avec ses monuments, ses places, ses rues" (434); the endless corridors of its basement warehouse "mettaient comme des boutiques souterraines, tout un quartier commerçant" (709); it is a phalanstery, "dont les ailes, multipliées sans cesse, dévoraient des quartiers jusqu'aux bois lointains de la banlieue" (799). And it is a woman's paradise, a lighthouse in the dark old quarter, an anthill, even a locomotive, huge and powerful, with a right to progress and expansion as the locomotive in motion has a right to its track.

But certainly nowhere is the device of hyperbole so apparent and so abused as in Zola's treatment of the concept that lies at the heart of Mouret's commercial success, the exploitation of woman. *Au Bonheur des Dames* is, taken from one point of view, an illustration of one of the fundamental theses of the whole Rougon-Macquart series, Zola's belief that the Second Empire was a time of unbridled "appetite," for money, for power, for sex, for luxury, and that the appetites of the time were very close to irresistible. Mouret, like Saccard of *La Curée* and *L'Argent*, is a man who knows how to make use of these appetites for his own ends and in his effort to succeed commercially he puts his perceptions to work most skilfully in subjecting his clients to the maximum of temptation in the form of fashion, *mode*, for he is convinced that no living woman is immune to the appeal of fashion. He sees woman, when subjected to the multiple temptations of a store like his, "cédant d'abord à des achats de bonne ménagère, puis gagnée par la coquetterie, puis dévorée" (461); and in the persons of some of the second-rank characters he demonstrates this process in action, the insidious progress of "la folie de la mode." Denise herself, in her first contacts with Au Bonheur des Dames, feels mingled temptation and fear (403), the emotions that Mouret's countless other "victims," for that is how he thinks of them, feel in the presence of the seductive monster.

Mouret's sole passion and his sole means of success lie in the conquering of woman, and he builds his great "temple" to have her at his mercy; his constant strategy will be to "la griser d'attentions galantes et trafiquer de ses désirs, exploiter sa fièvre" (612). At the conclusion of the last great sale "il se sentait le maître une dernière fois, il les [i.e. his female clients] tenait à ses pieds, sous l'éblouissement des feux électriques, ainsi qu'un bétail dont il avait tiré sa fortune" (798). It is certainly not accidental that in one scene a group of mannequins is seen without heads, and in another a second group is shown with a "petit manche de bois pareil au manche d'un poignard, enfoncé dans le molleton rouge, qui saignait à la section fraîche du cou" (630). This brutal exploiter, ready "comme un juif," Zola says, to sell women by the pound, so skilfully tempts and seduces them that not only do they become his willing—his ardent—victims, they lose all sense of their humanity in their half-crazed desire for the treasures of the counters. Progressively, in the last part of the novel, Zola proceeds to dehumanize the great crowds, composed almost entirely of women, who invade the store to wallow in the sales. The women become "une poussière humaine" (627), "un océan de têtes," "une marée montante" (631). Mouret sees "la houle désordonnée des têtes" (797)—the women are nothing more than "une foule de convoitise (402). With the calm brutality of a despot, he "possesses" them, ruins them collectively and individually, morally and financially (797).

His chief tactic is the use of sexual temptation. No novel of Zola's, not even *La Curée* or *La Faute de l'Abbé Mouret*, includes more—and more open—sexual imagery than *Au Bonheur des Dames*. Certainly this imagery is necessary in Zola's plan, but there is so much of it, in so many different forms, that we might reasonably conclude that here the chaste Zola's imagination became overheated and led him into exaggerations that do not add to the force of his argument or the validity of his observation of contemporary reality. But whatever its origins, this kind of imagery is much more dominant than machine imagery or military imagery. It appears early in the text and grows progressively more frequent and more violent until near the end of the novel it begins to seem obsessive.

It is of course not possible, in the space of the present study, to assess fully the role of sexual imagery here; the subject would require a monograph. But sex is everywhere. In Denise's first glimpse of the display windows she sees silk stockings which "montraient des profils arrondis de mollets," and the "nude" shades of these stocking have "la douceur d'une peau de blonde" (391). In another window "la gorge ronde des mannequins gonflait l'étoffe, les hanches fortes exagéraient la finesse de la taille" (392). And still further on, the materials themselves take on a human sexual form:

> Et les étoffes vivaient, dans cette passion du trottoir: les dentelles avaient un frisson, retombaient et cachaient les profondeurs du magasin, d'un air troublant de mystère; les pièces de drap elles-mêmes, épaisses et carrées, respiraient, soufflaient une haleine tentatrice; tandis que les paletots se cambraient davantage sur les mannequins qui prenaient une âme, et que le grand manteau de velours se gonflait, souple et tiède, comme sur des épaules de chair, avec les battements de la gorge et le frémissement des reins [402].

Much later, after the first of the three sales, the lace and lingerie scattered on the floors and counters make one think of a "peuple de femmes" who undressed there, "dans le désordre d'un coup de désir" (500). A glimpse of a dressing room sets Zola off on an impressionistic description of mannequins who have "une lubricité troublante d'infirme" and who display "des croupes énormes et tendues"; here the "déshabillé galant" begins, "un déshabillé qui jonchait les vastes pièces, comme si un groupe de jolies filles s'étaient dévêtues de rayon en rayon, jusqu'au satin nu de leur peau"

(780). Lingerie of all kinds is everywhere, "camisoles," "petits corsages," "peignoirs," "de longs vêtements blancs, libres et minces, où l'on sentait l'étirement des matinées paresseuses, au lendemain des soirs de tendresse" (780–781). And Zola becomes more explicit:

> C'était, aux trousseaux, le déballage indiscret, la femme retournée et vue par le bas, depuis la petite bourgeoise aux toiles unies, jusqu'à la dame riche blottie dans les dentelles, une alcôve publiquement ouverte, dont le luxe caché, les plissés, les broderies, les valenciennes, devenait comme une dépravation sensuelle, à mesure qu'il débordait davantage en fantaisies coûteuses [781].

The white sale is the apogee of this sexual theme; here nudity is implied everywhere, sometimes seen, and perhaps nowhere in all his work did Zola accomplish such a developed and so effective a long image as this. Hyperbole is universal: this is no "realistic" depiction of a sale in a department store of our time, it is a brilliant fantasy in which exaggeration is the generating agent of the principal effects. At the end of it, Mouret sees "la clientèle dépouillée, violée, s'en allant à moitié défaite, avec la volupté assouvie et la sourde honte d'un désir contenté au fond d'un hôtel louche" (797).

Some of Zola's contemporaries might well have objected violently to his insistence that the new passion for *la mode*, underlaid and generated by a thwarted sexual passion, has now become a religion, has indeed replaced the old religions of the cathedrals and is in a way to convert France from her ancient Catholic allegiance to the new materialism. Mouret, Zola says, creates the cult of woman: "il lui élevait un temple, la faisait encenser par une légion de commis, créait le rite d'un culte nouveau" (461); and Au Bonheur des Dames does become, not simply a "temple," but "la cathédrale du commerce moderne" (612):

> Sa création apportait une religion nouvelle, les églises que désertait peu à peu la foi chancelante étaient remplacées par son bazar, dans les âmes inoccupées désormais. La femme venait passer chez lui les heures vides, les heures frissonnantes et inquiètes qu'elle vivait jadis au fond des chapelles: dépense nécessaire de passion nerveuse, lutte renaissante d'un dieu contre le mari, culte sans cesse renouvelé du corps, avec l'au-delà divin de la beauté. S'il avait fermé ses portes, il y aurait eu un soulèvement sur le pavé, le cri éperdu des dévotes auxquelles on supprimerait le confessionel et l'autel [797–98].

And the tone of the last phrases is the key to Zola's ultimate daring, his final hyperbole: not only is *la mode* a new religion, a new faith, a new cult,

it satisfies the same sexual urges as religion once had done and the final
treasure of Au Bonheur des Dames, its enormous collection of lace, gives
Zola the opportunity to link his major theme and his major argument:

> Dans le salon, il faisait très chaud. Les clientes, qui s'y étouffaient,
> avaient des visages pâles aux yeux luisants. On eût dit que toutes les
> séductions des magasins aboutissaient à cette tentation suprême, que
> c'était là l'alcôve reculée de la chute, le coin de perdition où les plus
> fortes succombaient. Les mains s'enfonçaient parmi les pièces débor-
> dantes, et elles en gardaient un tremblement d'ivresse (64).

The white sale continues the effect. A tent made of white sheets is the
"autel de cette religion du blanc" (769) and the vast décor contains within
it elements of the tabernacle and the alcove: "on aurait dit un grand lit
blanc dont l'énormité virginale attendait, comme dans les légendes, la
princesse blanche" (769). In the last pages of the novel, the three elements,
fashion, religion, sex, attain to their ultimate expression:

> ... les guipures et les dentelles blanches volant dans l'air, ouvraient
> un firmament du rêve, une trouée sur la blancheur éblouissante d'un
> paradis, où l'on célébrait les noces de la reine inconnue. La tente du
> hall des soieries en était l'alcôve géante, avec ses rideaux blancs, ses
> gazes blanches, ses tulles blancs, dont l'éclat défendait contre les re-
> gards la nudité blanche de l'épousée. Il n'y avait plus que cet aveu-
> glement, un blanc de lumière où tous les blancs se fondaient, une
> poussière d'étoiles neigeant dans la clarté blanche [797].

The actual literary form which Zola chose for rendering the monstrous,
living organism he called Au Bonheur des Dames is anything but realistic
if "realism" is thought to partake of Balzacian precision and completeness
or Flaubertian distance and litotes. Zola's chosen vehicle, in spite of his
long lists of fabrics and colors, accommodates much less of ordinary, prosaic
reality than we might expect and is, in its total effect, largely impressionistic,
in both the literary and the painterly sense. There are not, for instance,
very many "complete" pictures of any aspect of the store or of its life. There
are significant scenes in large numbers, there is a profusion of telling details
all through the work, and some groups of such details have great importance
in creating the kind of panoramic effects which Zola seems to have been
seeking here; but often long metaphors replace truly "realistic" description,
inventory description as Thibaudet might have called it. When, for instance,
Denise observes Au Bonheur des Dames for the first time at dusk, this is what
she sees:

Mais, de l'autre côté de la chaussée, le Bonheur des Dames allumait les files profondes de ses becs de gaz. Et elle se rapprocha, attirée de nouveau et comme réchauffée à ce foyer d'ardente lumière. La machine ronflait toujours, encore en activité, lâchant sa vapeur dans un dernier grondement, pendant que les vendeurs repliaient les étoffes et que les caissiers comptaient la recette. C'était, à travers les glaces pâlies d'une buée, un pullulement vague de clartés, tout un intérieur confus d'usine. Derrière le rideau de pluie qui tombait, cette apparition, reculée, brouillée, prenait l'apparence d'une chambre de chauffe géante, où l'on voyait passer les ombres noires des chauffeurs, sur le feu rouge des chaudières. Les vitrines se noyaient, on ne distinguait plus, en face, que la neige des dentelles, dont les verres dépolis d'une rampe de gaz avivaient le blanc; et, sur ce fond de chapelle, les confections s'enlevaient en vigueur, le grand manteau de velours, garni de renard argenté, mettait le profil cambré d'une femme sans tête, qui courait par l'averse à quelque fête, dans l'inconnu des ténèbres de Paris [414].

The effect, of course, is powerful, almost hallucinatory, but the scene is not "real" in the sense that a Balzacian interior, for instance, is "real."

Here is an example of a slightly different technique, used to render a scene observed by the narrator himself:

Dans l'air immobile, où l'étouffement du calorifère attiédissait l'odeur des étoffes, le brouhaha augmentait, fait de tous les bruits, du piétinement continu, des mêmes phrases cent fois répétées autour des comptoirs, de l'or sonnant sur le cuivre des caisses assiégées par une bousculade de porte-monnaie, des paniers roulants dont les charges de paquets tombaient sans relâche dans les caves béantes. Et, sous la fine poussière, tout arrivait à se confondre, on ne reconnaissait pas la division des rayons: là-bas, la mercerie paraissait noyée; plus loin, au blanc, un angle de soleil, entré par la vitrine de la rue Neuve-Saint-Augustin, était comme une flèche d'or dans la neige; ici, à la ganterie et aux lainages, une masse épaisse de chapeaux et de chignons barrait les lointains du magasin. On ne voyait même plus les toilettes, les coiffures seules surnageaient, bariolées de plumes et de rubans; quelques chapeaux d'hommes mettaient des taches noires, tandis que le teint pâle des femmes, dans la fatigue et la chaleur, prenaient des transparences de camélia [492].

And still another, clearer in outline but no more complete than the others—and again a long metaphor:

Et la foule paraissait noire. On eût dit les patineurs d'un lac de Pologne, en décembre. Au rez-de-chaussée, il y avait une houle assombrie, agitée d'un reflux, où l'on ne distinguait que les visages délicats et ravis des femmes. Dans les découpures des charpentes de fer, le long des escaliers, sur les ponts volants, c'était ensuite une ascension sans fin de petites figures, comme égarée au milieu de pics neigeux. Une chaleur de serre, suffocante, surprenait, en face de ces hauteurs glacées. Le bourdonnement des voix faisait un bruit énorme de fleuve qui charrie. Au plafond, les ors prodigués, les vitres niellées d'or et les rosaces d'or semblaient un coup de soleil, luisant sur les Alpes de la grande exposition de blanc [770].

Scenes like this are everywhere, fine "impressions" of large spectacles, characterized by skilful use of light effects and spots of color, but really highly selective and designed to create only a single effect, not the effect of complex and prosaic reality. Here Zola writes above eye level, so to speak, and the great frequency of light and color effects supports the view that in this novel at least he did not desire to be taken for a realist—perhaps he had been all too much of a realist in the preceding novel, *Pot-bouille*. *Au Bonheur des Dames* is one of his "poems," the poem of fashion and elegant materialism and sex, just as *La Terre* is the poem of the soil and *La Débâcle* is the poem of war and destruction. And like a poet, he is often a visionary here, as he is in *La Curée* and *Germinal* and *La Faute de l'Abbé Mouret*, seeing *échappées* and *lointains* and *profondeurs* where we lesser observers would see little but grey corridors and dark corners. Some of his visions, more developed, are marvelous renditions of the half-seen. Denise passes through the store at night:

... il fallait traverser tout le magasin. Elle préféra ce voyage, malgré les ténèbres qui noyaient les galeries. Pas un bec de gaz ne brûlait, il n'y avait que des lampes à huile, accrochées de loin en loin aux branches des lustres; et ces clartés éparses, pareilles à des taches jaunes, et dont la nuit mangeait les rayons, ressemblaient aux lanternes pendues dans des mines. De grandes ombres flottaient, on distinguait mal les amoncellements de marchandises, qui prenaient des profils effrayants, colonnes écroulées, bêtes accroupies, voleurs à l'affût. Le silence lourd, coupé de respirations lointaines, élargissait encore ces ténèbres [532].

There are many visions like this, some of them much more developed, some more threatening and fearful; they indicate as nothing else could Zola's intention, here at least, to transcend reality and cause observation to rise to a higher level than the level of report. Any painter might envy Zola his impressionism, and it is as painter that he chooses to be seen in *Au Bonheur des Dames.*

Each of Zola's three main techniques in this novel contributes its part to the creation of the symbol of the new, Darwinian commerce. His animism, rendered chiefly by personification but appearing in many different guises, removes the "monster" from the level of the real, giving it personality, movement, and life that far transcend our normal experience with the entities we encounter in the world; his hyperbolical expansion of every element gives the phenomenon he calls Au Bonheur des Dames a stature and an impact that no entity created by humans can have, in the finite reality of our world, and it raises his account of the entity's life to the level of myth, where collective experience is codified in large images; his impressionism causes us to see parts of his "monster" with great clarity but leaves equally great parts of it in shadow and mystery, allowing us to divine a structure that we neither completely see nor comprehend. Perhaps the total effect of this novel, seen from the purely rhetorical point of view, is best perceived in this remarkable passage, symbol of a symbol (one of Mouret's men has pasted up a new advertising poster on the very window of the defunct Vieil Elbeuf, itself the symbol of the conquered opposition in the quarter):

... au milieu de cette devanture morte, salie des crachats de la rue, bariolée des guenilles du vacarme parisien, s'étalait, comme un drapeau planté sur un empire conquis, une immense affiche jaune, toute fraîche, annonçant en lettres de deux pieds la grande mise en vente du Bonheur des Dames. On eût dit que le colosse, après ses agrandissements successifs, pris de honte et de répugnance pour le quartier noir, où il était né modestement, et qu'il avait plus tard égorgé, venait de lui tourner le dos, laissant la boue des rues etroites sur ses derrières, présentant sa face de parvenu à la voie tapageuse et ensoleillée du nouveau Paris. Maintenant, tel que le montrait la gravure des réclames, il s'était engraissé pareil à l'ogre des contes, dont les épaules menacent de faire craquer les nuages. D'abord, au premier plan de cette gravure, la rue du Dix-Décembre, les rues de la Michodière et de Monsigny, emplies de petites figures noires, s'élargissaient démesurément, comme pour donner passage à la clientèle du monde entier. Puis, c'étaient les bâtiments eux-mêmes, d'une immensité exagérée, vus à vol d'oiseau avec leurs corps de toitures qui dessinaient les galeries couvertes, leurs cours vitrées où l'on devinait les halls, tout l'infini de ce lac de verre et de zinc luisant au soleil. Au-delà, Paris s'étendait, mais un Paris rapetissé, mangé par le monstre; les maisons, d'une humilité de chaumières dans le voisinage, s'éparpillaient ensuite en une poussière de cheminées indistinctes; les monuments semblaient fondre, à gauche deux traits pour Notre-Dame, à droite un accent circonflexe pour les Invalides, au fond le Panthéon, honteux et perdu, moins gros qu'une lentille. L'horizon tombait en poudre, n'était plus qu'un cadre dédaigné, jusqu'aux hauteurs de Châtillon, jusqu'à la vaste campagne, dont les lointains indiquaient l'esclavage [763].

And what a symbolic word, *l'esclavage*! For it may be that the "new" commerce is on its way to enslaving the world, just as Au Bonheur des Dames made willing slaves of the women who passed through its doors. Zola's symbol may prove to yield the truth.

PART IV

Poems

Wendell Berry

Ripe

for Wallace Fowlie

The wild cherries ripen, black and fat,
Paradisal fruits that taste of no man's sweat.

Reach up, pull down the laden branch, and eat;
When you have learned their bitterness, they taste sweet.

Alain Bosquet

Poème pour Wallace Fowlie

De chaque pierre naît le mythe de la pierre,
de chaque oiseau l'idéal de l'oiseau.
Là-bas le fleuve est amour de tout fleuve.
O lune, il faut que tu deviennes ta légende,
et toi colline l'élue des collines,
et toi vieux scarabée le dieu des scarabées.
L'azur s'emplit d'exemples pour l'azur.
Un vent qui court, et c'est déjà quelque musique.
Un sol, et c'est déjà un paradis, parfait,
très imparfait, très habitable
pour la belette et pour le serpolet.
La moindre chose est bienheureuse
comme bougie entre deux paumes,
comme caillou entre deux lèvres;
et l'ombre—oh! qu'importe de qui—
inspirée plus que la lumière.
Le premier mur pense à se faire temple,
et le premier genou à se plier,
et la voix à bénir.
Le monde est à l'abri de la souillure
si le monde se pense et s'empêche de vivre.
De la poussière vient le goût des puretés.
Sur le doute fermente un peu de certitude.
Le faucon plonge au cœur de quel faucon,
et c'est peut-être le paradisier?
L'arbre ne tombe pas s'il est l'esprit de l'arbre.
Le sacré dort
comme un insecte grimpant sur la vigne.
Le mot se tourne et se retourne
et sait qu'à force de se proférer
il devient vierge.

David Galler

'Look in thy heart and write'

for Wallace Fowlie

Many the mornings when the mind,
Filled with the need for utterance
Certain and clear,
Circles the heart's vast field to find
Some sharp detail to lift toward sense,
Despised or dear.

Hours perhaps the mind will soar,
Then swoop, then climb, but take no image
In its claws,
Preferring to hold out for more.
Unwilling to restrict its homage,
It knows no pause.

Wildly the heartscape tilts and veers,
Flashing its scenes and faces, bright
And myriad,
Till the mind stalls in the storm of years
And wings back slowly toward its height,
Silent but glad.

Arthur Gregor

Poem on the marvel of giving

1.

In need
not unlike those who've gone
hungry for too long

and not a landscape to provide
even a little

in short, not surrounded by
what other cultures have
provided

landscapes
that are reminiscent of
speak a language that
comprehends this need

not the overtones
from scenes such as this

—a canal
trees full at the top
the still reflection of
tall trees and of a man
sitting by its bank as though he
never moved and doesn't intend to—

not the reverberations of
a stillness such as this

the alternation of
clear light and shade

a glow barely seen

a blend barely heard

a simple old cottage in a simple garden

nothing like that
no distant peal of bells
to take us in and out
of sleep

2.

When you came
you entered as only you can

in that interval
that condition in between
that is to time, to thought
what water is to sea

you shine there
not because (as I figure it)
you mean to
any more than the sun
means to cast shadows
and creep into rooms

so distracting
grotesque or glittering
is the shape that
appears in
either side of two plates of glass

you whose place is in
the thin surface in between

are not noticed, are missed

but not by those who
not always knowing why
have called, cried out

O ihr Seligen, o ihr Heilen,
die ihr der Anfang der Herzen scheint

as Rilke said of those who
dispersed and ashen
without the sustenance that comes
only from you and from
things made, land tilled
in closeness to you

those whom
unbeknownst to them
heaven once touched

who, in the poet's words,
are the beginning of hearts

3.

A lutenist

the picture of
a lutenist in a dark interior

tells it

a lutenist
painted within
just the right amount
of light

the intense inwardness
the pleasure
of his look

Samuel Hazo

Radius

to Wallace Fowlie

Salted by rain, the ocean
    roughens into clashing circles.
They widen, arc by arc,
    toward predictable collisions
    with the shores.
                        After they shatter,
    you remember you're the core of every
    circle that begins with you.
Like any hub, you center
    six-times-sixty spokes
    that finger outward for the poles,
    the centuries, the stars.
                        You intersect
    a candled dinner at the Ritz,
    the oiled sculpture of a riflestock
    against a hunter's shoulder,
    hummingbirds blown wild as ashes
    in a hurricane.
                        If poetry is traveling
    without a ticket, you're a poet.
You follow every radius
    as far as you can dream.
                        No
    matter where your body's been
    or where it goes or what
    it leaves you to remember, all
    your dreams precede you . . .
Before the astronauts, you left
    your bootprints on the moon.
Pre-dating all the conquerors, you saw
    the cedars of the Lord.

                    The way
        you danced through Paris in your sleep
        makes Paris dance that dream
        awake each time you summer there.
Fulfilling all your prophecies
        by running into them, you're like
        the bull's eye of a world within
        a world around a core that opens
        in the always present to the never
        very far.
                When you stand still,
        you're one of many radiating suns
        until the air becomes the sum
        of circles interlocked like zeros
        on the sea.
                    Each circle's center
        never moves.
                        Each center's circles
        never stop.
                    To be both one
        and all is what they teach you.
Wait, and the rings will reach you.

Sandra Hochman

Celebrating lilies

I have made love to the yellow lilies,
Turned my face against their cool skin,
Led my lips and eyes to their stamens
While I cried to see anything as bright
As these golden lilies.
How I look for them!

There are people who do not explore the in-
Side of flowers, kissing them,
Resting their own tongues on their petals.
I must tell them. Where will I begin?

And I love
Earth, violently, and vegetables,
Stars, and all things that will not break.
My hair smells of melons, marl, jasmine.

Crystal-growing

I hear the sound. It is mostly
The sound of the sea, whining and weeping and suddenly
Letting out its great earthless roar.
It is deafening. I cannot get it out
Of my ears, my nostrils, my belly, my long hair.

It is clear as crystals growing
In a jar. It is the sound of dandelions going
To seed and blowing in the wind like huge great
Shadows which must disappear.

[161]

Barbara Howes

Time

May inch; or fall headlong
to splash through night,
drowning all rhythm.

    At times,
our day struggles one yard ahead:
Inner pedometer footless,
we grey with sloth, the heart cold as a trashcan,
around whose silver flutings we coil—
while the boisterous world
thrashes, gauze-miles away.

    At others, streamlined through hours
which escape backwards—
faces caught for an instant
in the opposite train—
we know one more day year has careened by,
witless as a balloon.

Sometimes, armed with love, the pace
    is just right, night comes when
    it should, after the day's chorale.
We have met again, and meet again
life's colors.

Play of light

My tangerine pig
      Comes from the Ural Mountains—
      A stone so fine
It seizes and holds light—
Light glides over his back,
Returning when he's tiptilted;
      Unlike grandmother's onyx
      Darning-egg, held, warming
Perhaps—my Ural piglet knits
Me—I am nearer stone,
Nearer light.

John Frederick Nims

The madness in Vermont this fall

Stripped of its summer wealth,
Must the bough be wan as a root?
Go dingy in spells of frost,
Untrimmed of its bird, its fruit?

No—trees go wild at the thought.
They know what they mean to do.
Wild trees, gone out of your head?
Do you burn to go south, you too?

Are you trying to be fruit, is it that?
Banana, wild cherry, or plum,
Lemon or apricot, grape
Glow of burgundy's from?

Even worse, are you envying birds?
Playing oriole, tanager—such?
Burn to be tropical wings?
Wildfire in the trees, too much!

Can we keep our heads in a world
With its yankee wit so lost
That the woods are a cry for fire,
And minding the fire is frost?

Reynolds Price

Damon's Epitaph: a translation of *Epitaphium Damonis* by John Milton

Argument. *Thyrsis and Damon, shepherds from the same place, studied together and were friends from boyhood, closest friends. Thyrsis, traveling to perfect understanding, got word of Damon's death. Home again, and the thing true, he deplores himself and his loneliness in this poem. By Da-mon is intended* Charles Diodati, *descended through his father from Etruscan Lucca but otherwise English, a young man singularly gifted in mind, learning, and the other brightest virtues.*

Nymphs of Himera—remember Daphnis, Hylas,
Old grief for Bion—keen down English Thames
Sicilian song, song Thyrsis moans
Imploring caves, streams, springs, deepening woods
For cutdown Damon, stumbling alone
In empty places, dead of night.
Twice now corn has cured on stalk,
As many harvests yellowed into barns
Since strong day swept Damon to dark
And Thyrsis not near—held in Tuscan city
By love of sweet Muse. But when full mind,
Neglected flocks, returned him home
He sat beneath accustomed elm—then knew friend lost,
Poured out the burden of enormous pain:
    "Home, lambs, hungry as I tonight.
Earth, sky, to what gods can I call
Now they have torn you down to death?
Damon, do you consent to go—unnamed—
To join the nameless crowd of shades?
Surely with golden bough the Guide of Souls
Leads you to worthy company,
Bays back dumb slugs of death?
    Home, lambs, hungry as I tonight.

Come whatever, know—if no wolf see me first—
You will not rot in grave unmourned;
Name will last, honored by shepherds
Second to Daphnis, sung second to him
Long as Pales, Faunus, love land—
If you chose well in keeping Old Faith,
Learning arts, loving a poet.
 Home, lambs, hungry as I tonight.
All that is yours now, all those prizes wait;
But Damon, me? Who'll cling in faith to me
Through cruel cold on iron ground
Like you, through parching weeds
Under hard sun to drive great lions
From our high folds, or avid wolves?
Who'll drug days with talk and song?
 Home, lambs, hungry as I tonight.
Who'll take my heart, soothe biting cares?
Who'll cheat long nights with gentle talk,
Pears spitting in fire, nuts splitting on hearth,
Bad wind crashing beyond in elms?
 Home, lambs, hungry as I tonight.
Or summer days impaled by noon—
Pan hid asleep in oakshade, nymphs swum
To cooler depths, shepherds crouched,
Plowman snoring under hedge—
Who'll bring me charm of your laughing
Greek salt, smiling wisdom?
 Home, lambs, hungry as I tonight.
Alone through furrows, pastures alone
I wander toward dense valleys, waiting night;
East wind and rain moan above
Making, canceling, shadows in the boughs.
 Home, lambs, hungry as I tonight.
My best fields—gone to rude weeds,
Corn molds on stalk, unwed grapes
Dry in clusters, myrtles count less
To me than sheep who beg for care—
 Home, lambs, hungry as I tonight—
As Tityrus calls me to his hazels,
Alphesiboeus to his aspens, Aegon to willows,

Beautiful Amyntas to rivers: 'Here cool,
Here sweet, here soft, here gentle; here arbutus
And water swap peaceful silence.'
They sing to stone. I plunge on deeper.
    Home, lambs, hungry as I tonight.
Mopsus—skilled in tongues of birds and
Stars—sees me returning: 'Thyrsis,
Why? Either love wastes you or
Bad star fixes on you ruinous.
Saturn has always hated shepherds,
Shot lead death through hearts of many.'
    Home, lambs, hungry as I tonight.
Then nymphs, astonished—'Thyrsis, what now?
No boy should bear such clouded face,
Frowning eyes. Boys run to dancing,
Laughing, love. Double pains, who wait to love.'
    Home, lambs, hungry as I tonight—
Then Hyas, Dryope, Aegle daughter of Baucis—
Skilled at music and lute but lost to pride—
Chloris from Blackwater: nothing to me.
Charms, soothing words—nothing here pleases, promises.
    Home, lambs, hungry as I tonight.
Even the cattle are playing together!—
All one-hearted, bound by one law
Yet none takes single mate from herd.
Wolves flock to eat, wild asses join
By turns at shaggy random.
Seas obey the law—on unknown shores
Seals calve in hordes. Vile sparrows
Flit from seed to seed companioned,
Return at dusk to mutual nests.
Let mate fall, hawk swoop,
Hunter strike—take nearest next,
Never break flight. But Man, hard man,
Flung by harder fate, mind cut from mind,
Heart hating heart. Find one in thousands—
Luck, blessed luck. And that one found—
Long prayer answered—day comes unseen,
Hour comes and claims him, leaves time desert.
    Home, lambs, hungry as I tonight.

What wild lust for moving dragged me off
To unknown land through white rock Alp?
What so precious in buried heart of Rome—
Even if she lay as in days of Tityrus
Who left flocks, country, to see her—
That I could leave you, sweet companion,
Set seas between us, crags, woods, streams?
Ah surely if I'd stayed they'd have let me—
One final time—touch your right hand,
Close dying eyes in peace, and say
'Farewell, through stars remember me.'
  Home, lambs, hungry as I tonight.
Still, I'll never regret you, Tuscan shepherds,
Young hands for Muse—your open charm.
Damon, you were Tuscan, through your line
Drawn from old Lucomo, ancient city.
And I—how grand I was, extended there
In poplar grove on bedded grass,
Arno cool and murmuring beside,
Picking now violets, now high myrtle,
Menalcas and Lycidas striving.
I even strove myself nor much displeased,
I think, since here are gifts I won—
Rush baskets, willow chains, pipes bound with wax—
And Dati and Francini, both Etruscans
Famed for song and study, taught my name
In song to native beeches.
  Home, lambs, hungry as I tonight.
Such things the damp moon told me
When, happy, I was penning kids alone.
Ah how often I'd say 'Now Damon's singing,
Baiting traps for hares, plaiting willows';
With simple mind I'd plan our wanted future,
See it there—'Friend, are you busy?
If nothing holds you, shall we lie
In shade and talk by waters of Colne
Or above at Cassibelaunus? You can tell me
All your medicines, herbs—hellebore, poor crocus,
Hyacinth leaf—tell me what cures
This pond grows, healing arts.'

Perish herbs, perish healing arts
That failed their master.
For me—eleven days and nights ago my pipe
Sounded unfamiliar grand notes.
I was shaping my lips to new reeds
When binding broke, reeds failed
Grave music. Doubting, still I'll speak—
Yield, country song, to what comes now.
    Home, lambs, hungry as I tonight.
I myself will sing Dardanian prows
On level seas Rutupian, ancient land
Of Inogene, Pandrasus' daughter, Brennus and
Arviragus both chiefs, and old Belinus;
British colonists of Bretony. At last
Then Igraine great with Arthur, guiled by Merlin
And the lying face that wore her Gorlois' arms.
Oh if I live, you shepherd-pipe
Must hang forgot on twisted pine
Or change to songs of home, cries of Britons.
Why them?—one man is not permitted all,
May not hope all. Enough for me—
Reward and honor though I go unknown,
Unglorified among all other nations—
If I be read by golden-headed Ouse,
And them who drink from Alne, twisting Humber,
Woods of Trent, above all Thames—if Thames
Will sing my songs, rusty Tamar;
Wave-racked Orkneys, far, learn me.
    Home, lambs, hungry as I tonight.
Those things I saved for you, in laurel bark,
Those and many like—cups
Mansus gave me, Mansus not the least glory
Of Chalcidian shores—wondrous works of art,
Wondrous himself, carved round with double legend:
In center, Red Sea rolls, spring and balsams
Scent Arabian distances. Among them Phoenix,
Godly bird, single on earth, flames cerulean
Mottled wings, awaiting dawn on glassy waves.
Elsewhere what seems Olympus, huge spread sky,
And armèd Love set forth in clouds,

Torch and brazen arrows flashing. But not at earthly herds
He shoots, frail vulgar souls—eyes blazing, rolling,
Aims toward heaven, steady target:
Hits. Whence saints burn ardent, essences of Gods.
You're there! Unless false hope deceives me,
Surely there—else, where your holy sweet simplicity,
Your lustrous virtue? Useless to hunt you
By Lethean Orcus, useless, to mourn—
I'll never mourn. Dry, tears. Pure Damon
Dwells in air, pure air; feet spurn rainbow.
Among heroic souls, eternal Gods, his sacred lips
Drink paradise, drink joy. And now that you
Possess the rights of heaven, stand on my right;
Show me mild favor however I call you—
Damon-that-was, here among our woods,
Or *Gift of God*, name holy, known by Gods.
Because you saved your blood of youth nor soiled,
Because you never drank the joys of bed,
For virgin you they serve you full rewards—
Head shining ringed with crimson crown,
Hands bearing palmleaf shades, you last
Through endless acts of endless Hymen
To song and mad harp threading choruses,
Wine feasts and orgies, sprouting wands of Zion."

Harvey Shapiro

Brooklyn streets

Verlaine's Paris rain
On the Brooklyn streets
Slick with sentiment.

Someone walking
Home, 2:30 in the
Morning, like an old song.

Every man

Every man lives his life
Against some question
If he lives at all.

To make this world perfect and full of splendor,
Was this indeed anybody's wish?
I look around me and inside me.

In my own night head,
Drinking slowly, smoking slowly,
The city at my back.
Both of us making
The long recovery to morning.

O Seasons

It seemed reasonable to expect an answer.
That was an early feeling, like owning something.

Urban dawn, and yet to hear the birds.
I must have that happiness.

Song

O'kay, it is night
And my own
Astral mind
Sings peace.

At the start and at the finish
What we want
Is to be close to the living,
Our heads against the skin
Of the song.

Karl Shapiro

T. S. E.

Coming slowly down the aisle,
Mounting the podium with baronial tread,
Very solemn and slightly stooped,
As if in awe of his stupendous stature,
The responsibility which he has created,
The hush he has summoned,
He carries his poems in two slim volumes,
Holding them lightly in one hand
And touched by the fingers of the other hand,
Sensing rather than carrying his books,
His mythic poetry that has stunned the world.

W. B. Y.

Shooting me in my study a cameraman
Panned upward to my highest shelf of books,
The X-Y-Z's that end the alphabet
Of poets of every flag, when suddenly
He spied a perfect spiderweb,
Invisible except to the cunning eye.
There from the ceiling delicately hung
The draglines and the swathing bands
Of viscid spider-silk caging and veiling
What journalists would call One of the Greats,
The poetry and prose of William Butler Yeats.

Theodore Weiss

The aerialist

dos moi pou sto

Even if you could
you would not change it, could
not get away.
         For what you had
to say, this thought gripping you
as much as passion, terror,
it must be Paris.
         Must be
the place—its chimney pots prim,
a smoke still wisping out of them
and with the laundry a St. Vitus
by the soaring cries of children
pouring forth—where it took place,

the moment like spring surprising
spring, its cocky feathers bobbing,
in that cloistered garden,
         surged
out of nubbly things, a light
nimbusing them and beyond them.

Only Paris could have made it
possible; only there could it
have happened in that particular
shape, thereafter fitting any
other place.
         A truth it was
swept over them, swept through,
needing all of them to be, to be
closely kin to them.

Yet different:
a moment like a glance opening
the world,
            then promptly lidding
down, the clay peering through
the flowers, the mud sounding out
the skylark's loftiest trill, as in
its clambering wings.
                    And still
mud, starting up, walks like a man,
stalks into each flower, feathers
off in flight and flutings
a lark gives itself to.
                    Stones
let's say, nuggets, dawn-glistening,
the shapely, rugged words a god
might bubble forth.
                    As you,
a Frenchman, come down for a moment
from your wire, your dapper over-
seeing of Paris, answer questions.

"Why do it? Because I love
the air up there, the solitude,
the one sure step—room for no other—
after another.
            Fear? I've none.
This work is exact."
                    So you have
gone beyond the topmost snow-
capped cliff, the exploits, of Everest;
alone, with no equipment, you stride
out on glassy crags, blue as
a gaze; do it because it's not there,

the frank and bracing air of Paris.

PART V

Symbolism and after

Henri Peyre

Poets against music in
the age of Symbolism

For Wallace Fowlie, scholar, critic, poet, musician

Of all the sources of confusion to which loose thinking and vague terminology expose unwary critics, none has proved more prodigal of mis-
understandings than the glib use, by commentators on poetry, of words
such as "musical," "melodious," "modulated," not to mention "counter-
point" or "fugue." Advocates of traditional wisdom like Irving Babbitt
denounced such confusion between the media of different arts and echoed
the warning once issued by Lessing in his *Laokoon*. Theorists of criticism
like René Wellek and Calvin Brown have pointed to the pitfall of borrowing
the terminology of one art and of applying it to a different one.[1] The peril
may be scant as long as one talks, in pleasantly metaphorical language, of
"the music of a picture" as did Delacroix, or lectures "On the Music of
Poetry," as T. S. Eliot did, very guardedly, in 1942.[2] It is greater when
writers on the Symbolist movement and apostles of pure poetry uncritically
adopt the striking and peremptory assertion of Walter Pater, in his essay
on the School of Giorgione, according to which "all art constantly strives
towards the condition of music." The assertion is patently gratuitous, since
neither the architecture nor the sculpture, not even the poetry of the centuries which preceded the nineteenth, ever aspired to the condition of
music. Even with the romantic poets who are most frequently dubbed
"musical"—Brentano, Heine, Shelley, Lamartine, Tuchev—very few were
keenly sensitive to music or consciously borrowed from that art. Were the

1. René Wellek, "The Parallelism Between Literature and the Arts," *English Institute
Annual* (1941); Calvin S. Brown, *Music and Literature: A Comparison of the Arts*
(Athens: Univ. of Georgia Press, 1948). See also a learned essay by Steven Paul Scher,
"How Meaningful Is 'Musical' in Literary Criticism?" *Yearbook of Comparative Literature*, 21 (1972), 52–56.
2. T. S. Eliot insisted, in that lecture in memory of the scholar W. P. Ker, that "the
music of poetry is not something which exists apart from the meaning."

French Symbolists any closer to either the vocal or the orchestral music of their time?

Verlaine never bothered to elaborate on the famous opening line of his "Art poétique." How much he cared for, or knew about, music is hard to tell. He was the brother-in-law of a musician, Charles de Sivry, to whom we indirectly owe the preservation of Rimbaud's *Illuminations*, which Verlaine had entrusted to him. A number of Verlaine's shorter poems (but few of the longer and more tragic ones) have been repeatedly set to music. They paradoxically earned for their author, who behaved more than once as an inebriated and uncontrollable faun, the reputation of a bard for coy virgins whom their mothers accompanied on the family piano. Verlaine seems to have been endowed with a more sensitive ear for music than many of his fellow poets. His sonnet on Parsifal, in the collective French tribute to Wagner in 1886, reveals a keener insight into Wagnerism than was evinced by the other contributors.

His exclamation "De la musique avant toute chose!" has been interpreted by some as an abdication of poetry before the sister art. In fact, all that Verlaine advocates is turning away from the plastic aspects of poetry which the Parnassians had favored and cultivating vagueness, mystery, suggestion, and what the psychologist Th. Ribot was to call a type of "diffluent imagination." Huysmans, who knew little about music and cared even less for it, praised Verlaine's poetry for "something vague about it, similar to a music which allows of dreams on the beyond." Among the less esoteric adjectives favored by the Symbolists were those which pointed to the allegedly "musical" qualities of poetry: "fluid," "evanescent," "melodious," "ineffable," and, more simply still, "indefinite." E. A. Poe had declared that true music requires "a suggested indefiniteness, bringing about a definiteness of vague and therefore of spiritual effect." The formula is not especially felicitous. The author of "Bells" and "Ulalume," whom Emerson derided as "the jingle man," has not usually struck English and American ears as the most delicately harmonious of poets. Foreigners on the other hand, and the French in particular, hailed him as a virtuoso of "l'indécis joint au précis," before Valéry made a lifelong cult of him as the paragon of lucid rigor. Somewhat similarly, French admirers of Wagner, who from 1880 on, atoning for the previous anti-Wagnerian outcry by French patriots, were more numerous and more ardent than the German men of letters, praised him for being one of the "Grands Imprécistes du XIXe siècle." Such is the surprising title of a book, celebrating Wagner alongside Turner and Corot, by Léon Arnoult (1930). In music, and in the literature which was thought to ape and to rival music, many French people cherished a dimly perceived meaning and a half-veiled beauty, laden with mystery and affording an initiation into the world of dreams.[3] Even such a would-be scientific theorist and atrociously jerky and flat versifier as René Ghil claimed to transfer into poetry "the music of flavors, of colors, of fragrances and of rumors," the last of those substantives implying more vague echoes than the mere word "sounds."

Only a few of the Symbolists had actually read much Schopenhauer. Still, they had absorbed from him a few notions on the privilege music enjoys of penetrating to the essence of things. The German pessimist had derided opera and poured his scorn on the music which resorts to speech and to attitudinizing. He probably would not long have acknowledged as his true disciple Wagner, with his claim to having founded the synthesis of the arts in his opera (Schopenhauer died in 1860, before *Tristan, Die Walkyrie,* and *Parsifal*). Truly great music to him was nonconceptual and could not assimilate words. The superiority of music lay in its being the one art altogether free from the world of appearances, which labors under the illusion that the phenomenal matters. For the French poets and theorists who heard about Schopenhauerian philosophy, "the real, because it is live," in Mallarmé's words, can be crossed off. Its scant and sordid function is to provide the raw material for a higher, symbolic interpretation.

The Symbolist poets of France composed a number of pieces which literary critics have been accustomed to term "musical" because they are delicate, fluid, and soft and often conjure up a world of dreams; they express a nostalgia for an "anterior life" or for the land of heart's desire, for a love purified from brutal desire, which addresses the loved one as "un paysage choisi" or a "blessed damozel." From Baudelaire's "Invitation au voyage" and Mallarmé's "Apparition" to poems by Léon Dierx, Albert Samain, and others, the list of pieces which attracted composers as lending themselves to be sung to their music is a long one. Later still, a poet who did not view himself as a direct heir to the Symbolists, Apollinaire, proved a favorite with composers. Other poets who had not particularly striven for what is commonly called musicality in poetry—Laforgue in his humorous ballads to or on the moon, Char with "Le Marteau sans maître"—have tempted and after a fashion inspired great composers. Often, however, the pieces favored by the musicians who wrote songs, from Duparc and De-

3. The book is mentioned in the remarkably learned and sensitive two-volume study, *Debussy: His Life and Mind,* by the late Edward Lockspeiser (London, 1962 and 1965). The author also discusses the enormous impact which Poe made on Debussy, who had projected an opera on "The Fall of the House of Usher."

bussy down to Poulenc, were the lighter works of Baudelaire, Verlaine, Mallarmé, or else the elegant "Odelettes" by Henri de Régnier, the more suave and dreamy poems in Moréas' *Cantilènes*, or in Stuart Merrill and Vielé-Griffin.

It would be a mistake, however, to believe that the verse written during the so-called Symbolist era and by poets who for a time gravitated around the Symbolist *cénacles* enjoyed a monopoly of tempting musical composers. In this domain, as in several others, no clear partition ever separated the Symbolists from their Parnassian predecessors or from Hugo. The fashion has been, for the middle of the twentieth century, to relegate Gautier and Banville to a secondary rank or even to a lower one, as poets for whom the exterior world existed almost exclusively. Foreign admirers of French poetry in Germany, Britain, Spain, thought otherwise. The lessons of technique to be learned from those two poets appeared to them at least as valuable as the models of languid and disembodied poetry provided by the Symbolists. The extraordinary, fruitful, and lasting impact of Gautier's verse outside France, the no less wide and prolonged appeal of Banville to a poet like Mallarmé (and to many others around him) should give us pause and perhaps invite us to revise our perspective on French poetry between 1840 and 1900. A similar revision, assigning an astonishingly exalted position to Romantic artists erstwhile dismissed as minor, or to Corot and to Millet, has been attempted since 1970 in the realm of painting.

It is more disturbing for literary purists to find that, along with pieces of great merit and indeed of rare "musical" charm such as Leconte de Lisle's "Fille aux cheveux de lin" and "Epiphanie," awkward, platitudinous, and on every count mediocre poems (by Jean Lahor, Sully-Prudhomme, Armand Silvestre) and weak, sentimental ones from Paul Bourget's "Les Aveux" have been selected by musicians, apparently with no revulsion against their banality. Do composers tend to grant their preference to a mediocre text, so that they can outshine it more easily? Are they unable to discriminate between the very great flowers in *Les Fleurs du mal* and the lighter and more facile ones there, or between "La Lune blanche" or "Les Sanglots longs" by Verlaine and his mature and deeper verse? Are they perhaps almost as insensitive to the literary qualities of a poetical text as men of letters so often are to music? "Soupir" and "Placet futile" by Mallarmé were easier for Debussy to use as a pretext for his music than the more truly Mallarmean pieces, and so for Webern were Baudelaire's hardly inspired poems on wine. We know how unenthusiastic Mallarmé felt about Debussy's composing a musical prelude to his most delicately sensuous poem, since he thought he had already endowed it with all the music it might need. Maeterlinck, who was practically deaf to music, came near to fighting a duel with Debussy about the singer who was to impersonate Mélisande. He was, understandably enough and for a less personal motive, irked when he heard it repeated around him that Debussy's *Pelléas et Mélisande*, and not his own text, was to be extolled as *the* masterpiece of Symbolism.

The estrangement between poets and musicians is probably a chronic one. Paradoxically, it appears to be much easier to speak of the symphonic structure of a novel than to apply musical terminology to the exegesis of poetry. We have heard enough, and perhaps too much, on the Wagnerian composition of Proust's saga novel. The recurrence of themes, *leitmotive*, through hundreds of pages, can be less obsessive and more palatable in a full-fledged novel than in a poem, even if the poem is Lamartine's "Les Préludes" or Swinburne's "Triumph of Time." Of all the novelists of the twentieth century, none felt closer to music or was better versed in it than Thomas Mann—far more so than Romain Rolland, who, an expert in musical history, avoided trying to impose a symphonic structure upon his series of stories on the career of the musician Jean-Christophe. *The Magic Mountain* constitutes the most expert and sustained attempt at enclosing a complex novel, replete with debates of ideas, in a subtly musical orchestration. Thomas Mann had proved even more successful in his shorter, Wagner-obsessed *Tristan* and in his early *Tonio Kröger*. "Here probably," he declared apropos of the latter, "I first learned to use music as a shaping influence in my art."

Much has been written, after diligent research and often from contrasting points of view, on the relationship between French Symbolism and the Wagnerian music drama, and more particularly on Mallarmé and music.[4] From all accounts by his friends and disciples (if Valéry may be called a disciple of the man whom he had, as he declared, adored), Mallarmé had very little musical culture and took only a scant interest, and even less

4. Kurt Jaeckel, *Richard Wagner in der französischen Literatur*, 2 vols. (Breslau, 1931, 1932) ; Léon Guichard, in *La Musique et les lettres en France au temps du Wagnérisme* (Paris, 1963), who repeatedly takes issue with Jaeckel's exaggerated claims for Wagner's influence on French writers; Suzanne Bernard, *Mallarmé et la musique* (Paris, 1959). Among the mass of articles on the subject, the one by Aimé Patri, "Mallarmé et la musique du silence," in the rich and fat issue of the *Revue Musicale*, No. 210, Jan. 1952, devoted to French literature and music since 1900, deserves a special mention.

pleasure, in concert music. He had gracefully, in "Sainte," evoked the quaint poetical charm of ancient musical instruments and ended that sixteen-line poem with a tribute to unheard melodies: "Musicienne du silence." He had been fascinated with the look of musical notes on the page, those hieroglyphics in a "grimoire," or wizard's book of scribbled spells, which only the initiated could decipher. He naturally heard much rapturous praise of Wagner from his friends such as the early French enthusiasts of the Master: Villiers de l'Isle Adam, Catulle Mendès. In 1885 Edouard Dujardin, the Frenchman who, with Théodore de Wyzewa, Polish-born connoisseur of music and of several literatures, directed the *Revue Wagnérienne*, took Mallarmé to the Sunday Concerts Lamoureux to listen to Wagner. Mallarmé listened dutifully, took down notes, attempted, from the fragments of Wagnerian operas thus heard, to form some notion of musical structure. The architectural value of those compositions and the hieratic, almost religious character of that music, keeping away the uninitiated, impressed him strongly. But he never seems to have perceived or enjoyed those extracts from Wagnerian operas *as music*, and he apparently was even less eager to listen to solos by violinists or cellists or to singers. His best-known prose essay on Wagner, which he found very difficult to write, was aptly subtitled "Reverie of a French Poet" apropos of the German composer. In it he vented what Valéry characterized as "his sublime jealousy." There, and in the oft-quoted introduction, or foreword ("avant-dire") to René Ghil's *Traité du verbe* (1886), repeated verbatim in "Crise de vers," Mallarmé rejected the claim of Wagnerian music drama to subordinate poetry to music. The intellectualist in him proclaimed, on the contrary, as Kant and Hegel had done, the primacy of poetry over music. "Le Livre," the Book that he dreamt of composing, would marry sense and sound; it would be read, and not just heard. Indeed, insofar as "Le Coup de dés" offers an approximation to that grandiose dream, it would be visual, and not auditive, poetry. In the face of the Wagnerian offensive, Mallarmé regarded it as the sacred mission and the duty of poets to "retrieve from music their own good." He saw, in the popularity of that imperialistic Wagnerian drama, the wreckage of his own dream of a Mallarmean theatre.[5]

5. Francis Vielé-Griffin, the American-born poet (more sensitive to music and better-informed on Wagner than most Frenchmen, as was also his compatriot Stuart Merrill), tried in vain to argue with Mallarmé that, the word being inaccessible to the masses, music, less forbidding than Mallarmean poetry, would "make Symbolist expression possible." See Vielé-Griffin's article, "Le Symbolisme et la musique," *La Phalange*, 15 Oct. 1908, pp. 193–98.

Paul Valéry made his own Mallarmé's war cry against music, and he
extended to the Symbolist movement in general that determination of
poetry to snatch back from music what was, and should have remained,
its own rightful possession. His own attitudes toward music, however, were
far more ambivalent or even contradictory. The publication of the *Cahiers*
in the two volumes of the Pléiade edition in 1974 will enable scholars from
now on to follow in detail, if not necessarily to reconcile, Valéry's con-
flicting statements on music and on Wagner in particular. When more
letters written in his younger years to the friends in whom he confided
most, notably Pierre Louÿs, come to light, it may become possible to put
together something approximating a philosophy and an aesthetics of the
musical art in that relentless foe of philosophy and of aesthetics. Allusions
to Bach are extremely few in Valéry's notes, and not especially warm.
Mozart is almost never mentioned. We know that Valéry had the recitatives
of Gluck in mind when he worked on passages in *La Jeune Parque*. One of
the insolent remarks, wilfully paradoxical (the French call them "boutades"
and like to stud their conversations, or monologues, with them) jotted
down by Valéry in 1916 in his *Cahiers* (II, 935–36) calls Beethoven "an
imbecile prodigiously gifted for the sonorous pantomime," which, strangely,
moves some natures. It ends with the irreverent question: "Must genius
obey what is most stupid?" (the word "bête" carries more connotations
than "stupid"). The answer is that the "bêtise" lies in ascribing profound
significance and mystery to powerful effects, more purgative than deep;
music is denounced as an "art of simulation." The one composer whom
Valéry, like Claudel, alternately admired and derided was Wagner. Indeed, the Parque's invocation to spring and her appeal to death, and the
delirium of the Pythia and other impassioned passages in Valéry have
more than once been recited as if they were sonorously and tempestuously
Wagnerian.[6]

The feelings generated in Valéry by music were those of envy and of
despair. "Beauty is what throws us into despair," he would repeat apropos
of Mallarmé. And music filled him with that sentiment almost as much as
did the perfection achieved by Mallarmé. One of the "few thoughts of M.
Teste" which follow the text of Valéry's short novel in the Pléiade edition
(II, 70) voices that negative tribute to the power of music. In 1914 he
compares music to a massage, "producing an electric effect on certain

6. Many a valuable remark touching on Valéry's jealousy of music will be found in
Edouard Gaède's remarkable volume *Nietzsche et Valéry: Essai sur la comédie de l'esprit*
(Paris, 1962). See also the article by J. Duchesne-Guillemin, "Valéry et la musique," in
the number of *Revue Musicale*, No. 210, Jan. 1952, pp. 113–21.

muscles and combinations of muscles, the simultaneous contraction of which corresponds to no known emotion" (*Cahiers*, II, 934). In 1917, when he was already the author of *La Jeune Parque* and exchanged many a letter with Pierre Louÿs on the prospective title and on the intent of his long poem, he warned that close friend of Debussy: "Let us not forget that we stand *against* music: Apollo against Dionysos." The allusion is of course to Nietzsche, and Valéry repeats the German philosopher's Latin warning: "Cave musicam." He accuses music of luring our will power into a slumber and of playing havoc with all our affective mechanisms. He confesses almost pathetically: "Music intimidates me, and the art of the musician throws me into confusion. He disposes of all the powers that I envy" (June 10 and 13, 1917). He attacks music even more frontally in the jottings of his *Cahiers* of the years 1916–17, well aware of his "injustice" to that dreaded art, going so far as to revile it as "an art of lies, of echolalias, of idiotic mimicries. . . . In the old days, it was used only at weddings, at ceremonies, military pageants and serenades . . ." (II, 936). He is not far from viewing it as a typically and dangerously Germanic art. True, 1917 was during World War I, when he feared for the survival of European culture and labored on his longest poem to offer a last homage to the French language. Still, he pretended to regret the time when Dionysos had been made by the ancients subservient to Apollo. "For a thousand years, the Boche had been restricted to his forests" (letters to Louÿs cited above).

Later, having become the friend of many a dancer and musician, Honegger among others,[7] Valéry expressed himself less bluntly, or more like a venerable Academician. Again and again, he recurred to Wagner, stating his admiration for his incomparable nervous energy (*Cahiers*, II, 973), seeing in him an illusionist without par, who gave the impression of being "the greatest man possible" (in 1933; *Cahiers*, II, 962). He had earlier defined him through an equation: "Shakespeare plus Beethoven," unknowingly echoing a remark by Nietzsche, as Gaède pointed out: "Shakespeare and Beethoven beside each other." And he confessed that he had learned much from Wagner, precisely because he was, by his music, plunged into despair (*Cahiers*, II, 979). Unable and unwilling to emulate the uncanny power of Wagnerian music upon our physical organism, unable, as he added, to tolerate hearing music very long—because it impeded the very thoughts that it had aroused in him (II, 476)—Valéry went back

7. Valéry had, with Honegger, composed his *Semiramis* and his *Amphion*. Still, he refused to write on him when the *Revue Musicale* invited him to (*Lettres à Quelques-uns*, 14 June 1942), making this confession: "Where music is concerned, I know only my ear, its pleasure or its displeasure, its demand or its refusal."

to the relative simplicity and (he, the obscurist) to the "clarity" of music before Bach and Wagner, to the recitatives of Gluck. He fled the confusion, the brutality, the power of Wagner, "the great power of unleashing inane tempests and of opening up empty abysses" (II, 706). Perhaps he also fled life. He, who disliked Flaubert inwardly, must have been stung by the same doubt as had assailed the author of *Salammbô* when the latter noted, in an anguished admission, the necessity of "through the beautiful creating nevertheless [*quand même*] something true and alive."

The jealous distrust of Wagner, extending to a more general dislike of music in many of the best minds of the years 1885–1920 in France, stemmed in part from an impatient reaction against the plethora of foolish and bumptious eulogies of Wagnerism which had been uttered by admirers of "the god Richard Wagner," as Mallarmé had called him in his sonnet. It had become the fashion, in Dujardin's *Revue Wagnérienne* and elsewhere, to identify Wagnerism and Symbolism. It had favored mental or simply verbal confusionism between the musical and the literary media. René Ghil, Albert Mockel, Paul Adam poured out declamatory effusions on and around music which the Parisian public, having lost (if it ever had it) all feeling for the ridiculous, applauded. Early in the history of Wagnerism in France, in 1857, in the official newspaper of the Second Empire, Théophile Gautier, who had no ear and little respect for music, had accumulated gaffe upon gaffe in appraising "technically" the merits of *Tannhäuser*. His daughter Judith, an authentic Wagnerian, had to confess in her memoirs her sense of shame at her father's imprudence. Huysmans, who had no more ear for music than Gautier, wrote even more pretentiously and ludicrously on the overture to *Tannhäuser* in the *Revue Wagnérienne* of 1885–87, at a time when he should have known better.[8] A very few Frenchmen evinced a real competence in judging the Wagnerian opera fairly, on its musical and technical merits. They forgot, or forgave, the partisan and callous prose writings of Wagner, in which he attacked indiscriminately the Jews, the French nation, and his own forerunners and childishly insulted the French for being defeated in 1871. The Alsatian Edouard Schuré proved by far the most sensitive and the best informed. Jules Laforgue, among the poets, kept his sanity and his sense of humor. But he did not live long enough to exercise any influence. In spite of his ill-advised intrusions into philosophy, politics, literature, and myth, Wagner had wished,

8. André Cœuroy has collected a number of judgments pronounced by French men of letters on Wagner and commented upon them shrewdly and acidly in a small book, *Wagner et l'esprit romantique* (Paris, 1965).

and deserved, to be judged on his music. He had warned that "the alleged intimate relation between music and poetry is a mere illusion." A poet then young and destined to greatness, Paul Claudel, who was later to be alternately fascinated and repelled by Wagnerian drama, proved more aware than others in the Symbolist circles of the harm that the confusion between music and poetry was causing among the poets. He was not yet thirty and still unknown when, having read Mallarmé's essay "Music and Letters" advocating independence from, if not hostility toward, music, he sent to the master a letter reprinted in the notes to the Pléiade edition of Mallarmé. The date was March 25, 1895:

> The proximity of that raving woman, music, has proved so harmful to many of today's writers that it is pleasant to see someone impose limits upon it authoritatively, in the name of the articulated word. If Music and Poetry are indeed identical in their principle, which is the same need of an inner noise to express, and in their end, which is the representation of a fictitious state of bliss, the Poet asserts and explains, where the other one goes shouting, like one who is seeking: one receives pleasure, and the other one possesses, his prerogative being that of giving a name to all things. No mind had, as much as yours, the right to claim that high privilege of Letters in which you are the acknowledged master: intelligence.

A French musical critic with a sincere love for music and a talent for intelligent popularization, B. Gavoty, asked the question, in the title of a book (1950): *Are the French Musical?* Not a few of his compatriots would probably answer negatively, and they would hardly feel apologetic about it. Valéry liked to argue that the very originality of the French language, with its softened vowels, its weak consonants, its hardly audible tonic accent, may account for the difficulty of making French verse musical (*Cahiers*, II, 1124). The explanation is a dubious one, coming from one who, elsewhere, rightly praised the "musicality" of Mallarmé's Faun. Large is the number of foreigners who have praised, above all other poetries, that of Racine, Nerval, Baudelaire, Verlaine, Valéry as being the most "musical" of all, precisely because it is not spoiled by strong beats and because its metrical possibilities are more varied and subtle. The French have not had, since the eighteenth century, as rich an output of *lieder* or of ballads as either their German or their British neighbors. They have evinced more reluctance than others to severing sound from meaning, and they have neither sought nor achieved much success with doggerel. To what extent is it a lack or a fault? T. S. Eliot, who disliked Swinburne for having more musical alliterations and assonances than content and who for a time berated Shelley for having settled, in his "Skylark," for sound without sense, declared, in his lecture "The Music of Poetry," that "a 'musical poem' is a poem which has a musical pattern of sound and a musical pattern of the secondary meanings of the words which compose it, and these two patterns are indissoluble and one."

Generalizations about the native national gifts of peoples and of races offer a fertile ground for adventurous and probably idle speculations. The number of poets who were insensitive to music is no less striking in other Western literatures than in the French. Walt Whitman—so writes an expert on the relations between the two arts[9]—"must have been practically a musical illiterate, for his references to music are of uniform and magnificent banality." None of the great English romantics seems to have had much fondness for music. W. B. Yeats enjoyed having Florence Farr, a beautiful lady and a musical one, playing a psaltery and singing or reciting his verse. "Her speech was music," he said. He made room for music, vocal or instrumental, in every one of his dramas. But he maintained that music was the servant of poetry and he was apparently tone-deaf himself. To a friend, Monk Gibbon, he avowed in 1931: "I have no ear for music, don't know one tune from another. Music impresses me, but I can no more judge of its quality than I can of thunder or the sound of the wind".[10] It is well known that Goethe altogether failed to enjoy or to understand Beethoven's music. He never bothered to acknowledge Schubert's "Erlkönig"; he never even answered Berlioz, who in 1829 had sent to him "Mephisto's Serenade," while he was praising the ballads of Béranger. He confessed to Eckermann his insensitivity to Mozart, and he never attended a single concert or opera while traveling in Italy. "The eye was the chief organ through which I embraced the world," he pompously declared in his memoirs. Schubert and Beethoven, on the other hand, often preferred mediocre poems to set to music, instead of the most sensitive and thoughtful ones by Goethe, Schiller, Eichendorff, Hölderlin. Max Brod remarked that Kafka, who could write a prose which we like to call euphonic, had no gift for pure music. He once stated that he could not tell *The Merry Widow* from

9. Calvin Brown, *Music and Literature*, p. 178.
10. These words are reported in Edward Malins, "Yeats and Music" in *The Dolmen Press Yeats Centenary Papers* (1965), (Dublin, 1969), pp. 490 and 507.

Tristan. He would refuse to accompany Brod to concerts and complained that Brahms' music rose like a wall around him and afflicted him with a sense of claustrophobia.

The list of Apollinaire's poems set to music is a very long one. It was published as an appendix to a volume of studies, *Apollinaire and Music,* first read at a gathering in Stavelot, Belgium, in 1965. The authors of the several articles in French in the book did their best not to betray their embarrassment, for they could not dodge the fact that Apollinaire had neither ear nor taste for music—"Music, of which I am totally ignorant," he confessed. All he had remembered from his younger days was Schumann's "Love Song" and the "Evening Star" in Tannhäuser. But Georges Auric, Arthur Honegger, Francis Poulenc, and others took over his poems and found in them inspiration for their musical compositions. Poulenc was discreet enough to leave most of the volume of *Alcools* alone, for he thought that its poetry was musical enough as it was; he chose rather to select pieces from *Il y a,* and he composed music only for "Rosemonde," a fifteen-line piece from *Alcools,* which hardly inspired him. He wisely remarked that "setting a poem to music is a way of letting the poet realize his own inadequacy." Apollinaire did not object. He merely acknowledged that the pictorial art attracted him more than the musical one. If his poems, "Chanson du mal-aimé," "le Pont Mirabeau," "O ma jeunesse abandonnée," count among the most "musical" in modern French, they are never mere sounds detached from thought or from feeling. At other times, as in "La Maison des morts" (in *Alcools*), he first wrote the piece in prose, then cut up the lines of prose so as to present them as unrhymed verses of unequal length, with total unconcern for the so-called musical values of the lines. "Le Musicien de Saint-Merry" in *Calligrammes* might just as well have been printed as a prose tale, from which a heart-rending pathos emanates. Indeed, the most experimental pieces in *Calligrammes* are nothing less than an attempt to displace auditive values in poetry in favor of the visual ones.

André Breton met Apollinaire while both served in the French Army, and he may have been confirmed by the older poet in his distaste for music. With Breton, the refusal to let musicians collaborate with poets amounts to a declaration of war. Painting, sculpture, the cinema were the only arts allowed by the Surrealist credo. Eluard, Aragon, Desnos, whose poetry is commonly judged to lend itself particularly to being sung, did not voice any more sympathy for music than did Breton.[11] In 1950 Breton launched

11. A very good essay—Michel Carrouges, "Le Surréalisme à l'écoute," *Revue Musicale,*

an angry antimusical manifesto entitled "Silence d'or": a clear allusion to the common French saying that "la parole est d'argent, mais le silence est d'or," often resorted to by parents who want to silence their talkative children at the dinner table. The text was printed in the anthology of Breton's prose and poetry published by Jean-Louis Bédouin in the Seghers collection "Poètes d'aujourd'hui."

Breton claimed, in his rejection of music, to speak not only in his own name (that of a poet who is impervious to the musical arts) but in that of "most of the artists of language: the poets worthy of the name and a small band of prose writers who care about verbal harmony." From music those choice minds are, and want to remain, alienated. In true Surrealist fashion (for these rebels, like all French revolutionaries, insisted upon appealing to ancestors), Breton invoked the precedent of the Goncourt brothers, who made no bones about confessing their total musical deafness. They relate in their famous and half-slanderous *Journal*, under the year 1862, how they paid a visit to Théophile Gautier at Neuilly. As the two brothers were alluding to their musical illiteracy ("we who only like, at the most, military bands"), Gautier beamed with pleasure and added: "I am exactly like you. I prefer silence to music. I barely succeeded, having lived part of my life with a woman singer, to distinguish between good and bad music, but it leaves me cold." Gautier, who liked to exaggerate and to entertain, called Gounod an ass and compared Verdi to the once popular author of melodramas Pixérécourt. He further justified his own dislike of music by attributing the same aversion to Balzac, Hugo, and Lamartine.[12] In many authors, Breton contended, there is either an aggressive attitude to music or indifference or complimentary politeness.

The high-priest of Surrealism then theorized about what he termed the antagonism between poetry and music, which reached its climax with Surrealism and the nineteen fifties. Far from deploring the misunderstanding, Breton strongly asserted that it should be interpreted as a warning that certain principles of the two arts had to be thought anew altogether. He refused to advocate a closer collaboration between the musician and the

---

No. 210, Jan. 1952, pp. 123–35—treats the relationship (a very cool one) between Surrealism and music.

12. We have, in a volume in French on Symbolism, included a quotation (borrowing it from an article by Jacques-Henry Bornecque, in *Revue des Sciences Humaines*, Nos. 77–78 [1955], p. 20) of Alexandre Dumas, in "A Dinner at Rossini's": "Poetry . . . as Hugo and Lamartine write it, has its own music. It is not a sister of music, but a rival: it is not an ally, but an adversary. Instead of lending its help to the siren, the enchantress struggles against it. It is the fight of Armide and of Fata Morgana; but its victory leaves it exhausted."

poet; he himself confessed to an absolute incompetence in the laws of musical composition. Still, he theorized none the less dogmatically about the need "to take by the horns all the antinomies of modern thought and to surmount them." And, cryptically and probably glibly, Breton, who saw the nucleus of all Surrealist thought and action in the worship of love, added: "It is in the expression of *love* that poetry and music may be united at a very high emotional temperature." With a patronizing condescension, he held out a hand to the composers and practitioners of music:

> As to the musicians, I would like them to observe that, in spite of a wide apparent lack of understanding, poets have marched forward to meet them more than halfway, on the only road which, in this day and age, proves to be safe and noble: that of a return to principles.

How could that be achieved? He preferred not to be specific on this point. Others around him, whom Surrealism attracted for a time, until Breton excluded them (Dali, Artaud), toyed with the notion of marrying some sort of music with their films or with their plays. Artaud, in particular, assigned to music a function of magical violence in the theater of the future which he fondly envisioned.

Literary criticism periodically aspires, not to the condition of music, but to the condition of what it believes to be science. The confusion between the arts and the profligate use of a vague and misleading terminology, supposedly borrowed from music, during the Symbolist era in France called for a reaction. Music claimed to reject any literary interpretation of itself which made signs and symbols out of sounds. The all too facile identification of "musical" with "formless," "smooth," "dreamy," has not served literary criticism well. It may be that the indifference to music of many poets past and present has not acted as a disservice to their own art. On the contrary.

Roger Shattuck

Vibratory organism: *crise de prose*

I

We rarely read a text "cold." Only literary editors and participants in experiments like those of I. A. Richards[1] face a poem or a passage without some equivalent of program notes. The author's name or even a century number is enough to prepare our reactions. Such information sets the work in context and fits it into a system of interlocking classifications that direct, or prejudice, the reading. The scholar virtually encases himself in such tendentious data before venturing out onto the frontiers of knowledge. Yet it is those of us who live with and by literature who most need to come back to the written word "cold turkey," without props and habits and protective garments.

I say all this in order to urge my readers to peruse the following quotation "naively and sincerely" as its author would have said. For this purpose the best method is to read aloud. Some scholars will recognize the words immediately; they might try feigning ignorance. I shall ask the others not to worry over the question of attribution. For heuristic purposes we can hold off the recognition scene as long as possible:

[a] Supposons un bel espace de nature où tout verdoie, rougeoie, poudroie et chatoie en pleine liberté, où toutes choses, diversement colorées suivant leur constitution moléculaire, changées de seconde en seconde par le déplacement de l'ombre et de la lumière, et agitées par le travail intérieur du calorique, se trouvent en perpétuelle vibration, laquelle fait trembler les lignes et complète la loi du mouvement éternel et universel.   [b]—Une immensité, bleue quelquefois et verte souvent, s'étend jusqu 'aux confins du ciel: c'est la mer.   [c] Les arbres sont verts, les gazons verts, les mousses vertes; le vert serpente dans les troncs, les tiges non mûres sont vertes; le vert est le fond de la nature, parce que le vert se marie facilement à tous les autres tons.*
[d] Ce qui me frappe d'abord, c'est que partout,—coquelicots dans les gazons, pavots, perroquets, etc.,—le rouge chante la gloire du vert; le noir,—quand il y en a,—zéro solitaire et insignifiant, inter-

1. See *Practical Criticism* (New York, 1929).

[193]

cède le secours du bleu ou du rouge.   [*e*] Le bleu, c'est-à-dire le ciel, est coupé de légers flocons blancs ou de masses grises qui trempent heureusement sa morne crudité,—et, comme la vapeur de la saison,— hiver ou été,—baigne, adoucit, ou engloutit les contours, la nature ressemble à un toton qui, mû par une vitesse accélérée, nous apparaît gris, bien qu'il résume en lui toutes les couleurs.

[*f*] La sève monte et, mélange de principes, elle s'épanouit en *tons mélangés*; les arbres, les rochers, les granits se mirent dans les eaux et y déposent leurs *reflets*; tous les objets transparents accrochent au passage lumières et couleurs voisines et lointaines.   [*g*] A mesure que l'astre du jour se dérange, les tons changent de valeur, mais, re-spectant toujours leurs sympathies et leurs haines naturelles, continu-ent à vivre en harmonie par des concessions réciproques.   [*h*] Les ombres se déplacent lentement, et font fuir devant elles ou éteignent les tons à mesure que la lumière, déplacée elle-même, en veut faire résonner de nouveau.   [*i*] Ceux-ci se renvoient leurs reflets, et, modi-fiant leurs qualités en les *glaçant* de qualités transparentes et emprun-tées, multiplient à l'infini leurs mariages mélodieux et les rendent plus faciles.   [*j*] Quand le grand foyer descend dans les eaux, de rouges fanfares s'élancent de tous côtés; une sanglante harmonie éclate à l'horizon, et le vert s'empourpre richement.   [*k*] Mais bientôt de vastes ombres bleues chassent en cadence devant elles la foule des tons orangés et rose tendre qui sont comme l'écho lointain et affaibli de la lumière.   [*l*] Cette grande symphonie du jour, qui est l'éter-nelle variation de la symphonie d'hier, cette succession de mélodies, où la variété sort toujours de l'infini, cet hymne compliqué s'appelle la couleur.

* Excepté à ses générateurs le jaune et le bleu; cependant je ne parle ici que des tons purs. Car cette règle n'est pas applicable aux coloristes transcendants qui connaissent à fond la science du contre-point.

If we found this passage as an anonymous fragment in an obscure pro-vincial collection, would we pause to examine it closely? Does this unitive vision seem excessive, or does it project a powerful sensibility in command of its medium? Does it immediately reveal its provenance? I shall assume that an inner voice, literary conscience or unconscious, has prompted us to look again.

The text opens with the phrasing of a mathematical demonstration. After the first clause, the style veers sharply toward sensuous-scientific descrip-tion of a strange landscape. The scene appears both abstract and visionary, like a painting that combines full-blown Impressionism with Magritte's petrified space. The only objects in the picture are either conventional (sea, sky, trees) or seemingly emblematic (poppies, parrots, rising sap). The first sentence focuses on an intense Brownian movement that animates everything within the encompassing stillness. The expanded scale of events forces us to confront molecules and seconds. This palpitating closeness gives way to a composition of vivid colors which, by an accelerating momentum carried over from the opening, fuses into the grey blur of a spinning top, [b]–[e]. Meanwhile we learn that a correspondingly fleeting consciousness (*me* [d]; *nous* [e]) is beholding the scene. In the second paragraph solar time enters the picture, [f]–[i], and shifts the pattern of tones inexorably toward the violence of sunset, [j]. Twilight, [k], restores the hush shattered by the dynamic movement of the opening sentence, and the closing sentence reinserts the composition into a vast cyclical pattern of time and change, [l].

A few words project out of this carefully developed passage: *vibration, mouvement universel, toton, reflets* (twice), *harmonie* (twice), *réciproque, mariage, variation.* They all depict some form of self-contained or reciprocating motion. Several verbs are made reflexive at key points. The beholding consciousness does not appear to stand outside the scene, but rather to join the dance with a minimum of syntactic separation. Because of these devices the entire composition develops as self-reflexive and self-beholding and gradually takes on an all-inclusive wheeling motion. The initial "vibration" becomes the rotation of an enormous top. As readers we are drawn into the elemental turning of the scene, of the earth itself as the sun "goes down," of the whole natural cosmos, and of the tiny human consciousness here appended to it, creating and observing it. The vocabulary and subtly circular style of the passage carry us to the edge of vertigo, the great grey blur of natural process.

One could say much more, about the imagery and the rhythm and the sonority. Does it add up to a text of any literary significance? Is this a page out of a journal by Van Gogh? or Kandinsky? Is it some third-rate Romantic foisting off on us an overwritten account of a howling drug experience? Why so much semiscientific color theory? Is this a fragment out of a larger work? In any case, the last line seems weak. The crescendo of visual display and intense feeling will not finally balance on the head of the word *couleur.* For by the end, the color theme has been overworked. Yet these confident effusions cannot be the work of a third-rater. The author has assembled a vivid and convincing sensibility.

No, not a third-rater. Baudelaire *fecit*—as many of you may have divined. The passage represents not typical but quintessential Baudelaire.

This self-contained text appears at the opening of the third chapter, "De la couleur," of the *Salon de 1846*.² Read beside the other 130 pages of his first important published work, it appears very much like a separate piece of writing half-embedded in the assemblage of notes Baudelaire must have pulled out of his drawers in order to meet his deadline. He claimed he composed the *Salon* in a week. It appeared as a printed book eight weeks after the vernissage. He was in top form.

Yet 1846 was a desperate year for Baudelaire, who at twenty-five was better known as a bohemian and dandy than as a poet. Two years earlier his family had put his inheritance into a trust from which he received an allowance. Financial need drove him to write the *Salon de 1845*, an ineffective pamphlet that earned him practically nothing. A month later he melodramatically and feebly attempted suicide. Meanwhile he seems to have been reading widely, particularly in the works of Swedenborg, Hoffmann, and probably Fourier. The historical significance of the text I have quoted can be succinctly conveyed by listing the various ways in which it represents a "first."

(i) These opening paragraphs from "De la couleur" represent Baudelaire's first *poème en prose*.³ He ends the previous chapter by saying, "Je veux écrire sur la couleur une série de réflexions qui ne seront pas inutiles pour l'intelligence complète de ce petit livre" (230). After the two initial paragraphs, the rest of the chapter on color breaks down into short paragraphs mostly of one sentence and of a discursive nature. Therefore the passage quoted even looks like a shaped fragment of heightened experience, and its style generally conforms to Baudelaire's major statement in the 1862 dedication of *Petits poèmes en prose* to Arsène Houssaye: "Quel est celui de nous qui n'a pas, dans ses jours d'ambition, rêvé le miracle d'une prose poétique, musicale sans rythme et sans rime, assez souple et assez heurtée pour s'adapter aux mouvements lyriques de l'âme, aux ondulations de la rêverie, aux soubresauts de la conscience?" (146). Baudelaire had made a first unsuccessful attempt to write a prose poem in the opening pages of *Salon de 1845*. Delacroix's painting, *Les Dernières Paroles de*

2. Baudelaire, *Œuvres complètes*, ed. Marcel A. Ruff (Paris, 1968), pp. 230–31. References to Baudelaire's work will be indicated by numbers in parentheses giving the pages in this edition.
3. A few critics have implied as much in passing, but without pausing to examine the merit of the idea. See André Ferran, *L'Esthétique de Baudelaire* (Paris, 1933), p. 140; and Enid Starkie, *Baudelaire* (New York, 1958), p. 159. Two other books have contributed substantially to my interpretations: F. W. Leakey, *Baudelaire and Nature* (New York, 1969); and Baudelaire, *Salon de 1846*, texte établi et présenté par David Kelley (Oxford, 1975).

Marc-Aurèle, is seen as a "harmonie de vert et de rouge," and the whole composition gives "l'effet d'un objet monochrome et tournant" (205). The following year Baudelaire dispensed with Delacroix and composed his own visionary landscape saturated with shrill colors. This 1846 text is well described by the title he proposed sixteen years later for his collection of prose poems. In the letter Baudelaire sent to Houssaye in 1862 with the manuscript, he proposed the general title, "La Lueur et la fumée."

Even though he may not yet have articulated and named the genre of *poème en prose*, all these circumstances permit us to see the color passage as a conscious attempt to write and publish such a work. Two comparisons reinforce the association. The second of the prose poems actually published as such, "Le *Confiteor* de l'artiste," employs a setting and a state of mind so similar to that of the color poem that they both seem to express the same vibratory response to a scene—"le *moi* se perd vite" (149). The later text expresses a more self-affirming and combative attitude toward nature and also replaces most of the color imagery with the concentrated point of a sail contrasting with the vastness of the seascape. Yet it is recognizably the same imagination at work.[4]

The other work of Baudelaire's that comes to mind in reading the 1846 color pasage is a poem whose date of composition is uncertain and which might be contemporary. "Harmonie du soir" embodies in its *pantoum* form a powerful turning movement that encompasses all the elements of the poem—rhyme, rhythm, air, sunset, and the poet's state of mind. Only the somewhat arbitrary last line gives the composition a different direction. These two works deserve the kind of joint reading we accord to other associated poems and prose poems.

For all these reasons I propose that the color text is not merely "like" a prose poem found in a critical essay. It actually is Baudelaire's first such text, explicitly set off as a separate whole, and reaffirming the early onset of Baudelaire's desire to develop a form of writing distinct from both formal verse and expository prose.[5]

(ii) The intensity of Baudelaire's writing in the color poem, as well as repeated terms like "harmonie" and "loi du mouvement éternel et universel" attest to the fact that this is his first treatment of the theme of *correspondances*. Though the word itself does not appear, the rest of the

4. One should also compare the prose poem, "Le Fou et la Vénus."
5. It may also be his first rendering of a drug experience. The evolution of Baudelaire's prose style shows us that he was able to insert into "Du vin et du hachisch" a number of passages transposed from poems—or out of which he formed poems. These exchanges also probably go back to the years just before the 1848 revolution.

chapter concerns nothing else and leads into the famous passage quoted from Hoffmann's *Kreisleriana*: "je trouve une analogie et une réunion intime entre les couleurs, les sons et les parfums" (232). Several details suggest that Baudelaire intended in this chapter to make his contribution to the reigning dispute over the relative importance of *ligne* (Ingres) and *couleur* (Delacroix). What came from his pen instead was a manifesto on universal analogy. There should be no need to belabor this point. In 1846 Baudelaire had already advanced a long way into his "forêts de symboles."

(iii) Because of the way he transposed his personal experience of sea-scape and color—either as he had seen them in the tropics, or in Dela-croix's paintings, or in hashish-induced hallucinations—Baudelaire cre-ated in the *Salon de 1846* a word tableau which we could call the first Impressionist painting. The text quoted speaks for itself. Everything is there to describe a Monet or a Renoir.[6] On the next page Baudelaire sets down a whole series of statements that open the way for Impressionist theory: "La couleur est donc l'accord de deux tons... ils n'existent que relativement" (231). "L'air joue un si grand rôle dans la théorie de la couleur que, si un paysagiste peignait les feuilles des arbres telles qu'il les voit, il obtiendrait un ton faux" (ibid.). He imagines himself a painter, and it is in this role that he makes the final affirmation of the chapter: "Les coloristes sont les poètes épiques" (232). Like the most extreme of the Impressionists at the height of their scientific experiments, Baudelaire yearns to obliterate the contours of objects in order to convey the pervasive vibration of molecules and light.

It is possible, moreover, that Baudelaire derived some of his color theory and vocabulary from Chevreul, the director of the Gobelins tapestry work-shop, a meticulous experimental scientist with an artist's eye. His magis-terial illustrated work, *De la loi du contraste simultané des couleurs*, had appeared in 1839. Directly, or indirectly through accounts in *L'Artiste* and elsewhere, Baudelaire probably became familiar with Chevreul's ideas. The "coloristes transcendants" in the footnote probably refer not only to painters but also to Hoffmann and Chevreul.[7] To a degree not yet fully

6. My colleague Paul Barolsky, who teaches history of art at the University of Vir-ginia, pointed out to me the painterly quality of Baudelaire's prose here and its strik-ing anticipation of Impressionism.

7. Chevreul deserves a footnote as long as I dare make it. In his effort to systematize the subjective process of color vision and interpretation, Chevreul has to develop a psychology of perception, virtually a science of sensibility. He distinguishes carefully between simul-taneous, successive, and mixed color contrasts, the last being an afterimage combined with a new color. In a long section on color and music, successive contrast comes out as melody, simultaneous contrast as harmony. The dynamics of color contrasts is compared

explored, the Impressionists (particularly Seurat, who had a strong scientific and optical bent) found verification and support for their practice in Chevreul's theories. After all, he was thinking in terms of juxtaposing colored threads in a tapestry in order to form a harmony of tones; the optical mixing of colors in the observer's eye is the implication that lies behind whole sections of his experiments and his account of them.[8]

(iv) I shall propose lastly that the quoted passage by Baudelaire instituted a line of thinking and looking that would eventually lead to nonfigurative or abstract painting. On the following page he states that "l'art n'étant qu'une abstraction et un sacrifice du détail à l'ensemble, il est important de s'occuper surtout des masses" (231). Of course he is using the word "abstraction" analytically more than aesthetically or historically, yet one cannot ignore the drift of his thought. A little later in the same chapter on color, he makes himself clearer. "La bonne manière de savoir si un tableau est mélodieux est de le regarder d'assez loin pour n'en comprendre ni le subjet ni les lignes" (232). He is asking us to consider the pure play of color. Veronese and Delacroix are both in his mind. He returned to the same idea seven years later in a famous passage about Delacroix in the *Exposition Universelle de 1855*. "On dirait que cette peinture... projette sa pensée à distance.... Il semble que cette couleur pense par elle-même, indépendamment des objets qu'elle habille" (369). What Baudelaire later begins to call *l'art pur* in the unfinished essay "L'Art philosophique" is probably a further exploration of the nonrepresentational possibilities of painting. In a phrase reminiscent of Coleridge and anticipating Mallarmé, he defines pure art as "une magie suggestive contenant à la fois objet et sujet" (424). Faint echoes of pure art survive in the *Salon de 1859* in the discussions of photography and the imagination. After that, in the last essays on Delacroix and Guys, this strand of critical thought gives way before the doctrines of modernity and spontaneity. Nevertheless, the evolu-

---

in the final section to mental processes in general. Chevreul lays it down as law that comparison exaggerates differences and needs correction. This law applies particularly in solitary thought, in a two-way conversation, and in teaching. "Absolute" judgment is not possible for us because of "relative" circumstances affecting all observation. Because analysis proceeds by dividing wholes into parts, it necessarily distorts. See M. E. Chevreul, *De la loi du contraste simultané des couleurs* (Paris, 1889), pp. 545–58. Chevreul wrote a remarkably modern text, in which one keeps hearing anticipations of Eisenstein on montage and of the Surrealists on the nature of an image.

8. I might mention that the Monet painting from which the name Impressionism was drawn had a subject closely related to that of Baudelaire's 1846 color text. Painted in 1872, *Impression, soleil levant* was one of the major entries in the first exhibit in 1874 of the Société Anonyme des Artistes Peintres. The painting shimmers as vividly as Baudelaire's prose poem.

tion of the idea of "abstraction" can be followed as far as 1859 from its beginnings in the 1846 prose poem on color. The theory is very tentative, but we learn what Baudelaire actually saw.

These last two "firsts"—that is, a prose poem straining to transform itself into an Impressionist painting, and the same prose poem projecting out of its swirling movement the possibility of an "abstract" color composition without identifiable objects—lead to the not unexpected conclusion that in the 1846 color passage Baudelaire was practicing a kind of imaginary ecphrasis. In highly rhetorical language he describes a work of art that can be attributed only to his own hand and that looks prophetically forward toward two major developments in European painting of the next hundred years.

II

With a little perseverance, therefore, one can place Baudelaire's early prose poem on color in a rich historical context that arrays his career as a writer beside the development of painting and art criticism in the nineteenth century. The two intensely written paragraphs begin to look like a remarkable anticipation of things to come. But once again I find myself impelled to ask the question with which I began. Without the historical and literary context, does one receive a direct impression of the literary significance and merit of this text?

When I try to put aside the rich associations evoked in the preceding pages and come back to it "cold," the color passage from the *Salon de 1846* leaves me with two principal impressions. The first is of the hortatory tone propelling the entire exposition, even the most personal responses. The text exceeds the bounds both of description and of meditation. The second impression is of the author's sustained effort to affirm a single principle that will embrace all the elements of his experience—physical and spiritual, moral and aesthetic.

Read aloud, the two paragraphs take on the sonorities of a sermon. Bossuet's periods move like a ground swell beneath the surface rhythms. In this light I believe we can begin to understand better the oddly addressed opening chapter, "Aux Bourgeois." You have taken over the government and the city, Baudelaire writes boldly; now in order to reach "cette suprême harmonie" you must learn to appreciate beauty. One sentence leads me to doubt the thesis that irony undercuts the words here: "Jouir est une science, et l'exercice des cinq sens veut une initiation particulière, qui ne se fait que par la bonne volonté et le besoin" (227). This helps us. For it suggests that the two paragraphs we have been discussing belong to a "special initiation." In his mid-twenties, Baudelaire still wanted to believe that he could convert the middle class to see and feel as he did. The initiation he proposed, encountered in its most concentrated form in the color text, consists in a direct presentation of what Baudelaire perceived under certain circumstances. The natural bent of his sensibility included a strong urge toward insight, clairvoyance, hallucination, distortion, abstraction. He was conscious of it and cultivated it deliberately and far longer than Rimbaud. The words *étrange, bizarre, dédoublement,* and the like stud his prose even when he is not concerned with drugs. And hashish can be seen as belonging to the systematic exercise of his heightened powers of vision. We can hear his resolute visionary intent, and the same hortatory tone, in the fragment on realism he wrote in 1855: "La Poésie est ce qu'il y a de plus réel, c'est ce qui n'est complètement vrai que dans *un autre monde*" (448). When, in 1862, Baudelaire states, "J'ai cultivé mon hystérie avec jouissance et terreur" (640), he feels the approach of madness because the process has gone on for fifteen years—since 1846 at least. The vision into which Baudelaire sought to initiate the bourgeois begins to sound like the "hallucination vraie" which Taine derived in part from his highly revealing correspondence with Flaubert about the imagination.[9]

Because of the special nature of his sensibility, Baudelaire was not content to cast his initiatory message entirely in words. He painted a picture; he directly depicted what he saw and what he implied we too can see. "Goût permanent depuis l'enfance de toutes les représentations plastiques" (617), he states in a biographical note. His fundamentally didactic purpose in writing about the arts is probably best expressed in the late essay on Guys: "peu d'hommes sont doués de la faculté de voir; il y en a moins qui possèdent la puissance d'exprimer" (553). He began in 1846 with the idealistic goal of converting the bourgeois; gradually he restricted himself to writing for fellow artists and poets. But until the very end the evangelistic manner continues.

One of the most apt terms to identify what Baudelaire saw and what he wanted others to see is the word he introduces forcefully at the very end of the *Salon de 1846*: "Le merveilleux nous enveloppe et nous abreuve comme l'atmosphère; mais nous ne le voyons pas" (261). He uses the word also in the essay on laughter (377) written at about the same period. It conveys Baudelaire's sense of wonder that so many parts of the world

9. *De l'intelligence,* 1870.

carry meaning, connect with one another, and speak to us. I believe it is a strong sense of the marvelous that radiates from his early undeclared prose poem—even if we know nothing about its provenance and circumstances. Eighty years later the Surrealists elected *le merveilleux* as their ideal. But by then the word had come to mean not so much *relation* as *rupture* with conventional modes of living and feeling. *Le merveilleux* testifies to the shifting ideology of modernism across two centuries.

The title of the chapter and the vocabulary of Baudelaire's initiatory prose poem appear to present color as the key to his vision. He probably thought so himself, in great part because of Delacroix's influence.[10] Samuel Cramer, the highly autobiographical hero of *La Fanfarlo* written the same year, consoles himself by composing a book on color symbolism (287). Yet closer inspection will show that the key is not so much the distribution and relation of tones as a deep-seated movement, a "vibration, laquelle fait trembler les lignes et complète la loi du mouvement éternel et universel" [a]. In the *Salon de 1845* he had tried out a weaker expression, "cette pondération du vert et du rouge" (205). In the final version, *vibration* pervades the entire scene beginning with the molecules themselves, an insight fully in accord with the theories of modern physics. An eternal and universal law carries the principle of vibration to its extreme limit and places it also at the seat of consciousness. The spinning top represents not only the ceaseless agitation of nature but also, enfolded into one rhythm, the operation of thought itself.

Here is the innermost burden of Baudelaire's prose poem. In the vibration of color he sees a supreme *correspondance*, linking external reality and the mind. This alternating rhythm finally becomes the subject of "Le Confiteor de l'artiste," which begins to throb between *immensité* and *petitesse*, between *les choses* and *moi* (149). Baudelaire returns to the universal law of alternation at a few other crucial moments of his writing. In "Conseils aux jeunes littéraires" he speaks of "la loi des contrastes, qui gouverne l'ordre moral et l'ordre physique" (268). Chevreul is audible again in this further attempt to find the unifying principle for all domains. Later, after writing on Poe, Baudelaire seemed to find a personification of the oscillating consciousness in the idealized figure of the dandy. But in 1846 he used vibration to express a dynamic combination of materialism and transcendence, in nature and in man. Therefore the strong hortatory tone of the prose poem finds its justification in the vastness of the principle or correspondence Baudelaire is affirming in it. The whole universe vibrates

10. See Ferran, pp. 139–50.

as one—if you can only see deeply enough into the world. Approximately ten years later in one of the journal entries collected as "Mon cœur mis à nu," Baudelaire caught the principle of vibration in two lapidary sentences that could stand as the inscription for his entire work. "De la vaporisation et de la concentration du *Moi*. Tout est là" (630). The systole and diastole of the universe itself is reproduced in the contraction and expansion of the mind, alternately concentrating its attention and then opening itself to all impressions. The text we have been studying implies, even more powerfully than a painting of the same subject, that the fascination of sunrise and sunset lies in the fact that these particular moments make sensible for us the earth's harmonious rotation, the generalized vibration of everything.

Whitehead too was deeply committed to what he called "vibratory organism." In the fifth chapter of *Science and the Modern World* he states firmly, on scientific grounds, that "In a certain sense, everything is everywhere at all times." Baudelaire hoped to initiate us to this vision: he could go no further.

III

For years I have believed that during the nineteenth and twentieth centuries music and painting were ahead of literature in their explorations of the potentialities of human thought. All poetry could do was to try to recover its rightful place.[11] On the one hand Hoffmann and Schopenhauer and Wagner made deep inroads on the aesthetic consciousness of Europe with their pronouncements on music. On the other hand, beginning with Manet and Monet (if not already with Turner and Delacroix) it looked as if the poets could do little more than jog along behind the painters of genius that formed the School of Paris. But an attentive and sympathetic reading of a text like "De le couleur" obliges one to suspend judgment and see the great artistic race as more evenly matched than one thought.

And I am spaking of a *prose* text, a *poème en prose* to be precise. Mallarmé just called attention to the *crise de vers* that descended on traditional poetry at the end of the century with the advent of free verse. Correspondingly one might speak of an effort in the novel since Flaubert to "reprendre à la poésie notre bien." In the great redistribution of roles and shift of powers that went on during the latter half of the nineteenth century, I feel sure that we could locate and identify a *crise de prose*. It concerns the

11. In "Crise de vers" Mallarmé speaks of the need to "reprendre notre bien"—a phrase Valéry echoes almost verbatim in "Avant-propos à *La connaissance de la déesse*" as the "commune intention" of Symbolism.

emergence of the prose poem in French, the claims to authority of certain
poètes fondés en peinture like Baudelaire and Apollinaire, and Baudelaire's
doctrine, powerfully relaunched by Eliot, that "tous les grands poètes
deviennent naturellement, fatalement, critiques... je considère le poète
comme le meilleur de tous les critiques" (517).

In order to grapple with these inchoate realignments of the arts and of
artists, Baudelaire, aged twenty-five, opened his initiatory prose poem
speaking like an engineer or a mathematician: "Supposons un bel espace
de nature ..."

Etiemble

Premier état d'un futur "mythe de Rimbaud en Roumanie" (1895–1945)

Mon cher Fowlie,
    J'aurais voulu vous offrir un travail digne de vous.
Ceci ne l'est peut-être pas. Voilà bientôt quinze ans
que j'accumule du matériau sur le sujet, et je suis
maintenant arrivé à obtenir, je l'espère, tout l'essentiel.
Au point que, trop riche de fiches, je ne pourrai traiter
que de la première période: des origines à la naissance
de la République populaire de Roumanie. Je vous offre
ici, avec toutes ses imperfections, la quatrième ou cin-
quième version (je ne sais plus au juste) d'un travail
tâtonnant, et l'état de ma santé ne m'a pas permis de
soumettre ces vingt-cinq ou vingt-six pages à quelque
Roumain compétent: à Lidia Bote, par exemple. J'es-
père obtenir son avis avant la correction des épreuves,
et vous faire alors bénéficier des amendements qu'elle
aurait suggérés. Ma seule consolation est que je ne con-
nais personne qui ait jusqu'ici traité le sujet dont je
m'occupe. J'ai lu, cela va de soi, les douze pages pu-
bliées par le professeur Gheorghi Calciu sur "Rimbaud
en Roumaine" dans le troisième cahier des Etudes
rimbaldiennes; *mais cela, quand j'avais écrit les pre-*
mières versions de ce travail, et l'on verra aisément
que je n'ai pas plagié les cinq ou six pages qui con-
cernent le demi-siècle dont je traite. Pardonnez-moi
donc les imperfections de cet essai, que je ne me ha-
sarde à livrer que parce que je sais que votre amitié
généreuse saura faire la part des circonstances atténu-
antes: exténuantes, dans lesquelles j'ai dû rédiger cet
hommage.

I

Le premier article important dont je dispose touchant l'œuvre d'Arthur Rimbaud, celui que publie en 1908 Ion Minulescu, est écrit par un homme qui se flattait d'avoir entendu un neurologue, Gheorghiu Marinescu, lui déclarer: "Je veux étudier ton cas parce que tu as, comme Rimbaud, l'audition colorée. Tu as cette audition colorée d'instinct sans que tu t'en rendes compte." Ce témoignage nous est fourni dans un entretien avec Valer Dona publié le 4 avril 1937 par *Adevărul literar și artistic*. Ainsi, en Roumanie comme ailleurs, c'est par "Voyelles" et cette prétendue poétique, dont j'ai longuement montré, j'espère, à quel point elle est dérisoire,[1] que l'œuvre du poète français touchera les milieux lettrés de Bucarest. Cette mode sévissait en Roumanie comme dans la plupart des pays européens. Témoin la thèse lucide de Lidia Bote sur le symbolisme roumain (*Simbolismul românesc*, Bucarest, 1966): on y apprend que, dès 1885, la revue transylvaine *Familia* entretenait ses lecteurs de cette illusion collective, au tome XXI, No. 49, pp. 383–84. Dix ans plus tard, le 21 août 1895, un journal socialiste *Lumea nouă* (*Le Monde Nouveau*) ne peut moins faire que de saluer cette nouveauté et de publier un article sur "la musique de la vue, ou le piano des couleurs." En fait de nouveauté, c'était ressasser la vieille idée du Père Castel, son *clavecin des couleurs*, son *clavecin oculaire*. Qu' importe! Trois ans plus tard, les poètes qui se veulent dans le vent se croient tenus d'en discuter. La revue *Carmen*, qui ne durera guère, publie le 21 juillet 1898 un essai "d'un obscur B. Gr. Buzea" sur "Les poètes et les couleurs," article qui fut relayé dans un autre périodique qu'on peut qualifier, quant à son intention du moins, de "symboliste," la *Revista modernă* (19 février 1901).

Il faut admettre d'autre part que "Voyelles" est connu en Roumanie dès 1895 au moins puisque, le 2 juillet de cette année-là, A. Macedonski traite du "symbolisme" dans *Tara* (*Le Pays*)[2] et critique en ces termes la complaisance de trop de gens à l'égard de cette prétendue "audition colorée": "Il est vrai qu'il existe des symbolistes qui, à propos des sons,

1. Dans *Le Sonnet des voyelles* (Paris: Gallimard, 1968).
2. Sur Alexandre Macedonski et le sujet qui nous occupe, voyez "Alexandre Macedonski et les lettres françaises," *Revue des Etudes Roumaines*, Institut Universitaire roumain Charles I (Paris, 1957), III–IV, pp. 36–55. Sur Macedonski et audition colorée, l'auteur de cet article, Titus Barbulesco, observe pertinemment: "les voyelles françaises ne sont pas les voyelles roumaines et, notamment, les diphtongues—bien plus nombreuses en roumain—ne suggèrent peut-être pas les mêmes instruments" que chez René Ghil; il conclut: "Il ne nous semble pas que Macedonski ait fait dans ce poème [*In arcane de pădure*, en français: *Dans les arcanes de la forêt*] l'application de la méthode de René Ghil en dépit du 'côté comédien' de sa personnalité qui eût pu s'y prêter" (p. 46).

vont trop loin: non contents d'accorder aux lettres une valeur musicale, ils leur confèrent une valeur colorée. A les en croire, la lettre *A* donne la sensation de noir, et ainsi de suite." *A noir*, c'est du Rimbaud. Il ne s'agit donc pas d'une coïncidence.

Hélas, ce même Macedonski se convertira aux pires extravagances du rimbaldisme revu et aggravé par René Ghil; et celui qui, en 1895, savait qualifier de "microbes du genre" ceux qui prenaient au sérieux l'*A noir* de Rimbaud composera, selon les "principes" de la méthode évolutive-instrumentiste, une épopée: *Thalassa*, dont en 1902 il définit ainsi l'ambition: "chaque chapitre doit donner la sensation d'une couleur, à cause des images employées; et chaque chapitre sera imprimé sur un papier de la nuance correspondante." Plus rimbaldien que Rimbaud, plus "décadent" que Des Esseintes, il entend que tous les sens contribuent au grand œuvre: odorat, vue, toucher collaborant avec la vue et l'ouïe pour constituer l'œuvre langagière. Dans un ouvrage sur *L'Imagination poétique colorée d'Alexandre Macedonski*, publié à Bucarest en 1944, V. G. Paleolog écrira que "le manuscrit de cette œuvre, devenue en français *Le Calvaire de feu*, commence à être transcrit avec des encres de couleurs différentes; on le confie à un disciple qui le publiera bien plus tard."

> A en juger d'après le fac-similé, tout ce qu'on peut constater, c'est une tentative avortée pour établir des correspondances entre les concepts et l'aspect graphique et coloré des mots qui les signifient. *Abis (abîme)* sera écrit en noir; *profondeurs*, en bleu; *vagues*, en vert, etc. Jusque là, rien d'obscur. Mais quand un mot est écrit de deux couleurs, les associations nous échappent. Dans le cas de *monstrueuses*, pourquoi la première syllabe doit-elle s'imprimer en noir, en vert les autres? Pourquoi sera-t-il *vert* le *mon-* de *montagnes*, alors que *-tagnes* commanderait le *noir* [*abîme, profondeurs, vagues, monstrueuses, montagnes*, sont en français dans le texte]? Tout devient jeu gratuit, qui prouve que la notion de correspondance n'avait pas été comprise par Macedonski.[3]

Autre écrivain roumain, D. Anghel, avait été initié à cette fameuse théorie selon Grüber, dont j'ai publié le système dans *Structure du mythe*, 3e édition, 1970, p. 79. Comparé aux divers bilans que je produis là, le tableau de Grüber prouve l'inanité de tous, y compris celle du sien. Mais on le prit au sérieux à Bucarest, comme à Paris et à Londres, où il

3. Toutes citations trouvées chez Lidia Bote, *passim*. Voir aussi, à ce propos: Adrian Marino, *Opera lui Alexandru Macedonski* (Bucarest, 1967), pp. 653–54; touchant la description des manuscrits polychromes, Al. Macedonski, *Opere* (Bucarest: V. Prozǎ, 1969), pp. 221–24, de l'édition procurée par Adrian Marino.

ébaubit les auditeurs en 1893 du Congrès international de psychologie
expérimentale.

Avec G. Călinescu, dans son *Histoire de la littérature roumaine des
origines à nos jours*,[4] faut-il soutenir que chez un écrivain au moins, G.
Bacovia, on discerne un estimable souci de symbolique des couleurs: "Le
noir lui donne une sensation de deuil; le violet est pour lui le crépuscule;
[...] le jaune, c'est la langueur, l'anémie [...] *ces derniers temps, je suis
obsédé par le jaune, couleur du désespoir. C'est pourquoi mon dernier
volume porte pour titre 'L'Etincelle jaune.' Le rouge représente le sang,
la vie tumultueuse.*" (Et revoilà notre Rimbaud, I, pourpres, sang craché...)
Voilà donc à Bucarest quelques-uns des méfaits de l'A noir et de l'I rouge;
ils ne sont ni plus ni moins graves que partout ailleurs.

En voici un autre qui ne fut largement divulgué qu'en 1968, grâce encore
à Lidia Bote, mais qui remonte en fait à l'époque dont ici je m'occupe.
C'est l'œuvre d'un contemporain de Rimbaud, mais qui lui survécut vingt-
trois ans, Mircea Demetriade:

SONURI SI CULORI

Alb, *A*; *E*, gri; I roşu, un cer de asfinţire
Albastru, *O*, imensul în lacuri oglindit,
U, mugetul furtunii şi-al crimei colţ vădit,
Alcovul criptei negre, lugubră prohodire.

A, rază săgetată de astru-n rătăcire
Cînd zorile în boabe de rouă s-au topit
Căzînd pe flori, pe iarbă, pe lanu-ngălbenit;
A, verbul peste ape născînd eterne fire.

E, gîndul meu de sceptic , simbol saturnian,
I, sînge şi incendii, fâşii învăpăiate,
Din trîmbiţe vestind-o virila libertate.

O, freamătul de coarde, un mit din Ossian,
Ciocniri de pietre scumpe, murmur colian
Pe harpele albastre de îngeri înstrunate.[5]

4. *Istoria literaturii române dela origini pâna in prezent* (Bucarest, 1941), p. 627.
5. En voici la traduction française:

Sons et couleurs

Blanc, *A*; *E*, gris; *I* rouge, un ciel crépusculaire
Bleu, *O*, l'immensité reflétée dans les lacs,

Jusqu'aux clairons, jusqu'aux anges, jusqu'à l'*I* rouge et l'*O* bleu, nous voici dans le rimbaldisme. Mais alors que Rimbaud ne se soucie nullement d'accorder son sonnet et la poétique supposée qu'il enseigne, Demetriade s'efforce d'accumuler sous chaque couleur les voyelles dont en l'espèce il s'agit de manifester la vertu. Plus rimbaldien que Rimbaud, beaucoup plus, par conséquent.

II

Il se trouve par infortune que ce Minulescu que l'on jugeait si doué pour l'audition colorée fut le premier introducteur de Rimbaud en Roumanie. Aurait-on voulu inventer un texte caricatural sur le mythe de Rimbaud en 1908, on ne pouvait faire mieux. Je traduis en m'efforçant de garder quand il le faut toute la gaucherie du texte original:

Jean-Nicolas Arthur Rimbaud, fils d'un capitaine de l'armée française, naquit à Charleville le 20 octobre 1854.

Sa jeunesse fut l'une des pages les plus tourmentées jamais écrites dans la vie d'un homme.

Vers 1870, à peine terminé le lycée, il réussit à terminer ses premiers vers; Rimbaud quitte la maison et commence à errer dans Paris, d'où il est forcé de revenir chez lui. Mais, à peine rentré chez soi, la nostalgie du vagabondage l'envahit à nouveau et le petit Rimbaud disparaît pour la deuxième fois.

Cette fois, on le voit lier amitié avec le critique André Gide [sic]. Mais au bout de quelques semaines, celui-ci est contraint de le chasser de chez lui, incapable qu'il était de supporter davantage le mauvais caractère et les manières du vrai "voyou" [ce mot en français dans le texte].

N'ayant pas les moyens de pourvoir à ses besoins, ni personne qui pût l'aider, Rimbaud s'engage dans les troupes révolutionnaires.

U, le mugissement de la tempête et du crime,
L'alcôve du caveau noir, messe funèbre.

A, rayon jailli de l'astre errant,
Quand l'aube fond en gouttes de rosée
Et tombe sur les fleurs, sur l'herbe, sur le champ jaune;
A, parole qui fait naître sur les eaux des fils éternels.

E, mon esprit sceptique, symbole saturnien,
I, sang et incendies, lambeaux empourprés,
Annonçant par des clairons la liberté virile.

O, frémissement de cordes, mythe d'Ossian,
Heurt de pierres précieuses, murmure éolien
Des harpes bleues, accordées par des anges.

Après leur défaite, il décide de rentrer à la maison; cette fois, pour de bon.

C'est alors qu'il écrit le fameux poème "Le Bateau ivre," à la suite duquel il engage une correspondance avec Verlaine; le voici de nouveau en route vers Paris.

Pendant dix mois il habite chez Verlaine, puis quelques mois chez Théodore de Banville, puis dans un hôtel de la rue Racine; enfin, grâce à une somme d'argent que lui prête Verlaine, il réussit à se faire meubler un appartement rue Campagne Première.

Là non plus, il ne séjourne pas longtemps. Un beau jour, il vend tout ce qu'il a chez soi et se met en route pour l'Angleterre avec Verlaine. De là, en Belgique où, après une querelle avec le "pauvre Lélian" [en français dans le texte], il se trouve pour tout profit avec une balle de revolver dans l'épaule. Verlaine est mis en prison, et Rimbaud transporté à l'hôpital Saint Jean.

Une fois guéri puis expulsé de Belgique, Rimbaud de nouveau regagne Charleville, où il publie *Une Saison en enfer*, autobiographie psychologique.

A peine paru le livre, le vagabond se met de nouveau en route. Cette fois il se rend directement à Londres où il devient professeur de langue française et où il prépare un voyage vers l'Orient.

Au mois de février 1875, il se trouve en Allemagne, à Stuttgart, et, vers la fin de l'année, en Italie.

Là, n'ayant pas un sou vaillant, Rimbaud décide d'aller en Espagne et s'engage comme soldat dans l'armée carliste. Mais après avoir encaissé la prime, il s'enfuit et s'établit de nouveau à Paris. A croire que les uniformes multicolores ont éveillé en lui un penchant pour l'armée: de Paris, il passe en Hollande et s'engage dans une unité de l'armée coloniale, qui à ce moment même se mettait en route pour l'Océanie. Mais à peine débarqué dans l'île de Java, Rimbaud déserte, échappe difficilement à la poursuite des autorités, s'engage comme interprète sur un vapeur anglais à bord duquel il regagne l'Europe.

La France ne lui suffisait plus. Il s'en va donc en Suède et devient contrôleur dans le cirque Loisset, à Stockholm.

Fidèle à ses habitudes, Rimbaud quitte également la Suède, s'embarque pour l'île de Chypre, d'où il se dirige vers Alexandrie d'Egypte; au mois de mars 1880, par le canal de Suez, il entre dans le golfe d'Aden où il débarque pour s'installer au Harrar. Dès lors, Rimbaud n'écrira plus une ligne.

Le littérateur vient de se transformer en une sorte d'explorateur-colonisateur-commerçant. Il importe de savoir que Rimbaud fut l'un des premiers Européens qui vendirent aux Abyssins les armes qui plus tard leur serviront dans la guerre contre l'Italie. Après dix ans de négoce, à cause d'une blessure qu'il avait au pied droit, Rimbaud s'embarque pour l'Europe—et ce sera la dernière fois—arrive à Marseille, entre à l'hôpital de la Conception; à la suite d'une intervention chirurgicale, il y meurt le 10 novembre 1891.

Si l'on excepte la prose, l'œuvre de ce précurseur de la poésie d'aujourd'hui se réduit à un millier de vers. Elle est rassemblée en trois volumes principaux: *Une Saison en enfer, Les Illuminations*, poèmes en prose publiés pour la première fois dans la revue *La Vogue* sous le patronage de Verlaine, et *Le Reliquaire*, volume de vers et de prose. Il est vrai qu'une grande partie des poèmes de Rimbaud s'est perdue.

Beaucoup de gens prétendent que Rimbaud fut une victime de Baudelaire. Gustave Kahn soutient qu'à l'âge où les autres enfants commencent à peine à lire Robinson, Rimbaud avait fini de lire *Les Fleurs du Mal*.

Les vers de Baudelaire, dont l'influence est perceptible dans les premiers essais de Rimbaud, sont à l'origine du goût de Rimbaud pour les vagabondages.

Mais on ne décèle cette influence que dans les vers écrits avant l'âge de dix-sept ans. Le reste de son œuvre—véritable phénomène littéraire—est tout ce qu'il y a de plus original.

On le trouve souvent si bizarre, si obscur et même absurde, que le talent de Rimbaud nous intéresse beaucoup plus qu'il ne nous plaît. En revanche, nous trouvons des pages vraiment incomparables, des pages qui, pour longtemps encore, marqueront dans la littérature française le sommet le plus élevé de la poésie.[6]

Document dont la gaucherie naïve enjolive la fable qui courait déjà la France: André Gide y remplace André Gill, trop peu connu sans doute, la *Saison* paraît à Charleville (alors qu'elle est restée en ballots à Bruxelles). La légende du chemineau s'enrichit en cheminant à travers l'Europe danubienne, mais édulcorée: si Rimbaud s'engage dans les troupes révolutionnaires (ce qu'il ne fit point) c'est pour la soupe, et non point par enthousiasme (au moins verbal) pour la Commune; voyage-t-il avec Verlaine, pas un mot ne trahit la nature homosexuelle de leur liaison. Le mythe du voyou s'étaie sur celui du bourgeois colonisateur. Seule surprise: pas un

6. Je donne cette version d'après le texte que j'ai reçu de Roumanie et qu'on m'assure correspondre à la référence qu'on trouvera ci-dessous dans la bibliographie, No. 3. Mais comme je n'ai pas vu, de mes yeux vu, le numéro de la revue dont il s'agit, je tiens à le signaler, en cas d'erreur possible. Combien d'heures j'ai passées, en préparant la *Genèse du mythe*, à chercher des références dont tous les éléments fournis par les bibliographies les plus sérieuses étaient faux! Ça m'a rendu prudent.

mot cette fois de *Voyelles,* ni de l'audition colorée, qui auraient dû être si précieuses à M. Minulescu.... Le vagabond-colonisateur phagocyte le poète, dont on se borne à citer l'inévitable "Bateau ivre" et quelques titres de recueils, assortis d'adjectifs tels que "bizarre," "obscur," "absurde" et d'autant plus "incomparable." Ceux mêmes, dont André Beaunier, dans la *Revue de Paris* du 1 septembre 1900 avait célébré le héros: "recueil bizarre," "obscurs morceaux," "extraordinaire Arthur Rimbaud." De ce Rimbaud à l'usage de la bourgeoisie marchande, capitaliste, colonisatrice, on élimine avec soin tous les poèmes de révolte sexuelle, politique ou religieuse. Une vie fabuleuse offusquera l'œuvre, trop dangereuse, celle-ci (et trop difficile aussi, avouons-le): voilà donc ce à quoi les Roumains auront droit de 1885 à 1914. Un seul article nuancera ce tableau: celui d'Ovid Densusianu, *Sufletul nou în poezie,* deux pages des *Conferențele 'Vieței Nouă,'* en 1910; s'il s'agit cette fois d'un "révolté," ce révolté n'est guère qu'un "rêveur," un "halluciné." Voici poindre la fable du "précurseur des Symbolistes," mais les adjectifs qui qualifient cette poésie nouvelle: "étonnant," "étrange," n'apportent pas de quoi préciser ceux de Minulescu.

III

La seconde image de Rimbaud qu'on ait proposée aux Roumains, à ma connaissance du moins, fut divulguée en 1930 par *Facla.* Le *Rimbaud* de Ruchon, celui de Marcel Coulon, celui de Jacques Rivière venaient de paraître en France, peu après celui de Renéville. Les séquelles du surréalisme et les débuts de la réflexion critique se livraient un combat douteux, généralement résolu en faveur des deux Rimbauds les plus abigotés, celui de Rivière (tripoté par sa veuve) et celui de Renéville. L'auteur de ce "Médaillon de Rimbaud" (Medalion Rimbaud) était le critique Lucian Boz. Voici le texte, où je ne fais qu'une coupure insignifiante:

> Rimbaud était sincère parce qu'il était jeune. De seize à dix-neuf ans, il écrivit les plus beaux poèmes en prose de la littérature française et quelques vers. En outre, il écrivit une confession-testament: "Une Saison en enfer."
>
> Puis il disparut dans les ténèbres; après n'avoir pu crier qu'une fois son appel, il s'en alla. Départ précipité, que les uns tiennent pour une faillite. D'autres ont pressenti que ce geste était fatidique.
>
> Au-delà du Finistère, il ne reste plus que l'Océan... l'auteur du poème *Le Bateau ivre* l'a préféré.

Entre la retraite honteuse (celle que choisit un Lautréamont) et la course au devant de l'avenir [...], Rimbaud préféra l'univers marin avec sa végétation monstrueuse et la nage ondoyante des poissons électriques.

Jacques Rivière voyait en lui un ange qui aurait abandonné sa mission à mi-chemin.

Mais plus proches de la vérité, de sorte que nous nous étonnons de n'avoir pas saisi, nous aussi, les dernières conclusions, il y eut Mallarmé et Duhamel. Rimbaud a donné un résumé de toutes les époques, de tous les styles. Violence philosophique de la poésie, puis des poèmes en prose... Mais Rimbaud le révélateur n'a pu comprendre que ce qui suit est organiquement lié au premier cycle de l'évolution. Dépassant son époque, las de la poésie, Rimbaud découvre la vie. Bien sûr, Rimbaud, tout comme Nietzsche d'ailleurs, est un exemplaire inaccompli. Il ne fait qu'annoncer ceux qui, dans l'avenir, donneront au problème toute sa force et sa solution. Si la destinée lui avait accordé les pleins pouvoirs, son désir frénétique d'anéantir le vieux monde aurait pu faire naître un nouveau Savonarole. Sur les places de Paris, au temps de la Commune, il aurait mis le feu à toutes les paperasses chères, à toutes les évasions vers des archipels imaginaires. Je me représente ce Rimbaud du temps où il travaillait à une sociologie révolutionnaire. Ecrivant le jour, la nuit courant les tavernes et collant sur les murs de Paris des affiches-manifestes adressées aux intellectuels-prolétariens et aux prostituées. Mais hélas: "J'avais en effet, en toute sincérité d'esprit, pris l'engagement de le rendre à son état primitif de fils du soleil,—et nous errions, nourris du vin des cavernes et du biscuit de la route, moi pressé de trouver le lieu et la formule." La formule s'était perdue, et nous marchions, écrasés par les ténèbres.

Nous autres poètes modernes subissons tous son influence. Accrochés à lui, il nous reste entre les mains cette peau multicolore appelée "littérature," qu'il avait rejetée, et dans laquelle chacun de nous se fait tailler une relique. Le poète errait encore dans les forêts de cellulose imprimée que Rimbaud, l'homme libre, gravissait les plateaux torrides de l'Afrique. De tous les visages des siècles, lequel est le masque et lequel est la vie? Si seulement nous avions dans l'âme la lampe d'Aladin, pour nous transfigurer!

Curieux texte, qui semble indiquer que le critique Lucian Boz avait une assez juste conscience du rôle mythique attribué à Rimbaud vers 1930, et de la diversité des avatars du nouveau dieu: "chacun de nous se fait tailler une relique." Plus encore toutefois qu'un "médaillon," Lucian Boz nous offre une façon d'icône. Qu'il tienne Rimbaud pour le héros de l'adolescence, sa première phrase en fait foi : d'autant plus frappante que moins fondée : "Rimbaud était sincère parce qu'il était jeune." Or quel âge de l'homme est plus que l'adolescence celui de l'artifice, de la pose, de l'insincérité ? Du moins Lucian Boz s'efforce-t-il de dépasser le voyou, d'aller à quelque chose d'essentiel. Comme vers ce temps-là le poète surréaliste Aurel Zaremba, dont Rimbaud était *le poète favori*, que Boz évoque l'angélisme et le satanisme de Rimbaud, c'est un autre thème de la fable. Qu'avec Zaremba encore, il se réfère à Duhamel, qui, pur effet de la légende, voyait en Rimbaud un "raccourci violent de l'histoire des littératures" (ce qui, pour un connaisseur même superficiel de l'histoire des littératures, est proprement ridicule), voilà qui manifeste que celui qui raille les tailleurs de reliques n'échappe point à ce vice de l'esprit humain. Thèmes légendaires en effet, ce "couple Rimbaud-Lautréamont," ce "couple Rimbaud-Nietzsche," tout bêtement calqués sur les formes françaises de cette thématique. Plus intéressant, parce qu'en ce temps-là, en ce lieu-là moins attendu, le thème de Rimbaud le communard : car nous sommes en 1930. Cette année-là, en Roumanie, Carol, qu'un conseil de Régence avait écarté du pouvoir, remonte sur le trône de son père le roi Ferdinand et s'attache à ruiner les éléments de démocratie qu'on avait inscrits dans la constitution après la guerre de 1914–1918. La crise de Wall Street a fait craquer le système capitaliste. Codreanu organise des troupes d'assaut qui deviendront la trop fameuse garde de fer. Le fascisme ne se cache point, mais le Parti communiste est mis hors la loi. On dirait pourtant que "le lieu et la formule" évoqués dans ce médaillon, c'est une variété de socialisme, ce que confirme l'évocation, parfaitement légendaire, mais exemplaire, d'un Rimbaud qui travaille le jour (alors qu'il écrit "Maintenant, c'est la nuit que je travaille"), et passerait ses nuits, parfait militant, à coller des affiches révolutionnaires. Lucian Boz fait de son mieux, et ça l'honore en un sens, pour lutter contre le fascisme en prêtant à Rimbaud une pensée factice : car le dernier alinéa de "Vagabonds," ce *lieu*, cette *formule*, ce ne sont ni les Tuileries en flammes, ni la semaine sanglante, ni l'autogestion ouvrière. Quand il écrit "Vagabonds," la Commune est morte et Rimbaud ne s'en soucie plus.

Je me demande par conséquent si le goût de Lucian Boz pour la "connaissance luciférienne" ne le disposa point à quelque sympathie pour le prétendu "satanisme" du poète français.

Le satanisme, au fond, c'est bien le *eritis sicut dii*: une forme déviante de la recherche de l'absolu. Vers 1930, on était un peu partout sensible à

cet aspect de Rimbaud. Témoin l'article de Al. Dumitru Păușești, "Cazul
Rimbaud" (Le "Cas" Rimbaud), dans *Unu*. Aux jugements de ce critique,
seul trouve grâce le livre de Jacques Rivière, qui seul échappe à la platitude
de toutes les vies de Rimbaud. Ce qui est fort bien vu. "Désaxé moderne,"
en quête d'un équilibre, le jeune Rimbaud se soucie moins de poésie, ou
d'agir, que de quêter l'absolu, de sorte que sa "chute" est "plus qu'humaine." A cet égard, le mythe roumain de Rimbaud se modelait assez
exactement sur la variante française.

IV

D'autant plus intéressant, d'autant plus courageux, Sașa Pană, qui ose
publier en 1936, dans *Sadismul adevărului* (*Le Sadisme de la vérité*) un
chapitre, le troisième, entièrement consacré à Rimbaud; livre dont les
surréalistes français ne jugèrent pas la couverture indigne d'être par les
soins de Paul Eluard reproduite dans le numéro 10 de *Minotaure* (Lettre
d'Eluard à Sașa Pană, datée de Paris, 20 septembre 1938). Ni le titre,
pourtant: "Rimbaud, geniul, Rimbaud, pribeagul" (Rimbaud, génie, Rimbaud, vagabond) ni la première phrase du texte, qui ressasse le dogme de
l'unicité de Rimbaud: "Intre geniim Arthur Rimbaud este unicul," n'in-
spirent confiance au lecteur armé d'un peu d'esprit critique. De fait, Pană
subit la légende telle qu'en France on la célèbre vers ce temps-là: il se
réfère quasi rituellement au "Shakespeare enfant"; à Gourmont, encore
que le "crapaud pustuleux" s'atténue en *crapaud* sans adjectif dépréciatif;
à Coppée, à son "fumiste réussi," à Claudel et Rivière. Ses qualificatifs
sont bien ceux que j'ai recensés, dénoncés dans le mythe en question : "enig-
maticul," "satanicul," ou encore: "Misterioasele scrisori cu cerneală sim-
patică" (mystérieux écrits à l'encre sympathique). Mais il n'ignore pas
que Rimbaud voulait qu'on brûlât ses premiers poèmes, il sait que "la
bibliographie de Rimbaud connaît un Rimbaud prophète, un Rimbaud
angélique, un Rimbaud diabolique, un Rimbaud vagabond, un cynique,
un autre blasphématoire"; chez lui, Rimbaud n'est plus seulement précurseur du symbolisme mais celui de toute la poésie, surréalisme compris.
Poète-prophète dès l'âge de dix-huit ans, ce serait avec lui que la poésie
commence à devenir obscure. On pourrait donc redouter que Sașa Pană,
vu les circonstances politiques, ne se réfugie dans le vague de ces propositions en somme peu subversives. Mais non! Il ose évoquer quelques-unes
précisément des "œuvres subversives" composées par le jeune homme:
"Paris se repeuple," ou "Les premières communions," dont il cite en

français les deux titres, comme il cite en français (prudence politique?) le sixain qui clôt "Le Mal": bref les œuvres où la révolte sexuelle se transmue, se sublime en révolte antireligieuse, en idéal révolutionnaire. Il le décrit même écrivant le légendaire "Mort à Dieu" sur les églises de Charleville: "scria cu cretă pe zidurile bisericilor, cu litere de o şchioapă 'MOARTE LUI DUMNEZEU' "; (merde à Dieu! non, cela ne s'écrit pas, surtout sur les murs d'églises). Ce qui n'empêche pas Rimbaud d'être aussi le "créateur d'une réalité supraterrestre," "Le Bateau ivre," par exemple (qui n'a rien, mais rien, de supraterrestre!) ou encore:

> Oisive jeunesse
> A tout asservie,
> Par délicatesse
> J'ai perdu ma vie.

Ou encore, mais oui: "Solde." Du moins comprend-il que si, dans le domaine des hallucinations verbales, Rimbaud et les surréalistes se superposent en quelque sorte, il n'en est rien quant à la technique générale du poème ("Dar nu de technică"). Alors que les surréalistes refuseraient le travail artisanal parce que les interventions postérieures aux "moments" de grâce ne sauraient que falsifier et dégrader le texte, les hallucinations de Rimbaud, elles, sont artistiques parce qu'il les a délibérément voulues belles. Mythe d'un Rimbaud surréaliste, par conséquent, mais revu, corrigé, atténué.

Sous un régime fasciste, tout cela ne manque pas de crânerie, et vaut bien la marque d'estime accordée par le *Minotaure*. Trop de vestiges légendaires, néanmoins, pour que l'esprit critique soit ici pleinement satisfait.

Ce que confirme hélas la biographie de Rimbaud, où s'entassent tous les lieux communs, tous les *topoi* de la fable: "unicité," je l'ai dit d'emblée; vers "hallucinants et prophétiques," "phénomène sismique inconnu jusqu'alors," "énigme," "Satan" qui accomplit en trois ans sa "mission"; et voici monter sur les barricades de la poésie, dès ses premiers vers, un enfant qui n'attend pas celles de la Commune. Cette vie est contée sur un fond d'hagiographie familiale, avec bientôt cette métamorphose du petit Satan en petit bourgeois, puis en bourgeois: "şef de carieră în insula Cipru," puis en grand bourgeois riche:"bogat, un business-man," et pour finir en nabab:"E nabab:posedă avere 40.000 de franci aur"; en nabab qui, selon sa légende, possèderait en effet quarante mille francs or de 1890... et qui serait devenu le "confident de Ménélik."

L'icône du bourgeois (engraissé dans le commerce colonial et le vertueux trafic d'armes) corrige donc l'image première du révolté, voire du révolutionnaire. Et la mort pieuse rachète l'ancien Satan: sous l'influence de sa sœur Isabelle, Arthur se convertit *in extremis* à la religion des siens (le 28 octobre 1891).

Sur deux points toutefois, Saşa Panǎ refuse l'orthodoxie: quand il évoque brièvement le coup de revolver administré à Bruxelles au "bel ephèbe" (frumosul efeb) et quand, au scandale des tenants de l'hagiographie cuifesque, il avoue que Rimbaud mourut d'un cancer. Mais, selon la famille, Rimbaud négocie l'ivoire, le musc et l'or, marchandises nobles entre toutes...

Article ambigu; en progrès par rapport à celui de Blaga, il dose, dirai-je habilement, dirai-je prudemment, quelques propos courageux, quelques vérités alors bonnes mais dangereuses à exprimer, et le vocabulaire vague, outrancier, de l'hagiographie familiale, bourgeoise, symbolarde et surréalisante. Bref, il reflète assez exactement l'état du mythe en France en cette année 1936 où nous le dénoncions, Yassu Gauclère et moi, dans les premiers chapitres du Rimbaud que nous sortions chez Gallimard,[7] mais qui n'eut aucun succès en Roumaine.[8]

Ce que disant, Panǎ reprenait un peu certaines idées éparses chez Geo Bogza, dont l'article "Exaspération créatrice" (Exasperare creatoare) amalgamait déjà Rimbaud avec plusieurs des idoles du surréalisme: Jarry, Lautréamont, Ribemont-Dessaignes, ou suggérées chez Const. I. Emilian, lequel dénonçait l'anarchisme poétique des *Illuminations*, voyait en Rimbaud un précurseur du dadaïsme (mais, curieusement plus spontané même que ces absolus spontanéistes) et n'appréciait guère, chez le poète français, que cette part de l'œuvre qui manifeste un précoce esprit révolutionnaire.

V

Indépendamment des quelques articles de peu de poids, mais qu'on trouvera cités dans la bibliographie dont je dispose pour les années 1895–1945, le dernier état du mythe de Rimbaud avant la création de la République populaire de Roumanie est celui qu'on décèle en étudiant l'ouvrage de Ion

7. Etiemble, Yassu Gauclère, *Rimbaud* (Paris, 1936), première partie: "Images de Rimbaud," p. 13–96; dans la troisième édition, 1966, collection Les Essais, ce chapitre se trouve aux pp. 17–105.
8. En 1936 paraissait à Paris le *Rimbaud* de Daniel-Rops, chez Plon. Sous-titré *Le drame spirituel*, il fut honoré de deux recensions favorables en Roumanie. Je les ai lues en leur temps, sur les coupures de presse que me communiqua l'auteur, mais dont les références étaient incomplètes, comme on le verra dans la bibliographie. Sur le *Rimbaud* que j'écrivis cette même année avec Yassu Gauclère, mon éditeur n'a reçu aucune recension de Roumanie; ce qui se comprend, vu le caractère marxisant et anti-religieux de notre interprétation.

Frunzetti:*Iluminările*, publié à la fin du régime fascisto-monarchiste du roi Michel, en 1945. Pour mon propos, seul importe le fait que ce livre soit sorti des presses et diffusé en Roumanie quand ce pays est gouverné par un fascisme allié au nazisme: Carol a dû céder le pouvoir à son fils Michel I, celui précisément à qui Ferdinand avait confié le trône en 1927. Le général Ion Antonescu devient alors le Duce, le Führer, le Conducător de l'infortunée Roumanie et devient en janvier 1941 le vassal du pouvoir hitlérien. Le 22 juin 1941, le Conducător entre en guerre avec l'Union soviétique. Telle sera la situation jusqu'au 23 août 1944. Ce jour-là, inquiet de l'offensive soviétique en territoire roumain, Michel I accepte qu'on arrête le Conducător et son homonyme Mihail Antonescu, ministre pro-nazi, un peu flottant, des Affaires étrangères. Pour sauver son trône, il demande aux Alliés l'armistice, déclare la guerre au IIIe Reich, marchande avec les Russes la Transylvanie contre la Bessarabie et un lambeau de Bukovine qu'exige l'impérialisme de Staline, ce nouveau tsar. C'est dans ces conditions que la Fondation royale pour la littérature et l'art publie l'ouvrage de Frunzetti, lequel annonce qu'il prépare un essai, *Arthur Rimbaud*, avec, en sous-titre français: *L'Homme aux verrues*, ce qui nous renvoie à la poétique de Rimbaud: "il s'agit de se faire l'âme monstrueuse: à l'instar des comprachicos, quoi! Imaginez un homme s'implantant et se cultivant des verrues sur le visage" (Lettre du 15 mai 1871).

Bien qu'il ne comporte aucune préface, aucune note, l'ouvrage est précieux en ceci qu'il nous offre le Rimbaud que pouvait accepter une Roumanie monarchiste, réactionnaire, fasciste.

Aux pages 7–19, douze traductions de ce qu'on appelle souvent les "premiers vers," savoir: "Sensation," "Tête de faune," "Le Dormeur du val," "Ma Bohême," "Oraison du soir," "Le Bateau ivre," "Voyelles," "Quatrain," "Roman," "Rêvé pour l'hiver." "Voyelles" et "Le Bateau ivre," on le sait, on ne le sait que trop, c'est l'essence, la quintessence du mythe. La plupart des autres poèmes choisis se distinguent par leur caractère anodin: historiettes d'amour rêvées, tableautins de la nature, qui ne choquaient pas non plus le camarade Staline. "Ma Bohême" et "Oraison du soir" ne sont peut-être pas édifiants; ils ont alors ce grand mérite: apolitiques. Mais ne doit-on pas admirer que, sous un régime férocement militariste, Frunzetti ait inclus "Le Dormeur du val," ce poème pacifiste, en tout cas souvent glosé comme tel? Lisons la version roumaine:

> Doarme, cu mâna pe piept: și'n plin soare
> Liniștea-i vată pe rănile—două—din șoldul său drept.

Bien atténués, les "deux trous rouges" au côté droit! *Adormitul văii*—au titre anodin—a donc pu se glisser dans cette anthologie, car on y peut fort bien admirer une idylle champêtre qui célèbre un vaillant guerrier, blessé dans une juste guerre. A lire la première partie du recueil, aucun Roumain, parmi ceux du moins à qui s'adressait Frunzetti: ceux qui ne pouvaient lire en français les textes de Rimbaud, ne pourrait soupçonner d'esprit subversif l'auteur de ces quelques pièces. Tout au plus, à cause de

Je pisse vers les cieux bruns,

qui devient:

Mă piş spre cerul brun,

pourrait-on le comparer à un espiègle *manneken-pis*!

Non moins édifiante, la seconde partie du recueil, pp. 25–57. Après ces "primele versuri" dont je viens de parler, elle rassemble, sous le titre arbitraire d'*Illuminations* (*Illuminările*), des textes qui, lors même qu'ils ne respectent plus la métrique traditionnelle, sont encore des vers, avec une prosodie où l'on discerne aisément des intentions de versificateur. Sous-titrés "vers nouveaux et chansons," ces poèmes avaient été publiés par Berrichon sous le titre général d'*Illuminations* dans son volume du Mercure de France. Ion Frunzetti s'en inspire évidemment et retient "Silence," "Larme," "La Rivière de Cassis," "Bonne pensée du matin," "Michel et Christine," "Comédie de la soif," "Honte," "Mémoire," "Jeune ménage," "Patience," "Eternité," "Chanson de la plus haute tour," "Bruxelles," "Est-elle almée?," "Bonheur," "Age d'or," "Fêtes de la faim," "Marine" et "Mouvement," c'est-à-dire, dans l'ordre de l'édition française, les poèmes classés par le beau-frère abusif; tous sauf un, le premier, par Berrichon intitulé "Vertige," bien que le manuscrit de la collection Bérès ne comporte aucun intitulé. Afin d'atténuer la virulence de ce cri, Berrichon renvoie donc, implicitement, à cette phrase de la *Saison* où Rimbaud condamne sa poétique: "Je fixais des vertiges". Il s'agirait donc, tout benoîtement, d'un *vertige*. Vertige à la rigueur, et dont *in fine* l'auteur sort très bien, très lucidement: "Ce n'est rien: j'y suis; j'y suis toujours." Mais ce vertige, ce "rêve," comme l'appelait Ernest Delahaye dans la glose qu'il en suggère, n'est pas anodin du tout:

> La pensée [en effet] est facile à suivre. Le révolutionnaire, voyant la défaite de sa cause, a des accès de rage. Il redirait bien *Les Incendiaires* (*) de son ami Vermersch:

(*) Poème de Vermeersch publié à Londres en 1871.

> Plus d'hésitations louches, plus d'équivoques:
> Bourgeois, tu mourras tout entier!
>
> Il nous faut au grand jour la justice farouche,
>   Sans haine comme sans amour,
> Dont l'implacable voix, plus haut que la tempête
>   Parle dans sa sérénité,
> Et dont la main tranquille au ciel lève la tête
>   De Prudhomme décapité!

Mais cette revanche impitoyable, ce quatre-vingt-treize intégral ne saurait lui suffire. Il veut la mise à mort, l'abolition d'absolument tout [...]. Catégories nationales et divisions géographiques ayant disparu, que reste-t-il à détruire?
> Les volcans sauteront! Et l'Océan frappé...
Toute excitation déréglée produit un besoin subit de repos, le délire intellectuel s'éteint.

En fait, l'échec de la révolte, celui de la révolution, égarent apparemment l'enfant Rimbaud jusqu'au nihilisme radical, jusqu'à rêver d'un retour universel au néant. Mais comme il s'agit d'abord d'exterminer tout ordre: "Industriels, princes, sénats" et jusqu'à la "justice," la "puissance" et l'"histoire,"

> Des régiments, des colons, des peuples, assez!

on comprend aisément que le nihilisme nazi, que financent alors les industriels, qui accumule les régiments, et qui veut implanter ses colons dans toute l'Europe (notamment l'orientale), n'ait pu tolérer ce poème chez Berrichon liminaire. Ion Frunzetti l'escamote, sans bien entendu préciser qu'il commet cette omission. En arrachant de la séquence des chansons plus ou moins "spirituelles" le cri de révolte absolue contre tout ordre bourgeois, militaire et colonisateur, le traducteur roumain trahit donc le poète français: le rend inoffensif.

Si je disposais d'autant de pages encore, que de réflexions s'imposeraient sur cette version "fasciste" du mythe de Rimbaud! Il me semble piquant, et significatif, qu'un volume intitulé *Illuminations* ne contienne en fait aucun des poèmes en prose que l'on a toujours rassemblés sous ce titre-là. Mais il faut un rêveur, un illuminé, un homme peu dangereux politiquement.Va donc pour *Illuminations*! Et comme il serait passionnant d'étudier en détail les traductions, pour voir si, oui ou non, les lecteurs de Frunzetti liront quelque chose qui ressemble à du Rimbaud. Pour les "vers libres" de "Marine" et "Mouvement," le sens est restitué assez honorablement; qu'on en juge d'après "Marină":

> Carele de argint și de arama
> Prorele de oțel și de argint,
> Bat spuma,
> Răscoală mărăcinilor tulpinile.
>
> Căile landei
> Și mătcile uriașe-ale refluxului
> Se răsusesc rotund spre răsărit
> Către coloanele pădurii,
> Către butucii digului,
> Izbit în colțuri de vârtejele luminii.

Mais c'était facile; c'est toujours facile de traduire du "vers libre." Quant aux autres poèmes! Soucieux à juste titre de rendre en vers roumains rimés les vers rimés de Rimbaud, le traducteur n'eut pas assez de talent, ou de patience, pour y parvenir; car c'est bien l'entreprise la plus nécessaire, mais la plus malaisée de toutes dans l'exercice de la littérature. De sorte que, les lecteurs roumains qui ne lisent pas le français ne pourront à travers Frunzetti ni connaître la pensée politique de Rimbaud, ni soupçonner les variations, les fins de sa poétique.[9]

Et pourtant, une trentaine d'années plus tard, dans un article à plus d'un égard judicieux qu'il publia dans *România literară*, Matei Călinescu, qui découvrit le poète français dans la version de Frunzetti, en conclut que son

---

9. Reconnaissons que la traduction de "Voyelles," toute rimée pourtant, restitue assez bien le sens de l'original: en voici la retraduction française:

> *Voyelles*
>
> *A* brun, *E* blanc, *I* rouge, *U* vert, *O* violacé. Est-ce que
> Je saurai jamais dire votre genèse intime?
> *A*, ceinture veloutée des mouches en nuées, brun
> Qui bourdonne sur quelque fraîche puanteur.
>
> Golfe lourd d'ombres. *E*, blanche vapeur, blanches toiles
> Glaciers aux lances étincelantes, rois blancs, corolles au vent.
> *I*, pourpres, sang phtisique, superbes bouches riant
> De fureurs, d'ivresses ou de pénitences pénétrées.
>
> *U*, cyclique vibration des mers verdâtres.
> Le repos parsemé de prairies et de troupeaux;
> Des silences gravant alchimiquement des traces au sommet du front.
>
> *O*, la trompette de l'éternité, stridences et défaites
> Le silence traversé d'astres et d'anges
> *O*, oméga, éclair bleu de Ses yeux.

émerveillement prouve que cette version était bonne. Par bonheur il reconnaît du même souffle que son enthousiasme fut sans doute aussi un effet de ce qu'après d'autres j'ai appelé le "mythe de Rimbaud." Pour Călinescu, ce mythe est "l'explosion de l'adolescence dans la poésie," ou encore "l'une des plus complètes expressions de la révolte juvénile." Bon. De tous les mythes élaborés à partir de l'infortuné Rimbaud, c'est en effet celui de l'adolescence qui seul est fondé en vérité historique à la fois et psychologique. Frunzetti éclairant Călinescu, voilà bien la dialectique de l'histoire, et son caractère quoi qu'on en dise contingent...

BIBLIOGRAPHIE (1895–1945)

Bien que je n'aie jamais pu me rendre jusqu'ici en Roumanie, où j'eus la chance d'être plusieurs fois invité, l'extrême obligeance de collègues roumains et français, jointe à l'inlassable vigilance d'Igor Stefanovitch Postoupalski, le savant critique soviétique, m'ont permis de me hasarder à traiter d'un sujet que je poursuis en tous les lieux où j'ai lieu de penser, ou de craindre, que je le trouverai. Sans ma collègue Agnès Sola, je ne disposerais pas du livre de Ion Frunzetti: elle eut le générosité de me le rapporter de son séjour en Roumanie. Sans le professeur Al. Dima, je n'aurais pas obtenu le texte roumain de plusieurs des documents dont j'ai pu traiter ci-dessus, et de plusieurs autres que j'emploierai quand je mettrai au point les années 1945–1975. Je lui dois également une bibliographie de seize numéros, dont certains, c'est fatal, se retrouvent dans les documents bibliographiques et les fac-similés que de Moscou me fit parvenir Igor Stefanovitch Postoupalski. Quant à Lidia Bote, outre que je lui dois une vingtaine de traductions de Rimbaud en revue, ou dans les anthologies, elle m'a fourni, avec une attention méticuleuse, trente et une références critiques qui complètent ou corrigent la cinquantaine de numéros que comptait mon fichier quand j'eus la chance d'entrer en relations avec elle et le professeur Adrian Marino. Je dois aussi divers renseignements à Mme Onfroy-Warusfel.Enfin, Mme Christina Ionesco, qui enseigne aujourd'hui au Canada, m'a souvent aidé à juger de la valeur des traductions de Rimbaud en sa langue. A tous, grand merci. Mais les reproches ne devront s'adresser qu'au signataire de cet essai. Il les attend, afin d'en faire son profit, en vue du livre qu'il prépare sur *Le Mythe de Rimbaud dans le monde socialiste.*

RO. 1. Alexandru Macedonski, "Simbolismul" (Le symbolisme), dans *Tara*, 2 juillet 1895.
    P. 625, allusion aux symbolistes qui, non contents d'assigner aux lettres de l'alphabet une valeur musicale, leur attribuent quelque couleur. *A noir* fait évidemment allusion à Rimbaud. C'est donc par "Voyelles," comme partout ailleurs, que Rimbaud fait sa percée en Roumaine.

RO. 2. Mircea Demetriade, "Sonuri și culori" (Sons et couleurs), dans *Antologia poeziei simboliste românesti (Anthologie de la poésie symboliste roumaine)*. Editie și prefața de Lidia Bote. Bucarest, editura pentru literatură, 1968, p. 35.

L'auteur de ce sonnet, à peu près contemporain de Rimbaud, reprend, mais en essayant de l'appliquer, la poétique dont le poète français se garde bien de se servir dans *Voyelles*.

RO. 3. Ion Minulescu, "Arthur Rimbaud," dans *Revista celor l'alți*, No. 2, avril 1908.

Cette revue, dont Ion Minulescu (1881–1944), écrivain délibérément tourné vers l'Europe occidentale, fut le créateur, fait à Rimbaud une place importante dès le second numéro.

RO. 4. Arthur Rimbaud, "Ofelia" (Ophélie). Trad. de George Duma, dans *Revista celor l'alți*, No. 2, avril 1908.

Complétant l'article de Minulescu, voici apparemment la première traduction de Rimbaud en roumain. Poème anodin.

RO. 5. Ovid Densusianu, "Sufletul nou în poezie" (L'âme nouvelle dans la poésie), dans *Conferențele 'Vieței nouă,'* Ire ser., 1909, pp. 7–8

Rimbaud comme précurseur des symbolistes; halluciné; qui fait entendre de nouveaux accents, etc....

RO. 6. N. Davidescu, "Estetica poeziei simboliste" (L' esthétique de la poésie symboliste), dans *Viața Românească*, XVIII, No. 1, janvier 1926, pp. 38–58; repris dans *Aspecte și Directii literare (Aspects et orientations littéraires)*, Bucarest, éd. Minerva, 1975, pp. 396–423.

Où l'auteur analyse encore le sonnet des "Voyelles," du point de vue des synesthésies. Après avoir exposé les sources du symbolisme français, on recherche ceux des écrivains roumains qui participent de la même esthétique, savoir: Eminescu, Macedonski, Petică, Minulescu, Demetriade; etc. Le style de Rimbaud est une sorte de "contraction nerveuse": grâce à lui, la littérature française s'est enrichie de quelques notes "uniques" du drame humain. L'*unicité* de Rimbaud: thème de sa légende. Mais quel écrivain, quel peintre, quel musicien n'est pas *unique*?

RO. 7. N. Davidescu, "Alexandru Macedonski despre poezia viitorului" (Alexandre Macedonski sur la poésie de l'avenir), dans *Flacăra*, VII, No. 33, 18 août 1922, p. 528; repris dans *Aspecte și Directii literare (Aspects et orientations littéraires)*. Bucarest, ed. Minerva, 1975, pp. 333–35.

L'auteur oppose ici la mélodie du vers roumain selon Macedonski à "l'instrumentalisme" de Ghil et à la poétique des "Voyelles" selon Arthur Rimbaud. Mais, depuis 1892, les poètes roumains ont tendance à se détacher d'Eminescu et à s'intéresser au symbolisme français: Macedonski, Petică, etc.

RO. 8. Lucian Boz, "Medalion Rimbaud" (Médaillon de Rimbaud), dans *Facla*, No. 337, 1930.

Préférable à la retraite "honteuse" de Lautréamont, la carrière de Rimbaud, en qui Rivière voyait comme un ange qui abandonne à mi-route sa mission: "înger care şi-a pierdut misiunea în drum." Rimbaud résume, à soi seul, tous les styles, toutes les époques. En outre il préparait une sociologie révolutionnaire. Bref, "Toţi poeţii moderni sântem influenţaţi de el": tous les poètes modernes ressentent, subissent son influence. Ce qui est alors le lieu commun de la fable.

RO. 9. Geo Bogza, "Exasperare croatoare" (Exaspération créatrice), dans *Unu*, février 1931.

Rapproche de toutes les figures hallucinantes qui dominent l'époque, Jarry, Lautréamont, Nietzsche, etc . . . . Exaspération: gage d'authenticité; ce qui convient aux Roumains, soucieux de ne pas s'ankyloser.

RO. 10. Al. Dumitriu Păuşeşti, " 'Cazul' Rimbaud" (Le "cas" Rimbaud), dans *Unu*, IV, décembre 1931.

Le seul *Rimbaud* de Jacques Rivière échappe à la platitude. La vie de Rimbaud est "l'effort suprême vers la négation absolue" (satanisme par conséquent, s'il est vrai que Satan est "der Geist der stets verneint"); mais satanisme manqué, à ce point puissante sur lui la tradition.

RO. 11. Const. I. Emilian, *Anarhismul poetic* (*L'Anarchisme poétique*). Bucarest, 1932.

Voir les pp. 79–80, où la poésie de Rimbaud est condamnée dans la mesure où elle est à l'origine de l'avant-garde anarchisante en poésie; où elle est acceptée, dans la mesure où elle manifeste un précoce esprit révolutionnaire.

RO. 12. Aurel Zaremba, "18 carate" (18 carats), dans *Unu*.

Saşa Pană, No. RO. 16, y fait allusion à propos de ce poète surréaliste, mort tuberculeux à 21 ans, et qui voyait en Rimbaud le lieu d'un combat cruel: "terenul unui permanete duel între satană şi înger, între ideal şi real, între cuvinte şi sunete"(lice d'un duel permanent entre le démon et l'ange, entre l'idéal et le réel, entre les mots et les sons). Rimbaud était le poète préféré de Zaremba.

RO. 13. Dr. G. Marisescu (membre de l'Académie roumaine), "Audiţia colorată" (L'audition colorée), dans *Muzica şi Poezie*, 1ʳᵉ année, No. 1, 1935, pp. 11–15.

L'auteur reproduit et analyse le trop fameux sonnet des *Voyelles*. Quarante ans après le No. RO. 1, on est encore là!

RO. 14. Anonyme, "Studiu critic despre Rimband [sic]" (Etude critique sur Rimband [sic]), dans *Adevărul*, 26 [mois inconnu], 1936.

Compte-rendu du *Rimbaud* de Daniel-Rops, lequel aurait traité son sujet avec beaucoup d'objectivité, "cu multă obiectivitate," ce qui est proprement dérisoire.

RO. 15. Anonyme, notule dans *Indreptărea*, Bucarest [jour et mois inconnus], 1936.

Autre compte-rendu favorable aux thèses indéfendables de cet hagiographe.

RO. 16. Saşa Pană, *Sadismul adevărului* (*Le Sadisme de la vérité*). Bucarest, collection Unu, 1936.

Ecrit en 1935, le troisième chapitre, pp. 31–43, concerne Arthur Rimbaud. L'auteur a conscience des divers avatars du nouveau dieu; il célèbre en lui le pionnier de toute la poésie moderne, tout en observant avec tact que la technique de Rimbaud n'est pas du tout celle des surréalistes. Une chronologie fabuleuse, pour finir.

RO. 17. George Hanganu, *L'Univers poétique d'Arthur Rimbaud* (en français). Brasov, s.d. [après 1936].
Je n'ai pas pu lire ces 29 pages.

RO. 18. George Hanganu, *Doi poeţi vizionari* (*Deux poètes visionnaires*) : *Charles Baudelaire şi Arthur Rimbaud*. Arad, 1938.
Où l'auteur, m'assure-t-on, reprend en roumain ce qu'il avait déjà rédigé en français. En insistant sur le caractère "visionnaire" des deux écrivains, on évite ce qu'il faudrait bien appeler, selon le jargon en usage, soit le réalisme, soit le naturalisme d'une partie des œuvres de Rimbaud.

RO. 19. Arthur Rimbaud, "Boema mea" (Ma Bohême), trad. de L. Iliescu, dans *Revista Fundatiilor Regale*, Bucarest, avril 1940.
Encore un poème anodin.

RO. 20. Dumitru Panaitescu, *Carnet inactual I* (*Carnet inactuel I*). Ed. Eminescu, Bucarest, 1970, pp. 81–87.
Où l'on reprend une étude parue dans *Vremea*, 19 et 26 avril 1942. Recension du livre de Robert Goffin, *Rimbaud vivant*; on observe que les affirmations ne sont pas toujours convaincantes, l'auteur travaillant de seconde main. Ce qui est vrai.

RO. 21. Arthur Rimbaud, "Chip de Faun"(Tête de faune), trad. d'Aurel Marin, dans *Vremea*, 26 avril 1942.
Encore un poème anodin.

RO. 22. George Hanganu, "Sensul tragic al existenţei la Arthur Rimbaud" (Le sens tragique de l'existence chez Arthur Rimbaud), dans *Saeculum*, juillet-août 1943, T. 1er, No. 4.
Comme si les premières interprétations existentielles de Rimbaud, celle de Benjamin Fondane, par exemple, atteignaient la Roumanie, avec naturellement un peu de retard.

RO. 23. Arthur Rimbaud, "Corabia îmbătată" (Le Bateau ivre), trad. de Mihnea Gheorghiu, dans *Meridian*, 1943, No. 17–19.
Première traduction, à ma connaissance, en langue roumaine d'un des deux poèmes en qui se résume la fable de Rimbaud: "Voyelles" et "Le Bateau ivre."

RO. 24. "Din Iluminarile lui Arthur Rimbaud,"trad. de Ion Frunzetti, dans *Universul Literar*, No. 18, 2 mai 1942.
On trouve ici "In urma potopului" (Après le déluge), "Barbara" (Barbare), "Flori" (Fleurs), "Zori" (Aube), "Copilarie" (Enfance).

RO. 25. "Poeme din Arthur Rimbaud"(Poèmes d'Arthur Rimbaud), trad. de Ion Frunzetti, dans *Vremea*, 15 août 1943.

On donne "Rugă de seară"(Oraison du soir), "Vocale" (Voyelles), "Vis pentru la iarnă" (Rêvé pour l'hiver), "Lacrimă" (Larme), "Mihai și Christina" (Michel et Christine).

Alors que tous les poèmes de 1943 sont repris dans le volume suivant, bien qu'il ne s'agisse nullement d'*Illuminations*, aucun de ceux de 1942, qui sont pourtant des *Illuminations*, n'est recueilli dans:

RO. 26. Arthur Rimbaud,"*Iluminarile,*"*precedate de poeme din "primele versuri.*" Traducere din limba franceza de Ion Frunzetti. (*Illuminations*, précédées de poèmes choisis parmi les "premiers vers." Traduits du français par Ion Frunzetti). Bucarest, Fundația regală pentru literatură și artă, collection Scriitorii Streini, 1945.

Le titre induit en erreur, puisque nulle *Illumination* proprement dite ne figure en ce volume. Mais on trouve ce qui figure sous cette rubrique aux pp. 114–61 de l'édition des *Œuvres d'Arthur Rimbaud* "mises en ordre" par Berrichon, avec préface de Claudel, au Mercure de France. Rien sur Rimbaud irréligieux, révolté, révolutionnaire.

RO. 27. Marcel Saraș, "Rimbaud," dans *Meridian*, 1944, No. 14–16, p. 12–18.

Article assez judicieux, qui n'est donc pas de mon gibier: l'hermétisme de Rimbaud n'a rien de commun avec le "formalisme précieux et obscur de Mallarmé," ni non plus avec "la technique virtuose et alambiquée" de Valéry. Rimbaud n'est pas un "innocent," mais il a le sens de la pureté. Il n'est pas athée, mais le Christ ne le comble point. Il veut changer la langue poétique. Soit.

RO. 28. Horia Lovinescu, "Rimbaud," thèse inédite, soutenue à Iassy en 1946.

Elle n'est pas à la disposition des chercheurs.

RO. 29. Miron Radu Parachivescu, *Tălmăciri după 8 poeți europeani (Traductions de huit poètes européens)*. Bucarest, 1946.

Je sais que Rimbaud figure parmi les élus, mais je n'ai pas encore pu voir le volume; je ne garantis donc pas l'exactitude scrupuleuse du titre.

Gilbert Gadoffre

Connaissance de l'Est et Mallarmé

I

"Mallarmé que j'ai fréquenté assez souvent à partir de 1887 m'intéressait mais n'a jamais eu aucune action sur moi," écrit Claudel dans son *Journal* en septembre 1924. Un an plus tard il avouait pourtant à Frédéric Lefebvre, au cours d'une interview, que *Connaissance de l'Est* était son "œuvre la plus mallarméenne,"[1] et peu de temps avant sa mort il convenait qu'il serait difficile de comprendre son œuvre sans tenir compte des conversations et des lectures de ses années de formation (1886–1893) qui l'ont orienté pour le meilleur et pour le pire. "Tout ce que j'ai appris à ce moment-là," a-t-il confié à Henri Guillemin, "est mêlé à ma substance."[2]

Ajoutons que malgré ses accès d'ingratitude à l'égard du maître de la rue de Rome, Claudel n'a jamais cessé d'affirmer qu'il lui devait une chose essentielle: l'aptitude à se placer devant un objet en disant non pas "Qu'est-ce que c'est?" mais "Qu'est-ce que cela veut dire?" Il n'y a aucun doute, affirme t-il à Amrouche dans *Mémoires improvisés*: "C'est certainement cette question là qui m'a guidé dans toute ma vie et qui m'a placé devant tous les êtres et les spectacles que j'ai vus avec la passion de comprendre, d'essayer de comprendre ce que cela veut dire."[3]

Le jeune Claudel des années quatre-vingt n'en est pas encore à mesurer l'admiration au maître. Fervent et sauvage, il assiste aux conversations du cénacle sans souffler mot, sauf aux rares moments où son agressivité de timide rompt son mutisme. "Chez Mallarmé, j'écoutais," confiera-t-il beaucoup plus tard, "je ne disais presque rien. Une fois, si, j'ai lancé une phrase contre Victor Hugo. Je me suis fait joliment ramasser, par Mallarmé lui-même. Lui qui était si poli, si gentil, il m'a 'contré' sec. Je me le suis tenu pour dit."[4] Dans la plupart des cas, semble-t-il, il ne discute pas avec le Maître: il a des conflits muets avec l'un ou l'autre des disciples, comme

1. Frédéric Lefebvre, *Les Sources de Paul Claudel* (Paris, 1927), p. 142.
2. Henri Guillemin, "Claudel m'a dit," *Le Nouveau Candide*, 2 (4 janvier 1962).
3. Paul Claudel et Jean Amrouche, *Mémoires improvisés* (Paris: Gallimard, 1954), p. 67.
4. Henri Guillemin, "Les confidences de Claudel à Henri Guillemin," *Le Nouveau Candide*, 2 (11 janvier 1962).

le laisse entendre la lettre de Mallarmé à Claudel alors chargé de mission à Fou-tchéou: "Vous me manquez aussi parce que vous auriez une façon de hausser les épaules furieusement, là, sur le petit canapé des mardis, laquelle me réconforterait intimement."[5]

Devant ce "parisien ironique et rusé à la Degas habitué à se faire comprendre à demi-mot,"[6] le jeune champenois, conscient de sa gaucherie, éprouve une vénération sans réserves accompagnée d'un sentiment très vif de sa "propre patauderie" de provincial sans usages et sans agilité.[7] Ce qui le stimule au plus haut point, c'est la recherche mallarméenne d'un instrument verbal souverainement précis qui lui permet de former "sa lèvre au vers exact et au mot absolu,"[8] recherche savante et subtile, mais non dépourvue d'éléments ludiques pour le plus grand désarroi des profanes qui ne voient qu'obscurité, dit Claudel, là où l'on trouve au contraire "la précision extrême et l'élégance d'un esprit habitué à de hauts jeux."[9] Mais les hauts jeux et la recherche d'un langage épuré déconcertent dans la mesure où ils sont liés à une vision du monde teintée de philosophie à l'allemande transposée par Villers de L'Isle Adam et Wyzewa, un univers où les seuls êtres virtuels sont les idées pures, les objets n'étant que des signes.

Claudel, dans la mesure où il s'applique à déchiffrer les signes et à établir entre eux et les idées une série de rapports bilatéraux qui les confirment dans leur existence, ne fait que rejoindre une tradition très ancienne, et mettre *Connaissance de l'Est* au confluent d'une triple tradition de symbolisme:[10] celle du symbolisme littéraire fin de siècle, celle des Pères de l'Eglise et de la liturgie remise alors en honneur non seulement par Huysmans mais par des agnostiques tels que Rémy de Gourmont[11] et la sym-

5. Lettre de Mallarmé à Claudel du 18 février 1896, *Cahiers Paul Claudel*, 1 (Paris: Gallimard, 1959), 48.

6. Paul Claudel, "La Catastrophe d'*Igitur*," *Œuvres en prose*, collection de la Pléiade (Paris: Gallimard, 1950), p. 510.

7. Lettre de Claudel à Mallarmé du 23 novembre 1896, *Cahiers Paul Claudel*, 1 (1959), 50.

8. Paul Claudel, sonnet offert en hommage à Mallarmé, publié dans Henri Mondor, *Vie de Mallarmé*, 38e éd. (Paris: Gallimard, 1946), p. 778.

9. Lettre de Claudel à Mallarmé du 25 mars 1895, *Cahiers Paul Claudel*, 1 (1959), 44.

10. Sur cette question, je me permets de renvoyer à mon article sur "Les trois sources de l'analogie claudélienne," dans *French Studies*, 13 (1959), 135–45.

11. Rémy de Gourmont, *Le Latin mystique* (Paris, 1890). L'année précédente dans son manifeste sur l'*Art symboliste*, G. Vanor avait aligné à l'appui de sa thèse une série de citations de pères de l'Eglise. Dans deux livres de Huysmans, *En Route* (1895) et *La Cathédrale* (1898)—ce dernier livre ayant paru la même année que l'étude magistrale d'Emile Mâle, l'*Art religieux en France au XIIIe siècle*—on pouvait trouver des tentatives de codification systématique de la symbolique médiévale.

bolique chinoise.[12] Mais lorsque Mallarmé pousse le haut jeu jusqu'à l'escamotage de l'objet après l'avoir laissé entrevoir, imagine-t-on Claudel suivant ses traces? Quand l'auteur d'*Igitur* ne confère plus aux objets qu'une présence en creux, quand il ne parle plus de fleurs ou de vases vides mais de "l'absence de tous bouquets," plus de tombes nues mais d'un sépulcre qui "Hélas du manque seul de lourds bouquets s'encombre," on pourrait croire Claudel immunisé par son tempérament et ses croyances à ces traits stylistiques visiblement liés à ce qu'il dénoncera plus tard comme une poétique de "l'absence réelle," qui "aboutit à ce blanc, à ce vide,"[13] à une imagination fascinée par le néant.

Un examen attentif de *Connaissance de l'Est* permet cependant de trouver plus d'un exemple de ces énoncés négatifs. Au terme d'une promenade dans la campagne du Fou-kien, quand de loin il aperçoit sa maison, Claudel précise: "Mon absence est configurée par cette île bondée de morts et dévorée de moissons."[14] La lampe, écrit-il dans *La Lampe et la cloche*, "atteste cela dont tout l'abîme est l'absence," et il donne de l'une et de l'autre des définitions négatives; "L'une mesure le silence, et l'autre approfondit l'obscurité."[15] La ligne d'horizon en haute mer se traduit par "la cessation de la couleur la plus foncée."[16] *Portes* multiplie les énoncés de ce type, depuis le début: "toute porte carrée ouvre moins que ne clôt le vantail qui l'implique," jusqu'au centre : "l'art de ce lieu restreint est de me dérober en m'égarant ses limites," et à la conclusion: "Que je ne cueille point la fleur de l'après-midi à un autre jardin... ."[17] Dans *L'Arche d'or dans la forêt* les dorures des temples de Nikko deviennent "la splendeur du trésor occulte, flambeau absent décelé par d'invariables miroirs."[18]

A ces définitions en creux s'ajoutent les propositions négatives qui tantôt se multiplient en donnant à toute une page sa structure, tantôt surgissent isolément et provoquent un point de rupture: ainsi des phrases telles que: "Nul cadavre n'est si suspect que d'exiger sur lui l'assoiement d'une pareille masse" dans *La Tombe*,[19] ou bien "L'appel brusque d'un paon n'accroît

---

12. Gilbert Gadoffre, *Claudel et l'univers chinois* (Paris: Gallimard, 1968), *Cahiers Paul Claudel*, 8 (Paris: Gallimard, 1968), 225 sq., 232, 239 sq., 278 sq., 287 sq.

13. Paul Claudel, "Notes sur Mallarmé," *Œuvres en prose* (Paris: Gallimard, 1913), p. 514.

14. Paul Claudel, "Le point," *Connaissance de l'Est*, éd. Gilbert Gadoffre (Paris: Mercure de France, 1973), p. 355.

15. "La Lampe et la cloche," ibid., p. 333.

16. "Dissolution," ibid., p. 367.

17. "Portes," ibid., pp. 189–90.

18. "L'Arche d'or dans la forêt," ibid., p. 258.

19. "La Tombe," ibid., p. 232.

pas moins l'abandon du jardin assoupi" dans *Halte sur le canal*.[20] Dans
La Dérivation, par contre,[21] les énumérations négatives sont serties dans
le mouvement rhétorique de la période: "ni la soie ... ni la profonde laine
d'un tapis de sacre ne sont comparables ... ni le nom du lait, ni la couleur
de la rose ... le fleuve ne m'apporte pas une richesse moindre.... Ne dites
pas ... car l'œil ne suffit point...."[22] Ici les négations cessent d'être facteurs
de rupture: elles sont, au contraire, le liant d'un alliage, et au lieu de raréfier
l'oxygène à la manière des formes privatives mallarméennes, au lieu de
susciter des zones de vide autour desquelles le poème s'enroule, elles sont à
l'origine des appels d'air qui s'organisent entre les zones de plénitude et
elles. Les *ni* en cascade qui jalonnent la période centrale nous conduisent
tout droit vers des évidences du toucher, du goût et de la vue ressentis avec
gourmandise: "ni le nom du lait, ni la couleur de la rose à cette merveille
dont je reçois sur moi la descente. Certes je bois, certes je suis plongé dans
le vin!" A ces affirmations des sens puissamment orchestrées répondent des
optatifs de conquête: "Que les portes s'ouvrent pour recevoir les cargaisons
de bois et de grains qui s'en viennent du pays d'en haut, que les pêcheurs
tendent leurs filets pour arrêter les épaves et les poissons, que les chercheurs
d'or filtrent l'eau et fouillent le sable: le fleuve ne m'apporte pas une
richesse moindre." Porté par un développement oratoire qui n'est pas ici
un ornement mais remplit une fonction très précise, le mouvement des
phrases contribue à lui seul à l'évocation du flux du Yang-tseu kiang dont
la présence physique s'impose à nos oreilles et à nos yeux.

II

Au début de son séjour en Chine, Claudel admire Mallarmé plus que jamais, sans méconnaître ce qui les sépare ni les sentiments d'infériorité qu'il
rumine. Il est encore un débutant à la recherche d'un langage. Partagé
entre deux admirations, Jules Renard et Mallarmé,[23] il doute de pouvoir
jamais "écrire d'une manière achevée dans un style ou dans l'autre," et
il ajoute: "De ma vie je n'ai pu écrire une phrase qui m'ait satisfait, proférer complètement une sentence accompagnée de l'ordre et du légitime
appareil des images et des rapports accessoires qu'est une phrase." Il termine sa lettre sur des cris de désespoir: "Je ne serai jamais un écrivain..."
et "il me faudra, malgré le sentiment de la beauté que je crois avoir, conti-

20. "Halte sur le canal," ibid., p. 245.
21. "La Dérivation," ibid., pp. 185–86.
22. Ibid., p. 186.
23. Cf. Introduction à l'édition critique de *Connaissance de l'Est*, pp. 17–23.

nuer à parler comme les hirondelles, dans un langage inconnu et barbare."[24]

On peut être surpris d'entendre ainsi parler Claudel à une époque où il peut déjà mettre à son actif quelques-unes des plus incontestables réussites de *Connaissance de l'Est*: "Le Cocotier," "Fête des morts le Septième mois," "L'Entrée de la Terre." Il a déjà découvert, sans en avoir pleinement conscience, le secret d'une prose de granite irradié, mais en tant que juge de soi-même et des autres il n'est pas encore complètement affranchi des critères de perfection de ses maîtres. Il jalouse la sécurité verbale que peuvent donner le laconisme de Jules Renard, avec "la courte proposition principale à deux notes qui constitue sa phrase,"[25] ou bien l'équilibre subtilement acrobatique de la phrase de Mallarmé où "dans l'aérien contrepoids des ablatifs absolus et des incidentes la proposition principale n'existe plus que du fait de son absence, se maintient dans une sorte d'équilibre instable et me rappelle ces dessins japonais où la figure n'est dessinée que par son blanc, et n'est que le geste résumé qu'elle trace."[26] Maîtrise de l'instrument verbal, cohérence classique de la syntaxe, sécurité jusque dans le risque, autant de privilèges que le débutant envie aux aînés.

La référence japonaise, remarquons-le, n'apparaît pas ici sans raison. Claudel ne cessera pas d'associer l'esthétique mallarméenne du blanc, le fragile équilibre entre l'énoncé et l'allusion, avec l'art japonais qui, précise *Connaissance de l'Est*, "n'exprime que les traits essentiels et significatifs, et laisse au seul papier à peine accentué çà et là par des indications furtives, le soin de taire toute l'infinie complexité qu'une touche vigoureuse et charmante implique encore plus qu'elle ne sous-entend."[27]

Voilà qui nous conduit bien loin des créations claudéliennes du quart de siècle qui va suivre, où le plein l'emporte sur le vide. Mais on peut noter aussi que les textes—il y en a—qui se conforment à ces principes ont été écrits au Japon: *Le Vieillard sur le mont Omi* (1925) et les *Cent phrases pour éventails* (1927).

Dans une préface à ce dernier recueil, il précisera que chacun de ces poèmes est fait de quelques mots "rejoints à travers le blanc par leur seule simultanéité, une phrase faite de rapports," ou mieux encore, qu'il entend laisser "à chaque mot, qu'il soit fait d'un seul ou de plusieurs vocables, à chaque proposition verbale, l'espace—le temps—nécessaire à sa pleine sonorité, à sa dilatation dans le blanc."[28]

24. Lettre de Claudel à Pottecher du 3 juin 1896, *Cahiers Paul Claudel*, 1 (1959), 103–4.
25. Ibid., p. 103.
26. Lettre de Claudel à Mallarmé du 23 novembre 1896, ibid., p. 49.
27. "Çà et là," *Connaissance de l'Est*, p. 267.
28. Préface à réédition (1941) des *Cent phrases pour éventails*, dans Paul Claudel,

Ce n'est pas le hasard qui lui a fait écrire au Japon, à la même époque, "La catastrophe d'*Igitur*" (1926), première tentative d'évaluation, avec un recul historique, du Mallarmé de sa jeunesse. Depuis ses années de formation jusqu'à l'apogée de sa carrière les données mallarméennes et japonaises se sont superposées au point de se confondre.

III

Il arrive dans *Connaissance de l'Est* que l'escamotage de l'objet se traduise non par des blancs, comme chez l'auteur d'*Igitur*, mais par une manière de soutirage du site, comme on peut s'en rendre compte en comparant certains poèmes en prose avec l'événement ou le lieu qui les a inspirés.

Prenons l'exemple de *Portes*, écrit à Hankeou au moment où Claudel, au printemps 1897, est chargé de négocier, de pair avec le consul de Belgique, un projet de chemin de fer Pékin-Hankeou qui serait construit par un groupe franco-belge et financé par des banques françaises et russes.[29] On peut, en se reportant aux agendas de Claudel, dater les entrevues avec le vice-roi Tchang Tche-tong qui se succèdent du 26 avril au 10 mai 1897. La délégation franco-belge se rend chaque fois au Yamen vice-royal, à l'écart de l'agglomération bruyante de Hankeou, dans la vieille cité patricienne de Wou-tchang, sur la rive droite du Yang-tseu. Telle est la situation résumée en deux lignes: "Plusieurs, d'un pas occulte, ont gagné le solitaire Yamen et cette cour qu'emplit un grand silence."[30] Voici les visiteurs dans la cour, ils gravissent les marches qui conduisent à la porte d'entrée du Yamen, s'annoncent par un coup de gong—et voilà que visiteurs, mandarin et Yamen disparaissent. Du Yamen il ne reste plus que la porte, ou plutôt l'entrebaillement de la porte—les "battants que disjoint la désirable fissure"—par lequel on entend la voix d'un serviteur proférer le nom des consuls. Et cet appel évoque aussitôt chez le poète le rituel chinois de la mort: les proches adjurant l'âme de réintégrer le corps, "car l'épouse ou le fils crie à l'oreille gauche du mort."[31] La porte disparaît alors elle aussi de notre champ visuel—on n'y fera plus allusion avant la phrase finale—les "plusieurs" du début se réduisent à un seul: le poète dans le jardin qui

Œuvre poétique, éd. de la Pléiade (Paris, 1967), pp. 699 et 701. Dans sa *Bibliographie* du recueil *Divagations* (1896) Mallarmé offre une définition assez proche: "Raison des intervalles ou blancs . . . remplacer par l'ingénuité du papier, les transitions, quelconques?" (Mallarmé, Pléiade, p. 1576).
29. Gilbert Gadoffre, *Claudel et l'univers chinois*, pp. 85 sq.
30. "Portes," *Connaissance de l'Est*, p. 189.
31. Ibid.

médite sur la mort et l'illusion, debout "sur la dalle plate qui continue le niveau de cette sombre mare,"[32] prêt à voir dans les formes tortueuses qui s'offrent à ses yeux tantôt le tracé d'un ancien souvenir, tantôt la scène d'un théâtre chinois que les acteurs viennent tout juste de quitter: "La Princesse, le Vieillard vient à peine de se lever de ce siège, et l'air vert cèle encore le froissement de l'illustre soie."[33]

Mais les acteurs ont disparu, il ne reste plus qu'un jardin sous le signe de l'illusion. En faisant jouer en fausse perspective les volumes des murs, des arbres, des toits de pavillons, les artifices du jardinier chinois ont désagrégé les repères de l'espace, rendu les limites invisibles, confondu les contours des pierres, des nuages, des feuilles: "Fabuleuse, certes, est mon habitation! Je vois dans ces murs, dont les faîtes ajourés semblent se dissiper, des bans de nuages et ces fantasques fenêtres sont des feuillages confusément aperçus par des échappées; le vent, laissant de chaque côté des languettes dont le bout se recourbe, taille dans la brume ces brèches irrégulières." Reclus dans l'invisible enceinte, le lecteur, avec le poète, voit ainsi la matière et les formes se volatiliser sous ses yeux.

La Mer supérieure présente un cas moins facilement discernable à première lecture. L'examen de l'agenda permet de préciser que ce court texte a été inspiré par une excursion en montagne de juin 1896.[34] Le poète a entrepris l'ascension du flanc d'une vallée brumeuse dans le massif du mont Kou chan, près de Fou-tchéou. Arrivé à un certain niveau il retrouve le soleil après avoir dépassé la nappe de brouillard qui recouvre les vallées, et il voit les sommets de montagnes en émerger comme des îles. Dans la première version manuscrite il n'est pas question de lac mais de "vapeur" ou de "nue," les mots de mer et d'îles n'étant évoqués qu'à titre métaphorique. Il n'y a pas non plus de batelière conduisant "son sampan à travers les eaux plates,"[35] mais un "paysan qui trotte par la rizière laissant posé à terre son double sac,"[36] et le voyageur lance son soulier "au travers de la nue" (n. 8). Entre la première et la seconde version le site réel a disparu. Il est remplacé par un paysage aquatique, la prolifération du champ métaphorique ayant envahi toute la surface du poème et la mer de brouillard étant devenue lac de montagne avec bateau et batelière. Fidèle au précepte de Mallarmé, Claudel ici a laissé l'initiative aux mots.

32. Variante manuscrite, ibid., p. 191 n.5.
33. Ibid., p. 190.
34. Ibid., p. 153. L'agenda précise également qu'au cours de l'excursion Claudel s'est foulé la cheville, ce qui éclaire l'avant-dernier paragraphe.
35. Ibid., p. 151.
36. Ibid., p. 153 n.5. Variante manuscrite.

IV

Le plus mallarméen, peut-être, des textes de *Connaissance de l'Est*, "la Lampe et la cloche," a été rédigé quatre ou cinq ans après la mort du maître de l'école symboliste, au cours du dernier séjour de Claudel à Fou-tchéou (1901–1905). Le rapprochement des deux termes du titre à lui seul est une indication. Quoi de plus mallarméen que le thème de la lampe, la "Lampe angélique" de *Don du poème*, la "clarté déserte" de *Brise marine*, et dans *Las de l'amer repos*: "ma lampe qui sait pourtant mon agonie."[37] Pour Mallarmé comme pour Claudel la lampe représente une continuité sereine, "Le calme doré de l'huile,"[38] dit l'un, "la durée même," dit l'autre, qui "contient son huile; par la vertu de sa propre flamme, elle se boit elle-même [...] Elle a sa provision d'or jusqu'à l'aube,"[39] relayant ainsi le soleil.

Chez Mallarmé il n'y a pas de point du jour et le soleil est rare. On pense au Minuit absolu d'*Igitur* dans le noir d'une "chambre du temps,"[40] le personnage unique du drame ayant une bougie à la main et son "âme fixée sur l'horloge."[41] L'association de la lampe et de la pendule reparaît d'ailleurs chez Mallarmé jusque dans ses écrits de circonstance. "Si j'ai accordé à la Pendule un privilège excessif" écrit-il dans la deuxième de ses *Trois lettres sur l'exposition internationale de Londres* "en lui assignant la première place... le reproche émane à coup sûr de quelque amateur studieux de la lampe, à qui la fonction de verser la lumière dans la chambre paraît plus remarquable que celle d'y jeter des heures retentissantes."[42]

Chez Claudel on retrouve les deux thèmes, mais dans "la Lampe et la Cloche" ils sont l'un et l'autre frappés d'ambivalence. La cloche au début se présente comme un appel venu de l'au-delà ou des profondeurs de l'âme, "La résolution de notre silence intestin."[43] C'est la cloche hydraulique du monastère bouddhique de Kouchan "que le battant intérieur, alors que se renverse la roue remplie d'eau, heurte d'un coup irrégulier"[44]—ce qui est redit d'une manière plus elliptique dans *Connaissance de l'Est*: "Quelque

---

37. Stéphane Mallarmé, *Œuvres complètes*, éd. de la Pléiade (Paris: Gallimard, 1945), pp. 40, 38, 35.

38. Mallarmé, *Proses diverses*, ibid., p. 736.

39. Paul Claudel, "La Lampe et la cloche," *Connaissance de l'Est*, pp. 333–34.

40. Mallarmé, *Igitur*, p. 435.

41. Ibid., p. 439.

42. Mallarmé, loc. cit., p. 669.

43. "La Lampe et la cloche," p. 334.

44. *Le Repos du Septième jour*, Claudel, *Œuvres complètes*, VIII, 259. Dans *Mémoires improvisés* il confirme l'identification de cette cloche avec celle du monastère de Kou chan (pp. 146–47).

chose s'accumule, mûrit dans le nul et vaste son nombre qu'un coup dé-
charge."[45] Cette cloche mue par une chute d'eau avait un son admirable,
précise Claudel dans ses *Mémoires improvisés*: "Je l'entends encore qui
résonnait à travers la forêt de cèdres quand je montais au temple de Kouchan."[46] Et cette cloche a un message, elle est celle "qui dit à toutes les
vanités et à toutes les amours de ce monde: *Non! Non! Non! Ré dièze!
Ré dièze! Ré dièze!*"[47]

Mais dès le milieu du texte on voit la cloche bouddhique peu à peu
devenir horloge, et une série d'interrogations sur le rythme ménage la
transition: "De quel tout est-elle la division? Quel est le mouvement qu'elle
bat? Quel, le *temps?* Voici pour le trahir l'artifice du sablier et de la
clepsydre; le piège de l'horloge contraint l'heure à éclater."[48] Mais une
autre mutation se prépare: le rythme de l'horloge en vient à se confondre
avec le battement du cœur: "Moi je vis. Je suis reporté sur la durée; je suis
réglé à telle marche et à tant d'heures. J'ai mon échappement. Je contiens le
pouls créateur. Hors de moi, le coup qui soudain résonne atteste à tout
le travail obscur de mon cœur, moteur et ouvrier de ce corps." Là encore
Claudel retrouve Mallarmé pour qui "toute âme est un nœud rythmique"[49]
et la chambre d'*Igitur* où l'ombre perçoit "l'oscillation hésitante et prête à
s'arrêter d'un balancier caché," un "battement régulier qu'elle reconnut
être celui de son propre cœur."[50] Il n'est pas sûr que la pendule existe hors
de l'esprit d'*Igitur* ou que le balancier soit autre chose qu'une douteuse
"perception de balancier expirant alors qu'il [*Igitur*] commence à avoir
la sensation de lui."[51] Chez Claudel, au contraire, pulsation et tic-tac ont
chacun leur réalité, et leurs rythmes ne se confondent que dans le cadre
d'une harmonie préétablie.

L'image de la lampe elle aussi change de signe en cours de route. Elle
était d'abord durée absolue, pérennité de l'huile qui "se boit elle-même,"
et voici que dans le dernier paragraphe elle devient phare tournant sur la
côte puis constellation d'astres, repère des navigateurs, et les deux thèmes,
comme dans le stretto d'une fugue, se superposent et se mêlent dans les
images cosmiques des phrases finales: "L'heure sonne, et par l'action de
l'immense ciel illuminé! De la pendule enfouie au cœur d'une chambre de

45. "La Lampe et la cloche," p. 334.
46. Claudel, *Mémoires improvisés*, p. 146.
47. Paul Claudel, "Préface à un album de photographies," *Œuvres en prose* (1950),
p. 398.
48. *Connaissance de l'Est*, p. 334.
49. "La Musique et les Lettres," Mallarmé, p. 644.
50. *Igitur*, ibid., pp. 445–46.
51. Ibid., p. 447.

malade au grand Ange flamboyant qui dans le Ciel successivement gagne tous les points prescrits à son vol circulaire, il y a une exacte réponse. Je ne sers pas à computer une autre heure. Je ne l'accuse pas avec une moindre décision."[52]

Ainsi la lampe devient-elle phare, puis étoile, pour s'identifier enfin avec le char solaire, à la fois lampe céleste et règle des heures. Comme la cloche bouddhique, elle a glissé du domaine de la vie contemplative à celui de la vie active et du mouvement pour se fondre dans un symbole cosmique apte à réconcilier tous les rythmes d'alternance dans l'harmonie universelle.

Nous voilà bien loin du Minuit absolu d'*Igitur*. Mais rien n'accuse mieux ce qui sépare Claudel et Mallarmé que les textes où les deux poètes semblent parler le même idiome.

---

52. *Connaissance de l'Est*, p. 335.

Anna Balakian

Anicet, or the pursuit of *pulchérie*

Among the astonishing areas of neglect in the criticism of twentieth-century literature is the substantial work of Aragon. The oversight is the more surprising in the light of resurgent interest in Dada and surrealism, extending to collateral references such as Jarry, Roussel, and Artaud. André Breton has fared better, although the current scholarly attention to narrative has overstressed the importance of *Nadja* and underestimated Breton's poetry.

In perspective, Aragon may well loom as the Victor Hugo of this century, and with luck and good health he may well make it to 1985. Like his predecessor he has had an active role in forming a literary movement, he has had his politically and patriotically inspired phases, his colossal narratives, and if he was not exiled at a certain period in his life like Victor Hugo, he has known what it is to be a stranger in his own land, evidenced in the poignant poetry of *En Etrange Pays dans mon pays lui-même*.

The current preoccupation with structural analysis puts Aragon at a great disadvantage. He writes plain, vigorous French, he is not neurotically subtle, he takes his structures where he finds them—in the satirical novel, the sotie, the historical romance, and a poetry largely conveyed in Romantic lyricism except for a brief early period in which he indulged in Dada *écriture*. In *Le Paysan de Paris* and in *Le Traité du style* Aragon crystallized and intellectualized the precepts of surrealism better than most of his colleagues who practiced the surrealist metaphor.

But in his earliest prose work, *Anicet*, he accomplished something even more significant: he gave the "materialization of a moral symbol in violent opposition to the morality of the world in which it emerged."[1] These are the words with which he was to characterize some years later the sense of the marvelous which he shared with Breton and a few others in their search for a concept of the Beautiful to replace the standard and tired ones. If the symbolism in *Anicet* is overt in its personifications, its negation of the ethics of the avant-garde of the historical moment makes it an unusual monument in the history of literature, not only in French literature but in

1. Aragon, "La Peinture au défi," in *Les Collages* (Paris: Hermann, 1965), p. 37.

its global and epistemological context. *Anicet* tells us how the spirit of surrealism was ignited; but beyond that, its satire of contemporary figures of the artistic world, lightly shaded, is a pretense and a screen for something much more fundamental that troubled Aragon in 1918 as he began his emblematic tale, something that remains one of the essential problematics of twentieth-century literature on an international level: the perilous struggle of the Beautiful in art and writing.

The central magnet of the "Panorama," as Aragon calls his narrative, is a woman named Mirabelle. If "belle" obviously stands for beauty, "mira" may well imply a reflection—which indeed makes her the center of a multifaceted courtship. But it also suggests the mirror vision, the false appearance, the semblance, implying the mistake that the generation of 1918 may have made in its definition of Beauty. Presumably, an old lover, Guillaume, characterized her as "Mire aux yeux d'argent,"[2] (untranslatable because the double connotation of silver/money does not come across in modern English, whereas in its French ambiguity lies an element of satire). As the *récit* progresses it becomes obvious that Guillaume was none other than Apollinaire, and that he was not referring to the color of her eyes but to their venal concerns. "That explains this court of masks around her, and its recruitment, and this symbol of beauty in the hands of the merchants" (p. x). Her gravitation toward wealth results in the choice she eventually makes of a husband: an American multimillionaire businessman wins her hand in a courtship in which his rivals are among the most talented artists of the time.

In identifying Mirabelle as the symbol of modern beauty, Aragon is stating a hypothesis, to be verified or demolished in the analogical progression of the work. At first, the most prestigious artists credited with having remodeled the concept of beauty at the dawn of the century are seen under veiled names and in Guignol exaggerations, arguing about her function:

—I tell you that she is a solar myth
—A conception of the mind
—An obsessive idea
—An image
—A symbol
—Shut up, said Anicet, she is a woman of flesh and bones, else we would not have found her so beautiful (p. 185).

2. Aragon, *Anicet*. I use the Livre de Poche edition from the Gallimard 1921 text, p. 214. All subsequent quotations will be from the same edition. The translations are all mine. The work has not been translated into English to my knowledge.

Mirabelle's background is examined, and it will not take too much de-
ciphering to realize that Aragon is giving the reader his version of the
history of the concept of Beauty from its beginnings. She first emerges in
the Western world through the constraining realism of a Mediterranean
maturation. She assumes a fatal power of seduction that destroys men; she
becomes an object of fear and persecution: "mothers threw stones after her
as they chased her from a village in Asturias where she had gone to hide
a painful secret" (p. 189). She eventually attracted the attention of the
bizarre—or shall we say "avant-garde"?—Harry James (a suicidal character whom we subsequently are led to identify with a veiled embodiment of
Jacques Vaché).[3] The attraction produced instant results: "suddenly he
leaned toward Mirabelle, drew her to himself and made her a mother" (p.
190). Retrospectively, Mirabelle passed judgment: "Nobody in the world
has ever done so much good and so much harm at the same time" (p. 193).
In fact, the Mediterranean Beauty's illicit alliance with the Absurd produced an offspring which, according to Mirabelle's account, was sold as
trash.

In Paris, the mecca for the worship of Beauty, the adulterated and
modernized version embodied by Mirabelle was wooed by seven identifiable archetypes: a titled crook, an actor, an artist, two poets, a dandy, and
a metaphysician. Bringing her their gifts as masked scavengers, they offer
her a wide range of alternatives, all resulting from "three preliminary conditions" without which modern Beauty cannot be courted: "theft, lie,
mystery" (p. 63).

The glass ball presented by the first suitor is a kaleidoscope that has presumably powers of transcendence. But modern Beauty is capable of using
it only to contemplate her own image as the center of all the universe,
limiting thus the infinite potential of vision to a confined and narcissistic
perspective. The agility of word and movement, the flair for creating illusion, the prestidigitator's aplomb constitute pointedly the stylized stereo-
type of Jean Cocteau.

The second gift is a polygon of iridescent taffeta containing a beautiful
face in its design. In ripping off a piece of the cloth the thief has cut into
the face. The iridescence is an illumination of reality; yet there is an element of clumsiness that destroys the beauty inherent in the ever-changing

3. Jacques Vaché was the young wounded soldier Breton had befriended in a hospital in
Nantes, where he had been on medical service during World War I. Vaché was to symbolize for him, and through him for the surrealists in general, the anti-establishment
spirit of cold defiance and grim humor which Breton amalgamated into the surrealist
archetype.

colors. Despite its damaged appearance it is more powerful than the kalei-doscopic luminosity of the first character's ball, which, placed upon the magic though mutilated cloth, loses all its transfigurative quality. The speech of this second masked figure with the lofty lip contains the lexical characteristics which were to become associated with the future leader of surrealism: iridescence, enchantment, the marvelous, the personal spectrum that extends from grey to rose.

The third suitor is a clown, the Charlie Chaplin archetype, the first great star of the new medium for the representation of Beauty on celluloid. Under the name of Pol, he roams through Aragon's novel, giving it the ragtime version of Beauty, the mechanical, accelerated sense of reality. His contri-bution to modern Beauty is an elixir in the form of a tangerine: "this bizarre little fragrant sun" (p. 60). He procures it at great and comic risk to himself and disrupts the systematized structure of a theater audience as he snatches the precious golden apple from a vendor. All he can do to remunerate her is to give her a spectacular acrobatic performance of his flight. Much valor is displayed, and stunningly succulent is the fruit, but rapidly consumed. Aragon gives a succinct indictment of the value of the cinema to aesthetics: brilliant, gilded, savory but ephemeral—so much effort for so short a satisfaction. We are here very far from the high hopes that Apollinaire had entertained for film as an eventual replacement for the word in the making of poetry, i.e. the Beautiful.

The accent of the fourth suitor suggests that he is either a high-class Italian or a low-class Slav; he brings a diplomatic document, which, if leaked, could cause catastrophic wars. It seems not too far-fetched to con-clude that the allegory of the gift and the ambiguity of the place of origin of the giver suggest the involvement of a foreign conspiracy in the shaping of the so-called modern version of the Beautiful. There are elsewhere direct references to futurism and overt ones to Dada. It is interesting to note that Aragon gives neither of these in any guise an important role in the shaping of the new aesthetics; but the foreign suitor in whom they seem to be amalgamated is among the most shady of the whole secret society seeking to espouse Mirabelle

The fifth bearer of a gift is Omme, which is a homonym for Man and for the unit of electrical resistance. Although some critics have identified Omme as Jarry, Aragon's own 1931 preface names Valéry, who indeed fits more logically here as the suitor who brings a resistor and an element of measure, stolen from the Institut des Arts et Métiers. His concern for philosophic truth and rule-oriented humanism, pronounced in what Aragon calls a "white" voice, sums up the self-serving hyperbole of Omme: "the most useful present, the most urgent, and the most worthy of your character and of mine" (p. 63).

The next, a painter, whose manifest and later confirmed model is Picasso, has lifted the signal which railroad stations use to prevent collisions of trains. He compares the gadget to a red flower and reminds Mirabelle of the cataclysmic consequences of his theft: the possible collision of two rapid trains originating from distant points. Here the conquest of modern Beauty demands the sacrifice of order and risks terrible destruction. Had not Picasso caused, indeed, the collision and explosion of long-established and orderly systems, the breakdown of standardization and of accepted relationships?

The last donor brings the faded photograph of a Beauty of a past generation, of the time of the Blue Danube and of *Pêcheur d'Islande*. One thinks of Rimbaud's *Letter*, in which he chastized those whose search for novelty only led them back to "the spirit of things dead." Aragon is here passing a devastating judgment on Chipre, under whose mask is Max Jacob, generally presumed to have been an avant-garde figure.

If there are seven suitors in this scene, the secret society assures the new aspirant, Anicet, that the number of those seeking modern Beauty's hand is not fixed; it is flexible and ever-fluctuating, and she is indeed an equal-opportunity employer, which makes it possible for Anicet to join the ranks immediately. His gift is a stanza of verse, which is received with derision. He will have to do much better than that to prove a worthy contender for the favors of Beauty: "Don't be surprised by anything," said the fourth masked figure, "and act according to the dictates of your desire for beauty; thus by your actions we shall judge of your aesthetics better than we can by the six mediocre lines of verse you have produced" (p. 73).

A composite methodology for the conquest of modern Beauty emerges out of this allegorical ritual: it is solipsistic, clumsily enchanting, ephemerally glittering, deliberately orderly, perilous, intriguing, superannuated, and amateurishly versified. As narrator, Aragon has not favored any one of the suitors, not even the one with whom he identifies. There is a definite distancing between the two roles he plays: that of participant, in the guise of Anicet, and of third person narrator.

Of his identification with Anicet he makes no secret. What is the meaning of his name? Since he mentions at one point "the fresh fragrance of anise," it can be surmised that he is a fresh, young, somewhat hallucinated being—a small pinch of anise. Anicet/anisette, the drink that he and his companions took when they were not drinking grenadine! The white and the red liquors of their youth were symbolic of that unusual combination of the pure and the sanguine which was to mark the special quality of surrealism among a host of avant-garde movements: the sensual reality of red, the power of dreams and the search for absolute beauty that the white hallucinatory potion provoked.

Anicet's story could have consisted simply of a solipsistic adventure in which he might have imagined himself as the champion of Beauty, delivering her from the beasts that surrounded her. He could have cast himself as the white knight in shining armor triumphant over a series of unappetizing Minotaurs. The cloak-and-dagger imagery of *Anicet* is reminiscent of Breton's poetry of the same vintage, but in Aragon's story it contains a measure of realistic irony, which eventually leads his not quite heroic protagonist to prison, to face the indignation and rancor of public opinion; the accusations against him are so grievous that they may well drag him to the guillotine. His achievements in the defense of Beauty have had a destructive rather than constructive character. He succeeded in eliminating two of the unworthy suitors: the metaphysician of "white" poetry and the American multimillionaire. In the course of a tumultuous presence in the arena, he also managed to burn a number of classified museum possessions representing the Beauty of the past: paintings by Boucher, Meissonnier, Millet, Greuze, and Pissarro were destroyed by his libertarian vandalism. He burned his personal bridges as well: "the chains fall: I cease to be the slave of my past" (p. 78). He even pretended to burn the money that his bourgeois family had sent him for his sustenance. It is a pretense recognized as such by Anicet himself, for even as he assumes the role of disinterested rebel, he calls his own bluff and replaces the 1000-franc bill he had destroyed by another one he had kept in reserve.

True, he may have cut himself off from his family, but he dragged his ancestors behind him in the figures of an aged Rimbaud in the first chapter and an aged Lautréamont in the last. Both are presented as superannuated factors, suggesting that even the most powerful firebrands of aesthetics wane in time and that the position of avant-garde is short-lived as youth itself. As Rimbaud tells of his disillusionment, in a lengthy monologue, the reader realizes how rejectable he is becoming in the eyes of Anicet. At the end of his encounter with Rimbaud, Anicet discovers that he has slept with the same Hortense whom Rimbaud loved and then abandoned—in other words the young rebel had pursued an aging concept of Beauty at the very moment when he was thinking of himself as avant-garde. "I noticed what old-fashioned potions I was using, I did not want to persist in my error, and I went off in search of the modern idea of life, of the line that marked the horizon of our contemporaries" (p. 43).

But at the end of the scene with the seven suitors just as he is declaring his dedication to Beauty and to love, the lights go out. He is left in the figurative dark, for if Hortense was second-hand, Mirabelle is fake; the sense of adventure generated in her pursuit is vain and futile. What she had really done is to open Anicet's eyes to the inauthenticity of what is called the new art. Anicet's function is to single out every one of the false pretenders to avant-garde beauty and to bring out their ineptness.

The methodologists also come under attack: "they looked within themselves with a system of mirrors. They did not care about their objectives. All they enjoyed was the method to be used to attain a goal. The world was governed by minds which reasoned about themselves" (p. 141).

The most compelling scenes are those with Chipre and Bleu. Max Jacob's mating of poverty with poetry comes off as an artificial stance. Bleu's most recent triumphs are revealed as academic disgraces. The chapter in which Aragon describes Bleu's rise and fall is called, tellingly, "Decease." His *natures mortes* gave the viewer a wonderful sense of living forms, says Anicet, whereas his latest so-called masterpiece in praise of living form, called "Praise of the Body," is lifeless and stilted. "Anicet suddenly understood that Bleu had passed from the domain of love to that of death and glory" (p. 118). The self-appraisal which Aragon puts candidly into the mouth of Bleu is even more devastating: "What a nonentity it is just the same!" (p. 183). The last glimpse of Bleu in this ignoble gallery of false gods is in a newspaper account of his deposition at the trial of Anicet. He shows himself disloyal and unfriendly toward the young defendant. He speeds off to America to become the subject of much adulation and the recipient of much financial reward under the sponsorship of art critics such as Mr. Bolonais (undoubtedly a variation of the ambivalent sausage) whose function will be to establish and dictate tastes in art not only for the current generation but for posterity. Aragon is here not only challenging the validity of the new art of his immediate predecessors but questioning the operations whereby art is promoted and prestige is artificially generated. His satire casts the artist and the critic not in the intellectual battle against each other, which has for so long been the accepted dichotomy, but in an astonishing and shady conspiracy against a gullible public.

Was there anyone who could still salvage Beauty from false creators and promoters? There is the poet with the haughty lip and the clumsy hand who mutilated iridescently beautiful patterns of a face on cloth in the scene of the suitors. His name, we later learn, is Baptiste Ajamais. "He must have been born at the end of a great river in some port on the ocean for his eyes to have caught the grey glow and his voice to have acquired a certain sonority of shells when he said 'the sea.' Somewhere in his childhood, low docks slumbered in the heavy summer evening, and on their still waters there were sailboats that would not leave before the rising of the breeze" (p. 114).

An extraordinary change of style occurs when Aragon is speaking of his friend Breton; the banal and pedestrian tenor of the conversation of the art establishment fades, and the poetic longing that was to characterize and distinguish surrealism from all the other avant-gardes is for a moment fixed on the strange young man coming from the funeral of Harry James, who, having buried the prototype of the absurd, floats in a state of transit, in search of something new.

Whereas Aragon's self-portrait is without glamour, and indeed full of candor and auto-criticism, he adorns his portrait of Breton with an aura of mystery, catches and isolates the rhythm of his speech. Whereas he is Anicet, the subject of transitory excitation, the name Baptiste Ajamais suggests prophecy and permanence, the infinite character of the search. Baptiste is the only one not impressed by the charms of Mirabelle. He tells Anicet: "The conquest of Mirabelle is but an episode, don't forget it, it is the first step in life toward a mysterious end, that I can perhaps discern" (p. 132). When Mirabelle tries to seduce him by undressing before him, Baptiste, unmoved, stares at her coldly. By using Baptiste as his alter ego Aragon demonstrates the ambivalence of his own stand at that moment of youthful incertitude when he might have jumped on the bandwagon of his elders' definition of modernism but didn't. The trouble with the world, according to Baptiste, is that nothing has happened since the world began (cf. p. 237).

Yet where does this purity of posture lead? Baptiste's saintliness is by no means total. He is seen playing with fire, but is cautious not to get burned. Anicet, on the other hand, is shown holding a lamp in one hand and a revolver in the other. The atmosphere that was charged with adventure and vertigo turns into a climate of confusion. All three principals of the narrative are condemned as inept. Mirabelle's beauty was a fraud, and she failed even as a fortune hunter. Anicet was in prison for having pursued false gods and false goods: did he not try to steal Bleu's latest paintings, only to find out that they were worthless? As for Baptiste, he beat a quick retreat to the country and was content to share the fate of Anicet vicariously through newspaper accounts of the trial. He was in the company of two old habitués of a café, one a certain M. Prudence who bore a strange resemblance to Harry James, and the other an old gentleman by the name of Lautréamont. Was Aragon making prophecies about all the graveyards of the avant-garde?

Anicet is indeed the portrait of the author as a young man, but the viewing of the young man is distanced—just as Candide is and is not Voltaire. Candide was the mocking of an attitude of optimism espoused and then corrected by the creator of the persona; in the same manner Aragon was Anicet before he created Anicet, and Anicet's illusion and subsequent disillusionment are crystallized in a self-critical portrayal. When commentators of Aragon quote from Anicet to illustrate permanent attitudes of its author, and when they equate Mirabelle with Aragon's notion of modern beauty, they forget that *Anicet* is but the record of an historical moment, and as Aragon has said: "I don't think people can understand anything about me if they overlook the dates of my thoughts and my writings."[4]

Historically *Anicet* makes an assessment of the avant-garde of the first two decades of the twentieth century. His rejection of the reigning champions of so-called modern Beauty makes this early work a significant document in the history of the modern arts. Whereas at a half-century distance the attitude of most literary and art critics has been to unite the avant-gardes in a continuous flow from cubism to futurism, to Dada and then on to surrealism, a scrutiny of *Anicet* opens a different perspective. Aragon viewed the early years of the century as apocalyptic rather than as avant-garde. He saw his elders in the pursuit of a false aesthetics and found his own contemporaries floundering even though they may have been rejecting the false prophets of a new Beauty. Despite his confusion, the young hero of *Anicet* conveys a deep sense of jeopardy in his handling of the symbolism of Art and Beauty to suggest the perilous state of what he calls "the last divinities of men" (p. 162).

From the narrator's point of view the triumph of Bleu is as great a threat to the discovery of a new concept of beauty as the imprisonment of Anicet and the immobilization of Baptiste. Moreover, Aragon makes it clear at the end of the book that the spirit of absurdism, made incarnate in Jacques Vaché/Harry James, is not in his view the true spirit of modernism either. When Baptiste finds under the guise of M. Prudence his old

4. Epigraph to *Aragon, une vie à changer* by Pierre Daix (Paris: Seuil, 1975). The translation is mine.

friend whom he had thought dead, his devastating remark to the red-haired character is: "Harry James, I did not really believe you could have died, but now can no longer believe that you are living" (p. 255).

In *Anicet* Aragon shows the threats to the cult of beauty in the twentieth century, but he offers no solutions. He leaves his young characters in a quandary and suggests that they had better not look to their elders for guidance or inspiration. Indeed, if we remember, this was the very time when Breton had lost confidence in Valéry and when his fondness for Apollinaire had lapsed from a professional to a personal level. The situation at the end of *Anicet* has a significant historical validity; it makes it clear that whatever future aesthetics was to emerge, the composition of a new *cénacle* would not be that of master and younger disciples, but a fellowship of peers, shedding the past and looking forward together but without a concerted platform. This phenomenon also explains why as a *cénacle* surrealism would be subject to constant disruptions as each participant found his own direction.

In the pursuit of a new sense of beauty (beyond the desire to prevent the demolition of the aesthetic principle), the next step in the strategy to save Beauty for our time was to come from Breton in his declaration at the end of *Nadja* that Beauty must be convulsive or not be at all. The championship of Beauty from *Anicet* to *Nadja* suggests a continuity that the Dada episode did not succeed in breaking up. The effort to dislodge Beauty from the passive center of an arena toward which the opportunists gravitated, observed in *Anicet*, was not an anti-art reaction: Beauty was thought to be a catalytic force shooting off lightning and producng upheaval. The desire for an aesthetics of dynamic power over minds is inherent in *Anicet* and was to be overtly expressed in the theoretical writing of Breton. In fact, surrealism was to distinguish itself from all other avant-garde movements of the century precisely in its efforts to prolong some semblance of the notion of the Beautiful in a world where the Harry Jameses appear to have triumphed, demolishing both ancient and convulsive Beauty.

In 1929 Valéry, who survived Aragon's verbal annihilation of him along with the other perpetuators of what he considered a false notion of Beauty, reactivated the question, and his prognosis for the survival of the Beautiful was pessimistic and prophetic:

A science of the Beautiful? . . . But do the moderns still use that word? It seems to me that they no longer pronounce it except in jest. Or else . . . they are thinking of the past. Beauty is a kind of corpse. It has been supplanted by novelty, intensity, strangeness, in a word by all the values of shock. Base excitement dominates the soul these days; and the current function of literary works is to tear us away from the contemplative state, from the passive happiness whose image was previously connected in intimate fashion with the general idea of the Beautiful. . . . In our time, a 'definition of the Beautiful' can, therefore, be considered only as an historical or philosophical document. Taken in the ancient fullness of its meaning, this illustrious word is about to join, in the drawers of the numismatists of language, many other verbal coins that have gone out of circulation.[5]

In reiterating the alarm of the young Anicet, an aging Valéry was confirming Aragon's worst fears.

The truth of the matter is that the image of a precarious "pulchérie" has been with us for well nigh a hundred years. In the midst of the Symbolist movement, which was presumably centered on the cult of the Beautiful, Mallarmé was foreseeing in cryptic terms the litigation of Beauty in "Prose pour Des Esseintes" in 1882.

He was telling us that beyond the blatant hyperbole, the sorcery, the futility of imaginary landscapes ("de vues et non de visions") the artifices of faded or exaggerated flowers ("Pulchérie/Caché par le trop grand glaïeul") the resurrection of Beauty by the Symbolists had been only a survival on paper ("Anastase: Né pour d'éternels parchemins"). Mallarmé's fatal oracle unfolds as a testament of silence:

> Oh! sache l'Esprit de litige,
> A cette heure où nous nous taisons
> Que de lis multiples la tige
> Grandissait trop pour nos raisons.

In his last poem, *Un Coup de dés jamais n'abolira le hasard,* he had already given up aesthetics to pass on to his episteme.

Were they right, these masters of Symbolism, like Mallarmé and Valéry, to be so faint-hearted toward the future of the cult of Beauty? As we notice how seldom the concept emerges in current literature except in coarse perversion, Aragon's innocent prescience is noteworthy. Unimpressed by the dazzling promises of all the avant-gardes that surrounded him, he had been able to identify Beauty as the major casualty in modern literature.

---

5. Paul Valéry, *Léonard et les philosophes,* in *Œuvres complètes,* Pléiade ed., II, 1240.

Linda Orr

The limit of limits:
aphorism in Char's *Feuillets d'Hypnos*

The enslavement of poetry parallels the enslavement of man.

Age of Surrealism (on Eluard)

Enregistré ainsi, tout émoi ressemble à une sentence qui dans l'esprit du lecteur grandit en
gravité et acquiert une mesure.

La Pureté dans l'art (on Mallarmé)

—Wallace Fowlie, aphorist

The smallest books have the largest aspirations. *Feuillets d'Hypnos* is a
modest volume of notes, a soldier's *carnet*, that would stand in for all that
is worth saving, all that is valued, against the forces of opposition. Holding
steadfast in the dwindling "inaccessible field" of fantasy, the notebook
would first resist so as to repossess everything later. Spanning the highest
and lowest possibilities, it would be either *feuillets* or fire-writing on stone,
the great blue tabulae of a god or the scribblings and scraps of someone in
particular and everyman: leaves of grass.

Before the reader arrives at the first aphorism, the central drama has
already transpired. The title should register the owners of the deed or the
act hinted at in the epigraph, but Hypnos—a pseudonym for Captain Alexandre of the Resistance, another pseudonym—is destined to go up in flames
like dry grass and paper: "Hypnos saisit l'hiver et le vêtit de granit. L'hiver
se fit sommeil et Hypnos devint feu. La suite appartient aux hommes" (p.
84).[1] The epigraph explains the ritual of all beginnings in which there is
an initial combat between *frères ennemis* or doubles (winter and Hypnos),
and out of their fission and transfusion issue two opposite elements: stone

1. Page references to the epigraph and "introduction" or "forward" (as I call the three
short paragraphs preceding the body of aphorisms) correspond to *Fureur et mystère* (Paris,
1967). On the other hand, aphorisms from *Feuillets d'Hypnos* will be referred to by their
numbers (A.1, etc.).

[248]

and fire. (Other binaries are suggested by the initial couple—death/life, defeat/triumph, sleep/wakefulness—though "fire" makes the positive term seem a temporary one in a continuous circle.) The rest or what follows ("la suite") is literally the text or the ashes which are what man is left with after the conflagration: leavings.

The event passes in myth and then comes the word or world of man: history, or journalism, perhaps no more than notes. So a brave apologetics follows as a kind of introduction. Its tone is not necessarily false modesty, but it is written in a double time:

> Ces notes n'empruntent rien à l'amour de soi, à la nouvelle, à la maxime ou au roman. Un feu d'herbes sèches eût tout aussi bien été leur éditeur. La vue du sang supplicié en a fait une fois perdre le fil, a réduit à néant leur importance. Elles furent écrites dans la tension, la colère, la peur, l'émulation, le dégoût, la ruse, le recueillement furtif, l'illusion de l'avenir, l'amitié, l'amour. C'est dire combien elles sont affectées par l'événement. Ensuite plus souvent survolées que relues.
>
> Ce carnet pourrait n'avoir appartenu à personne tant le sens de la vie d'un homme est sous-jacent à ses pérégrinations, et difficilement séparable d'un mimétisme parfois hallucinant. De telles tendances furent néanmoins combattues.
>
> Ces notes marquent la résistance d'un humanisme conscient de ses devoirs, discret sur ses vertus, désirant réserver *l'inaccessible* champ libre à la fantaisie de ses soleils, et décidé à payer le *prix* pour cela [p. 85].

The writer of notes implies that he will not be categorized in traditional genres, that he is not a lyric poet, a story writer, a maker of maxims, a novelist. When he implies that he has no debts to pay to tradition, he suggests that his enterprise either modestly falls short or, more arrogantly, outdistances the others. At first the "leavings" act as the reflection of history's passing: the broken *fil* where blood flowed and was buried, the biosphere of many fleeting emotions, the *affectation* of event. As a body is "affected" by great pain, so a text is affected by the holocaust. Yet: "il est difficile," warns the extended definition of *affecter* in the Littré, "qu'une véritable douleur s'affecte." For affectation is artifice and exaggeration. So the attempt to mark history's passage is perhaps presumptuous. But, as the "introduction" continues to argue, the "mimétisme," the sameness of surface and artifice, must be avoided at all cost for the sake of man's underlying life. Still, if recording history and interpreting the meaning of individual existence are not impossible enough tasks, the writer of *Feuillets* would also mark the sanctum of retreating humanistic culture. He would stand at these limits, drawing the line past which no decent society could go, and from there regroup, redefine the basic duties and virtues. Though "discreet," does this goal not echo Nietzsche's similarly modest title: "Revaluation of All Values"? "Revaluation" in the context of both Nietzsche and his philosopher-poet descendants should mean a demystification of morality and sympathy with a "revolutionary" consciousness. Aphorism, as a form, should guard, by its very nature, against the (Kantian) moral imperative that works its fallacious logic. It must, by definition, invite a new economy, for economy is ultimately the substance of its form and vice versa.

After Rimbaud's imperative to find a new language, can one do other than renew his imperative language? *Feuillets d'Hypnos* is the way a tall, self-confident *méridional*, one of France's greatest living poets, gives power to the people and instructs them in power, but it is also a meditation on the essential problems of writing (that are not necessarily invoked in a short story or maxim). Here he is preoccupied with how history (especially a holocaust) can enter a text, with what roles his act (his stand) and his concern for value play, and with how any writer can participate in the economy of aphorism (of any text) without aiding and abetting the greater economy of an ambiguous tradition and politics. "J'écris brièvement. Je ne puis guère *m'absenter* longtemps. S'étaler conduirait à l'obsession" (A.31).

Writing seems to be a "break" from the arena of presence and history, from the place of serious responsibility. It resembles an indulgence like sex, where one spreads (*étaler*) one's needs and wares, a prostitution. The temptation it evokes is both repeatable and uncontrollable (as obsessive-compulsive) and demonic (obsession as possession). The image projected by the "foreword" is of a man insisting on his economic independence, on his lack of possessions (I owe nothing to literary history; I am paid up); he is determined to keep the last, precious "reserves" out of the degrading exchange, but in his enthusiasm, even self-righteousness, is pulled in by the commerce he would disdain. "Destiné à payer le *prix* pour cela" turns the argument on its head: is the price a last, lonely stand (s'il n'en reste qu'un...), or a headlong plunge into the fray, or both, that is, the tension of their impossible reconciliation? Is the *price* doubly dear— the loss of lives whose trace is certainly not apparent in this place of literary prostitution, this *néant* without importance? Or is the price that one pays for being an oracle who would concern himself with duty and value, the publication of scraps that such *étalement*, such explaining, entails where one must, though obliquely, attach one's name and open up to vulgar interpretations having very little to do with one's "self": la suite appartient aux hommes. What would be a *Bible de l'Humanité* (Michelet), a *Decline and Fall of the Roman Empire* can, in all good faith . . . , only be notes, and yet have these "notes" lost the shadow of their heritage, do they really owe nothing?

Notes make history and not the other way around. They mark the resistance, i.e. what should resist time, oblivion. First, given the avalanche of speech or events, it is imperative that notes choose what will be retained. He who "covers" an event scratches words down as they escape him, misquoting, misreporting, or, listening, jots down what catches his "fantasy." While notes seem anodyne, they are the beginning of important moral decisions and judgment. A superior who notes his underlings holds their fate in his pen. "C'est une note qu'il portera toujours" (Littré). Often a dispatch or note between diplomats of two countries decides a question of war or peace. There is one such message inserted like a document in *Feuillets d'Hypnos*. Hypnos writes to "LS" and because of the aphoristic content of the letter, it provides an ironic commentary on the whole collection; this telescoped version of the whole is both tragic and comic (like all synecdoche?). Though the advice sounds moralistic and pedantic ("Filles et cafés dangereux plus d'une minute"), only such obsessive care saves lives: "inspirez celles que vous en voulez pas trop tôt voir mourir." A piece of paper becomes a matter of life and death: and this is the only text that is literally signed, though it is signed "Affection. Hypnos." And followed by the punctuation of a period which indicates that the letter is a literary affectation. A footnote, however, takes over the responsibility of the "real," for it specifies the true name of the letter's addressee, LS: "Léon Zyngerman, alias Léon Saingermain," as if the difference were clear between alias and identity, between artifice and orders, dimestore books of advice and survival kit.

This fundamental ambiguity of the aphoristic form prevents one from deciding if it is actually, by essence, "collaborative" (in the largest sense) or "resistant." Its literary heritage (which *Feuillets* is hesitant to admit) comprises two tendencies: one (to be avoided), a "closed," sophisticated, moralistic literature; the other, an "open," disruptive, more philosophical and speculative form. Nietzsche, whose *Twilight of the Idols* includes a section called "Maxims and Arrows" (arrows deflate the maxims?), warns of the self-defeating ambitions behind the moralistic impulse. Trying to promote a rebirth of morality, the moralist only reveals "signs of decline, of disbelief in life, a preparation for pessimism."[2] Nietzsche, for whom moral values are "immoral affects," realizes, however, that he runs the risk of falling into the dialectical temptation, becoming as "seduced" by the search for immorality. Though *Feuillets d'Hypnos* expresses a desire for the same moral renewal ("afin d'élever et d'élargir notre action comme notre morale"; A.100), its author is careful to distinguish himself from the famous seventeenth-century French "moralist" tradition, victim of the gilded society it reflected. Yet the word *discret* sounds a dissonant note, since it echoes a title from the grandfather of that salon-based movement: *El Discreto* (1646) by Baltasar Gracián. The title was later translated (by the same man who translated *Il Principe* of Machiavelli) as *L'Homme de Cour* (1648). Certainly the tradition, stemming perhaps from Gracián, was concerned with how to cope in its contemporary society, how to see clear, finally how to succeed. The title of Gracián's anthology, *Oraculo manual y arte de prudencia* (1647), focuses on the ironic cross-purposes of the oracle that publishes a practical (not spiritual) manual. The fact that the humanism of *Feuillets d'Hypnos* is "discret sur ses vertus" does not console, for "discreet," while denying the presence of "affectation," may also mean a respect for property, which is a price too great to pay.

The second aphoristic tradition (though this division is arbitrary) is varied in its targets and thinking: Theophrastus, Heraclitus, the pre-Socratics in general, Montaigne, Bacon, Lichtenberg, Schlegel, Nietzsche, Wittgenstein, Cioran. Perhaps it is true that the "moralists," La Rochefoucauld, or Pascal could be reintegrated into this more "radical" movement since any aphorism prompts "re-examination of the author's assumptions—and our own."[3] Yet in such writers as Bacon and Lichtenberg an ideology stands behind the choice of form. Bacon's well-known quote ("Aphorisms, representing a knowledge broken, do invite men to inquire farther; whereas Methods, carrying the show of a total, do secure men, as if they were at the farthest") sheds disbelief on all systems, and on the pursuit of truth in general. Lichtenberg, especially, seems to have chosen the aphorism as the only way of saying anything—and even then perhaps too elaborate and suggestive; his goal was a longer form (he wanted to write a Fielding novel) and well-grounded scientific discovery, but each

2. *The Will to Power*, ed. W. Kaufmann (New York, 1968), p. 149.
3. John Cruikshank, *French Literature and Its Background* (London, 1969), II, 140.

time he started to build knowledge, he ended by breaking it off: "Since the middle of the year 1791, something that I can't really describe as yet has been stirring the whole economy of my thoughts. It is an extraordinary distrust of all human knowledge, except for mathematics."[4] Finally Lichtenberg reasoned that the form of all thought should take the merchant's ledger as its model, for this was, after all, the basic text of economy:

> The merchants have their *Waste Book* [Lichtenberg uses the English]; there they record from day to day everything they buy and sell, one after the other, without any order. From there the entries go into the *Journal* where everything is recorded more systematically, and finally it goes to the *Ledger at Double Entrance* [ed. Mautner, p. 12].

Feuillets d'Hypnos is, then, a Waste Book where the writer keeps his accounts: "Additionnez, ne divisez pas" (A.87). "Accumule, puis distribue" (A.156). The genre of *Feuillets d'Hypnos*, specified as *carnet*, is first and foremost "un petit livre que les négociants, courtiers, agents de change, portent dans les bourses et marchés pour inscrire immédiatement leurs opérations" (Littré). The philosopher-poet-historian-journalist of *Feuillets* is both a moralist and a merchant (synonyms?). In the fray he tallies the rise and fall of values ("Le poète, susceptible d'exagération, évalue correctement dans le supplice"; A.154); he metes out the judgments of culture, calling for change, and meaning just that, with his empty hand extended or extending the always unpaid *addition*. One part of his image is uninvolved with tradition and exchange while the other pays the price by picking the people's pocket over and over, giving them back their own linguistic leavings, what they have never noticed being spoken, stealing the same notes again and again ("Ensuite plus souvent *survolées que relues.*" Read: purloined to the saturation point). We think our money and commonplace wisdom have been whitewashed by a publication signed by a god. And yet the miracle is we read ourselves with delight and even joy.

The attempts to define aphorism have, finally, had to vacillate or combine certain dialectical limits. Open or closed? The end of a philosophical process or inspiration? Coal or diamond? Shell or pearl? A banal *reductio ad absurdum* or insight? A "spot of time" or a hidden narrative? Jean

---

4. Georg Christoph Lichtenberg, *The Lichtenberg Reader*, trans. and ed. Franz H. Mautner and Henry Hatfield (Boston, 1959), p. 21.

Onimus, writing specifically on the poet of Isle-sur-Sorgue, wants to privilege the pearl but ends by constructing an oxymoron to encompass the contradictions:[5]

> Un aphorisme est une pensée dense qui fait la "perle" qui se roule en boule et se clôt sur elle-même, isolée, sans environnement affectif ou logique, sans lien avec quelque pensée voisine dont elle serait la conséquence ou la source.... Il y a donc deux sortes d'aphorismes: ceux qui referment la pensée et ceux qui l'ouvrent.... Mais dans certains cas la solidité n'est que dans le cadre et, telle une fenêtre donnant sur un vaste paysage, l'aphorisme n'a d'autre but que *d'enclore* l'illimité."[6]

In *Maxime und Fragment* (Munich, 1934), Arthur-Herman Fink plays the aphorism off of two extremes he calls maxim (too complete, "zu vollendet") and fragment ("zu formlos"). He finally describes aphorism as a surprise and somewhat satisfying end (though not Being) that can also yield a new aphorism, a new "ending" such that aphorism's doorway is seen (Fink uses Nietzsche's words) as both *Zugänge* and *Durchgänge*. The general consensus of aphoristic theoreticians[7] conceives of a two-staged experience of reading: a refreshing sense of temporary coherence leading for some readers onto "a moving contour" where change is "not quite completed."[8] The resulting effect is one of expansion/contraction and perhaps some rippling movement of change. Another theoretical dialogue between Franz Mautner (who speaks of aphorism as *Einfall* or *Klärung*) and Albert Schneider (who would blur this arbitrary distinction) has used the same quote from Marie von Ebner-Eschenbach as its paradigm definition: "der letzte Ring einer langen Gedankenkette (chain of thoughts)."[9]

Aphorism, then, reproduces a horizon effect: *apo*, away from, and *hori-*

5. For a discussion of dialectics in Char, see Robert W. Greene, "Char, Poet of Contradiction," *Modern Language Review*, 61 (1971), 803–9. See also Mary Ann Caws, *The Presence of René Char* (Princeton, N.J., 1977).

6. *Expérience de la poésie* (Paris, 1973). For a larger study of Char's poetics in general, see Virginia La Charité, *The Poetics and the Poetry of René Char* (Chapel Hill, N.C., 1968).

7. See especially Corrado Rosso, *La maxime: saggi per una tipologia critica* (Naples, 1968), and Pierre Missac, "Situation de l'aphorisme," *Critique*, 30 (1974), 374–83.

8. Quoted from Stevens, "Notes Toward a Supreme Fiction." See Beverly Lole, "An Anchorage of Thought: Defining the Role of Aphorism in Wallace Stevens' Poetry," *PMLA*, 91 (March 1976), 206–22.

9. For a résumé which gives "der letze Ring einer langen Gedankenkette," see Albert Schneider, "Lichtenberg et l'aphorisme," *Etudes Germaniques*, 25 (jan.-mars 1970), 62–65; Franz Heinrich Mautner, *Lichtenberg, Geschichte seines Geistes* (Berlin, 1968); Albert Schneider, *Georg Christoph Lichtenberg, l'homme et l'œuvre* (Nancy, 1954).

zein, to limit. It is "cette suite d'impasses sans *nourriture* où tend à se perdre le visage aimé" of sense or knowledge. It feeds into the next impasse without being fed, like paying over and over without earning. Stealing in and out of pockets and hallways. Unlike maxim and axiom its etymology does not guarantee legitimacy and results. Maxim has the empirical and democratic sanction of the majority behind it;[10] axiom is, by nature, what acts (*agere*), what has value (Gk. *axios*). The first "aphorisms," written by Hippocrates, were already a catch-all between the principles of a burgeoning medical science and folk wisdom, but their "origin" as hypothesis was conveniently forgotten, like the first metaphorical meanings of catechresis, so that an aura of "general truth" slipped in. One walks, as Heidegger notes, *into* a horizon, sighting a promise and coming up on it as it dissipates, re-sighting and always walking. These fits-and-starts ("Rosée des hommes qui trace et dissimule ses frontières..."; A.160) that characterize the aphoristic form[11] describe, finally, a universal phenomenon ascribed to the function of metaphor,[12] the process of thinking itself, or the generation of any utterance which is history.

Distinguishing aphorism from its related genres—epigram, *pensée*, saying, sentence, maxim, gnome, fragment—is a lesson in futility. One can say that *Feuillets d'Hypnos* does not look like Bacon's titled essays, nor do they have headings like in Pascal, nor an initial phrase (in italics) that orients the discussion, as often found in Gracián or Nietzsche (*Human All Too Human, Mixed Opinions and Maxims*). They look more like La Rochefoucauld's numbered sentences, Nietzsche's "Maxims and Arrows" (*Twilight of the Idols*), Schlegel's or Lichtenberg's fragments. But *Feuillets d'Hypnos* gives evidence of a wide variety within an "economical" form, incorporating aspects of many fictional genres: poetry, history, novel, and philosophy. Curiously, the aphorism's content seems predetermined by its length, though not always. Under five or six words is often a fragment based on metaphor; a complete sentence leans toward definition (using "is"); two sentences are a definition and qualification; three, a nascent syllogism; beyond three, an argumentative essay (like Bacon's induction and dis-

10. La Bruyère was nervous about the pretensions of maxims and protected his *Caractères* by saying "Je n'ai ni assez d'autorité, ni assez de génie pour faire le législateur."

11. See Jonathan Culler, "Paradox and the Language of Morals in La Rochefoucauld," *Modern Language Review*, 68 (Jan. 1973), 28–39: "Paradox rests on a fragile illusion, an apparent contradiction that is dissipated by the very process of understanding" (and put again into contradiction, and so on).

12. See Jean Cohen, *La Structure du langage poétique* (Paris, 1966).

qualification)[13] or a story. The longest text in *Feuillets d'Hypnos* can pass for historical rapportage or fable. The shortest, one compound word, also passes for the point and the ripples.

LA FRANCE-DES-CAVERNES (A.124)

In the middle of *Feuillets d'Hypnos*, an obvious sign yawns. The text we enter is also the territory of Free France: this aphorism might have been the "title" of the collection. We are led through the labyrinth of the political Underground that is disguised in codes and indirectly recounted in anecdote. We are taken on a "literal" tour of the Midi, site of Lascaux and the gorges of the Tarn River. The aphorism composed of a proper noun is, therefore, already a metaphor with its own rhetorical genesis. The proper noun is the chameleon of names: neither object nor subject, it is the Name-of-the-Mother, that is, the spot in which one decides arbitrarily to begin. Yet, this is not all of geographical France, but only the caves. The diegetic movement has already begun, or, as Gérard Genette explains: "sans métonymie, pas d'enchaînement de souvenirs, pas d'*histoire*, pas de roman."[14] The cavernes are both synecdoche and metonymy: Fontanier explains the possible ambiguity or doubleness of the figure: "Mais quand c'est le nom d'une ville, la figure est ordinairement double, et il y a tout-à-la-fois *synecdoque* et *métonymie: synecdoque*, la ville pour le pays; *métonymie*, la ville pour ses habitans."[15] LA FRANCE-DES-CAVERNES imitates a sign on the highway locating the "true France."

The "map" of Master Tropes[16] leads from metaphor to metonymy and synecdoche and finally to irony, but in aphorism (as perhaps in all texts) there is literally no time for the text before the onset of irony. This no-time is the space of lyric poetry and *Feuillets d'Hypnos* gives lip service to it in all the topoi of the "moment" (all that flashes or *scintille—diamant, coup, éclair, foudre*—usually followed by the despairing cry: "Franchise de courte durée!" A.37). I am using irony in the sense of a trope that undermines; that is, not simply contradiction, paradox, negation, or reversal. Actually I would prefer that it be understood simply as what impression an ending gives. After all, the text has to try to stop itself. Wallace

13. See Stanley E. Fish, *Self-Consuming Artifacts* (Berkeley, 1972), pp. 78–155.
14. *Figures III* (Paris, 1972), p. 63.
15. *Les Figures du discours*, ed. G. Genette (Paris, 1968), p. 89.
16. See Harold Bloom's discussion of Vico, Burke, Nietzsche, and de Man: *A Map of Misreading* (New York, 1975), esp. p. 94. Also see Hayden White's *Metahistory: The Historical Imagination in Nineteenth-Century Europe* (Baltimore, 1973).

Stevens gave out the formula in "Notes Toward a Supreme Fiction" by saying "It must be abstract," i.e. it must begin (pull away, define from, "aphorize"); "It must change" (turn, trope), i.e. it must middle; and finally "It must give pleasure," it must end. "Literally" (etymologically) it must "level off,"[17] flatten as into a tombstone, into a sign. From sign to sign.

LA FRANCE-DES-CAVERNES, a definition of place, marks the interim between the flash of one word and the history of a country. Supposedly there is no connection between lightning bolts of aphorism, but white space on a page does not preclude narrative. On the contrary. The sign that surprises for a moment is a part of a metonymic (narrative) chain, for the temptation to link points is impossible to resist though the outcome can only enhance the irony of any movement. The aphorism preceding §124 disclaims any notion of prophecy; the narrator speaks of a future "dont je ne saisis pas les présages." Immediately thereafter we are at the oracle's door: LA FRANCE-DES-CAVERNES. But we are as soon reminded of the autoroute and how we are left to our own devices without an ordnance map, without other ostensible signs from our narrator-guide. "Mettre en route l'intelligence sans le secours des cartes d'état-major" (A.125).

The multileveled narrative continues to function from fable to farce, punctuated by irony. Like LA FRANCE-DES-CAVERNES, all place names are compound (EVE-DES-MONTAGNES, Fontaine-la-pauvre) as if the genius loci were personified or the people were their own place, as in times of myth or the timelessness of a Southern village. *Feuillets d'Hypnos* describes this "émerveillement communiqué par les êtres et les choses dans l'intimité desquels nous vivons continuellement" (A.61). Though Hypnos is straight out of myth, the other characters belong to the allegory of a medieval romance, a novel of Chrestien de Troyes: *l'Elagueur, Passereau, l'ami du blé, l'Homme-au-poing-de-cancer, le grand Meurtrier, Olivier le Noir, les ogres.* But the atmosphere of fable is pierced by the high mimetic mode (Northrop Frye) which displaces it: Robert G and "LS," who stand for persons of low mimetic history: Emile Cavagni and Léon Zyngerman. Equally present are the figures of farce: Arthur le Fol or Colonel Eslabesang (Blood-gushing or Blood's-slave) who is a kind of Hitler-Chaplin (treated with black humor after his death: "La serviette du colonel était pleine d'intérêt"; A.121). The untellable story of the holocaust is minimally tell-

17. The Indo-European root *plakē*, to be calm, yields *placēre*, as well as *plancus* and (Gk.) *plax* (*American Heritage Dictionary*).

able in the broken forms of this mixed genre ("But unity of impression is precisely what the Holocaust experience cannot evoke . . ."[18]), though tragedy is the central outline of the mythical farce. In the first aphorisms, a feeling of daring and courage colors the activity of recruitment; friends and partisans seem inseparable. Then come the executions and betrayals, the dis-appointments; the flash misfires, the airplane does not deliver its arms on target. The individuals, the only *points de repère* in the almost mapless story, begin to die as does the poem. Hypnos can only exist through them and in the pages of their action; otherwise he is stone and sleeps. The names carry the weight of the poem. Though the emptiest of signs, so are they fullest.

One of the most moving aphorisms is a list of names: the litany and ledger of a war memorial. A name (perhaps Roger Chaudon is the closest to being the hero) is the "nakedness, a point./Beyond which fact could not progress as fact" ("Notes Toward a Supreme Fiction"). If life and history enter the poem, they enter it here:

> A coté d'un Joseph Fontaine, d'une rectitude et d'une teneur de sillon, d'un François Cuzin, d'un Claude Dechavannes, d'un André Grillet, d'un Marius Bardouin, d'un Gabriel Besson, d'un docteur Jean Roux, d'un Roger Chaudon aménageant le silo à blé d'Oraison en forteresse des périls, combien d'insaisissables saltimbanques plus soucieux de jouir que de produire! [A. 65].

But then, one could argue that these names are metonymies . . . At aphorism 157 (out of 237), the poem doubles back toward its "end": "Nous sommes tordus de chagrin à l'annonce de la mort de Robert G." After this comes the general descent: "Je vois l'espoir, veine d'un fluvial lendemain, décliner dans le geste des êtres qui m'entourent" (A.192). Finally, the sign of closure, though not "chronological," is Roger Chaudon's last words. As in a "new novel," we do not know exactly when in the narrative he died, nor were we witnesses. We have known since halfway through (A.146) that Roger Chaudon is dead/will die, for his wife and friend (the poet) mourn him. His execution—too much the intimate holocaust—cannot enter the text, as perhaps "B's" can. The last "canto" (?) of the poem, which is the only one to have a title and no number ("La Rose de chêne"), is recognizable not only as a "prose poem" but as an epitaph that would be inscribed on the patriarch-oak or across the sky. It would literally be the war me-

18. Lawrence L. Langer, *The Holocaust and the Literary Imagination* (New Haven, 1975), p. 12.

morial abstracted to spell "Beauty," metamorphosing all the names to one that would, in the writing of it, bring hope:

> Chacune des lettres qui compose ton nom, ô Beauté, au tableau d'honneur des supplices, épouse la plane simplicité du soleil, s'inscrit dans la phrase géante qui barre le ciel, et s'associe à l'homme acharné à tromper son destin avec son contraire indomptable: l'espérance.

The Hugolian gesture has a Whitmanian content, and the echo of Eluard's "J'écris ton nom," which defies the critic's need for disguises, creates a nostalgia for the "political poem."

Tradition is somehow too finicky to account for the span that would narrate *Feuillets d'Hypnos*, for though its roots are Romantic, it would link in a flash, in one sign, the caves of Lascaux and the autoroute. The origins of Free France are the womb and the cave and mouth of first syllables. Hermann Fink's fantasy, that aphorism might have come from the same root as Aphrodite since it emerges as from foam, conveys the effect of freshness the short form would produce—or the effect of being the only, fragmentary remains of something lost. If the hyphens do not hold, neither does the center, and the place and text of resistance is gone. The *caverne* is an inverted world, either the crux of the matter or the empty hollow of a hand the palm-reader raises to her eyes.

The final irony of signaling LA-FRANCE-DES-CAVERNES is that the minute the underground sets up its sign, advertises itself, it is no longer underground. It literally fades from existence like the face of the beloved. But the continuous urge to name where we are/wish we were/ have been is hard to halt: we keep thinking that the next step will lead off the ledge and into meaning, the village, history; or that we will have finally opened onto Being. Heidegger keeps trying to think the Other outside of the infinitely regressive perspective of horizon. He keeps walking over and over the same ground, stalking something with thought, trying that tactic, rather than the leap:

> *Teacher*: What is evident of the horizon, then, is but the side facing us of an openness which surrounds us; an openness which is filled with views of the appearances of what to our re-presenting are objects.
> *Scientist*: In consequence the horizon is still something else besides a horizon. Yet after what has been said this something else is the other side of itself, and so the same as itself. You say that the horizon is the openness as such, if we disregard that it can also appear as the horizon of our representing?

Teacher: It strikes me as something like a *region*, an enchanted region where everything belonging there returns to that in which it rests.[19]

On the other side of the horizon, its inverse or unimagined self, on the other side of our representations, lies an *inaccessible champ libre* which is both already falsely claimed or not discovered yet and would dissipate if it was. "Il renonce à se dire, son site" (Heidegger, in *Cahiers de l'Herne*, No. 15, p. 181).

Or the only site is the signifier which is never securely located between its limits. The ideal is the explosion and deliverance, but when the smoke clears, the snaky connotations are seen to follow. "Etre du bond, n'être pas du festin, son épilogue" (A.197). The *bond* (glossing over the easy association with bonding, bondage, double bind) can exist as a leap only in the context of a ricochet, a motion already in motion ("Nous nous battons sur le pont jeté entre l'être vulnérable et son ricochet aux sources du pouvoir formel"; A.183). *Bond* comes from *bombire*; the deep hollow sound, perhaps a rumbling (from a cave) or a buzzing as from a bomb or boomerang. ("Nuit, de toute la vitesse du boomerang taillé dans nos os, et qui siffle, siffle..." A.71). In the fifteenth and sixteenth centuries, *bond* was used in a context where we would use the modern *tour* (trick) or *change*: "il lui avait baillé le bont; lui donner le bond" (Littré). So the leap is a part of a metaphorical spiral: it must come back (change) and it comes back different, for it turns against itself. When located and represented, the *bond* becomes the *borne* of LA FRANCE-DES-CAVERNES, not only a milestone, but often a simple reinforcement at the angle of a building or wall close to the road, protecting it from swerving vehicles (*bouteroue*), from passing events: what in the end stands between (if standing for) the speaker or witness and history. The *bond* should be the bomb that splits open the *borne*, though often it is quoted and "used" or turned against itself in the words of an after-dinner speaker, the well-nourished bourgeois. *Borne*, then feeds into *borde*, for historically the words cannot be separated. (*Borde*: "large ouverture de fond, destinée à laisser écouler toute l'eau de l'étang quand on retire le tampon qui la bouche ordinairement"; Littré). As sense fills out the text, so does the text empty itself of sense. From *bond* to *borne* to *bonde*. And back again. Harold Bloom talks of the making and breaking of vessels. Or it is like a well with a plug so that when one stoops to drink, it dries up, *Fontaine-la-pauvre*. "Nous errons auprès de margelles dont on

19. Martin Heidegger, *Discourse on Thinking* (New York, 1966), pp. 64–65.

a soustrait les puits" (A.91). The water has literally been pulled out from under (like a rug) its markers of stone, leaving the dusty ruins of another Stonehenge, another one of our broken zeros. Sing, then, sing your *soif irisée*, never to be irrigated, the hallucinations of your march in the desert showering you sometimes with an ineffable knowledge of life's desperate diamond: "connaissance ineffable du diamant désespéré (la vie)" (A.3).

To go on would be to continue turning against oneself: "La même mécanique qui les [des canailles] stimule, les brisera-t-elle en se brisant, lorsque ses provisions hideuses seront épuisées?" (A.29) Yet the machine is beautifully seductive, a diabolical combination of child-princess (*infans*, nonspeaking) and motor. So is the poem.

Ponge calls the alternatives *crevette* and *char* (*homard, langouste*, etc.). In his piece called "La Crevette," he temporarily takes the side of the diaphanous nothing: "Non, à n'en pas douter elle [la crevette] vit tout autant que ces chars malhabiles, et connaît, quoique dans une condition moins terre à terre, toutes les douleurs et les angoisses que la vie partout suppose." "Ainsi le blindé tendait-il à devenir lui-même la meilleure arme antichar" (Larousse Encyclopedia). As Char circles, his own artillery covers him ("La place demeure vide mais le couvert reste mis"; A.131). The notes become notches in a ratchet wheel that automatically loads the guns: a colt (A.50), a revolver (A.217), machine guns (A.121, A.128). If aphorisms have to do with economy, they bring about that economy through violence. The act of separating, of forcing boundaries, of drawing definitions was the "immoral beginning" of language and society. In such a way historians and lawyers impose their perspectives. "Welche willkürlichen Abgrenzungen," exclaimed Nietzsche:[20] "What arbitrary delimitations!" Style itself has developed its means of terror beyond the stylus to the machine gun. The author of *Feuillet d'Hypnos* is constantly confronting the duplicity of the act of writing: to combat the oppression of language, one uses ferocious instruments: the pen of diamond that cuts stone, the barrel of a gun. Yet somehow they fizzle "comme un essaim de fusées engourdies" (A.141). One cannot shoot in a nightmare; a "volet de crystal" separates entities that are identical but mutually exclusive. The *Feuillets d'Hypnos* is the fable of this resistant separation; its aphorisms repeat the virginal violence of speech and sign and the ensuing degradation which never touches them. ("L'acte est vierge, même répété"; A.46.)

The few overtly "historical" scenes in *Feuillets d'Hypnos* describe the voyeur-writer-marksman, powerfully armed but paralyzed to *do* anything.

---

20. *Das Philosophenbuch/Le Livre du philosophe* (Paris, 1969), p. 176.

The chilling impotence of watching B's execution: "Nous étions sur les hauteurs dominant Céreste, des armes à faire craquer les buissons et au moins égaux en nombre aux SS.... Je n'ai pas donné le signal parce que ce village devait être épargné *à tout prix*" (A.138). Finally a last limit must be maintained or all communication, civilization itself, succumbs. To imagine no bar between words and acts, signifier and signified, history and the writing of it is to imagine no distinctions, is not to imagine any more, is not to . . . is unimaginable and perhaps as "horrible" as the execution itself. The writer finally is of the bondage and the boundary as much as he is of the bomb: he is his best at epilogues.

The longest text in the *Feuillets d'Hypnos* (A.128) recounts in excruciating detail the frustration of trying to control whether writing will speak and betray or whether it will resist. Hidden behind "des rideaux jaunis," like the "vapeur jaune flamboyante" of the broom plants in the execution of aphorism 121, the narrator watches with cocked gun to see if his double, his *porte-parole*, will reveal where he hides. "Mes mains communiquaient à mon arme leur sueur crispée, exaltaient sa puissance contenue. Je calculais que le malheureux se tairait encore cinq minutes, puis, fatalement, il *parlerait*. J'eus honte de souhaiter sa mort avant cette échéance." But the text, knowing and not knowing the secret intentions, does not speak. The spectator-narrator is under the illusion that he has been saved because of a very clever *plan concerté*, orchestrated by the whole village. Later he reconsiders and requalifies everything in a footnote, flipping the text over once again. "N'était-ce pas le hasard qui m'avait choisi pour prince..." If no one talked, it was not because of a stratagem or his own magnetic power, it was chance.

Finally what one says has little to do with what was planned. Char would have liked to present his friends—who died for the Resistance—in their glory; he wanted their last words to speak, but his text is a busy house whose employees go about their business gaily unconcerned (as in *The Gay Science*): "Je n'ai pas vu d'étoile s'allumer au front de ceux qui allaient mourir mais le dessin d'une persienne qui, soulevée, permettait d'entrevoir un ordre d'objets déchirants ou résignés, dans un vaste local où des servantes heureuses circulaient" (A.214).

Here the writer becomes his own reader, a process which is put into motion when he signs, but a process which is perhaps too painful and thus impossible. "Tu ne peux pas te relire mais tu peux signer" (A.96). Char has paid his price for the deed to work his text, his parcel of the "truth"; he has understood the terms of the bondage: "La vie commencerait par une explosion et finirait par un concordat?" (A.140). Yet the compromise, the contract, accompanies the explosion from beginning to end, for are they not one and the same? If the poet is *souverain*, he is also "ce nouveau fermier général" (A.216). When he wrote his notes, denying the authority of legislatures (maxims), and of history (*roman*), rejecting the presumptions of philosopher and scientist, he had nothing left but the authority of authority itself. His Revaluation of All Values pretends to be all and nothing. "Evaluation sans objet" (A.85). One of the poet's darkest visions and greatest insights lies in aphorism 37, in which he explains that man reached the height of evil genius when he slipped sheer authority between action and truth: "Le génie de l'homme, qui pense avoir découvert les vérités formelles, accommode les vérités qui tuent en vérités qui *autorisent* à tuer." Then the swastika, the double S's, all initials, start to turn, like the damned body of Don Juan turns in the French television film of that Molière play. The petals of the dark flower eternally turn and fall in an endless abyss, becoming itself a black sun nearing and ever distant from its imploding other, the Sun. What does a word do in this somber whirlpool? "La fleur *tracée*, la fleur hideuse, tourne ses pétales noires dans la chair folle du soleil. Où êtes-vous source? Où êtes-vous remède? Economie vas-tu enfin changer?"

The aphorism breaks off here at the limits to begin again, and the hypnotic cycle from stone to fire begins again just as carbon passes from one allotrope to another via amorphous forms. From time to time, there is the illusion of diamonds; more often, graphite pointing to points. Or another kind of fire, invisible and clean, burns in the cave where we cannot see: "Le camp ne sera jamais montré. Il n'existe pas de camp, mais des charbonnières qui ne fument pas" (A.87). These ashes and leaves held in the palm are carbon paper and gold.

Neal Oxenhandler

Nihilism in Le Clézio's *La Fièvre*

We know more about nihilism than we like to think.

> W. J. Dannhauser, from a lecture

Si vous voulez vraiment le savoir, j'aurais ne préféré ne jamais être né.

> J. M. G. Le Clézio, Preface to *La Fièvre*

I

The fictions of J. M. G. Le Clézio unfold on a devastated and devastating world. Few other writers in the tradition of Kafka and Sartre have celebrated as powerfully the emptiness of the contemporary cityscape. Numerous images of emptiness are brought into play to convey the reductive power of a nihilistic imagination.

The question I will put to Le Clézio's fiction has to do precisely with the meaning and extent of his nihilism. I wish to pursue this nihilism into various motifs of the stories, seeing what shapes it assumes and how it repeats itself. Once Le Clézio's nihilism has taken shape and substance we will be able to pose the question of its extent or limits. Obviously, if Le Clézio were a totally unrelenting nihilist he would not write stories. So the nihilism must be mitigated in some way. And perhaps it may even provide its own antidote. Is there escape from this nihilism—some possibility of redemption from (or perhaps through) it? I put this question to Le Clézio's book of stories *La Fièvre* because I think it his best work to date. Paradoxically, he poses the question of the meaning and limits of nihilism more effectively here than in his straight philosophical essays. One might ruefully apply to the Le Clézio of the later works, a novelist turned essayist, Rimbaud's devastating line on the misuse of talent: "Une belle gloire d'artiste et de conteur emportée!" (*Une Saison en Enfer*, "Adieu").

II

Le Clézio's hero lives in a world of matter in motion:

Le mouvement renaîtrait dans le petit appartement, avec des à-coups, avec des ratés de moteur encrassé. Le mouvement viendrait. Il passerait sous la porte et se mettrait à ramper sournoisement, comme un reptile, vers le lit du malade [p. 48].[1]

This molecular motion creeps in everywhere—nothing can resist it. Le Clézio calls it "l'extase matérielle," and it encompasses all of creation. It includes human consciousness and the world of created objects. All-invading and all-encompassing, it reveals a monistic universe, one with only local differentiation. All things ebb and flow between nodal points of energy.

Language is the privileged matrix of *extase matérielle*, since it is here that the flux turns back upon itself in a loop or fold and so contains itself by a reflexive act.[2] Language as Le Clézio uses it is a *material* force: hence it is not primarily used to perform a cognitive act, i.e. to denote concepts or relationships. It is used as a magical power whose function is to change the material relations of the user. Language does not stand for an object; it *is* an object. It is not merely a symbol of the object but rather a material sign that contains it own referent. In what is the best article on Le Clézio to date, Gerda Zellner makes the point that Le Clézio uses language in a way diametrically opposed to the way it is used by the formalists of the Tel Quel group.[3] He is fascinated with names because they somehow contain the essence of the thing named:

Qu'est-ce qui est marqué sur cette dalle? Les noms des morts, sans doute, et les empreintes spiralées des vivants. Les signatures aussi. Les dates des jours et les chiffres des heures, les numéros des années, les phases de la lune, les vents, marées, éruptions solaires. Le nombre des feuilles des arbres. Les écailles des serpents, les pattes des scolopendres. Arêtes, vieux vestiges, reliefs du festin, miettes, miettes! C'est cela mon domaine, ma prison. Je n'en sortirai pas; mais je veux compter les grains de sable et leur donner un nom à chacun, puisque c'est la seule raison de ma vie.[4]

The world is a trash heap littered with names, dates, graffiti. There are splendid remnants of the biological order—snake scales, spider legs. The

1. All references are to *La Fièvre* (Paris: Gallimard, 1965) unless otherwise indicated.
2. Le Clézio's fascination with matter and his exaltation of matter as an ecstatic force that implicitly contains consciousness as its inner dimension is reminiscent of the view of Teilhard de Chardin.
3. "Jean-Marie Gustave Le Clézio: le roman antiformaliste," in *Positions et oppositions sur le roman contemporain* (Paris: Klincksieck, 1971).
4. J. M. G. Le Clézio, "Comment j'écris," in *Les Cahiers du chemin* (Paris: Gallimard, 15 Oct. 1967).

writer's task is to rescue these remnants from the indeterminacy of the trash heap and to give them momentary prominence by the act of insertion in the mental order, an order which is directly cognate to their own, since it too is part of the *extase matérielle*.

This conception of the function of language no doubt has its roots in Symbolism with its view of the magical power of name-giving.[5] Yet perhaps the clearest link is with the alchemical view of poetic language held by Rimbaud. Like Rimbaud, Le Clézio uses language to change the world. He possesses Rimbaud's acute awareness that this banal, daily world is somehow not the real one; and like Rimbaud, he uses language to void the world and penetrate through it to something else. That "something else" is Nothingness. No matter where one begins in a Le Clézio story one is always carried back to that emptiness at the center of his vision. Yet how one *sees* or interprets the void is the central issue for arriving at an understanding of Le Clézio's poetic ontology.

The flux of the literary text reveals itself in a constant process of making and unmaking. It is characterized by continual change and openness which is opposed to the deathlike sterility of the cityscape. And yet the flux of the text seems to be a directed process, a dialectic propelled by some inner urgency toward a meaningful opening-out.

Certain motifs return over and over again in these stories. A classification of these motifs would run as follows:

1. The walk through the city. This is the motif that occurs the most frequently in *La Fièvre*. The characters wander aimlessly through the teeming streets of a Mediterranean city (based on Le Clézio's own Nice), where they have a number of random encounters:

> Il traversa à nouveau toute la ville, tout ce dédale sonore plein de coups de douleur et de frissons, cette espèce de blockhaus asphyxiant et sale où les couloirs partaient dans toutes les directions, pour mieux vous tromper, où les chambres se ressemblaient toutes, avec leurs meurtrières minces et leurs coins noirâtres, où se croisaient près du béton armé de lourdes odeurs de croupissures et d'excréments [p. 34].

2. Encounters in the city. The most powerful presence in the city is the crowd, which seems to live its trance-producing existence like an affliction or plague. The solitary walker is constantly on the verge of succumbing to the crowd's power, but the presence of human flesh awakens nausea in the hero and deep feelings of paranoid fear:

5. One is also reminded of the Sartrean view of poetry's ability to "unveil" or "disclose" a reality sunk in shadows until it is named.

Au centre de cette viande suante, criarde, bariolée, des yeux vivaient, d'une vie presque indépendante, petites bêtes glauques et voraces.... Il était cerné par ces murailles de vivants, tenu fixement au milieu du trottoir, attaqué de tous côtés, en proie à toutes les sortes d'hommes, ceux qui marchent, ceux qui sont assis, ceux qui rient, ceux qui parlent, ceux qui sont derrière, ceux qui regardent, ceux qui dorment [p. 121].

Other encounters, however, are less menacing. There is, for instance, in *Le Procès verbal* (published in 1963, two years before *La Fièvre*) the extraordinary sequence during which the hero follows a dog for hours on end, abandoning his own autonomy to that of the animal. More frequent than encounters with animals, however, are those with children. There are a number of these in *La Fièvre*; all communicate a Rimbaud-like fascination with the nondiscursive intelligence exhibited by children. Perhaps most poignant is the child's ability to remove himself from the inhumanity of the city and to immerse himself in an imaginary world. Yet childlikeness does not provide an effective antidote to the constant aggression that the hero meets as he wanders through the city. Much of Le Clézio's paranoia seems to focus on the automobiles encountered during the city walk:

... il se dégageait de toutes ces machines à l'arrêt une sorte de rumeur confuse, qui n'était plus du bruit et pas encore le silence.... J'étais en quelque sorte nourri de cette rumeur. Elle entrait par mes oreilles et par toute ma peau et s'installait à l'intérieur de mon corps, déclenchant des mécanismes inconnus, des rouages. Au bout de quelque temps, j'étais devenu une sorte de voiture, moi aussi, une machine d'occasion sans doute [p. 93].

The automobile is the prime example that indicates the adversary relationship between the Le Clézian hero and all material objects. No doubt this follows from the dehumanization and pollution of the city by the automobile. Yet, at the same time, there remains a deep fascination with the car as a primary locus of fantasy life.

3. Encounters between man and insect. The insect presents to man a minuscule version of his own vulnerability. Often the text focuses down like a high-power microscope:

Martin pencha la tête vers la bête immobile au creux de sa main et la contempla longuement. Il vit le corps rond, noirâtre, la rainure des élytres, la tête et les antennes rentrées... il comprit tout de suite que le charançon était vivant, et qu'il faisait le mort pour qu'on le laisse tranquille. Il vit ça tout de suite, au premier coup d'œil, à cause de l'application que mettait le petit animal à rester levé sur lui-même, et peut-être aussi à cause d'un imperceptible mouvement de vibration dans les antennes pliées. C'était cela, la peur, ce petit grain de poussière, ce pauvre pépin de fruit, tout noir, tué sur lui-même, le temps arrêté, le corps à l'envers, les pattes serrées sur son abdomen où la vie palpitante se cachait [pp. 156–57].

Later in the story Martin himself will become an insect, when he is attacked by a ruthless band of children. Le Clézio is fascinated by the way in which the insect presents to man a reduced and elemental version of his own place in the cosmos.

4. The enabling emotion. Le Clézio's text is a crossroads of all the intellectual and aesthetic currents that precede him. As a continuator of the existentials, notably Sartre, he makes it clear that any important insight must be grounded in the body and must be accompanied by a powerful emotion. Le Clézio's heroes, updated versions of Sartre's Roquentin, are frequently subject to nausea. The prime example of an enabling emotion is the fever which gives the whole collection its name. The overwhelming vertigo and panic which crash down upon the character Roch are described at length as they overwhelm his mind and body. The fever mounts in him like a wave; he shivers and feels that his body is on fire; objects melt under his gaze or become part of a nebula. In this truly Rimbaldian story the hero reaches apocalyptic heights as he destroys the world with his glance. The world becomes an enormous cancer; and one thinks of Roquentin's intuition that being is "de trop" as he stares at the roots of the chestnut tree in the park of Boueville.

Like Roquentin, Le Clézio's hero, Roch, perceives objects as secretions:

Les choses sécrétaient, sans arrêt, laissaient couler des liquides brûlants. Il y avait des glandes partout, des cloques invisibles qui bouillonnaient au plus profond de la matière [p. 31].

It is, of course, the insertion of man into the world that makes reality viscous, since he must dye it with the stuff of consciousness before he can apprehend it. Emotion, which occurs at the endothymic juncture between body and soul, is for Le Clézio a guarantee (albeit a weak and fallible one) that man, anchored to the world through his tormented and fever-ridden body, is still viable, even if threatened.

If we ask what it is that threatens the Le Clézian hero, we return to the theme of nothingness which was our original starting point. For the intuition of the void seems to underlie every perception, every act. Finally, we realize, the Le Clézian hero must go *through* the void if he is ever to attain appeasement.

Nothingness functions not as a "motif," but rather a permanent basso continuo always present at any point in the work's unfolding. The hero aspires to dissolve himself and vanish into the emptiness of space:

> Ce qui était bizarre, offusquant, c'était que je me sentais vivre, dans la plus profonde évidence, et qu'en même temps, il me semblait être devenu transparent sous la lumière. Les vibrations de l'éclairage passaient à travers moi comme à travers un bloc d'air, et me faisaient onduler doucement du haut en bas. Tout mon corps, tout mon corps vivant était attiré invinciblement par la source lumineuse, et j'entrais longuement dans le ciel ouvert; j'étais bu par l'espace, en plein mouvement, et rien ne pouvait arrêter cette ascension [p. 91].

This is certainly one of the most positive of the Le Clézian hero's many transformations. It is important because it expresses the underlying monism of Le Clézio's work, his view that all reality is finally one. If we went further and added that the One or Underlying Principle is nothingness, nirvana, then we would not be far from the view of Buddhism. It is clear that Le Clézio is close to Buddhism in other respects: his view that all human existence is suffering is profoundly Buddhist. And from Buddhism we can borrow insights that will help us to understand the role of nothingness in Le Clézio.

Le Clézio's work must be approached with the understanding that it is deeply paradoxical, as is any text that attempts to express the meaning of life. Man is diminished yet retains, through his power to name, an awesome ability to create existence where before there was nothing. His heroes deny any meaning to existence while at the same time they endlessly record that meaning (or absence of meaning). All things, Le Clézio maintains, are one, yet he draws up endless lists of material objects. Perhaps the greatest paradox lies in the appeasement that comes, for apparently no reason, after the frantic wanderings (through material and imaginary space) of heroes such as Roch or Paoli or Beaumont or Martin. We see that the text is dialectically organized in such a way as to make this outcome necessary. The appeasement seems logical and inevitable; yet how explain it, how justify it in such an apparently comfortless cosmos?

The appeasement that is attained by Le Clézio's hero may come after a period of frantic efforts as it does to Roch, after his long bout of fever (p. 59). When finally the narrator is able to control movement (synonymous with change and hence life itself), then he will be wholly appeased. Appeasement thus seems linked with some kind of negative or downward closure on existence. Tranquillity comes as he vanishes, as he dissolves the apparent solidity of the self and evaporates into the night air. This attainment of nothingness, of nirvana as the goal toward which the self moves, is presented even more strikingly in a passage that appears earlier in the same story:

> Il semble même que les pensées se répandent au-dehors, qu'elles sortent par mon nez et mes oreilles et vaquent dans l'espace, me font un lit. Les désirs forment des boules non loin de moi. Dans le fond d'une caverne noire, une impulsion palpite, isolée, enfin de moi visible. Je peux toucher mes mots, mes visions. Et moi, ce qui s'appelle moi, n'est plus rien. Vidé, soulagé, ma tête immense m'abandonne. Je suis enfin libre. Je suis enfin libre. Je n'ai plus de nom, je ne parle plus de langage, je ne suis qu'un néant. J'appartiens à la vie, morte, anéantie, transfigurée par la splendeur de l'évacuation. Un souffle. Je n'ai plus de pensée, mon âme est un objet. Je gis [pp. 198–99].

The central paradox here amounts to a reversal of the Cartesian cogito: I think and perceive, therefore I am not. This is only an apparent paradox to one who has some understanding of the Buddhist goal of nirvana.

The affirmation of the nothingness of the self lies beyond the principle of contradiction and, at the very least, must be viewed as an unresolvable paradox. Yet there are a variety of meanings that can be attributed to the affirmation that the self is empty and strives to unite its emptiness with the absolute emptiness of nirvana.

There is, first, an effort to define the self as a protean and immaterial principle, a principle that has all forms and no forms, that dies and yet survives death. The very paradox quoted earlier, "Je n'ai plus de pensée, mon âme est un objet," is dense with meanings. If I have *this* thought, how can I have no thought? Because, no doubt, I am an immaterial substance, that is, one occupying neither time nor space. Yet, he claims, the soul is an object. There is a Sartrean echo here, for the soul seems to lack any particular ontological privilege. Yet the surging, spontaneous, protean quality of the very passage quoted seems to place the "soul" in a category above and beyond all objects.

For Le Clézio, the soul is a pilgrim in quest of some dimension, some realm where it can subsist without the constant threat of annihilation. This realm, if it could be attained, would be nirvana. Yet here we return to paradox, for the only way the soul could exist would be to cease to exist. A further extension of the paradox of the soul's emptiness would be to read it as a vector pointing toward a profound or deep self, as opposed to the superficial self that functions in most of our daily transactions. This would be a view consonant with the depth psychologies or the psychology of Marcel Proust, whose entire fictional work is a descent into the depths of lost or vanished selves.

Still another possible interpretation would be to insist that the second term of the assertion (nirvana) is not merely a "vide" but a "vide-plein," to borrow the terms of the scholar of Buddhism, Joseph Masson. Masson sees in the asceticism of Buddhism the traditional steps: negation of the world and of attachment to the world; negation of the self, in preparation for the attainment of nirvana. He writes: "C'est en supprimant, théoriquement et pratiquement, le Soi, la personne, que l'on peut dépasser toutes les douloureuses limitations et parvenir à l'expérience béatifiante et illimitée de la mystique; c'est alors qu'il peut y avoir nirvana."[6]

So much is clear in regard to the first stages of the mystical ascent. But beyond this point lies the vexed question whether nirvana is pure negativity or might not be rather a *via negationis* for arriving at the absolute, in other words, a "vide-plein." This question must no doubt be answered differently for each of the different Buddhisms, not to speak of the different Buddhists. The Zen scholar D. T. Suzuki comes out strongly in favor of nirvana as a transcendence toward an absolute ground of being. Masson echoes this position:

> Bien conduite, l'opération de dépouillement "doit déboucher," semble-t-il, sur tout autre chose que le rien pur et simple; sur une "négation," "un vide," un "anéantissement" qui ne sont nullement le néant.... Nous serions ici en face... d'une via negationis vécue, anéidétique, et para—ou supra—conceptuelle... qui use du vide et de l'abolition pour connaître comme inconnue l'existence substantielle de l'âme.[7]

The Oriental scroll-painting, known as the mandala, presents a pictogram of spiritual states through which an individual must pass on his journey to enlightenment. In the center is the abode of the deity. This is contained within the palace of inner being, surrounded in turn by the different gates through which the pilgrim must enter. All these stages or way-stations,

---

6. *Le Bouddhisme* (Paris, 1975), p. 173.
7. Ibid., p. 182. The quotations are from an article by Jacques Maritain.

simultaneously present on the illuminated surface, impel the pilgrim to advance along his meditative way. Carl G. Jung took the mandala, essentially a meditative ritualistic device, and adapted it to therapeutic use, as a means for the neurotic to achieve self-centering.

One might see Le Clézio's stories as representing the different aspects of a quest from neurosis and toward enlightenment or at least appeasement. The Le Clézian persona moves through different spiritual and psychological states, all equally synchronous as he runs his predetermined course. He too follows a spiritual path, usually unrelentingly downward, into the throbbing city streets that lead him inwards, on his spiritual journey. Each hero seems to be drawn irresistibly toward the void, only to regain consciousness at the last moment, just before he succumbs to its hypnotic power and plunges into oblivion. Each story is a litany of negations and denials, a stripping of all camouflage and all defense from these characters until they are revealed totally naked.

Perhaps the immediate literary ancestor of Le Clézio's persona is the officer in Kafka's tale "The Penal Colony." When the execution machine starts to run amok, the officer strips and lies down on the bed, allowing his body to be riddled and mutilated by the deadly needles of the harrow. One might add that there is a strong Oriental strain of impassivity and submission to suffering in Kafka, just as there is in Le Clézio.

But, after all, although he has a strong streak of the exotic, Le Clézio is not a Buddhist. And yet the Buddhist multivalent use of nonbeing helps to circumscribe Le Clézio's struggle with nothingness, helps to situate and schematize it. Le Clézio's personae move through nothingness and assimilate it or are assimilated by it as they progress along a spiritual path. The nature of their spiritual experience can never be stated once and for all. So it is that the writer uses metaphor and negation as he attempts to deal with this experience. And he begins the story over and over again. In a very profound sense each of these stories is the same story repeatedly told. Perhaps this explains Le Clézio's doubting and abandonment of the traditional narrative form. He seems to be making no progress, seems to be repeating himself. Again and again, the same motifs occur. Again and again, the story makes closure on an incommunicable experience, till finally he makes the decision to abandon the fictional form altogether and to seize the core experience directly, by a different kind of discourse. Like Rimbaud and like that contemporary Rimbaud, Jean-Luc Godard, Le Clézio may eventually abandon the struggle with the narrative form altogether. Yet this will not bring him any closer to nirvana.

Le Clézio is like the man in the parable that ends Kafka's *Trial*. He waits patiently, year after year, for a gate to open—not knowing that it was open all the time. In the mysticism of the void, to search is to have found; to desire is to be appeased; and yet there is no finding and no appeasement.

Bibliography of Wallace Fowlie

BOOKS

Poetry

Matines et Vers. Paris: Figuière, 1936. Pseudonym Michel Wallace.
From Chartered Land. Seven fragments on the world and the poet, prefaced by an essay on the poet and the mystic. New York: William Scott, 1938.
Intervalles. Préface de Pierre Louis Floquet. Brussels: Cahiers des Poètes Catholiques, 1939. Pseudonym Michel Wallace.

Criticism in French

La Pureté dans l'art. Montréal: L'Arbre, 1941.
De Villon à Péguy: grandeur de la pensée française. Préface par Henri Focillon. Montréal: L'Arbre, 1944.

Criticism in English

Ernest Psichari: A Study in Religious Conversion. London: James Clarke, 1939; New York: Longmans, Green, 1939; Dublin: Browne and Nolan, 1939.
Clowns and Angels: Studies in Modern French Literature. New York: Sheed and Ward, 1943. Under the title *Spirit of France,* London: Sheed and Ward, 1945.
Rimbaud: The Myth of Childhood. New York: New Directions, 1946; London: Dennis Dobson, 1947.
Jacob's Night: The Religious Renaissance in France. New York: Sheed and Ward, 1947.
The Clown's Grail: A Study of Love in Its Literary Expression. London: Dennis Dobson, 1948; Denver: Swallow Press, 1948. Reprinted as a Midland book under the title *Love in Literature: Studies in Symbolic Expression,* Bloomington: Indiana Univ. Press, 1965.
Mallarmé as Hamlet: A Study of Igitur. Yonkers, N.Y.: Alicat Bookshop Press, 1949. With a portrait of Mallarmé by Picasso.
The Age of Surrealism. New York: William Morrow, 1950; London: Dennis Dobson, 1953. Reprinted as a Midland Book, Bloomington: Indiana Univ. Press, 1960.
Mallarmé. Chicago: Univ. of Chicago Press, 1953; London: Dennis Dobson, 1953. Reprinted as a Phoenix Book, Univ. of Chicago Press, 1962.

Paul Claudel. In the series Studies in Modern European Literature and Thought. London: Bowes and Bowes, 1957; New York: Hillary House, 1960.

A Guide to Contemporary French Literature: From Valéry to Sartre. New York: Meridian Books, 1957.

Dionysus in Paris: A Guide to Contemporary French Theatre. New York: Meridian Books, 1960; London: Victor Gallancz, 1961; German translation, *Dionysos in Paris,* Munich: Langen-Müller, 1961.

A Reading of Proust. An Anchor Original. New York: Doubleday, 1964; London:Dennis Dobson, 1967. Second edition, Chicago: Univ. of Chicago Press, 1975.

André Gide: His Life and Art. New York: Macmillan, 1965. Reissued in paperback, Collier-Macmillan, 1966.

Rimbaud: A Critical Study. Chicago: Univ. of Chicago Press, 1965. Reissued as a Phoenix Book, Univ. of Chicago Press, 1967.

Jean Cocteau: The History of a Poet's Age. Bloomington: Indiana Univ. Press, 1966.

Climate of Violence: The French Literary Tradition from Baudelaire to the Present. New York: Macmillan, 1967; London: Secker and Warburg, 1969.

The French Critic: 1549–1967. Carbondale: Southern Illinois Univ. Press, 1968.

Stendhal. New York: Macmillan, 1969.

French Literature: Its History and Meaning. Englewood Cliffs, N.J.: Prentice Hall, 1973.

Lautréamont. Boston: Twayne, 1973.

Correspondence

Letters of Henry Miller and Wallace Fowlie. New York: Grove Press, 1975. Translated by Paul Verguin as *Correspondance privée, Henry Miller et Wallace Fowlie.* Paris: Editions Buchet/Chastel, 1976.

Novel

Sleep of the Pigeon. London: Harvill Press, 1948.

Autobiography

Pantomime. Chicago: Regnery, 1951.
Journal of Rehearsals: A Memoir. Durham, N.C.: Duke Univ. Press, 1977.

Translations

Sixty Poems of Scève. Introduction, translation, and commentary. New York: Swallow Press and Morrow, 1949.

Rimbaud's Illuminations: A Study in Angelism. London: Harvill Press, 1953; New York: Grove Press, 1953.
Mid-Century French Poets. Introduction, critical notices, translation. New York: Twayne, 1955. Evergreen Book 26, Grove Press, 1955.
The Journals of Jean Cocteau. Edited and translated, with an introduction. New York: Criterion Books, 1955. Reprinted as a Midland Book, Bloomington: Indiana Univ. Press, 1964.
Saint-John Perse, *Seamarks.* New York: Bollingen Series, 1958. Reprinted as a Harper's Torchbook, 1961.
Paul Claudel, *A Poet Before the Cross.* Chicago: Regnery, 1958.
French Stories—Contes Français. A Bantam Dual-Language Book. New York: Bantam, 1960.
Two Dramas of Claudel: Break of Noon (Partage de Midi) and Tidings Brought to Mary (L'Annonce faite à Marie). Chicago: Regnery, 1960. Each play, reprinted separately, in Gateway Paperbacks, 1960.
Classical French Drama (The Cid, Phaedra, The Intellectual Ladies, The Game of Love and Chance, The Barber of Seville). New York: Bantam, 1962. Reprinted in Bantam World Drama Series, 1968.
François Mauriac, *What I Believe.* Edited and translated. New York: Farrar, Straus, 1963.
Baudelaire, *Flowers of Evil and Other Works/ Les Fleurs du Mal et œuvres choisies.* New York: Bantam, 1964. A Bantam Dual-Language Book.
Molière, *The Miser.* Translated with an introduction. Woodbury, N.Y.: Barron's Educational Series, Inc., 1964.
Molière, *Don Juan.* Woodbury, N.Y.: Barron's Educational Series, Inc., 1965.
The Complete Works of Rimbaud. Chicago: Univ. of Chicago Press, 1965. Reissued as a Phoenix Book, Univ. of Chicago Press, 1967.
Selected Poems by Alain Bosquet. A translation of forty poems. Athens: Ohio Univ. Press, 1972.

EDITIONS

The Paul Valéry issue of the *Quarterly Review of Literature*, Vol. 3, No. 3 (March 1947) : 211–326. Reprinted as Special Issue Retrospective, *Quarterly Review of Literature*, 20:92–168 (1976).
Honoré de Balzac, *Père Goriot.* Jane Sedgwick, translator. New York: Rinehart, 1950.
The Postwar French Poets issue of *Poetry*, 80:311–368 (1952).
Four French Poets issue of *Poetry*, Vol. 104, No. 5 (Aug. 1964).
François Mauriac, *Le Désert de l'Amour.* Waltham, Mass.: Blaisdell, 1968.
A Mauriac Reader. Introduction. New York: Farrar, Straus and Giroux, 1968.

The Major Texts of French Literature. Vols. 1 and 2. Englewood Cliffs, N.J.: Prentice-Hall, 1973.

ESSAYS IN BOOKS

"Petrouchka's Wake," in Henri Peyre, editor, *Essays in Honor of Albert Feuillerat. Yale Romanic Studies,* 22:249–253 (1943), and in *Accent,* 3:182–185 (Spring 1943).

"Masques du héros littéraire," in *Les Œuvres Nouvelles,* IV. Paris: Editions de la Maison Française, 1944, pp. 39–117.

"Shadow of Doom," in Reginald Moore, editor, *Modern Reading 11 and 12.* London: Wells, Gardner, Darton and Co., 1945, pp. 204–211. Also appeared in *The Happy Rock,* Bern Porter, editor, Berkeley: Packard Press, 1945, pp. 102–107; and in *Of-By-and-About Henry Miller,* Oscar Baradinsky, editor, Yonkers, N.Y.: Alicat Bookshop Press, 1947, pp. 18–24.

"Eliot and Tchelitchew," in Kerker Quinn and Charles Shattuck, editors, *Accent Anthology.* New York: Harcourt, Brace and Co., 1946, pp. 603–609.

"The Pilot," in Saint-Exupéry, *Transformation IV.* London: Lindsay Drummond Ltd., 1947, pp. 132–135.

"André Gide," in *Writers of Today.* London: Sidgwick and Jackson, 1947, pp. 29–42.

"Mauriac's Dark Hero," in B. Rajan, editor, *The Novelist as Thinker, Focus Four.* London: Dennis Dobson, Ltd., 1947, pp. 92–106.

"The Fountain and the Thirst," in R. B. West, editor, *Essays in Modern Literary Criticism.* New York: Rinehart, 1952, pp. 489–501.

"Catholic Orientation in Contemporary French Literature," in Stanley Romaine Hopper, editor, *Spiritual Problems in Contemporary Literature.* New York Institute for Religious and Social Studies, 1952, pp. 225–241.

"Mid-Century French Poetry," in R. Richman, editor, *The Arts at Mid-Century.* New York: Horizon Press, 1954, pp. 97–102.

"French Theater," in Julian Park, editor, *The Culture of France in Our Time.* Ithaca, N.Y.: Cornell University Press, 1954, pp. 104–133.

"Salvatore Quasimodo," in Stanley Burnshaw, editor, *The Poem Itself,* New York: Holt, Rinehart and Winston, 1960, pp. 326–327; New York: Meridian Books, 1962, pp. 326–327; London: Penguin Books, 1964, pp. 326–327.

"Introduction," in *Four Modern French Comedies* ("Ubu roi" by Alfred Jarry; "The Commissioner" by Georges Courteline; "Professor Taranne" by Arthur Adamov; "Clérambard" by Marcel Aymé). New York: Capricorn Books, 1960, pp. 7–12.

"Introduction," in Honoré de Balzac, *Cousin Bette,* translated by Anthony Bonner. New York: Bantam, 1961, pp. v–xv.

"Maritain the Writer," in Joseph William Evans, editor, *Jacques Maritain: The Man and His Achievement.* New York: Sheed and Ward, 1963, pp. 46–57.

"French Poetry," in *Encyclopedia of Poets and Poetry.* Princeton: Princeton Univ. Press, 1965.

"Introduction," in *What Is Literature?* by Jean-Paul Sartre. New York: Harper Colophon Books, 1965, pp. vi–xvi.

"L'œuvre pure de Saint-John Perse," in *Honneur à Saint-John Perse.* Paris: Gallimard, 1965, pp. 262–265.

"The French Novel: Quests and Questions," in Siegfried Mandel, editor, *Contemporary European Novelists.* Carbondale: Southern Illinois Univ. Press, 1968, pp. 39–68.

"Valéry," in *Explication de texte.* Englewood Cliffs, N.J.: Prentice Hall, 1970, Vol. II, pp. 147–157.

"Introduction" to *The Stranger* by Albert Camus. Del Mar, Cal.: Limited Editions Club, 1971.

"Baudelaire: The Beginning of a World," in *Regards sur Baudelaire.* Paris: Minard, 1974, pp. 11–26.

ESSAYS IN PERIODICALS

1937

"Villon," *Colosseum,* 2, no. 14:39–49.
"The Bennington Experiment," *French Review,* 11:93–101.

1938

"Baudelaire," *Colosseum,* 4, no. 17:18–26.
"The Conversion of Ernest Psichari," *Colosseum,* 4, no. 19:200–208.
"The Poet and the Mystic," *Examiner,* 1:28–46.

1939

"Racine, Poet of Grace," *French Review,* 12:391–400.

1941

"André Gide," *La Nouvelle Relève,* 1, no. 3:150–156.

1942

"The Novel of Jules Romain," *Southern Review,* 7:880–892.
"Claudel," *Amérique-Française,* 1, no. 5:12–16; no. 6:14–19; no. 7:16–18.

"La Paix de Dieu," *La Nouvelle Relève*, 1, no. 8:486–488.
"Tragedy in the Plays of Cocteau," *French Review*, 15, no. 6:463–467.
"Swann and Hamlet: A Note on the Contemporary Hero," *Partisan Review*, 9, no. 3:195–202.

1943

"Villon, poète de la foi," *Lettres Françaises*, no. 7–8:34–40.
"Le rôle de la poésie dans *Pilote de guerre*," *Amérique-Française*, 2, no. 6: 21–24.
"François Mauriac," *Kenyon Review*, 5:189–200.
"The Juggler's Dance: A Note on Crane and Rimbaud," *Chimera*, 2, no. 2:3–14.
"Narcissus, an Essay on the Modern Spirit," *View*, 3, no. 3:72–73, 91, 96.
"Méditations sur Héloïse," *Gants du Ciel*, 2:81–89.

1944

"Ballet," *France-Amérique*, 11, no. 557.
"The Poetic Tradition of Saint-John Perse," *Chimera*, 2, no. 4:338–43.
"Memory of France: April 1944," *Kenyon Review*, 6:570–572.
"Shadow of Doom: An Essay on Henry Miller," *Accent*, 5, no. 1:49–53.
"Nerval," *Hemispheres*, 1, no. 4:39–43.
"The Two Monarchs: A Study of Lautréamont," *Circle*, 1, no. 4:14–21.

1945

"Eliot and Tchelitchew," *Accent*, 5, no. 3:166–170.
"The Religious Experience of André Gide," *Quarterly Review of Literature*, 2, no. 2: 142–145.
"Méditation sur Pascal," *Gants du Ciel*, 9:101–108.
"The Example of Max Jacob," *View*, 5, no. 4:8.

1946

"Paul Valéry," *New English Review*, 12, no. 1:42–48.
"Le mythe de l'enfance," *Arts et Lettres*, 1, no. 1:53–59.
"Existentialist Theatre," *View*, 6, nos. 2–3:32.
"Homage to Valéry," *Sewanee Review*, 54, no. 2:250–257.
"The Fountain and the Thirst," *Accent*, 6, no. 2:67–76.

1947

"Selections from Mélange," *Quarterly Review of Literature*, 3, no. 3:215–221.
"Selected Moralities," *Quarterly Review of Literature*, 3, no. 3:306–309.

"La Jeune Parque's Imminent Tear," *Quarterly Review of Literature*, 3, no. 3:318–326.
"The Theme of Night in Four Sonnets of Mallarmé," *Modern Philosophy*, 44:428–458.
"Europa in Boston," *Perspective*, 1, no. 1:3–7.
"The Meaning of Love in *Manon Lescaut*," *Western Review*, 2, no. 2:85–93.
"Henry Miller," *Arts et lettres*, 1, no. 5:115–122.

1948

"Existentialist Hero: A Study of l'Age de Raison," *Yale French Studies*, 1:53–61.
"Under the Equanimity of Language," *Quarterly Review of Literature*, 4, no. 2:173–177.
"Myth in Mallarmé's *Hérodiade*," *Yale Poetry Review*, 8:11–24.
"The French Literary Mind," *Visva-Bhatati Quarterly*, ser. 2, vol. 14, pt. 2:82–99. This also appeared in *Accent*, 8, no. 2:67–81.
"Hero Taking His Time: The Journals of André Gide," *Kenyon Review*, 10, no. 1:161–164.
"Mauriac's Dark Hero," *Sewanee Review*, 56, no. 1:39–57.
"Mallarmé's 'Afternoon of a Faun,' " *The Tiger's Eye*, 1, no. 7:9–23.
"Three Masks of Mallarmé," *Zero*, 1:4–15.

1949

"Paris Letter," *Hudson Review*, 2, no. 1:113–117.
"Mallarmé as Hamlet: A Study of Igitur," *The Outcast Chapbooks*, 16:1–21.
"Rimbaud in 1949," *Poetry*, 75, no. 3:166–169.

1950

"Mallarmé's Island Voyage," *Modern Philology*, 67:178–190.
"The Religious Experience of Van Gogh," *College Art Journal*, 9, no. 3:317–324.
"Recent French Literature," *Measure*, 1, no. 2:186–198.
"Mystery of the Actor," *Yale French Studies*, 5:5–11.
"Paul Valéry," *Poetry*, 76, no. 5:279–287.
"Eluart's Doctrine of Love," *Accent*, 10, no. 2:85–99.
"Apollinaire," *Poetry*, 77, no. 3:162–167.

1951

"Saint-John Perse," Waiçlim Yip, translator, *Modern Literature*, 7 (15 March):51–55.

"Mallarmé as Ritualist," *Sewanee Review*, 59, no. 2:228–253.
"Jules Laforgue," *Poetry*, 78, no. 4:216–222.
"Et Vous, Mers," translation, *Poetry*, 79 no. 1:11–22.
"Saint-John Perse," *Poetry*, 79, no. 1:31–35.
"Legacy of Symbolism," *Yale French Studies*, 9:20–26.

1952

"Gide's Earliest Quest: *Les Nourritures terrestres*," *Essays in Criticism*, 2:285–294.
"Mallarmé," *Poetry*, 80, no. 1:37–41.
"The French Literary Scene," *Commonweal*, 56, no. 8:201–208.
"Marianne Moore," *Sewanee Review*, 60, no. 3:537–547.
"The Child's World in Rimbaud's *Illuminations*," *Accent*, 12, no. 4:159–179.
"Choderlos de Laclos: Dangerous Acquaintances," *Accent*, 12, no. 4:250–252.
"Who Was André Gide?" *Sewanee Review*, 60, no. 4:605–623.
"Rimbaud in the Sorbonne," *Partisan Review*, 19, no. 6:723–724.

1953

"Henri Michaux," *Poetry*, 81, no. 4:265–268.
"Rimbaud as Mystic," *Western Review*, 17:211–228.
"Baudelaire Today," *Poetry*, 82, no. 2:86–95.
"A Note on Jules Laforgue (1860–1880)," *Newberry Library Bulletin*, 3, no. 3:94–100.
"Raymond Radiguet (1903–1923)," *Sewanee Review*, 61, no. 3:527–532.
"The Poetics of St.-John Perse," *Poetry*, 82, no. 6:345–350.
"Mid-Century French Poetry," *New Republic*, 129 (7 Sept.):15–16.
"A Note on René Char," *Poetry*, 82, no. 1:49–54.
"Prologue to Tobias," *Botteghe Oscure*, 11:354–366.

1954

"A Note on Jean Cocteau," *Poetry*, 84, no. 2:185–188.
"From the Crucifixion," translation, *Poetry*, 84, no. 1:80–85.
"The Poetry of Leonie Adams," *Commonweal*, 61, no. 8:224–226.
"Claudel and the Problem of Sacred Art," *Accent*, 14, no. 1:3–21.

1955

"Seamarks," by Saint-John Perse, translation, *Yale Review*, 44, no. 3:389–410.
"Petrus Borel," *Accent*, 15, no. 2:145–146.

"Poetry and Prophecy," *Poetry*, 86, no. 2:108–111.
"Vocation of the Poet," *Commonweal*, 62, no. 8:199–201.
"Some Notes on Mortality," *New Republic*, 132, no. 24:16–18.
"Mer de Baal" and "Mer de Mammon" by Saint-John Perse, translation, *Poetry*, 86, no. 4:187–227.
"Contrasts in Elegance," *Commonweal*, 63, no. 4:82–85.
"Claudel: The Tidings That Are the Poem," *Poetry*, 87, no. 3:169–173.
Poems of Paul Claudel: "Dialogue from 'La Ville,' " "Heat of the Sun," "From the 'Art Poétique,' " "From the 'Magnificat,' " "The Infant Jesus of Prague," "The Virgin at Noon," "Saint Joseph," "Parable of Animus and Anima," "December 25, 1886," translations, *Poetry*, 87, no. 3:130–146.
"Epilogue to the Story of Tobias," *Botteghe Oscure*, 16:293–300.
"The French Theater and the Concept of Communion," *Yale French Studies*, 14:23–39.

1956

"Claudel as Dramatist," *Sewanee Review*, 64, no. 2:218–237.
"French Chronicle: Recent publications," *Poetry*, 88, no. 6:408–410.
Paul Chaulot, "A Stranger," translation, *New World Writing*, 10:94–95.
Michel Manoll, "A Sea Chant for Dylan Thomas," translation, *New World Writing*, 10:95–96.

1957

"Poetry of Silence," *Commonweal*, 65, no. 20:514–516.
"Crisis of Belief," *Commonweal*, 65, no. 25:636–638.
"Jorge Guillen, Marianne Moore, T. S. Eliot: Some Recollections," *Poetry*, 90, no. 2:103–109.
"First Modern Poet," *Commonweal*, 66, no. 12:304–305.
"Return to Paris: 1957," *Yale Review*, 46:586–596.
"David Hayman: Joyce et Mallarmé," *Symposium*, 11, no. 2:328–332.
"A Commemoration: *Les Fleurs du Mal*," *Poetry*, 90, no. 6:376–385.
"Péguy as Poet," *Commonweal*, 66, no. 24:594–595.
"French Chronicle: Recent Publications," *Poetry*, 91, no. 1:36–40.
"Poem to Phaedra," *Botteghe Oscure*, 19:211–218.

1958

"French Chronicle: Recent Publications," *Poetry*, 93, no. 1:40–45.
"René Char and the Poet's Vocation," *Yale French Studies*, 21:83–89.

1959

"Giraudoux's Approach to Tragedy," *Tulane Drama Review*, 3, no. 4:6–15.
"Letter from Haiti," *Poetry*, 94, no. 6:398–404.
"The New French Theater: Artaud, Beckett, Genet, Ionesco," *Sewanee Review*, 67, no. 4:643–657.
"The Poets on Haiti's Map," *Portfolio*, 1:105–111.

1960

"Albert Camus: 1913–1960," *Commonweal*, 71, no. 20: 549–550.
"Surrealism in 1960: A Backward Glance," *Poetry*, 95, no. 6:365–372.
"Paris Letter," *Poetry*, 96, no. 6:371–374.
"New Plays of Ionesco and Genet," *Tulane Drama Review*, 5, no. 1:43–48.
"The Case of Jean Genet," *Commonweal*, 73, no. 5:111–113.
"Paul Valéry's Theatre," *Poetry*, 97, no. 2:121–124.
"Exercices," *Botteghe Oscure*, 25:65–67.

1961

"Chronique by Saint John Perse," *Poetry*, 99:194–196.

1962

"Jorge Guillen," *Poetry*, 99, no. 4:243–246.
"Letter from the Midi," *Poetry*, 99, no. 4:258–265.

1963

"Julien Green," *Ramparts*, 1, no. 4:82–90.
"Avant-Garde: The Experimental Theatre in France," *Ramparts*, 2, no. 2:84–86.
"Oiseaux" by Saint-John Perse, translation, *Portfolio*, vol. 7.

1964

"Four French Poets," *Poetry*, 104:187–192.
"French Poetry Today," *Poetry*, 104:273–328.
"The Christian Critics in France," *Ramparts*, 3, no. 4:51–56.

1965

"Homage to Jean Cocteau," *Ramparts*, 4, no. 5:39–42.

1966

"Baudelaire and Eliot: Interpreters of Their Age," *Sewanee Review*, 74:293–
   309.
"Mallarmé and the Painters of His Age," *Southern Review*, 2:542–558.
"Pages from a Journal," *Bennington Review*, 1 (Fall).

1968

"Light Years," a poem by Marc Alyn, translation, *Mundus Artium*, 1:25–29.
"On Austin Warren," *Sewanee Review*, 76:665–668.

1969

"Earth Writes Earth," a poem by Alain Bosquet, translation, *Mundus Artium*,
   2:6–15.
"Stendhal's Armance," *Novel: A Forum on Fiction*, 2, no. 3:230–240.

1970

"Rimbaud's Desert as Seen by Pasolini," *Evergreen Review*, 74:27–29.
"Stendhal the Writer," *Sewanee Review*, 78, no. 2:310–340.
"A Stocktaking: French Literature in the 1960's," *Contemporary Literature*,
   2, no. 2:137–154.

1971

"Rimbaud and the Commune," *Massachusetts Review*, 12, no. 3:517–520.

1973

"Mundus Artium: the Guest Word," *New York Times Book Review*, 9 Dec.,
   p. 55.

1974

"Jean Cocteau: The Artist as Clown-Angel," *Prose*, 8:93–110.

1975

"A Return Visit to Paris," *Virginia Quarterly Review*, 51, no. 1:80–94.
"Teacher and Student as Critics," *Mosaic*, 8, no. 2:13–18.

BOOK REVIEWS

1951

Horace Gregory, *Selected Poems of Horace Gregory* (New York), *New York Times Book Review*, Aug. 19, p. 5.

Walter de la Mare, *Winged Chariot and Other Poems* (New York), *New York Times Book Review*, Oct. 28, p. 4.

Martin Turnell, *The Novel in France* (New York), *Renascence*, 4:66–67.

1952

"The Quest of a Writer Obsessed," Graham Greene, *The Lost Childhood* and *Other Essays* (New York), *New York Times Book Review*, Feb. 17, p. 1.

Matthew G. Lewis, *The Monk* (New York), *New York Times Book Review*, June 1, p. 6.

"Rhythms in France," Joseph Chiari, *Contemporary French Poetry* (New York), *New York Times Book Review*, June 1, p. 6.

"In Love with Truth," Emmanuel Bondot-Lamotte, *To the Happy Few: Selected Letters of Stendhal*, translated by Norman Cameron (New York), *New York Times Book Review*, Nov. 2, p. 5.

1953

"Yes and No," *The Correspondence Between Paul Claudel and André Gide*, edited by Robert Mallet, translated by John Russell (New York), *Saturday Review*, 36 (Jan. 17) :12.

"An Ironic Poet Without Heroes," Warren Ramsey, *Jules Laforgue and the Ironic Inheritance* (New York), *New York Times Book Review*, Aug. 2, p. 7.

"Figures from Two Tortured Generations," Martin Turnell, *Jacques Rivière* (New Haven), and Iris Murdoch, *Sartre, Romantic Rationalist* (New Haven), *Commonweal*, 59 (Nov. 15) :144.

1954

"The Greatest European Poet of His Century," Martin Turnell, *Baudelaire: A Study of His Poetry* (New York), *Commonweal*, 60:18.

"The American Word for La Fontaine," *The Fables of La Fontaine*, translated by Marianne Moore (New York), *New York Times Book Review*, May 16, p. 1.

"Pleading the Absurdity of Human Existence," Louis-Ferdinand Céline, *Guignol's Band*, translated by Bernard Frechtman and Jack T. Nile (New York), *Commonweal*, 60:346.

Charles Chasse, *Les Clefs de Mallarmé* (Paris), *Romanic Review*, 45:304–305.

1955

"Severity as Humanism," Norman Suckling, *Paul Valéry and the Civilized Mind* (New York), *Poetry*, 85:300–303.

"Petrus Borel," Enid Starkie, *Petrus Borel, the Lycanthrope: His Life and Times* (New York), *Accent*, 15:145–146.

"Poetry and Prophecy," Amos N. Wilder, *Modern Poetry and the Christian Tradition* (New York) ; Joseph Chiari, *The Poetic Drama of Paul Claudel* (New York) ; Francis Fergusson, *Dante's Drama of the Mind* (Princeton), *Poetry*, 86:108–111.

"Adventure and Voyage," Valéry Larbaud, *Poems of a Multimillionaire*, translated, with an introduction by William Jay Smith (New York), *New York Times Book Review*, June 5, p. 30.

Henri Peyre, *The Contemporary French Novel* (New York), *New York Herald Tribune Book Review*, July 24, p. 6.

"Three Poets," Isabella Gardner, *Birthdays from the Ocean* (Boston) ; Edwin Honig, *The Moral Circus* (New York) ; Ben Belitt, *Wilderness Star* (New York), *Accent*, 15:237–240.

"The Mystery of the Ordinary," Marcel Adéma, *Apollinaire*, translated by Denise Folliot (New York), *Commonweal*, 62:333.

"Art as a Mode of Salvation," Germaine Brée, *Marcel Proust and Deliverance from Time*, translated by C. J. Richards and A. D. Truitt (New Brunswick, N.J.), *Commonweal*, 62:524.

"Work of a Wanderer," Robert Gibson, *The Quest of Alain-Fournier* (New Haven), *Renascence*, 7:148–149.

Wanderer's Progress," Robert Champigny, *Portrait of a Symbolist Hero* (Bloomington, Ind.), *Renascence*, 8:99–100.

"The World in His Hands," John Logan, *Cycle for Mother Cabrini* (New York) ; Ernest Kroll, *The Pauses of the Eye* (New York) ; William Carlos Williams, *Journey to Love* (New York), *New York Times Book Review*, Dec. 18, p. 4.

1956

"A Reflection of Self," Henry Miller, *The Time of the Assassins* (New York), *New York Times Book Review*, March 4, p. 20.

"Faraway Childhood," Saint-John Perse, *Eloges and Other Poems*, translated by Louise Varese (New York), *Saturday Review*, 39 (Aug. 18) :19.

"Life, Death, and Verse," Stéphane Mallarmé, *Un Coup de dés n'abolira jamais le hasard*, translated by Daisy Alden (New York) ; Pierre Emmanuel, *The Mad Poet*, translated by Elliot Coleman (Baltimore) ; Saint-John Perse, *Eloges and Other Poems*, translated by Louise Varese (New York), *New York Times Book Review*, Sept. 2, p. 7.

"Within Our Most Elaborate Literary Construction," J. M. Cocking, *Proust* (New Haven), *Commonweal*, 64:130.

"An Anthology of the Lyric," Kenneth Rexroth, *One Hundred Poems from the Japanese* (New York), *Poetry*, 88:116–118.

1957

"New Judgments on the French Novel," Raymond Giraud, *The Unheroic Hero in the Novels of Stendhal, Balzac, and Flaubert* (New Brunswick, N.J.) ; Germaine Brée and Margaret Guiton, *An Age of Fiction: The French Novel from Gide to Camus* (New Brunswick, N.J.) ; Walter A. Strauss, *Proust and Literature. The Novelist as Critic* (Cambridge) ; Milton Miller, *Nostalgia: a Psychoanalytic Study of Marcel Proust* (Boston) ; Samuel Beckett, *Proust* (New York), *Sewanee Review*, 65:666–676.

"Of Human Time," Georges Poulet, *Studies in Human Time*, translated by Elliot Coleman (Baltimore), *Prairie Schooner*, 31:181.

"Triumph and Disaster," Lawrence and Elisabeth Hanson, *Verlaine: Fool of God* (New York), *New York Times Book Review*, Nov. 10, p. 5.

"Intrusion of Evil into the Ordinary Life," Julien Green, *The Transgressor*, translated by Anne Green (New York), *Commonweal*, 65:640.

David Hayman, *Joyce et Mallarmé* (Paris, 1956), *Symposium*, 11:328–332.

1958

"Training a Sensibility," Marcel Proust, *On Art and Literature*, translated by Sylvia Townsend Warner (New York), *Saturday Review*, 41:34.

Roger Shattuck, *The Banquet Years: The Arts in France, 1885–1918* (New York), *New York Times Book Review*, June 29.

"Poet-Protagonist Against Mankind," James Ramsay Ullman, *The Day on Fire* (Cleveland and New York), *Saturday Review*, 41 (Sept. 20):26.

"Fallen Out of the World," Samuel Beckett, *The Unnamable*, translated by the author (New York), *New York Times Book Review*, Nov. 23, p. 4.

1959

"To Write Was His Life," André Gide, *So Be It or the Chips Are Down*, translated by Justin O'Brien (New York), *Saturday Review*, 42 (June 13):57.

"On a Study of Camus," Germaine Brée, *Camus* (New Brunswick, N.J.), *Evergreen Review*, 2:198.

"Weavers at the Loom of Language," *On Translation*, edited by Reuben A. Brower (Cambridge), *New York Times Book Review*, July 5, p. 4.

"Like Heroes, Like Author," Robert M. Adams, *Stendhal: Notes on a Novelist* (New York), *New York Times Book Review,* Aug. 2, p. 4.

"Writer's Lives," Leon Edel, *Literary Biography* (New York), *New York Herald Tribune Book Review,* Sept. 20, p. 13.

1960

"Eyewitness to Adventure in the Air," Marcel Miego, *Saint-Exupéry,* translated by Herma Briffault (New York), *Saturday Review,* 43 (June 11) :31.

"Two Biographies of Molière," Ramon Fernandez, *Molière, the Man Seen Through the Plays,* translated by Wilson Follett (New York, 1958), D. B. Wyndham Lewis, *Molière, the Comic Mask* (New York, 1959), *Kenyon Review,* 22:515–518.

"Paul Valéry's Theater," *Paul Valéry, Plays,* translated by David Paul and Robert Fitzgerald, with an introduction by Francis Fergusson and a memoir by Igor Stravinsky (New York), *Poetry,* 97:121–124.

"Neither Hero nor Stoic," *The Complete Works of François Villon,* translated by Anthony Bonner (New York), *Saturday Review,* 43 (Dec. 10) :34.

1961

Armand Lanoux, *Rendez-vous at Bruges,* translated by Francis Fenaye (New York), *New York Herald Tribune Book Review,* Jan. 15, p. 34.

"Latter-Day Disciples of the Muse," M. L. Rosenthal, *The Modern Poets: A Critical Introduction* (New York and London), *Saturday Review,* 44 (Jan. 28) :23.

"Ideas Are Not Separate from Ideals," François Mauriac, *Second Thoughts: Reflections on Literature and on Life,* translated by Adrienne Foulke (Cleveland and New York), *New York Times Book Review,* Feb. 19, p. 7.

"The Poet's Chronicle," Saint-John Perse, *Chronique,* translated by Robert Fitzgerald (New York), *Poetry,* 99:194–196.

1962

Robert Lowell, *Imitations* (New York), *Jubilee,* 10:53–54.

"Camus: Contradiction Accepted," Philip Thody, *Albert Camus: A Biographical Study* (New York), *Commonweal,* 62:90.

William S. Rubin, *Modern Sacred Art and the Church of Assy* (New York), *Arts Magazine,* 36:68.

1963

"Machines and the Poetic Imagination," Paul Ginestier, *The Poet and the Machine* (Chapel Hill), *Poetry,* 101:292–294.

"Not Bards So Much As Catalyzers," Hayden Carruth, *The Norfolk Poems* (Iowa City) ; John Ciardi, *In Fact* (New Brunswick) ; Robert Bly, *Silence in the Snowy Fields* (Middletown) ; Charles Edward Eaton, *Countermoves* (New York), *New York Times Book Review*, May 12, p. 36.

"Eternal Problems," François Mauriac, *Young Men in Chains*, translated by Gerard Hopkins (New York), *Saturday Review*, 46 (May 18) :32.

"The Method of Sainte-Beuve," *Sainte-Beuve: Selected Essays*, translated by Francis Steegmuller and Norbert Guterman (New York), *Poetry*, 103:183– 184.

1964

"The Art and the Conscience of Jean Genet," Jean-Paul Sartre, *Saint-Genet, Actor and Martyr*, translated by Bernard Frechtman (New York, 1963) ; Jean Genet, *Our Lady of the Flowers*, translated by Bernard Frechtman (New York, 1963) ; Joseph H. McMahon, *The Imagination of Jean Genet* (New Haven and London, 1963), *Sewanee Review*, 72:342–348.

Jean Delay, *The Youth of André Gide*, translated and abridged by June Guicharnard (Chicago and London), *Ramparts*, 2, (No. 4) :93–95.

"Man as He Is and as He Would Be," *Julien Green: Diary, 1928–1957*, selected by Kurt Wolff, translated by Anne Green (New York), *New York Times Book Review*, Sept. 27, p. 7.

1965

"The Poetry of Ben Belitt," Ben Belitt, *The Enemy Joy* (Chicago and London), *Poetry*, 105:324–325.

Simone de Beauvoir, *Force of Circumstance* (New York), *Boston Herald*, May 9.

1966

"Puzzles of a Life of Tumult and Creation," André Maurois, *Prometheus: The Life of Balzac* (New York), *Commonweal*, 84:641–642.

1967

"The Complete Picasso," Georges Brassai, *Picasso and Company*, translated by Francis Price with a preface by Henry Miller (New York), *Nation*, 204:694– 695.

"Notes on a Spiritual Odyssey," Jean Cocteau, *The Difficulty of Being* (New York), *Saturday Review*, 50 (June 17) :28–29.

1968

"Three Critical Approaches to Poetry," Marcelin Pleynet, *Lautréamont par lui-même* (Paris); Bernard Weinberg, *The Limits of Symbolism: Studies of Five Modern French Poets* (Chicago and London); Georges Poulet, *Metamorphosis of the Circle*, translated by Corley Dawson and Elliot Coleman, in collaboration with the author (Baltimore), *Poetry*, 112:41–44.

William Troy, *Selected Essays*, edited with an introduction by Stanley Edgar Hyman, and a memoir by Allen Tate (New Brunswick), *Poetry*, 112:116–118.

"Correspondences with Heaven," Kathleen Raine, *Defending Ancient Springs* (London, 1967), *Sewanee Review*, 76:541–543.

"The Search for Stability," Austin Warren, *The New England Conscience* (Ann Arbor, 1966), *Sewanee Review*, 76:665–672.

1969

Frederick Brown, *An Impersonation of Angels: A Biography of Jean Cocteau* (New York), *Commonweal*, 89:622–624.

Victor Brombert, *Stendhal: Fiction and the Theme of Freedom* (New York); Robert M. Adams, *Stendhal: Notes on a Novelist* (New York), *Commonweal*, 90:208–209.

"Bovarysme," Enid Starkie, *Flaubert: The Making of a Master* (New York, 1967), *Sewanee Review*, 78:333–338.

Self-Portraits: The Gide-Valéry Letters, 1890–1942, edited by Robert Mollet, abridged and translated by June Guicharnaud (Chicago and London, 1966), *Sewanee Review*, 78:521–525.

"Seven Years When the World Was Rebegun," John Berger, *The Moment of Cubism and Other Essays* (New York), Pierre Reverdy, *Selected Poems*, translated by Kenneth Rexroth, illustrated by Juan Gris (New York), *New York Times Book Review*, Nov. 19, p. 76.

1970

Parker Tyler, *Underground Film: A Critical History* (New York), *Commonweal*, 91:623–624.

1972

Vivian Mercer, *The New Novel from Queneau to Pinget* (New York), *Commonweal*, 96:172–173.

"The Banal Transmuted into Poetry," Maurice Nadeau, *The Greatness of Flaubert* (New York), *Nation*, 215:341–342.

"Will and Instinct, Order and Sensibility," Germaine Brée, *Camus and Sartre: Crisis and Commitment* (New York), *Nation*, 215:374–375.

1973

The Anaïs Nin Reader, edited by Philip K. Jason with an introduction by Anna Balakian (Chicago), *New York Times Book Review*, Sept. 9, p. 76.

1974

"University Press Books: Some Outstanding Books of the Year," *Accent: An Anthology*, edited by Daniel Curley, George Scouffas, and Charles Shattuck (Champaign) ; Marjorie Perloff, *The Poetic Art of Robert Lowell* (Ithaca) ; Robert Greer Cohn, *Poetry of Rimbaud* (Princeton) ; Arthur King Peters, *Cocteau and Gide: An Abrasive Friendship* (New Brunswick) ; Larken E. Price, *Marcel Proust: A Critical Panorama* (Champaign), *Commonweal*, 100:286–287.
Robert Speaight, *George Bernanos: A Biography* (New York), *Commonweal*, 101:89–91.

1975

"Four French Novelists," Jonathan Culler, *Flaubert: The Uses of Uncertainty* (Ithaca, 1974) ; V. S. Pritchett, *Balzac* (New York, 1973) ; Geoffrey Strickland, *Stendhal: The Education of a Novelist* (Cambridge. 1974), William Sansom, *Proust and His World* (New York, 1973), *Sewanee Review*, 83: 316–324.

1976

"New Studies on Proust," Céleste Albaret, *Monsieur Proust: A Memoir*, edited by Georges Belmont, translated by Barbara Bray (New York) ; Serge Doubrovsky, *La Place de la Madeleine* (Paris, 1974) ; André Maurois, *The World of Marcel Proust*, translated by Moura Buberg and Barbara Creed (New York, 1974) ; Jean-Pierre Richard, *Proust et le monde sensible* (Paris, 1974), *Sewanee Review*, 84:334–341.
"Hungering for History," Jean Lacouture, *André Malraux* (New York), *Commonweal*, 102:442–443.

1977

"The Novelist of 'le Petit Peuple,'" Raymond Queneau, *The Sunday of Life*, translated by Barbara Wright (New York), *New York Times Book Review*, July 10, p. 33.

Index

Abbott, Charles, 88
Adam, Paul, 187
Adrian VI, 129
Ambri, Paola Berselli, 124n
Anacreon, 66
Ancelot, Virginie, 85n, 87, 91
Anghel, D., 207
Anthony, Saint, 77n
Antonescu, Ion, 218
Apollinaire, Guillaume, 181, 190, 204, 238, 240, 246
Aragon, Louis, 60, 190, 237–247
Archimedes, 55
Aretino, Pietro, 127
Aristotle, 13–15, 17, 19, 55, 56
Armstrong, Edward A., 66n, 69n, 74n
Arnault, Antoine Vincent, 87
Arnoult, Léon, 180
Artaud, Antonin, 192, 237
Aspasia, 52
Auerbach, Erich, 20
Auric, Francis, 190

Babbitt, Irving, 179
Bach, Johann Sebastian, 187
Bacon, Francis, 252, 255
Bacovia, G., 208
Baldensperger, Fernand, 93n
Balzac, Honoré de, 7, 114, 130, 132, 140, 146–147, 191
Banville, Théodore de, 182, 210
Barante, Prosper de, 82n
Barbulesco, Titus, 206n
Barolsky, Paul, 198n
Baudelaire, Charles, 5, 50, 124n, 135, 181–182, 188, 193–204, 211
Beaumont, Lucile and Pauline de, 68
Beaunier, André, 212
Beckett, Samuel, 53, 57–60
Bédouin, Jean-Louis, 191
Beethoven, Ludwig van, 185–186, 189
Béranger, Pierre Jean de, 189
Berdyaev, Nicolas, 37n
Berkeley, George, 48–49, 53–54, 58
Berlioz, Hector, 88
Bernard, Suzanne, 183n

Berrichon, Paterne, 219–220, 226
Berry, Charles, Duc de, 68, 82
Berry, Duchesse de, 68
Beyle, Henri, *see* Stendhal
Blackmur, Richard P., 21
Blaga, Lucian, 213
Blake, Howard, 3
Bloom, Harold, 256n, 260
Bogza, Geo, 217, 224
Boileau, Nicolas [Boileau-Despréaux], 94, 101
Boissel, Jean, 121n
Boorsch, Jean, 90n
Borgerhoff, J. L., 82
Borgia, Cesare, 124–125
Bornecque, Jacques Henry, 191n
Bossuet, Jacques Bénigne, 73, 200
Bote, Lidia, 205–208, 222
Boucher, François, 242
Boulenger, Jacques, 115n
Bourget, Paul, 182
Boz, Lucian, 212–214, 223
Bradley, Andrew Cecil, 24
Brahms, Johannes, 190
Brentano, Clemens, 179
Breton, André, 50, 53–54, 59–60, 190–192, 237, 242, 244, 246
Brieux, Auguste, 94
Brod, Max, 189–190
Broglie, Achille Léon Victor, Duc de, 100
Brown, Calvin S., 179, 189n
Brown, Robert, 195
Bruno, Giordano, 59
Brunschvicg, Léon, 48–49
Buddha, 269–272
Buffon, Georges Louis Leclerc, Comte de, 66, 68
Bugeaud, Thomas, 68
Burckhardt, Jacob, 125
Burke, Kenneth, 256n
Buzea, B. G., 206
Byron, George Gordon, Lord, 82n

Calciu, Gheorghi, 205
Calinescu, G., 208